CASES IN EDUCATIONAL ADMINISTRATION

Katherine K. Merseth

Harvard University

LONGMAN

An imprint of Addison Wesley Longman, Inc.

New York • Reading, Massachusetts • Menlo Park, California • Harlow, England
Don Mills, Ontario • Sydney • Mexico City • Madrid • Amsterdam

Acquisitions Editor: Ginny Blanford
Supervising Project Editor: Lois Lombardo
Project Coordination and Text Design: York Production Services
Cover Designer: Kay Petronio
Manufacturing Manager: Hilda Koparanian
Electronic Page Makeup: ComCom
Printer and Binder: R. R. Donnelley and Sons Company, Inc
Cover Printer: Phoenix Color Corp.

Library of Congress Cataloging-in-Publication Data

Merseth, Katherine Kilppert.
    Cases in educational administration/Katherine K. Merseth.
        p.   cm.
    Includes bibliographical references and index.
    ISBN 0-673-99003-6
    1. School management and organization—United States—Case
    studies. 2. School supervision—United States—Case studies.
    I. Title.
    LB2805.M437   1997
    371.2'00973—dc20

96-16823
CIP

ISBN 0-673-99003-6

5678910---DOC---0302

CONTENTS

Preface vii
Acknowledgments xi
Foreword xiii

INTRODUCTION   1

SECTION 1
Professional Development   13

Quiet Time, Julia Ames Van 16
It Ain't Fair!, Katherine K. Merseth 21
The Prince and the Principal (A),
 Roger Shouse 27
The Prince and the Principal (B),
 Roger Shouse 33

SECTION 2
Community Relations   37

The Science Fair Incident (A), Mark Cosdon
 and Al Thurman 39
The Science Fair Incident (B), Mark Cosdon
 and Al Thurman 48
Promise and Fear (A), Debi Phillips 55
Promise and Fear (B), Debi Phillips 70
Promise and Fear (C), Debi Phillips 79
Rash Decisions (A), Edward Barnwell
 and Sean Reardon 81

Rash Decisions (B), Edward Barnwell
and Sean Reardon 92

SECTION 3
Governance 101

An Apple for the Teacher, Katherine K. Merseth and Jeffrey Young 103
Who Goes? Edward Barnwell 108
The Allen School, Darryl Ford 116
Augusta County—Beech Mountain Institute, Sean F. Reardon 122

SECTION 4
Organizational Design 149

Dante Alighieri High School (A), Edward Miller 151
Dante Alighieri High School (B), Edward Miller 164
Ottawa High School, Michelle Bauerly 166
What's Your Plan, Mr. Sommers? Claudia Johnson 188

SECTION 5
Curriculum and Assessment 203

Joe Fernadez and the *Children of the Rainbow* Guide (A), Ed Kirby 205
Joe Fernadez and the *Children of the Rainbow* Guide (B), Ed Kirby 219
Imagining the World, David Beare 222
Lake Wobegon West High School, Edward Miller 229
Who Knows Best? Claudia Johnson 238

SECTION 6
Personnel and Labor 247

On the Cutting Edge of Education Reform, Michele M. Pahl 249
The Case of Bernice Demovsky, David Kuechle 256
Ascot School District (A), Richard Fossey and Katherine K. Merseth 266
Ascot School District (B), Richard Fossey and Katherine K. Merseth 275
The Case of Jack Buick, Katherine K. Merseth 282
Supporting Teachers at Somerset High, John Ritchie 291

Bibliography 303

PREFACE

This exploration of administrative practice represents the confluence of two personal passions: case-based instruction and K-12 education. From the moment I first participated in a skillfully led case discussion, I sensed that cases and case-based instruction could serve as a powerful pedagogical approach to explore the complex world of schools. Now nearly twenty years and many case discussions and school experiences later, I have learned that cases and case methods offer an engaging and effective medium to enhance both the practical and reflective capacities of school leaders. Cases can serve as a bridge to bring the reality of administrative practice into a seminar or professional development setting for careful analysis, examination, and discussion.

During my first year as a doctoral student at the Harvard Graduate School of Education in 1978, I decided to enroll in a class offered at the Harvard Business School. Drawing on my experience as a public school teacher and administrator, I wanted to learn about management techniques that would help me become an effective school leader. In reviewing the Business School catalogue, only one course caught my eye. It wasn't just an ordinary business class on accounting, marketing, or business policy; rather it was a class titled "Developing Effective Discussion Leadership Skills."

From the first class meeting, I realized that the instructor didn't fit the stereotype of a university professor who delivered lectures, stood behind a podium, and entertained questions from students only at the end of class. No, this professor was different, very different. He exemplified the view that "teaching is a social art, necessarily involving a relationship between people. . ." (Gragg, 1940). His classes were occasions where teacher and students both taught and learned. And while his title was "Professor of Business Administration," he taught me more about teaching than he did about business. His name was C. Roland Christensen.

The name Christensen is synonymous with case method teaching at Harvard University. Without question, this skillful pedagogue has done more through his writings, teaching, and quiet encouragement to promulgate the use of cases and case-based instruction than any other individual. His influence is widely felt in a variety of professional fields including business, education, government and public policy, public health, and medicine. He touched my professional life profoundly.

Thus by the early 1980s, my love affair with cases and case-based instruction was solidified. Drawing upon my experience in the Christensen seminar, I began to explore the use of cases in the training of educational practitioners. My work first focused on the use of the case method in educational administration programs, tracing their use of cases as far back as 1924. Curiously, however, cases and case-based instruction never became a prominent pedagogical approach. While there was a brief burst of interest in case-based instruction to train educational administrators in the 1950s and 1960s, enthusiasm seemed to wane in the 1970s.

When I became the Director of Teacher Education at Harvard in 1983, I extended my interest in case-based instruction to the field of teacher education. Here it seemed, case use might be effective to help new teachers develop analytic and problem solving skills before entering the classroom. I found that while there had been proponents of the case method in teacher education for more than a half a century, the situation in teacher education was similar to that of administrative education. Very few programs or faculty were actually using cases in teacher education programs.

In the mid to late 1980s, interest in case-based instruction for educational practitioners received a boost from a number of prominent individuals and influential organizations. In teacher education, for example, the Carnegie Forum on Education and Economy issued a report titled *A Nation Prepared: Teachers for the 21st Century*. This report declared that "an approach to instruction that should be incorporated. . .is the case method, well developed in law and business, but almost unknown in teaching instruction. Teaching 'cases' illustrating a great variety of teaching problems should be developed as a major focus of instruction" (Carnegie Commission 1986, p. 76).

Similar calls were made for case use in educational administration programs. For example, Derek Bok, President of Harvard University opined that

If past experience is any guide, school administrators will face a host of difficult problems during their careers that cannot be anticipated today, let alone incorporated into the curriculum. The basic habits of problem-solving conveyed through the repeated use of the case method offer the best preparation for coping with these novel issues when they arise (Harvard University Annual Report 1987, p. 56).

During this time and well into the 1990s, more and more calls were made for the use of cases and case-based instruction in the training of educational practitioners. As these exhortations increased, it became clear that at least two significant barriers stood in the way of widespread case use in professional education. These barriers were the lack of well developed case materials and a mechanism to make case materials widely available. As a colleague at the time said, "It makes great sense to use cases to train practitioners, no question about it. But where do I find the cases? I hope you don't expect me to research and write them! I don't have the time."

This collection of cases about administrative practice seeks to ameliorate this situation. By providing high quality case materials in an easily accessible format, this volume will help staff developers and higher education faculty have access to the necessary case materials. The cases in this collection portray actual events and real individuals engaged in educational reform. Current reform topics such as standards and assessment, tracking, site-based management, staff development, and multicultural education are represented in these cases.

The case narratives represent complex, multi-faceted situations that can enable educational practitioners to practice techniques of sophisticated analysis and problem solving. In addition, the materials invite the assessment of possible strategies and the development of viable action plans—all in the safety of a seminar or other educational setting. In essence, these materials provide the reader with a freeze-framed account of a moment in administrative practice that encourages the reader to examine, explore, dissect, and reflect more deeply about the essential elements of administrative practice. In this way, these materials provide a picture of administrative practice that is both realistic and instructive. Taken as a whole, a great deal can be learned about administrative practice through the study of these cases.

Katherine K. Merseth

ACKNOWLEDGMENTS

Cases, such as those presented in this text, represent real-life experiences. As such, they exist only when individuals who have lived the experience are willing to share information, perspectives, and circumstances with others. Offering to be the subject of a case can be a mixed blessing. On one hand, it is an honor to have a case writer spend hours and hours exploring the event, interviewing subjects, examining documents, and writing a cogently balanced description of the situation. On the other hand, being the subject of a case means that one's decisions, actions, and professional judgment will be scrutinized, sometimes ruthlessly, by many individuals. The willingness and courage of the individuals whose professional practices are represented here make this book possible.

The genesis of this book comes from the support and encouragement of many individuals. First and foremost, C. Roland Christensen of the Harvard Business School and the Harvard Graduate School of Education deserves recognition for inspiring literally thousands of individuals to explore and utilize cases in teaching. By teaching graduate students in business administration, conducting seminars for faculty on discussion method teaching, and writing prolifically about case methods throughout his career, he has single-handedly stimulated the use of cases in a wide range of professional fields.

The MacDougall Center for Case Development and Teaching at the Harvard Graduate School of Education supported the development of many cases in this book. Established in 1989 through the generous support of the Roderick MacDougall family, the center encourages the development and use of cases to facilitate the education of educational practitioners. To make the case resources developed by the MacDougall Center available to a broad audience of educators was a prime motivation for this book. Other cases in this collection were written by higher education faculty, graduate research assistants, graduate students, and practitioners. The professional attention to detail given by each case writer contributed significantly to this material.

Special recognition is due to Debi Phillips, special assistant to the Dean, Harvard Graduate School of Education, who played a significant role in the development of this book. She exercised major responsibility in the organization and management of the case manuscripts. Her administrative acumen coupled with her knowledge of educational practice and cheerful attitude made the creation of this book a pleasure. Other individuals who contributed significantly to the preparation of this case book include Mary Askew, Nancy Bradley Capasso, Michelle Comeau, Mark Cosdon, and Elizabeth Walker. Colleagues who have been supportive of case development work in education include Carne Barnett, Larry Cuban, Richard Elmore, Helen Harrington, Jerome Murphy, Judith Kleinfeld, David Kuechle, Dan Lortie, John Mauriel, Lee and Judith Shulman, Rita Silverman, and William Welty.

FOREWORD

The use of case studies has come relatively late to the field of educational administration. Case teaching has been a more or less routine fixture in the teaching of business administration since its inception at the Harvard Business School in the 1920s. In the late 1960s and early 1970s, case teaching began to influence instruction in schools of public policy and management, largely due to the development of an extensive collection of teaching cases by Harvard's John F. Kennedy School of Government. With this collection of cases, Katherine Merseth opens the possibility of systematic use of case teaching in the field of educational administration—a long-overdue development. She has, by her single-minded and thoughtful advocacy of case teaching, coupled with her skillful nurturing of talented case writers, drawn the field of educational administration into a deeper conversation about pedagogy and content.

Every exponent of case teaching can tell a personal story about some pivotal event that drew them into the use of cases. Katherine Merseth's story, described in her preface, grows out of her experience as a graduate student taking a course at the Harvard Business School. My own story grows out of a fateful experience I had during my third year teaching in a graduate public policy and management program at a large public university. It was an evening class. The students were a wonderful mix of experienced and inexperienced practitioners of public management, many of them tired after a long day of work. I stood in front of the class doing what I imagined university professors were supposed to do: lecturing, brilliantly (I thought) weaving the theoretical literature of the field together with practical anecdotes, and the occasional joke. The students sat, in rapt attention, diplomatically jotting the occasional note, laughing at the appropriate moments, dutifully raising the occasional question about some obscure point in my lecture. I had a modest reputation for being an engaging lecturer, and my students were doing what dutiful students do in the presence of a modestly talented lecturer: They were giving me the periodic reinforcement I needed to plow through the two-hour session, and I was reciprocating by giving them the occasional stimulating remark that would stave off their drowsiness. About fifty minutes into this particular lecture, I had an epiphany. I suddenly heard my voice bouncing off the back wall of the classroom, a disembodied echo. It occurred to me that I was talking largely to myself. It occurred to me that I had no idea—none whatsoever—what my students were actually thinking, what knowledge they were accumulating, or what their understanding was of what I was trying to say. It occurred to me, in short, that I had no idea what I was actually teaching, if teaching was defined as creating an occasion for student learning. I stopped in mid-sentence. I posed a hypothetical problem, and I asked a succession of students what they would do if they were confronted with that problem. Something miraculous and mysterious happened. I began to hear what students were, or were not, learning, rather than listening to my own disembodied voice. From that point, I began a long odyssey that eventually led me to the systematic use of cases in my teaching, and a long love affair with the miracle of student learning. I use cases because they teach me about student learning; cases open a window into the minds of students. Cases have taught me how to observe and understand minds at work. Now, nearly twenty years after that fateful evening, I cannot imagine teaching any other way.

Teaching, to repeat, is the creation of occasions for student learning—the systematic, thoughtful, and reflective observation and guidance of minds at work. Case studies are one way to create these occasions—and, to be sure, not the only way—but, in my judgment, a particularly powerful way. Case studies are also an antidote to the rampant professorial disease of substituting teacher-talk for active student learning. Using cases in the classroom has been, for me, an exercise in the discipline of listening, listening to what students think, and thereby learning what students actually know and how they come to know it.

An unfortunate mystique has grown up around case teaching: that case teaching is either too "hard" for ordinary mortals to do, or alternatively, that it is too "easy" in that it substitutes mere opinion for hard-edged analysis in classroom discourse; that there are "right" and "wrong" ways to teach cases and that only initiates to the priesthood of case teaching can do it successfully. Good case teaching requires discipline and thoughtfulness, preparation and forethought, but so, too, does good teaching of any kind. Using cases successfully in the classroom is just a special case of good teaching in general. Try a few cases, ask a colleague to observe you teaching and tell you what they see, ask your students what was more and less successful about their experience, regroup, and try again. It's worth the effort, and a lot more fun than listening to your voice bounce off the back wall of the classroom.

The cases in this volume open up the opportunity for a new kind of pedagogy in educational administration. The cases included here are also significant in another way: They portray educational administration as the management of teaching and learning in schools. Katherine Merseth's background in teacher education and mathematics teaching serves her well in this volume because she puts the business of teaching and learning at the center of educational administration. Engaging students in a discussion of these cases sends the message that they should define their role as administrators in terms of their capacity to enable teachers to teach.

I use a number of these cases in my own courses in educational policy and administration. *It Ain't Fair,* a case that is nominally about a beginning teacher trying to master a new kind of instruction, can be used to provoke a broader discussion of the organizational conditions that promote good teaching, the problems of supervision and accountability in teaching and administration, and even the broader problems of teacher recruitment and induction. *An Apple for the Teacher,* a case that is nominally about what kind of computers to purchase, can be used to provoke a discussion about the ground rules of site-based management and decentralized decision-making in school systems. *On the Cutting Edge of Educational Reform,* a case that is nominally about one principal's and one teacher's problems explaining alternative student assessment to a parent, can be used to provoke a more general discussion of what student assessment means and how it is used in schools and school systems. *Dante Alighieri High School,* a case that is nominally about one parent's and one student's reaction to an episode in the classroom, can be used to provoke a broader discussion of grouping and tracking practices in high schools and how they affect students' access to learning. *Augusta County-Beech Mountain Institute* and *Chancellor Joseph Fernandez and the Children of the Rainbow Guide* raise profound questions about the relationship between what gets taught in schools and what are the surrounding community values about education. The common theme in these and other cases in this volume is the centrality of teaching and learning to the process of educational administration.

We owe Katherine Merseth a considerable debt for her determined and productive advocacy of the case method in the field of education. We can discharge that debt by using these cases, and creating others, in a way that causes us all to be more reflective about how we teach and what we teach.

Richard F. Elmore

INTRODUCTION

Educational administrators intending to practice in the twenty-first century need professional preparation that helps them work effectively in a world characterized by accelerating change, exploding knowledge, growing diversity, galloping technology, and increasing uncertainty. Such demands require preparation that not only equips administrators with cutting edge knowledge but also with the capacity and appetite to continually improve their practice. Administrators must develop skills to manage complex, ever-changing challenges while leveraging personal strengths through collaborative work with others.

Programs in educational administration seek to influence both what practitioners know and how they act. These programs employ a variety of materials and activities to achieve these goals. Traditionally, knowledge definition and theory development have occurred in settings removed from the world of practice—in university classrooms, research seminars, and libraries. In these settings, students read and examine work that documents and illuminates administrative practice. Much of this effort is passive and reflective, relying heavily on the capacity and imagination of the student to make important connections between theory and practice. To influence how administrators act, education programs often rely on field placements and internships where students directly experience the world of practice. These situations offer an opportunity to engage, under close supervision, in administrative ways of thinking and acting. Typically this work is fast-paced and active; sometimes it is non-reflective.

Traditional educational administration programs have tended to conceptualize knowledge and action in these disparate locales. Not only are the learning environments separated physically, with one taking place in the higher education setting and the other in the field, but they also are separated in time. A student may spend months in libraries and lecture halls before stepping into the field. Other programs place singular emphasis on the field; here the dominant philosophy is "to learn by doing." However, innovative programs for administrators now recognize that effective preparation must embody approaches and materials that constantly, purposefully, and explicitly connect the worlds of theory and practice. In today's complicated, complex school environment, a deep and interactive understanding of both knowledge and action are fundamental to competent educational leaders.

❖ WHY USE CASES IN EDUCATIONAL ADMINISTRATION PROGRAMS?

Cases offer a unique pedagogical approach that bridges the gap between theory and practice. While they are not intended to replace the development of theory or the observation of practice, they provide an approach to examine theory and practice together in specific contexts and settings. Cases also enhance the development of important skills required to lead in uncertain, rapidly changing environments. Educational administrators often are confronted with situations requiring decisions and actions that depend on the careful analysis of the context and the development of comprehensive strategies. In these contexts, successful administration relies on fundamental knowledge, disciplined techniques of analysis, generation of multiple and creative action plans, skill to connect action plans to probable outcomes, and the capacity to evaluate the effectiveness of outcomes. Cases afford one opportunity to develop these skills.

Arguments for the use of cases in professional administration programs abound. Perhaps the strongest assertion is that cases, well known in the professional education of doctors, lawyers, and businessmen, help practitioners gain skills of critical analysis and problem solving (Carter & Unklesbay, 1989; Christensen & Hansen, 1987, 1994; Greenwood & Parkay, 1989; Hunt, 1951; Kleinfeld, 1991; Merseth, 1990, 1991; McNair, 1954). These researchers argue that the structure of cases and their pedagogy foster the capacity to analyze ill-defined situations, to formulate action plans, and to evaluate those plans with respect to specific context variables.

A second advantage attributed to case-based instruction is the opportunity to engage directly in one's own education. Successful learning from cases employs a constructivist approach to the development of knowledge. Educators now recognize that learners bring their own conceptions to the learning process and if these assumptions are left unexamined, they can block new learning. Through case-based instruction, administrators have opportunities to build their own understandings as they interact in these public environments. This public/private thinking afforded by case work provides students with the tools, structure, and substance to articulate, explore, and revise their personal conceptions and to construct new knowledge.

Third, cases offer an opportunity to develop important group process and teamwork skills. The capacity to present and defend one's viewpoint, to persuade and convince others, to collaborate and build on the ideas and knowledge of others as well as the ability to listen carefully are all developed through effectively led case discussions. Advocates stress the synergy that develops when multiple learners engage in the same task of analysis, action planning, and evaluation.

Case based instruction assumes that learning in supportive groups holds the potential to be more effective than learning alone. The collective exploration of the situations enhances the development of multiple interpretations and points of view. Such learning environments require that students not only take responsibility for their own learning by being active, engaged participants, but also contribute significantly to the learning of others. This experience of shared problem solving fits especially well with the increasing emphasis on shared governance in educational settings. Offering an opportunity to experience an environment of collaborative inquiry before entering the workplace is an extra benefit of case-based instruction.

Another advantage of case-based education for administrative education is the capacity to expose readers to multiple settings that would otherwise be inaccessible. Physical and geographic realities limit the number of settings students can experience in preparation programs. Through cases, those individuals with experience in suburban settings, for example, can examine and learn from a case situated in an urban setting. Case discussions also emphasize multi-disciplinary perspectives; a case that initially appears to focus on governance may, through analysis, be found to draw upon knowledge of finance and human resources. In this way, students come to appreciate the role of the specialist and the generalist in the role of the administrator. Similarly, students have the opportunity to study diverse roles—from the kindergarten teacher to the superintendent—to gain a more complete understanding of the entire educational system. In this rapidly changing world, the capacity of cases to impart information about multiple and diverse settings and functions can play an important role in the preparation and continuing education of practitioners.

The purpose of professional education programs is to offer opportunities for practitioners to develop skills and knowledge and the propensity to act that will enable them to be effective educational leaders. Cases and case-based instruction offer one pedagogical approach to achieve this purpose.

❖ ABOUT CASES AND CASE METHODS

Many professional fields, including business, public policy, medicine, social work, law, and educational administration use cases and case methods to influence the knowledge and actions of professionals. Cases, it is believed, help impart professional skills. However, mentioning cases and the case method of instruction in any of these fields is certain to expose different definitions, purposes, and uses of these materials and pedagogical approaches. Definitions range widely depending upon the field and the context in which the materials are used. Sometimes these differences even exist within the same professional field.

The purpose of cases and case-based instruction in any professional field relates directly to the nature of the body of knowledge that exists in that particular field. In business education, for example, a case "provides data—substantive and process—essential to an analysis of a specific situation for the framing of alternative action programs, and for their implementation recognizing the complexity and ambiguity of the practical world." (Christensen & Hansen, 1987, p. 270). The purpose is to develop an understanding of what needs to be done and how to do it. In legal education, court decisions are used as case material to encourage future lawyers to trace threads of legal precedent in order to develop an understanding of legal theory and judicial reasoning. The study of cases helps students appreciate the meaning of the law through the study of particular, specific examples; the determination of legal precedence is fundamental.

In teacher education, educators use cases in a variety of ways—as exemplars to study and emulate, as instances to practice analysis and contemplate action, and as stimulants to personal reflection (Merseth, 1996). As exemplars, their purpose is "to exemplify the desired principle, theory or instructional technique" (Sykes & Bird, 1992, p. 480), while for the analysis and decision-making purpose, cases are used "as pedagogical tools for helping teachers practice the basic professional processes of analysis, problem solving, and decision making" (Doyle, 1990, p. 10). Some teacher educators have students create self-reported cases, not for the purpose of large class discussion, but rather to create the opportunity for personal disciplined instruction. In this instance, "preparing cases involves developing skills central to reflective practice" (Richert, 1991, p. 139).

Practitioners and faculty engaged in the design of educational administration programs frequently take decision making as central to administrative practice. Thus cases are employed in these programs to offer opportunities to practice analysis, problem solving, action planning, and evaluation. The emphasis is on the application of theory to analyze and solve problems of practice. As Christensen and Hansen of the Harvard Business School state: "The minimum end product of a case discussion is an understanding of what needs to be done and how it can be accomplished" (1987, p. 30).

❖ CASE METHODS

There is no single approach to teaching and learning with cases. A wide variety of methods work for different individuals in different situations. Case methods can stimulate individual study and reflection as well as offer a springboard for group problem solving. Some individuals use a combination of individual and group approaches to explore the content of the cases. For example, case readers may study a case individually, reviewing important data, and addressing previously suggested study questions. Some instructors require the preparation of written "case briefs" for submission prior to group discussion. Depending on the size of the discussion group, students may gather into small "study groups" of five to six individuals to share insights and questions that the preliminary analysis of the case has uncovered. Others may choose to employ role plays or dialectic exchanges to highlight differing perspectives in the case.

Clearly the role of the case discussion facilitator is important. This individual acts as a guide, who may probe, direct, challenge, or simply observe the discussion process. This is not an easy task. The demands of leading effective case discussions are significant. As Christensen and Zaleznick note "dealing with concrete situations is a far more complex and demanding task than working with any set of generalizations or theories" (1954, p. 215).

What are the characteristics of good case facilitators? First and foremost, the facilitators must know the subject. They must understand the theoretical foundation and knowledge base implicit in the case, and they must guide the discussion so that it is grounded in substantive knowledge. Many poorly led case discussions degenerate into "opinion-swapping" where analyses and action plans are not subjected to close analysis and exploration. The role of the instructor is to guard against loose talk and flabby thinking.

Proponents of case-based instruction often stress that the analysis of cases does not necessarily yield a single point of view. There are no "right answers" in case-based instruction. And yet, case-based instruction is not hopelessly mired in relativism; there are certain points of view and approaches to issues in administrative practice that are more effective than others. It is the role of the instructor to help the participants differentiate among these points of view and to bring a level of disciplined analysis and inquiry to the case discussion that produces thoughtful strategies and effective action plans. The case instructor accomplishes this task by grounding the discussion in the data of the case while reflecting the knowledge and theoretical foundations for the decisions.

In essence, effective instructors prepare not only the case but also to teach the case. This means focusing on the students and the discussion process at the same time as focusing on the content. Indeed, some experienced case discussion leaders suggest that the biggest change for faculty moving to case-based instruction is the need to focus on the teaching process—the teaching methods—used in the classroom (Welty, 1989). No longer is it sufficient to know the material well: case-based learning requires facilitators who consider the nature and characteristics of their learners and the dynamics of group interaction (Christensen, 1981; Christensen & Hansen, 1987, 1994). In so doing, they develop a set of teaching objectives and construct careful teaching outlines that include key concepts and related questions for use during the discussion, continually mindful of how to frame and connect the contributions of the students (Wasserman, 1994). Joseph Schwab summarized the characteristics of the effective discussion leader: The instructor must

> know the work under analysis through and through. Second, he must be equally familiar with the varieties of questions and attacks which can be made on such a work. . . . Third, he must be alertly and sensitively mindful of what each student is saying and doing, not only in the moment but in the whole course of the discussion (1969, p. 66).

These characteristics of case-based instruction place new demands on students as well. Learning with cases demands a different form of preparation and study by students. Instead of a loose confederation of individual learners, case-based instruction requires the creation of a community of learners with the responsibility for learning shared by all members of the community.

❖ THEORETICAL FRAMEWORK—DECISION MAKING IN EDUCATIONAL ADMINISTRATION

Educational administrators often act in the face of serious dilemmas, ambivalences, and paradoxes. Dilemmas of practice, as Lampert (1985) points out, are rarely solved. Instead they are managed. However, managing in the complex, ever-changing educational environment requires both a recognition and an ability to analyze the multiple influences on the environment. Three kinds of influences define this environment.

The first are those influences extrinsic to the event or decision. These may emanate from sources such as the political motivations of others, the economic constraints of the system, or the social and ethical mores of the organization. Administrators often acknowledge these factors and include them in their environmental analyses. Sometimes these influences are described as "politics" or "culture."

Intrinsic or internal factors make up the second set of influences and include features and characteristics inherent to the situation. For example, if an administrator wants to implement a new assessment program for fourth graders in mathematics, implicit and fundamental assumptions about what children at this level should know and be able to do as well as the nature and structure of mathematics will influence the design and implementation of the new program. Depending on the sophistication and experience of the practitioner, these intrinsic influences may or may not be acknowledged and addressed.

Practitioners also respond to a third influence—their own set of core beliefs, values, and personal philosophies about education. Personal beliefs often act as an invisible lodestar for educators as they think, plan, and undertake the work of administration. In particular, leaders with strong values and a clear vision can respond intuitively as well as analytically to the complex context of education. Many practitioners, however, have not articulated this core set of beliefs—their influence unspoken and unacknowledged. Whether an individual values confrontation over compromise or change over stability will significantly influence deliberation, analysis, and action. Making these personal beliefs more explicit can help administrators as they face the recurring tensions and dilemmas of educational practice.

These factors form the core of the educational enterprise and influence, in varying degrees, all forms of educational practice. In reality, however, much of the work of practitioners has a tendency toward detachment or isolation, ignoring or denying the existence of one or more of these influences. Urban school superintendents, for example, may drift away from implicit issues of teaching and learning as they administer food or transportation services; classroom teachers may "close their doors" to ignore the political and social realities swirling outside their classrooms. Thus it is the role of innovative practitioner education programs to make these influences explicit and to help practitioners gain the skills, dispositions, and habits of mind to acknowledge and understand these influences.

❖ RECURRING DILEMMAS OF EDUCATIONAL ADMINISTRATION

Dealing effectively with the recurring and persistent dilemmas of educational practice requires a recognition and analysis of the extrinsic and intrinsic elements of the situation as well as the administrator's beliefs and values. What are the recurring dilemmas—dilemmas that are more commonly managed rather than resolved? One dilemma that appears consistently in educational administration focuses on managing for the individual good versus managing for the common good. Examples of this dilemma appear in decisions about instructional program: How do you treat each child as an individual while still adhering to high standards for all? They also appear in personnel decisions: When does the right to privacy prevail over the right of the public to know? This dilemma also appears in setting system-wide budgetary priorities: Is it better to reduce all programs by ten percent, to close one elementary school, or to eliminate one program entirely?

Another common dilemma in educational administration focuses on decentralization versus centralization. When does it make sense to manage schools and their instructional programs centrally rather than individually? Should economies of scale supersede individual preferences? When should a principal or superintendent reward differences and manage for diversity rather than strive for uniformity? Other administrative dilemmas concern style and tempo: When is it best to act quickly rather than slowly? When are short term goals more important than long term objectives? When is confrontation ever preferred to compromise? When is flexibility preferred over precision?

Educational administrators operate in complex environments where change is the only certainty. Much of the skill in educational administration focuses on making decisions, designing strategies to enact the decisions, taking action, and assessing the results. Cases offer an opportunity to practice these administrative skills. The environments in which administrators practice are influenced by extrinsic, intrinsic, and personal factors that must be acknowledged by the administrator. To lead effectively in such environments, practitioners need integrity and courage to select appropriate actions.

❖ A GUIDE TO THE CASES IN THIS BOOK

A number of criteria guided the selection of cases for this book. First, all the cases in this collection depict actual events that occurred in administrative practice. They are real, not fictional. As such, the cases are descriptive research documents that seek to convey a balanced picture of a real-life situation. They represent concrete examples of common yet complex dilemmas and challenges present in many educational settings. The cases satisfy the criterion that they "bring a chunk of reality" into the professional classroom (Lawrence, 1960).

A second criterion for inclusion is that the cases reflect the reality of administrative practice. None of the cases evoke a clear "right answer or action." Instead, they illustrate the messy, complex situations that characterize administrative practice and seek to guard against the oversimplification of the educational environment. Complex cases stimulate and foster multiple perspectives and levels of analysis. This aspect of the pedagogy exposes the novice to differing interpretations of complex situations that often characterize the thinking of more experienced practitioners. Furthermore, reasonable, well-grounded analyses of these cases will differ, multiple interpretations abound. Depending on background, personal beliefs, and individual skills, individuals can analyze the same case in very different ways. The cases offer an opportunity to explore the complicated nature of administration.

The book presents cases in six categories which correspond to substantive areas in which administrators frequently make decisions and take action. It is important to note that the categories are *not* mutually exclusive; they only provide the reader with a general guide to the issues and topics presented in the cases. Many of the cases explore multiple concepts and thus may be used to explore many different issues. For example, the same case may exemplify professional development, labor relations, and organizational change issues. Nearly all of the cases in this collection offer opportunities to explore the important topics of politics and organizational culture. The categories include Professional Development, Community Relations, Governance, Organizational Design, Curriculum and Assessment, and Personnel and Labor.

Further descriptions of the cases and the categories appear at the beginning of each section. In addition, at the end of each case, readers will find suggested questions to guide initial reflections and analyses of the cases.

❖ A GUIDE FOR STUDENTS

For students, the use of cases in the classroom can signal the development of new study habits, alternative forms of preparation and participation, and new levels of collaboration with fellow students. Because of their participatory nature, case discussions require that students prepare explicitly for each class by reading the material, discussing the case informally with classmates, and coming to class ready to contribute to the learning of others. Case discussions, in order to be effective, must be student-driven.

Those new to case discussions will notice a number of differences in case-based classrooms from more traditional lecture-based learning. First, in case-based discussions, students take more responsibility for their own learning and for the learning of others in the class. Unlike traditional lectures, students do not sit idly receiving information from the course instructor. In case discussions, students actively participate. Productive learning from cases relies on a strong learning community where respect for ideas and alternative viewpoints abounds. Through the case discussion process, members of the learning community combine individual ideas and perspectives together to create new understandings that very few could build alone. Ideas developed in this collective and respectful way ideally will present a whole that is richer and more substantive than the sum of the parts.

Second, norms of student collaboration may differ from other more traditional classrooms. While some classes may stress the independent preparation of students of problem sets or papers, case-based learning is enhanced by student collaboration both within and outside the classroom. Instructors may ask that students join informal "study groups" to discuss the case prior to the large class meeting. The purpose of this informal discussion is to offer an opportunity for the students to hear the ideas and thoughts of their classmates. These informal discussions also provide learners with an opportunity to examine their own personal beliefs and knowledge and to "try out" new ideas before moving to the larger group context. In the classroom, some case instructors assess the performance of participants not only on the quality of their own ideas or case analysis, but also on the participant's ability to affect the learning of others. The focus on the group construction of a strategy, not on individual performance, differs from more traditional settings. Collaboration is encouraged. Great advances in complex problem analyses are most commonly the result of cooperation and mutual respect.

Learning to be a good listener is another skill that may seem new to case participants. Carefully listening to the contributions of others in case discussions serves two purposes. First, it enables the listener to examine, compare, and explore, in private, his or her own understandings with regard to that of the speaker. And second, careful listening will enhance the group problem solving process, avoiding unnecessary repetitions and false starts.

Students participating in case discussions should expect to spend time reflecting individually on the content and concepts of the cases, both before and after the class. Throughout the entire process, case-based learning assumes an actively engaged respectful participant; it also assumes that all who participate in the discussion, either through listening or building on the ideas of their colleagues, will have fun.

❖ A GUIDE FOR FACILITATORS

To achieve the widely cited advantages of case-based instruction, case discussion facilitators need to develop expertise in a number of facets of the case discussion process. A case discussion leader has multiple responsibilities: to guide a disciplined and theoretically grounded analysis of the case; to elicit and sustain multiple points of view in order to construct a deep understanding of the issues in the case; and to facilitate positive personal interactions among the participants in order to create a positive learning environment.

Teaching with cases often represents a new experience for instructors and students. As such, it offers an opportunity to explore alternative arrangements in the classroom and affords an occasion to expand one's pedagogical repertoire. For those who are new to this pedagogical approach, the following suggestions may offer a helpful starting guide. These suggestions are divided into four categories: preparation; discussion facilitation; physical arrangements; and student participation.

❖ PREPARATION

Teaching with cases requires significant preparation time. Some instructors suggest that discussion leaders read the case at least three times before its discussion. The first review helps gain a sense of the overall context, the second explores the major issues and concepts, and the third focuses on the development of leading the case discussion with a particular group. Case facilitators need to have a firm grasp on the details of the case including characters, context, plot, major and minor themes, and fundamental issues. It is often helpful to ask "What type of case is this?" as one prepares to lead a case discussion and "Why have I decided to use this case at this time?"

All of the cases in this book have multiple themes and issues. While many of the issues are interrelated and intertwined, facilitators should not expect to explore all the issues and topics in the case during one discussion session. Sometimes it is best to identify the two or three critical issues in the case and focus on those rather than trying to "cover the waterfront." Instructors may elect to use multiple sessions to explore different facets of the same case.

Case facilitators must prepare both the content of the case as well as the discussion process itself. Leaders should plan the discussion, keeping in mind the particular experiences, perspectives, and personalities of the participants. It is not the role of the facilitator to simply lead a review of the facts and details of a case; rather, the role is to stimulate analysis, problem solving, and higher order thinking. Effective and thought-provoking questions combined with the prior identification of individual perspectives are key elements in this planning process. Simultaneously tracking the content and the process of a case discussion is perhaps the most challenging aspect of case teaching.

❖ DISCUSSION FACILITATION

During the discussion, case facilitators should not be concerned with silence and reflection. A cacophony of voices does not necessarily indicate that learning is taking place. Discussion leaders should try to encourage an analytic process that is grounded in the context of the case. Usually it is not wise to assume additional or hypothetical information not stated in the case. Speculation about additional facts in the case can lead to "opinion swapping" and loose thinking. If the case doesn't state a fact, the best interpretation is "We simply don't know."

Case discussion leaders must model and encourage good listening skills. Whenever possible, ask participants to direct their statements to their classmates and to relate their comments to previous discussion points. Redirecting comments with statements such as, "How does your view relate to the point that so-and-so just made?" signal the importance of listening and building on the interpretations of others.

In addition, case leaders should monitor "air time" and be sure that all participants have an opportunity to contribute to the discussion. In this context, it is important to protect those who take risky or unpopular positions. Discussion leaders will want to model respect for all learners and their viewpoints in the case discussion classroom. Without a respectful environment, learning from discussions will be difficult, if not impossible.

❖ PHYSICAL SETTING

Case discussions are enhanced by the ability to see the faces of all of the participants. Thus arranging the classroom in a "U" or in a circle is advised. Facilitators usually stand during a case discussion in order to maintain eye contact with all the participants and to access to the blackboard or other recording devices. Blackboards can help create a map of the discussion and document key points. Recording the comments of participants on the blackboard encourages participation and provides ample evidence of the group's efforts. At the end of a session, leaders may use the blackboard to take a few moments to review the key points made during the discussion.

Facilitators often ask one participant to "lead off" or initiate the discussion. Requests made before class or as the class is assembling are called "cool calls" whereas direct calls, "Karl, would you lead off today?" are known as "cold calls." Depending on the setting, either approach can be effective. Productive and effective discussions of cases in this book can easily occupy 90 minutes at a minimum. If facilitators decide to extend the discussion time, a stretch break is advisable.

❖ STUDENT PREPARATION

Because case discussion may be as new to the participants as it is to the facilitator, it will be helpful to stress the need for careful listening, detailed preparation, and active learning and participation by students before launching into the first case discussion. Students should understand that the case discussion leader will not deliver the "right answer," and that the major advances in learning and understandings will come from their active participation with others in the classroom setting.

Case questions found at the end of each case are intended to guide the pre-discussion and small group consideration of the case. A case facilitator should assume that these questions have been explored and answered. Essentially these questions form a common platform for further investigation by the group. Case leaders may wish to assign additional questions either for written "case briefs" to be submitted before the discussion or for additional reflection following the discussion. In other instances, the facilitator may wish to utilize role plays or the acting out of small vignettes from the cases as methods to engage student participation.

❖ A MATRIX OF TOPICS, CONTEXTS, AND PROTAGONISTS

1. Quiet Time
2. It Ain't Fair
3. The Prince and the Principal
4. The Science Fair Incident
5. Promise and Fear
6. Rash Decisions
7. An Apple for the Teacher
8. Who Goes?
9. The Allen School
10. Augusta County—Beech Mountain Institute
11. Dante Alighieri High School
12. Ottawa High School
13. What's Your Plan, Mr. Sommers?
14. Joe Fernandez and the *Children of the Rainbow* Guide
15. Imagining the World
16. Lake Wobegon West High
17. Who Knows Best?
18. On the Cutting Edge of Education Reform
19. The Case of Bernice Demovsky
20. Ascot School District
21. The Case of Jack Buick
22. Supporting Teachers at Somerset High

Protagonist	1	2	3	4	5	6	7	8	9	10	11	12	13	14	15	16	17	18	19	20	21	22
Superintendent	X						X			X			X	X					X	X		
Assistant Superintendent																						
High School Principal				X	X		X					X				X					X	X
Middle School Principal			X	X		X		X	X									X				
Elementary School Principal											X											
Assistant Principal	X	X										X			X	X					X	
Department Head																					X	X
Curriculum Coordinator	X	X	X	X	X	X	X	X			X	X	X	X	X	X	X	X		X	X	X
Teacher(s)	X	X	X	X	X	X	X	X	X		X						X	X		X	X	X
Parent(s)	X	X		X	X						X						X					
Student(s)		X																				
Other					X		X			X	X		X	X	X	X	X		X	X		

Level of School/Organization	1	2	3	4	5	6	7	8	9	10	11	12	13	14	15	16	17	18	19	20	21	22
District	X	X	X							X	X	X	X	X	X	X					X	X
High School				X	X		X				X	X			X	X				X	X	X
Middle			X			X		X	X								X	X				
Elementary																	X	X	X			
Other																			X			
Public	X	X		X	X		X	X		X	X	X	X	X		X	X		X	X	X	X
Private															X				X			

Location	1	2	3	4	5	6	7	8	9	10	11	12	13	14	15	16	17	18	19	20	21	22
Urban	X								X		X			X					X	X		X
Suburban	X					X	X	X				X	X		X	X	X	X	X		X	
Small Town					X	X		X		X		X		X	X		X					
Rural				X		X	X			X				X								

Category	1	2	3	4	5	6	7	8	9	10	11	12	13	14	15	16	17	18	19	20	21	22
Professional Dvlp./Staff Relations	X	X	X								X	X	X	X	X	X	X		X	X	X	X
Labor Relations			X									X	X	X			X	X	X	X	X	X
Curriculum Assessment Instruction		X		X		X	X	X	X	X	X			X	X	X	X	X	X	X	X	
Community Relations and Politics	X			X	X	X	X	X				X	X	X			X	X	X	X		X
Governance			X	X	X	X	X			X	X	X	X	X	X	X						
Organizational Development	X									X	X											
School Board Member										X												

PROFESSIONAL DEVELOPMENT

Creating a positive and supportive culture where staff members feel valued and have the opportunity to develop professionally and personally is an important responsibility of educational administrators. Whether in the role of superintendent, principal, staff developer, department chair, teacher, or central office employee, decisions and actions to improve the human capacity of the members of the community are central to the creation of a positive learning environment for all. The cases in this section explore the opportunities for professional growth in various learning communities and the actions that educational administrators and teachers can take to enhance professional development. The cases in this section also offer an opportunity to examine the political environment and its influence on the educational culture.

❖ QUIET TIME

Westbay was considered a "model" school for many years, but recently it has experienced a serious decrease in enrollment. The community blames the teachers and the fallout is low staff morale. Hoping to support her teachers' professional development and boost morale, Gloria Wilson, head of the English department, has found funding to give each of her teachers a day off each semester for professional enrichment, but she runs into trouble with the other departments.

❖ IT AIN'T FAIR!

First-year teacher Laurie Cabot has been working hard during the first two months of school to motivate her racially and ethnically diverse sophomore English students, but nothing seemed to work. Her fourteen departmental colleagues in this large urban school are all much older than she and seem too busy to help her. Laurie decides to try something different—Cooperative Team Learning. Things don't work out the way Laurie expects.

❖ THE PRINCE AND THE PRINCIPAL (A AND B)

After a year of vigorous but friendly efforts to improve the school environment and to engage faculty in improving learning, Betty Tyler, principal, finds
only seven or eight teachers with whom she can work and an "old guard" that
is literally harassing her. A district supervisor gives her the following advice:
Read Machiavelli's *The Prince* and then mobilize your seven or eight good
teachers.

Suggested Readings

Barth, R. (1990). *Improving schools from within.* San Francisco: Jossey-Bass.

Lampert, M. (1985). How do teachers manage to teach? Perspectives on problems in practice. *Harvard Educational Review, 55,* 178–194.

Lieberman, A., and Miller L. (1991). *Staff development for education in the
'90s: New demands, new realities, new perspectives.* New York: Teachers
College Press.

Little, J. (1993). Teachers' professional development in a climate of educational reform. *Educational Evaluation & Policy Analysis, 15,* 129–151.

Sarason, S. (1996). *Revisiting the culture of the school and the problem of
change.* New York: Teachers College Press.

Sykes, G. (1990). Fostering teacher professionalism in schools. In R. Elmore
(ed.), *Restructuring schools: The next generation of educational reform* (pp.
59–96). San Francisco: Jossey-Bass.

Quiet Time

Julia Ames Van

It was 5:45 on a Thursday afternoon in mid-September. The halls of Westbay High School were quiet. Gloria Wilson, head of the English department, was still at her desk. "What a day," thought Gloria as she sipped her tepid coffee. A new school year always meant dealing with one problem after another. And, on top of today's crises, she'd needed to spend a couple of hours preparing for her morning meeting with Westbay's principal, Bob Singer.

For several months the previous year, faculty members from the English department at Westbay High accumulated research on the value of reflective time for educators. The idea was that teachers needed "quiet time" to reflect on their teaching, to brainstorm new lessons, to set goals, and more. The English teachers were excited and intrigued by what they read and presented their information at the June department meeting. Gloria reviewed the research her teachers presented and found it very convincing.

In fact, Gloria and the fourteen members of the English department pursued the "quiet time" idea with a small but powerful group of parents called the Patron's Group. It was a fundraising organization for schools in the district and regularly funded proposals from teachers and departments. The group was progressive and particularly receptive to proposals for classroom reform.

Over the summer, Gloria and two other English teachers wrote a proposal requesting $2,800 to hire substitute teachers. According to the proposal, every English teacher would have a substitute teacher, one day each semester, and use the time outside the classroom to improve their teaching. English teachers might attend a seminar, work on a new lesson, or reflect on teaching habits. The proposal was submitted to the Patron's Group in late August and, in early September, the English department was notified that the initiative would be funded contingent on the principal's approval.

Gloria had phoned Bob Singer during the summer to brief him on the progress of the proposal. She was meeting with him in the morning to explain the program in detail and receive his formal approval.

❖ WESTBAY HIGH SCHOOL

Westbay High was a medium-sized high school located in a middle-class suburb of a large, metropolitan city in the Pacific Northwest. The school enrolled 1,200 students in grades 9 through 12. The student body was homogenous; only 6 percent were students of color. Westbay High was considered a "model" school in the late 1970s and early 1980s but now was rumored to be on a "downswing." The building site, though pleasant when it was built in the 1950s, was showing signs of age. Moreover, the area's youth population was dwindling at the same time as a number of students were leaving the district for a new series of magnet schools in the city. The community routinely blamed district teachers for the decline in enrollment. Many residents felt the district teachers were old, inflexible and too close to retirement to care about innovation.

Gloria was relieved when the district hired Bob Singer as the new principal of Westbay High. Bob was appointed the year before and charged with "turning things around at the high school." His predecessor was a "by the book kind of guy." Many thought he'd been unresponsive to local and district requests for change. Gloria and the other department heads felt stifled under his direction.

Bob Singer seemed different from the start. On his first day at Westbay High, he called an all-faculty meeting to introduce himself and explain his management style and educational philosophy. Bob's manner was warm and jovial. He told a string of corny jokes throughout the meeting. Everyone was pleased and hopeful.

Bob was a recent graduate of an elite east coast university. During his first year at the school, his initiatives impressed everyone. He said he believed in an open door, hands off policy. He welcomed new ideas and encouraged experimentation. "What we need to worry about is what's best for the kids," he said. "If that means we all need to wear our shirts inside out, then that's what we'll do." He expressed the same philosophy to his five department heads. Gloria was encouraged. She was eager to implement new policies after years of maintaining the status quo. *Quiet Time* was the first in a long list of initiatives she wanted to realize.

❖ THE NEXT MORNING

"You see, Bob, the English department is growing fragmented and unfocused," Gloria explained. "Getting through the English curriculum can be so burdensome that I worry the teachers never have time to sit back and think about their teaching or the big picture. They initiated this idea and I think it's a good one. I want to support them."

Bob looked over the three page proposal. "You'll take care of coordinating the scheduling? I don't want the entire department taking *Quiet Time* simultaneously," he replied.

"No problem. I don't anticipate that being an issue. Also, I'm not going to require the teachers to take their *Quiet Time* here in school. They can just as easily reflect at home sitting at the kitchen table as they can here," said Gloria. "Each teacher will be asked to file a report describing how they spent their time and explaining how *Quiet Time* helped them in the classroom."

Bob leaned back in his chair. "Keep me posted on your progress," he said. "Let's see how it goes this year before we make it permanent."

"Terrific! I'll tell my department this afternoon." Gloria was pleased. This was definitely a step in the right direction.

❖ GLORIA WILSON

After graduating with a degree in secondary education from a large midwestern university, Gloria Wilson spent five years teaching English in a high school on the lower east side of New York City. She met her husband there and moved with him to the Pacific Northwest twelve years ago. After teaching English at Westbay High for eight years, she became head of the department.

Gloria was thrilled when she was named head of the English department. She'd always had ideas for impacting the way English was taught at the high school and was excited to have the opportunity to implement them. When Bob came on board, Gloria had been department head for three years. She felt ambivalent about her accomplishments. It also disturbed her that her staff referred to her as "The General." Gloria tried to solicit teachers' input but frequently felt compelled to make unilateral decisions. She knew this didn't sit well but she couldn't seem to avoid it. People often didn't respond to her requests; they seemed tired and uninvolved. Gloria hoped *Quiet Time* would generate goodwill and be the beginning of a new era in the English department.

❖ THE ENGLISH DEPARTMENT

Fourteen educators composed Westbay High's English department. They were known for being a cohesive group and some were thought to be innovative teachers.

But problems were emerging. Gloria was receiving complaints from parents about her teachers being "unresponsive." They weren't returning phone calls or responding to parent suggestions. At the same time, department meetings were beginning to disintegrate into gripe sessions. Gossip and back stabbing were on the rise.

"Dymillah, Barbara, Tony and the rest are all putting in sixty and seventy hour weeks," Gloria confided to Stuart Greenburg, the head of the science department. "The problem is we're in a continual state of crisis management, just barely keeping up with classes and paperwork. We run from one fire to the next. I feel like I have talented people who never have time to think about anything but the task at hand. It's a waste."

In private, Gloria acknowledged that her staff and the rest of the faculty were reacting to other conditions, as well. Decreasing enrollments meant staff reductions and those who remained were overworked. Bob Singer was the third principal at the high school in ten years. Parent-teacher antagonisms were worse than Gloria had ever experienced. Westbay High's reputation was in decline and so was morale. Gloria was affected by low morale, too. For the first time in her career, she found herself avoiding her staff and some of her duties.

❖ QUIET TIME UNFOLDS

As promised, Gloria announced the *Quiet Time* funding in the department meeting that afternoon. The English teachers were jubilant and began making plans for their day off.

Dymillah was the first to use her time and was very prompt in submitting her report. "I spent my morning studying Howard Gardner's *Multiple Intelligences*," she wrote. "I pulled out an idea for a student poetry slam that I had last year and used my afternoon to draft some ideas, research potential sponsors and poets in the area and work up a rough timeline. It's amazing what a day of peace and quiet will do!"

Later that week, after receiving Dymillah's report, Gloria went downstairs to a meeting of department heads in Bob's office. The minute she walked in the door she knew it was going to be a long one. Pam Walsh, head of the social studies department, started off. "What's this *Quiet Time* all about Gloria? That's all I hear from my staff, 'How come the English department can take days off and we can't?'"

Enrico Dominguez, head of the foreign language department, chimed in. "Look Gloria, I'm sure this is a great thing for the English department, but think how it looks to the rest of the building. My teachers think you all just take days off and go to the beach."

Bob spoke up. "Look, this is an idea that Gloria brought to me in August and we decided to try it out for the year. We just wanted to see what would happen. At the end of the year, I'll take a look at the reports her department prepares and decide if I think the program is worthwhile. If I like what I see, I'll reprogram enough funds to provide subs for all the departments. Until then, let's give it a fair chance. Now, let's get back to the agenda. . . ."

After the meeting, Gloria found a message taped to her chair, "Call Bonnie Myers as soon as you get back." Bonnie Myers was the parent of a student in Dymillah's senior AP English class and president of the Westbay High PTA. Gloria, an active PTA member, worked with Bonnie several times through the years and the two women had developed a comfortable rapport. Although Bonnie could be difficult, Gloria greatly respected her commitment to Westbay High, its students and its faculty.

"Gloria, what is this I hear about teacher *Quiet Time* in the English department?" Bonnie asked. "My daughter tells me she had a substitute teacher in her class last week because Dymillah was planning some poetry thing. Listen, I believe in professional development, but I don't want my kids subjected to no-brain substitutes. Since when can Dymillah take a day off to work on extracurricular activities?"

Gloria heard the edge in Bonnie's voice. The thought crossed Gloria's mind that a lot more was going on here than Bonnie's concern for her daughter's hour with a substitute. It was a fact that the PTA and the Patron's Group vied for influence in the high school. The two groups rarely agreed on anything. Gloria suspected that this phone call was really related to the PTA–Patron's Group rivalry. She replied, "Well, I'm trying something new with the English department. Each term, every teacher can take one day off to reflect on their teaching, work on a new project for the classroom, attend a seminar, or whatever—as long as it's professionally related. I got the funding from the Patron's Group to pay substitute teachers for those days."

"Look, let me be honest with you, Gloria. I've been getting complaints from parents about Dymillah's day off. This idea of a 'free day' is not going over well. You and Bob are going to be getting a lot of phone calls from angry parents on this one—especially as more teachers take time off. I think a major brouhaha is on its way. I just wanted to get the scoop from you and let you know what's going on. Did Bob okay this?"

"Yes, we couldn't accept the funding without his approval. Bob agreed to try the program for the year to see how it works," Gloria replied.

Bonnie said, "Well, I'd like some input on that decision. Will you transfer me to Bob's office?"

Gloria transferred Bonnie and leaned back in her chair. "Oh great, here we go," she thought. There was nothing to do but wait for Bob's call.

And ten minutes later, the phone rang. It was Mitra, Bob's secretary. "Gloria, do you have some time this afternoon? Bob wants to see you. . ."

❖ CASE PREPARATION QUESTIONS

1. Gloria Wilson has developed a plan to provide much needed "reflection time" for the teachers in the English department. Was Gloria's plan a good one?

2. Gloria is a "manager in the middle." Who should have a say in the design of professional development programs for teachers? Teachers, department chairpersons, principals, parents? Should Bob Singer have approved Gloria's plan?

It Ain't Fair!

Katherine K. Merseth

It was Sunday night. Laurie Cabot felt her stomach tighten as she switched off the TV and walked reluctantly down the hall toward her desk and the pile of student essays awaiting her comments. As she gazed out the window at the blinking Christmas lights, she recalled Tony's angry words before his stormy exit from her room at Gardiner High School on Friday afternoon:

> How come I gotta do essays and Maria don't? Huh?? How come Maria gets the same grade as me when she don't do the work? Dumb SPIC!! How come, Miss Cabot? IT AIN'T FAIR! Group work sucks and so does this class!!

As Laurie looked back at her desk and the papers, she knew she needed to do something about tomorrow. Indeed, she had told Maria two weeks ago that she would not have to make up her missed essays; she felt Maria simply could not handle the pressure. On the other hand, Laurie was convinced Tony had talent but had never been pushed. Tony's words, "How come, Miss Cabot? It ain't fair!" kept ringing in her head.

❖ LAURIE CABOT

After graduating with a B.A. degree in English, Laurie chose an M.A. program in teaching at Longfellow University. Laurie received her certification to teach English and joined the faculty of Gardiner High School. She felt lucky to get the job because jobs for white teachers were difficult to get in the inner city. Mandates for racial balance required personnel offices to seek minorities as new hires. Often, however, minority teachers could not be found because so few minorities elected teaching as a career. For Laurie, this meant that she got her job on Friday, August 29th and was to report to Gardiner the next Tuesday, the day before school opened on September 3.

Laurie's commitment to urban education stemmed in part from the influence of her mother who had been a kindergarten teacher for 18 years, and from her work as an undergraduate in a dual history and literature and urban studies concentration. She enjoyed school, loved learning new things and had always been surrounded by others with similar values. Her father, a successful corporate lawyer, and her brother, a third year medical student, weren't so sure why Laurie had such a passion for education, and urban education at that. When Laurie visited home over Thanksgiving break, her father commented, "If you really like teaching that much, why don't you just come back to Evanston and teach at Deerfield High for a few years? You could live at home and save some money in case you decide to go back for a doctorate in a few years." Laurie often wondered if her father feared for her physical safety in an urban school or whether he disapproved of the use of a Longfellow education for teaching. She never asked him.

❖ GARDINER HIGH SCHOOL

Gardiner High School was a large, urban school of 2600 students, known for its superiority in athletics and its eight-story physical plant complete with escalators connecting the floors. Because Gardiner was the only high school in the city, students reflected varied social and economic backgrounds as well as intellectual talents and interests in learning.

Gardiner High was 70% minority with over 70 different countries of origin and languages represented in the student body. The racial make-up of the school was 35% African-American, 30% Caucasian, 25% Hispanic, and 10% Asian. Gardiner had not always been so racially and ethnically diverse. In fact, the mix of students had changed drastically over the last 10 years since the major employer, National Steel, had closed the mill. These changes in student and town demographics were not reflected in the teaching staff who were predominantly white and over 40.

As a first year teacher, Laurie was given four classes with three different preparations, lunch duty, and bathroom patrol. Her classes were two general 9th grade English classes, one 10th grade remedial English class, and a senior elective in composition for students in the Vocational-Technical track. Laurie knew it was a tough schedule, but she knew it was typical for a first year teacher. Classmates at Longfellow had told her that schools often give the toughest schedules to the new teachers. Something about experience and seniority left the advanced placement classes for the veteran teachers.

Laurie was the only new hire in the English department. She had heard that there was also a new teacher in math and a new soccer coach who taught health. She had never met them, since they didn't have the same "prep" periods, and Laurie taught on the fourth floor while math and science were taught on the seventh floor.

Laurie felt reasonably comfortable in the English department with a staff of 14, even though she was more than 20 years younger than the next youngest member. Nearly all were married and had jobs after school. While most were friendly, few seemed to have the time or interest to help a rookie learn the ropes. In one of the monthly department meetings, Laurie asked if she could observe some classes. Two teachers said it would be alright, but she felt by their response that her request was an unusual one.

❖ SYSTEM POLICIES

The chairman of the department, Paul Kelly, talked with Laurie during the first week of classes. He gave her a tour of the bookroom (which by then was in a sorry state after the veteran teachers had taken their books) and reviewed some of the system policies. According to a system wide plan instituted the prior year, Paul informed Laurie that all teachers were to turn in plans every 9 weeks to the Superintendent's office. The purpose of this activity was to enable administrators to know what was being taught in each class in order to conduct unannounced evaluations of teachers on any given day. In addition, teachers were required to write their objectives and class plans on the board each day. The principal of Gardiner routinely checked to see if this information was available as instructed. Laurie had heard a rumor that a teacher had been fired last Spring for not having this information on his board. Finally, there were mandatory instructional activities that must be observable in every lesson including: initiating the class; stating the objective; recalling the immediate pre-requisites; reviewing the study assignments; introducing new information; providing practice and feedback; and offering a closing summary.

These requirements made Laurie's head swim, but she conscientiously prepared her 9 week and daily plans, although there was precious little match between her plans and reality. "How can I know how long this essay will take?" she thought to herself. The harder she worked, the worse the results were in the classroom. This upset her; hard work in college had always produced good results for her. It was so different being a teacher than being a student. She constantly worried about her evaluations. The principal had come to her room once, but luckily was immediately called on his walkie-talkie and had to leave before he could ascertain what she was teaching.

❖ LAURIE'S IDEA

Laurie continued to work hard, spending evenings and weekends planning and preparing materials, but she was not having any success with her sophomores. The class seemed lethargic and bored. The kids, when they came to class, sat with their arms folded, saying nothing. Others would mumble a response if asked a question or put their heads on their desks and sleep for part of the period. It was just after Thanksgiving that Laurie decided to try something different.

Laurie stopped Paul Kelly in the hall and asked what he thought about implementing small working groups in the class. He was not enthusiastic. "It is hard enough to control a class of sophomores with everyone doing the same thing," he warned. "Control should be your first concern. If you use a whole-class lecture approach you can concentrate on the subject. Besides, it's a lot of work to have groups and some of your students may not like it." Laurie also knew that Paul wondered how she would incorporate the mandatory instructional activities into her lessons with students working in groups. She could sense that he was about to mention this when his secretary joined them and reminded Paul he had a meeting. It was clear that Paul was trying to discourage her without being completely negative.

Laurie wanted to try anyway. In her classes at Longfellow, the faculty had discussed Cooperative Team Learning techniques and pointed out the advantages of such an approach for students of mixed abilities and different social and ethnic classes. Laurie dug out her Longfellow class notes about cooperative learning and teams. In her notebook Laurie had written, "Two important effects of cooperative learning—creation of friendships among students of different ethnic or social backgrounds and an increase in self esteem of kids." As she reflected on the way her Latino students sat on one side of her room and the Black students sat in the back, she decided, "This is just what I need."

❖ MARIA

At the same time as Laurie was trying to find a solution to lack of motivation in her classes, she also found herself thinking about individual students. Maria Rodrigues was one of them. Maria had entered Gardiner in early October, after moving to town with her mother and two younger brothers. Maria was very shy, her English was extremely limited. When she came to class, she sat near the windows and said nothing.

At first, Laurie had tried to encourage her, holding her to the same standards as the rest of the class. But late in October, after only a few weeks in her class, Laurie sensed Maria was slipping. One day, she asked Maria to come back after school and, when she returned, Laurie explained that she was worried about Maria's performance. Sounding a little like her own high school English teacher, Laurie said:

> Sophomore English is a significant course for you. The curriculum covers many important plays and novels. Everyone in English 10 must learn to write a good essay. The same standards for this course are applied to everyone and include meeting due dates, coming to class prepared, and submitting homework. I know you can do it, Maria. I know you can; it just takes hard work.

Laurie felt good about her talk with Maria. She knew it was important to have clear and high standards.

But Maria continued to slip. She would be absent two or three days each week. When she came to class, she would not have her homework, and for the in-class writing assignments, she would submit a single page of poor quality. Laurie felt she had to do something. She invited Maria to come see her to go over her missed assignments. Nearly two weeks had passed when Maria quietly walked into Laurie's room. During the meeting, Maria hesitantly described her responsibilities caring for her younger brothers and working in a donut shop after school. Tears welled up in her eyes. The family needed her paycheck, she stuttered, to pay for groceries.

Laurie felt an ache of frustration within her. She resolved then to take certain steps to help Maria. Since the class was starting group work after Thanksgiving, Laurie decided it would be a good time to make different arrangements for Maria. Feeling great sympathy for Maria, Laurie offered her a different grading system:

> Maria, you don't have to complete your past essays; we'll just ignore those and I will give you a special competency exam to demonstrate your skills. When you come to class, do what you can. If you miss an assignment because you are absent, I will excuse you.

Maria was grateful. Laurie decided not to press Maria. She now felt it best to accept Maria where she was.

❖ COOPERATIVE LEARNING AT GARDINER HIGH

Laura's tenth grade English classes were reading *Catcher in the Rye* by J.D. Salinger and she planned her group work around the novel. At the end of one week of reading, and writing, and revising essays, the small groups were to produce a final group report that addressed the development of the main character, Holden—the conflict he faced, how he came to realize the conflict, and how he chose to deal with it. When Laurie introduced the assignment to the class, she stressed the importance of revisions:

> Today, we'll be working in groups (groans from the students) on *Catcher in the Rye*. Each of you is to select one of five questions about Holden and write a 5 page essay. Wednesday and Thursday we will read each other's essays, making comments and revisions. On Friday, you will bring the final version of your essay to class and you will meet as a group to make final comments on the essays and to plan a group report for Monday that uses everyone's work. The grade for the group report will be the equivalent of a chapter test for each of you. Now listen, while I announce the teams. Team One: Tommy Young, Captain; Maria Rodrigues; Tony D'Angelo; Isa Fan and Armando Rey. Team Two. . . .

Laurie had put Tommy Young in charge of one of the six groups she had created for the 32 students of the class. Tommy seemed a natural for a group leader. Intelligent, articulate, interested in reading, he seemed, too, to enjoy helping other students. Laurie deliberately placed Tony D'Angelo in Tommy's group because she thought Tommy's good work habits might motivate him. Laurie also hoped the group experience would increase Tony's self esteem. And, at the last minute, Laurie added Maria Rodrigues to the group because she thought Tommy was mature and compassionate enough to make room for Maria's limited language abilities.

❖ THE RESPONSE

"You wouldn't believe what happened then!" Laurie told her roommate. "I looked up and Tony and Tommy were yelling and pushing each other. A desk was overturned; kids moved away, anticipating a fight. Tony said something like 'I ain't gonna take no crap from you about my essay. Who in the hell do you think you are to tell me it stinks.' Then Tommy said something like, 'But we all have to work on it for a group grade. If our group fails, it's *your* fault.' Then Tony glared at me, shook his fist, and walked to the door. 'I ain't gonna be no part of no stupid group! Besides, how come I gotta do essays and Maria don't? Huh? How come Maria gets the same grade as me when she don't do the work? Dumb SPIC!! It ain't fair! Group work sucks and so does this class!!'"

❖ CASE PREPARATION QUESTIONS

1. There are a number of problems at Gardiner High School. What are they and whose problems are they?

2. Describe the culture of Gardiner High and the English department. Whose responsibility is it to support beginning teachers like Laurie Cabot?

3. Describe Laurie Cabot's responsibilities as a teacher.

◆ ◆ ◆

The Prince and the Principal (A)

Roger Shouse, principal co-author, assisted by Darryl Ford, Paula Kleine-Kracht, and Susan Ryan

It was mid-December and Betty Tyler sat alone on her living room sofa, under the light from the nearby Christmas tree. A year before, the flickering glow might have warmed her heart, but now it seemed an inconvenience barely thwarting the cold night. It was just a year ago, Tyler remembered, she had been ready to begin an exciting new career as principal of the Florence Elementary School. Now, she wondered if her career as a principal was near its end.

Tyler prided herself on not giving in easily. She recalled an incident that had occurred several years earlier, at the end of her twelfth year teaching kindergarten in a Chicago school. She and her principal had been engaged in an ongoing professional dispute that had finally become unbearable. Rather than obey unacceptable directives from her principal, she had threatened to quit. "You can't," said the principal. "I happen to know that you just bought a new car!" But Tyler was not bluffing. "I'm not a woman you can say *can't* to," she realized. She submitted her resignation the same day.

For the next several years Tyler worked as a sales representative for an educational publishing company, a job that sent her to as many as a dozen schools a day. She'd become a keen observer, able to sense the mood of a school within moments of entering the building. And as she observed, her knowledge deepened, not only of the interactions among students, teachers, and administrators, but also of the contributions that she could make to improving schools. In her mid-forties—an age at which many professionals "settle in" and look towards retirement—Tyler decided to put her knowledge to use. She returned to teaching and took the Chicago principal's exam. That was two years ago. She began her new career teaching seventh and eighth graders for a short time, but, once again, she felt frustrated by an unsupportive principal. If she wanted to work in a school that was run well, she thought, she would have to run it herself.

❖ FLORENCE MIDDLE SCHOOL

Tyler first visited the Florence Middle School, on the south side of Chicago, shortly after being appointed the new principal. It was mid-year. Her assignment would begin in a few weeks, at the beginning of the second semester.

Tyler was visiting the school on a bleak winter day. Entering the building, she was immediately struck by its dismal interior. The school's hallways were dark. Instead of holiday decorations, the walls were adorned with graffiti and litter. Students ran by, laughing and making noise. An angry teacher shouted at them to stop. She was not comforted coming in from the cold. The Florence School looked to be a "dark, depressing mess."

Arriving at the office, Tyler asked to speak with Mr. Anthony, the Assistant Principal. The secretary, Mrs. Potter, told Tyler that Ralph Anthony was meeting with some parents in the "Parent Room." With directions to the Parent Room, Tyler retraced her steps down the hall, all the while looking for anything that might contradict her earlier impression of the school. When she arrived at the Parent Room, she found several people lounging in front of a television, enjoying a soap opera, coffee, and snacks. One was Anthony, who looked at Tyler suspiciously and asked, "Can I help you?" After Tyler introduced herself, he responded tactfully, but seemed cold and uninterested.

Ralph Anthony had long hoped to become Florence's principal, and everyone had expected him to fill the position when the previous principal retired. However, he had twice failed the principals' exam, the second time by a single point. Discouraged, but determined to obtain a promotion, he had begun the current school year as the acting principal. Tyler was told by her district superintendent that Anthony might be a reluctant partner.

Tyler began her principalship as planned, in January, with Anthony as her assistant. She scheduled a teachers' meeting for 7:30 a.m. on the morning of her first day. Tyler wanted to begin on the right foot with the faculty supporting her. Her agenda was set and Mr. Anthony agreed to formally introduce her. Unfortunately, at 7:30 a.m., two thirds of the staff were still missing. Anthony told Tyler, "We can't wait too long. We got classes to teach." The assistant principal brought the meeting to order five minutes later. At 7:45 a.m., teachers were still trickling in, many with coffee, doughnuts, and fast food breakfasts. The latecomers seemed to attract more attention than the new principal. Tyler was trying to get through her agenda with doors clicking open and shut, coffee slurping, and bags rattling. For Tyler, this was the limit.

"Look people!" she spoke forcefully. "Leave your food alone, and put your coffee down. You know 7:30 means 7:30, and I would appreciate your cooperation!"

The room fell silent and Tyler felt embarrassed. This was not the right foot Tyler had hoped for. After all, only seven or eight people out of thirty were causing problems. Still, the teachers' behavior only reinforced her first impression of Florence School. This school was dismal in more ways than one.

❖ TAKING STOCK

After her outburst at the teachers' meeting, Tyler made a conscious decision to refrain from making any comments or taking any action for at least three weeks. She wanted to hold back and observe the situation at Florence more closely. Tyler's observations showed her that the school had an unclear curriculum, outdated and poorly used materials, and a staff that was largely resistant to change or innovation. She often overheard teachers ridiculing their students behind the kids' backs and to their faces. Corporal punishment was not uncommon. Many teachers kept paddles and taped-up rulers in visible places in their classrooms as an ever-present threat. "Order," rather than "learning," seemed the watchword at Florence.

The staff, however, seemed anything but orderly. Tyler noticed that teachers had no assigned duties outside of teaching. Some spent their free time, and even class time, gossiping or engaging in private business activities with other teachers. The principal noticed other traits, as well. Teachers argued over parking places and seats in the lunchroom, in spite of the fact that there was a distinct "pecking order" within the Florence faculty. A group of eight or nine teachers reigned at the top, controlling the culture of the entire school. And, as Tyler continued to "lay back and observe," she began to think this group, lead by Ralph Anthony, might be trying to undercut her power.

The principal's suspicion was confirmed when she tried to become involved in the process that determined the use of ECIA (Education Consolidation and Improvement Act) Chapter One funds. ECIA expenditures had to be approved by the Parent Advisory Council and Anthony strongly encouraged Tyler not to attend the Council meetings. His implicit message was, "You stay in your office and let us worry about taking care of business!"

Betty Tyler was incredulous at Ralph Anthony's attitude. She wouldn't consider not participating in such important decision making. Tyler knew her school was scheduled to submit a needs assessment to Central Office, and, as yet, there had not been an adequate exploration of how the money should be spent. Tyler was not surprised when she discovered that the "power clique" already had a plan for the money. Ralph Anthony and his group wanted to buy a new mimeograph machine, upgrade the parent room, and continue to pay for a "School Community Representative."

But, as far as Tyler could tell, the Parent Room was little more than a TV room and the School Community Representative was one of the people who, more often than not, could be found sitting and watching soap operas. And though a case could be made that a mimeograph machine was a reasonable request, it was low priority for Tyler. The school needed to upgrade its curriculum, buy new materials and supplies, motivate students and teachers, and improve the quality of instruction. To Tyler a mimeograph machine meant more work sheets and less creativity and innovation.

❖ **TAKING ACTION**

One of Tyler's own priorities was to find more computers for the school. After only a couple of months, she had already obtained a small grant to renovate the computer room; a forgotten space that was never used. She had also provided in-service computer training for teachers. She didn't know if she could persuade the Parents Advisory Council that computers were critical learning tools but she was going to try.

The new principal also tried to persuade teachers to take part in Florence's needs assessment and to make more of an effort to improve the school, generally. She organized committees around curriculum topics and instructional questions and held weekend retreats for them. She tried hard to foster more teacher participation in policymaking, which she hoped would lead to better instruction and a more productive educational environment.

As the Spring progressed, Betty Tyler watched her activities increasingly threaten the traditional power structure of the school. It was not just the core group of eight or nine teachers that she had to worry about. By her conservative estimate, nearly a third of the faculty, some who had been at Florence since it opened in 1961, were firmly fixed in their views and agendas. And if the rest weren't openly hostile to change, they were generally apathetic.

Tyler's tenure at the Florence was evolving into a lonely search for support—from adults. A large number of students were eager to support their principal. Betty loved children and her natural instincts were to try to develop a warm, trusting relationship with them. Children at Florence seemed starved for attention and Tyler responded as best she could providing countless hugs. Anthony's predecessor had spent his last years coasting to retirement and little had been done to ease the local effects of violence and poverty. The middle class Black neighborhood of 1961 had finally given way to the violence of gangs like the Blackstone Rangers. Over the years, the school had come to co-exist in a neighborhood of knives, guns, gangs, and fights and had done little to help Florence students feel safe.

For a time Tyler despaired for Florence students. They seemed to have, "no hope, no dreams, no aspirations." She was especially worried about gang problems. School doors were not locked during the day, so students and non-students went in and out, unsupervised. Kids roamed freely around the neighborhood and often broke into yards and homes. Teachers refused to monitor the playground saying, "It's not my job," and students often failed to return to school after recess. Bottles and remains of cigarettes and joints littered the playground. Tyler finally began supervising the playground herself and students presented her with a big pole that she could use to keep the "bad kids" in line. She tied flowers and yarn to it, used it as a baton, and marched around the playground with the children. By giving attention that had never been given before, Tyler felt that she was winning many students over.

❖ THE FIGHT

Tyler couldn't rely on Anthony and found more and more of her time being spent on disciplinary issues. The principal was running up and down the hall, breaking up fights, having long talks with the perpetrators in her office—it all left her drained. Often, the police had to be called. On one occasion a student hit her. Tyler responded by pressing charges. On another occasion, a fight broke out across the street from the school. Students were attacking each other with chains. Tyler grabbed her "baton," ran outside, separated those involved, and marched them back into the school. Parents and police were called and a "flare up" in the school office ensued. A group of parents began criticizing Tyler because the police were brought in. Anthony joined the complaining parents. Betty Tyler couldn't believe this reaction. She had the police brought in so children would be safe. But the parents wouldn't hear her. Their complaints escalated and Tyler "blew up." She told the parents to "Be quiet," and told Anthony to "Go home now."

The next day, despite Florence's open campus policy, Tyler placed students under "house arrest," and directed all teachers to supervise their students during lunch.

Teachers opposed this decision and many in the "old guard" attempted to use the PTA to overthrow Tyler's "house arrest" policy. The PTA consisted of ten teachers and eight parents. Many of the parents were former students of the PTA teachers. If anything, they represented the informal power structure that Tyler could not seem to budge. Not surprisingly, the PTA voted to reverse the "house arrest" decision but Tyler held her ground. By letter, she reminded the group that the PTA was not an authorized governing body. The letter was copied to the district superintendent. Betty Tyler's decision held. And teachers grumbled over their "lunch duty" the rest of the year.

By June, Tyler thought she might be beginning to build a small power base. There was a small group of teachers that she could regularly rely on. Tyler encouraged this group and others to attend the summer's city-wide Administration Academy. She hoped the Academy would inspire a sense of leadership and ownership in her teachers. But the word was out—don't do anything that might make Tyler "look good." Only four teachers attended the academy.

❖ MAKING A NEW START

The following August, Tyler, and the four Academy teachers met daily at the school. They scrubbed away graffiti, painted the main hall, and decorated every wall and bulletin board. They had a new, energetic agenda to implement at Florence and the first "bullet" was the school's appearance. When teachers arrived on the first day of school, they were offered a variety of new teaching materials, most of which came from the Administration Academy. Tyler again wanted the first staff meeting to set an optimistic, cooperative tone.

It was not to be. From behind the podium, Tyler immediately sensed the hostility. Anthony was sprawled in his chair at the back of the room, with his arms folded across his chest, and a slight smirk on his lips. In the middle of the room, a large group of teachers sat sideways, talking to others seated behind them, making no effort to hide their disregard for Tyler. Tyler didn't want to lose her temper. She made her announcements, made some remarks about the new year, and adjourned the meeting.

When she returned to her office, Tyler was confronted by the building union representative and eight other teachers, each ready to hand in a completed grievance form. How, she wondered, had they had time to fill out grievance forms on the first morning of school? It was, she saw clearly, organized harassment. When she left the office, she saw Anthony removing a hallway bulletin board display. "The teachers complained about this," he said.

From September through December, Florence was a war zone. Tyler stepped up her classroom observations and began preparing files on teachers she considered incompetent or insubordinate. In turn, teachers, aided by the union representative, stepped up the barrage of grievance forms. The district supervisor, Mr. Brantley, who had hired Tyler on the basis of glowing reports from one of his advisors, tried to encourage Tyler to find a solution. Over the phone he told her, "Betty, you've got a serious problem. Now I know how teachers are and I know what you've tried to accomplish at your school. I appreciate it tremendously. But your teachers are working hard to run you out of there. They've complained to the Superintendent about you. Some parents have also complained. Do you understand the position we're both in? Now listen Betty," Brantley went on, "there must be some teachers at the school who are on your side. I suggest that you get with those people and try to turn things around."

"I've tried," she explained. "But there are only seven or eight I can work with anymore."

"No, no. You don't understand. Your job could be at stake. Listen, go to the library and find a dusty, old book called *The Prince*, by Machiavelli. Read it carefully. After you've read it, I want you to mobilize your seven or eight good teachers. Don't wait until after vacation, start now!"

Sitting on her sofa in the glow of the Christmas lights, Mr. Brantley's words echoed in Tyler's mind. A well worn library book, a list of teachers' names and phone numbers, and Tyler's telephone lay around her. It was late in the evening, but perhaps not too late. Could she solicit support from these teachers? Betty Tyler looked down at her telephone and wondered.

❖ CASE PREPARATION QUESTIONS

1. Critique Betty Tyler's performance during the first year of her principalship. What would be your entry plan for Florence?

2. Describe the culture of the Florence School from the point of view of the staff, the principal, the parents? What concrete actions would you employ to change this culture?

3. What lessons does this case hold for the professional development of teachers?

◆ ◆ ◆

The Prince and the Principal (B)

Roger Shouse, principal co-author, assisted by Darryl Ford, Paula Kleine-Kracht, and Susan Ryan

"Sure, no problem . . . you have a Merry Christmas, okay? Goodnight, Mrs. Tyler." Tom Van Pelt hung up the phone. It was midnight and he had spent the last forty minutes talking to his principal. He related the conversation to his wife, Lynn.

"That was Betty Tyler. It's strange, she wants to have a meeting next week."

"Don't you always have a meeting the first week after. . . "

"No, I mean next week, before New Year's. And not everybody, just a few teachers, over at Ray Harshaw's. . . "

"Some kind of party?"

"Not hardly," answered Tom, amused by the irony of his wife's question. "She's upset."

"From what you've told me over the past year, she's got good reason to be."

"I guess upset isn't the word. Determined is more like it. I haven't heard her talk this way in a long time. She's seemed kind of depressed lately with all those teachers making her life so miserable."

Tom had seemed depressed lately, too, thought Lynn. She knew how much he liked and respected his principal, and how excited he used to get over ideas and projects that the two of them would plan for the school. And she remembered the day, the previous fall, when Tom came home upset after an afternoon staff meeting. Several of his colleagues had displayed such a lack of attention and respect for Tyler that he had, "wanted to get up and bang a few heads right there on the spot."

When Tom had begun teaching at Florence three years ago, he would tell Lynn about events inside his classroom: his students' progress, attitude, behavior, etc. Tom hoped to become an administrator, and his observations had lately turned towards the teaching methods and behaviors of other teachers. Frequently, he told Lynn "horror stories" of unprofessional and even bizarre conduct by other Florence teachers. Lynn knew that Betty Tyler had become a role model for Tom, and that he was beginning to share her frustrations over the conditions of the school.

Tom and Lynn said little as they prepared for bed. Tom had so much on his mind. Lynn had nearly fallen asleep when Tom spoke again, "You know, Betty's got some teachers over there who really support her and appreciate what she's trying to do. We've been kind of holding back and not saying too much. With Anthony's crew we're walking on eggshells over there. Maybe it's time we broke some."

A week later, Tom and six other teachers had the first meeting of what came to be known as "The Team." Its members included Ray Harshaw, Rita Burns, Donna Slater, and Harriet Price, the four who had attended the Administration Academy, and Tom Van Pelt and Betty Tyler.

Tom and the others knew Betty Tyler as a woman who was businesslike and matter-of-fact. Now, there was an emotional tension in her voice. As others spoke, the meeting took on a therapeutic quality, each sharing their feelings and frustrations over the situation at Florence.

Much of the discussion focused on the "old guard." These were the eight or nine teachers who had been at Florence so long that, in Tom's words, "they must have come in with the bricks." Ray Harshaw told how one of them did nothing all day long but, "pass out work sheets and paddle kids."

"At least she passes out work sheets," replied Donna. "The woman next door to me hardly does that. And every time I walk by, she's got pizza or doughnuts or Kentucky Fried Chicken sitting on her desk." For the first time, laughter broke through the tension and the group began to feel more at ease. Talking about food made them realize they'd been ignoring the refreshments. They filled their plates and continued talking late into the night.

Less than a week later, the team met again, this time at a local restaurant. Having finished *The Prince,* Tyler spoke resolutely about power and strategies for seizing and holding it at Florence. Others spoke up and the team discussed ideas and goals. "The fact that we stand for something gives us some power in itself," commented Rita Burns. "The old guard teachers don't really stand for anything."

"But they do have strong support in the community," replied Donna Slater. "Look at who controls the Parent Advisory Council and the PTA. You see the same ten or twelve parents and teachers showing up at all those meetings."

"It seems to me," suggested Betty, "that you've just helped us to identify two important targets."

"How about the union?" added Ray Harshaw. "We've got thirty-one voting members. At least nine of them are definitely against us, including the union rep, and with others on their side we're up against it." Betty Tyler needed little reminding about the union. She had a file drawer full of petty grievances, and their number grew every week.

After a moment, Tom spoke, "Okay, now we've got something to think about. We've agreed that we want Florence to be more academically stimulating for students. Well, the PAC is sitting on over a hundred thousand dollars of ECIA money." The money he referred to consisted of federal grants for compensatory education resulting from the Education Consolidation and Improvement Act. The existing Parent Advisory Council, influenced by the old guard, had indeed spent much of the money on a mimeograph machine and on the salary of the School Community Representative.

"We agree that we want Florence to be a safer, more nurturing place for our students," continued Tom, "but we've got teachers who won't supervise their kids, and a union that opposed closing campus at lunchtime." Although Tyler had closed campus the previous spring, she was unable to continue the policy after summer vacation, because district policy indicated it would require union approval—a fact that Ralph Anthony was only too eager to point out in September.

It was near closing time in the restaurant when Betty Tyler summarized the team's accomplishments and what lay ahead. "We've got a mission here, people. Like Rita says, we stand for something. But we've also got an enemy standing in the way." It was the first time anyone had used the word "enemy," and the word seemed appropriate. "Now, we've got some untapped resources. For example, with over six hundred students, we must have at least five or six hundred adults whose children attend the school. If we can persuade just one hundred of them to support us, we'll outnumber our opposition on the PAC and PTA by nearly ten to one. If we can build that kind of power base outside Florence, we can also be extremely persuasive inside the school. If we all show some leadership, I think we'll win over those teachers who are sitting on the sidelines.

Betty continued, "This will be a tremendous challenge for all of us. Over the coming weeks, I'm going to follow certain teachers around with a clipboard and write down every unprofessional act or contract violation I see. I'm going to be inside their classrooms so much that they'll think I'm part of the furniture.

"This could put a lot of pressure on you all, but we've got to work together. We've got to be more together, better organized, and sneakier than the people we're fighting against."

Heads nodded in agreement. "This sounds like war," someone commented.

"That's right," said Tyler. "Tonight we're declaring war."

Tom left the meeting encouraged but a little doubtful. "What kind of atmosphere will we create at Florence? What if we fail? The long stretch to June might be stressful, and lonely too, if the support doesn't come from parents and other teachers." Through his doubts, however, Tom kept remembering words like "mission," "organized," and "sneakier."

The next morning Tom arrived at school early, as did Tyler and the rest of the team. He walked past the stairs that led to his second floor classroom, and continued down the hall to the Parent Room. He unlocked the door, and, with screwdriver in hand, walked to the television at the end of the room, removed the back panel, and delicately took out a small tube. He pocketed it, replaced the panel, and headed to his classroom.

The war had begun.

COMMUNITY RELATIONS

A key decision for educational administrators is the degree to which schools and other educational organizations reflect the values and beliefs of the community. How should the community be defined? Beyond the individuals who reside within a community, many external agencies focusing on social and juvenile justice, public health, and the family also help define the community. All of these individuals and institutions are increasingly engaged with educational institutions. Conflicts over purpose, role, and objectives are common. The cases in this section explore the actions of administrators in these complicated communities.

❖ THE SCIENCE FAIR INCIDENT (A AND B)

The presentation of results of a science fair project conducted at the Braden Middle School in the midwest raises issues of racism and censorship. The science teacher, Mr. Richter, feels that the results should be presented in order to call attention to the school's climate of covert racism. The principal and the parents do not agree with Mr. Richter. Students demonstrate and the media becomes involved.

❖ PROMISE AND FEAR (A, B, AND C)

Erica Suzman is a promising new principal at a suburban middle school in an area experiencing dramatic population increases. She's overwhelmed learning about the school community and making plans for what she believes are needed reforms. On the first day of school, Erica encounters Royal Collins, a troubled little boy who, as the year unfolds, requires increasing involvement by more and more members of the school community, including legal and social service advocates.

❖ RASH DECISIONS (A AND B)

After a thunderstorm floods part of Reynolds Elementary School during a summer roofing project, teachers and students returning to school in the Fall complain of hives, rashes, and respiratory ailments, mostly undocumented by doctors. Despite tests conducted by the state's Department of Public Health (DPH) at the request of principal Bill Eberly, the cause remains mysterious. Teachers and staff increase pressure on Eberly to do something.

Suggested Readings

Danzberger, P., et al. (1987). School boards: The forgotten players on the education team. *Phi Delta Kappan, 69,* 53–59.

Epstein, J. (1986). Parents' reaction to teacher practices of parent involvement. *Elementary School Journal, 86,* 277–294.

Epstein, J. (1992). School and family partnerships. In M. Alkin (ed.), *Encyclopedia of Educational Research* (pp. 121–136). New York: Macmillan.

Greene, M. (1993). The passions of pluralism: Multiculturalism and the expanding community. *Educational Reformer, 22,* 13–18.

Johnson, J. (1995). *Assignment Incomplete: The unfinished business of educational reform.* New York: Public Agenda Foundation.

◆ ◆ ◆

The Science Fair Incident (A)

Mark Cosdon and Al Thurman

Located in the rural, gently rolling hills of Ohio, Grainsville was a small, solidly conservative community of 35,000 people—just one hour from a major metropolitan city and 20 minutes from several large, affluent suburbs. Western Ohio State University (WOSU) was located in Grainsville, as well as Heartland Technologies, a major agricultural research and production company. WOSU and Heartland were the dominant employers in the area. Largely due to WOSU, the community and its schools were becoming more racially and culturally diverse. The Grainsville School District consisted of five elementary schools (K-5), two middle schools (6-8), and a high school. According to a recent census, the Grainsville School District was 92% White, and the remaining 8% was almost entirely African American.

Braden Middle School, located on Grainsville's Main Street, was the oldest building in the district. And, forty years of continuous use had transformed the edifice into a gloomy, gray brick building housing just over 500 students. Most of Braden's teachers had been at the school for nearly 20 years. All of Braden's 35 faculty members and five administrators were White.

❖ ROBERT CAGE

Braden Middle School's increasing number of minority students was evident to Principal Robert Cage as he watched students clog the hallways, hailing each other on their way to their next class. Garish, heart-shaped posters announcing the upcoming Valentine's Day dance decorated the corridors. In his five years as principal, Cage had witnessed the African American population grow from 5 students to almost 40. These few minority students formed a tightly-knit group. They ate lunch together, sat next to each other in classes, and tended to socialize with the other minority students. It bothered Cage that his school was integrated but his students were not integrating.

Glancing at the stragglers moving into their classes, Principal Cage pondered the challenges and opportunities this new mixture of students brought to his school. Uppermost in his mind was the recent graffiti adorning the walls of the girls' restroom. In his head he could still see the hate words screaming from the walls in black and red markers

NIGGERS GO BACK TO YOUR GHETTO!
NIGGERS ARE NOT WANTED HERE—GO BACK TO AFRICA!!
ALL BLACK BITCHES ARE <u>WHORES</u>!

Although the custodial staff had scrubbed the tile to remove the offensive remarks, one could still barely make out the indelible writing—a sad and constant reminder of someone's ignorance.

And, recently, there had been several fights between African American and White students. He recalled a particularly brutal clash earlier that month between Lawanda Michaels, one of the most academically gifted African Americans, and Amanda McKenzie, a White student. Strolling to a parent conference, he came upon the brawl. Lawanda had managed to pin Amanda to the floor and was punching her in the face. It had taken Cage and two custodians to separate the girls. Investigating the genesis of the fight, Principal Cage heard from several bystanders that Lawanda had been "dissing" Amanda's sneakers. Because there was no evidence to suggest that Amanda was at fault, she was given five days of lunch time detention. Consistent with district policy, Lawanda, the perpetrator, was suspended for the mandatory three days. Cage hated doing it; in his mind, it had cost Braden Middle School the loss of the *Academic Decathlon* to cross-town rival Sherwood.

❖ RACIAL TENSIONS

Principal Cage shook his head as he thought about the four White students he had reprimanded last month for using racial slurs. A lunchroom monitor overheard them using a stream of inflammatory epithets while talking about the Grainsville High School basketball team—which was nearly all Black.

"What brought all of this on?" Cage demanded.

Sheepishly, Chris Tremain said, "We didn't mean any harm. Honest. We were just talking about how good the team was."

"Regardless," said Cage. "That doesn't allow you to use derogatory language."

"We weren't using derogatory language," replied John Reynolds. "You should hear the Blacks! They say nigger and stuff all the time. Why shouldn't we? I mean why is it okay for *them* to say it but not us?!"

Later that same day, after his discussion with Cage, in a social studies discussion about civil rights, John Reynolds stated, "Blacks have gained equality but still aren't nothing but a bunch of niggers. I mean *they* even call themselves *niggers*."

The few African American students in the class were offended by the comment and demanded an apology. Mr. Weimer, who had taught social studies at

Braden for over 22 years, said that no harm was meant and that the class should get back to the lesson at hand.

For the remainder of the week following this incident, tensions around the school were at a peak. Principal Cage, unsure of what action to take, could only hope that things would settle down. They didn't.

On Thursday afternoon, a small group of students, mostly girls, gathered at the back entrance of the school and taunted each other with some pushing and shoving. Leaving for the day, math teacher Mrs. McGlynn overheard the White students calling the African American students "niggers" and "big-lipped Black bitches." Mrs. McGlynn took three of the White students to Principal Cage's office, despite their protests: "The Blacks have been making fun of *us*!"

Principal Cage was looking over the school budget when Mrs. McGlynn burst into his office with the three pupils. "I overheard Emma, Kerri, and Lisa leading a group of eight or nine other girls in name-calling," said Mrs. McGlynn.

"Really?" Principal Cage took a deep sigh. "And what were the names?"

After a moment of silence, Mrs. McGlynn prodded Emma Greenleaf, "Go on! Tell him!"

Trying to stifle her laughter, the girl said, "Uhm, nigger. Blackie. Porch monkey. Stuff like that." The two other girls burst into laughter.

"That's not funny!" yelled the principal. No one had ever heard Principal Cage raise his voice before. He had startled even himself. The laughter ceased. The principal gathered his composure and then continued, "All of you, Blacks and Whites alike, *need* to get along. Your races may be different, but you're all still the same. You need to respect and appreciate each others' cultures—not debase them with this name calling. Do you understand me?"

The three, looking at the floor, nodded their heads in agreement.

"I won't tolerate this name-calling in my school any longer. It will stop as of this day." He paused and a moment later added, "You may leave."

The three girls nearly tripped over each other hurrying out of the room. After Principal Cage thanked her for bringing the matter to his attention, Mrs. McGlynn excused herself too.

The following day, Principal Cage issued a school-wide statement which was read in all homerooms and prominently posted:

ANY STUDENT USING RACIAL, ETHNIC, OR RELIGIOUS SLURS OF ANY KIND WILL BE PROCESSED APPROPRIATELY AND WILL RECEIVE DISCIPLINARY ACTION.

❖ GREG RICHTER AND THE SCIENCE FAIR

It was late February, cold and clear, with fresh white snow on the ground. Greg Richter watched the last of his eighth graders troop through the door and contemplated the Science Fair, his favorite event of the year. Ten years of teaching middle school had demonstrated that the Science Fair powerfully motivated students to research, learn, and report on major science issues. This one event made February and March bearable for the teacher. During the year, he constantly reminded students about the March Science Fair and encouraged them to think about their projects.

Mr. Richter was a veteran teacher. He had worked in the Grainsville schools since his graduation from the University of Illinois, serving five years at the high school and the last ten in the middle school. He was well liked by the administration and the students, and received glowing evaluations from Principal Cage. Mr. Richter was a popular teacher and was always able to inspire his students to do more than they thought they were able. Twice in the past five years, he had been voted best teacher in the district. As faculty advisor to the Braden Student Council, he had been instrumental in helping the students secure film and video courses, Macintosh computers, Internet access, and vending machines from the rather traditional, conservative school board. Moreover, because of his honesty and his outspoken support of better working conditions for teachers, he had been selected two years earlier to serve as one of the co-presidents of the teachers' union.

Mr. Richter was particularly popular with the minority students at Braden and they often sought his counsel. Having grown up in an integrated Chicago neighborhood, Richter felt it important to acknowledge the needs of all students, regardless of race. To that end, Richter went out of his way to listen to and spend time with the small number of minority students. In turn, the minority students trusted him—not something they would say about other staff at Braden.

With a wide smile, Mr. Richter greeted his third period class. "You know this is my favorite time of the year," he beamed. "All of you are headed for one of the most extraordinary adventures of your lives—your Science Fair projects." A chorus of skeptical guffaws emanated from the class. He explained that they could engage in broadly conceived projects involving chemistry, physics, biology, statistics, geography, or earth science. Mr. Richter further noted that all projects should include a literature review and original information gathered through surveys, interviews, focus groups, or other approved methodologies.

The teacher also reminded the students that all projects were to be approved by him and were to be done in teams of two or more. However, the work of individual students should be detailed in the written description of the project. Mr. Richter also said that he would like to see a rough draft of the project and results before students finalized their displays.

Traditionally, the final projects had been displayed in Richter's classroom; but this year the teacher had an exciting announcement to make. "During lunch," he said, "Mrs. Dougherty [the school librarian] gave me some terrific news. She's agreed to let us display this year's Science Fair projects in the Media Center!" Excited chatter greeted the announcement. "Now the *entire* school will be able to see your poster board description and summaries," he continued.

Bill Spears, an unruly student, called out, "Come on! What do they care?"

Without flinching Mr. Richter encouraged him, "*I* care. And I think your friends will care about the work you choose to do." He paused a moment, mostly for dramatic effect, then concluded, "It's important we show our projects to *everyone* at Braden so they can come to see how important science is to our lives."

Before commencing the day's lesson, he reminded the students that he was available for consultation and help at any stage of their research.

❖ MARGIE CONRAD AND LORETTA CULLER

Two days later, Margie Conrad and Loretta Culler, two of Mr. Richter's best students, came in to let him know that they planned to work together on a project about gender and racial attitudes. The description of their project was brief and indicated only that they were planning to develop a word association instrument which they would give to students at Braden Middle School.

Margie was born in Grainsville. Besides being active in the Girl Scouts and playing on the school soccer team, she had shown signs of academic excellence in her earliest years. Margie was White. Until recently, she had been best friends with Georgette Williams. Like Margie, Georgette was an honors student and played soccer on the school team. Georgette was an African American. Margie and Georgette had been almost inseparable until the previous year, when Loretta Culler had transferred into Braden.

Loretta moved to Grainsville from Champaign, Illinois where her father had worked at the University of Illinois. The family had moved to Grainsville because Loretta's dad was offered an appointment at WOSU's College of Engineering. Margie's dad was a faculty member in the College of Business. Almost immediately, Loretta and Margie began sitting next to each other in the gifted classes and became good friends. They also participated in several of the same after-school activities. Like Margie, Loretta was White.

Mr. Richter quickly read Margie and Loretta's project description, nodded, and said that it looked okay and they could go ahead with it. "Wonderful! So you're planning a survey using students at Braden?" he asked.

"Yes," replied Loretta, "We'll be compiling the results from between 75 and 100 surveys."

"Yeah, see we want to get a good sampling, based on the population of Braden," chimed in Margie. "But we don't want so many that we're overwhelmed by the data."

"Very wise; very wise," Mr. Richter said. "When will you do this surveying? Not during science class I hope."

"Not to worry," assured Loretta. We're probably gonna do it at lunch time. It's when we'll have the most people around."

"Ah! Catch them before they eat?" smiled Mr. Richter.

"Exactly," said Loretta.

❖ A FEW WEEKS LATER. . . .

Though he never checked their progress, and had not seen a rough draft, Mr. Richter could tell Margie and Loretta were actively engaged in their project. He saw them working together after school in the library and in the newly refurbished computer lab on several occasions. A few weeks later, he saw the girls sitting at a table outside of the lunchroom, while several grinning students completed their surveys. He was grateful for their self-sufficiency as he was literally overwhelmed helping other students who needed assistance. A dedicated teacher, he was usually seen leaving the building late in the afternoon with a briefcase loaded with papers to grade. He often thought to himself that if he had more students like Loretta and Margie, he might be able to keep more reasonable hours.

❖ THE SCIENCE FAIR

On Tuesday, March 14, the Braden Media Center was busier than usual. It was the day the science project posters and displays went up. Margie and Loretta were very excited and ran to Mr. Richter's room. Mr. Richter was using his much-coveted teacher preparation period to hurriedly complete his class plan for that afternoon's earth science lesson. Knocking on the door as she entered, Margie said, "Mr. Richter, come see our project!"

"Yeah!" said Loretta, following closely on Margie's heels. "We stayed up most of the night at my house finishing it up!"

Given the girls' enthusiasm, he knew he couldn't say no. Laying his pen aside, he figured he could finish his planning during lunch. "Let's go!" he said.

Walking with Margie and Loretta to the Media Center he said, "You know, I've watched you girls work and I'm pleased with the effort you gave." It was moments like this, he thought, which really made teaching worthwhile.

A few students and faculty aides were already examining several of the displays. This made Mr. Richter feel good, reminding him that the Science Fair's new home in the Media Center would be visited by many more people than when it was located in his classroom. While Loretta and Margie stood proudly at his side, Mr. Richter's eyes were attracted to the letters forming the title of the project at the top of the poster:

DOES GENDER AFFECT RACIAL ATTITUDES?
A Social Science Research Project
by
Margie Conrad & Loretta Culler

Do girls and boys have different attitudes towards Blacks?

RESULTS

Boys associated Blacks with: Niggers, lazy, strong, good athletes, stealing, good basketball players, can jump high, ghettoes, loud music, crime, dumb, good football players.

Girls associated Blacks with: Ugly, muscular, niggers, loud, thick lips, kinky hair, Africa, strong, athletic.

CONCLUSIONS

There is a gender difference in attitudes toward members of a different race. About Blacks, boys are more apt to notice athletic characteristics and girls are more likely to notice physical characteristics.

Methodology Used: Word Association Survey.

Population Sampled: 100 Braden Middle School 7th & 8th Graders.

Late for a faculty meeting, Mr. Richter quickly scanned the poster, skipping to the conclusion. He read aloud:

CONCLUSIONS: There is a gender difference in attitudes toward members of a different race. About Blacks, boys are more apt to notice athletic characteristics and girls are more likely to notice physical characteristics.

"Great," Mr. Richter said. "I'm proud of you!"

❖ STUDENT REACTION

Within hours of placing the poster in the Media Center, word about Margie and Loretta's project spread throughout the school. Doubters and believers alike made their way to the Media Center to see for themselves that "the WORD" had been posted in the middle of the school.

At lunch, Georgette Williams overheard Suzan Parks talking about the project. She was unable to believe that her once-close friend Margie would post something so insulting. Excusing herself from the corner table where the African American students normally ate, she walked down to the Media Center. When she entered the room, three White boys were huddled over the morning newspapers' comics. She walked past a number of displays looking for the offending poster. Reaching Margie and Loretta's exhibit, she recognized her friend's handwriting. Her eyes scanned the offensive list of adjectives and came to rest on the word "nigger."

Georgette felt nauseous. As a child of African American professionals, one of whom was a member of WOSU's Affirmative Action Committee, she was not hesitant to act. The sophisticated adolescent angrily pulled the poster off the Media Center's wall while the boys watched in mild amusement. She heard them laughing at her as she marched down to Mr. Richter's room.

When she came into the science classroom, Mr. Richter was standing by his file cabinet. "Mr. Richter," she began.

"Georgette, what's new?" He gazed warily at the poster in her hand.

"I'm upset, Mr. Richter," Georgette responded, "and I think you know why."

"Go ahead," said Mr. Richter.

Pointing to the poster, Georgette said, "Did you let those girls put *this* up in the Media Center?!"

"Georgette, that project isn't about you—it's about perceptions. It's a scientific study."

"That's what you call it," rejoined Georgette, "but I call it about *me* and my *race,* and I can't believe you let anybody make such a poster and then put it up for the whole school to see!"

Affected by Georgette's intensity, Mr. Richter was surprised at the intensity of his own reply, "Georgette, the poster isn't the problem; it's *about* the problem."

"No, Mr. Richter, the poster *is* the problem, and many of the African American students, including me, want it down!"

"Am I hearing you right? Are you asking me to repress scientific evidence because you and your friends don't like it?"

Several sixth grade students began to drift into the classroom. "Call it any way you want," said Georgette, "but this poster is insulting to me, to my friends, and to my heritage. It *had* to come down!"

"I disagree," said Mr. Richter as the bell rang. "Listen, I've got to start class. Give me the poster." Georgette hesitated a moment before angrily throwing the poster to the ground and storming out of the room.

Stunned, Mr. Richter somehow got through his lesson on plant reproduction. After class, he brought the poster to the Media Center and reattached it to the wall. As he was pushing the second thumbtack into the corkboard, his eye was drawn, for the first time, to the word "nigger."

He felt an icy shudder work its way up his spine as he finally recognized the cause of Georgette's anger. He thought about Braden Middle School's recent spate of racial turmoil. After a moment of silent contemplation, he felt the poster needed to be displayed. The school's covert racism, in his opinion, demanded the inclusion of Margie and Loretta's project. The simmering racial attitudes needed to be addressed once and for all.

The teacher reached for the third and fourth thumbtacks.

❖ CASE PREPARATION QUESTIONS

1. Principal Robert Cage is managing a changing culture. To whom does he have responsibility? Students, parents, teachers, superintendent, school board members, other community members?

2. Community involvement in school affairs can have a strong impact on the culture of a school. To what degree should the community members have a say in school affairs?

3. Is Mr. Richter a racist? Should he be fired?

◆ ◆ ◆

The Science Fair Incident (B)

Mark Cosdon and Al Thurman

Displayed in the Braden Middle School's Media Center for just one day, Margie and Loretta's Science Fair project was already the center of a storm of controversy. Hundreds of students and faculty members flocked to the normally quiet Media Center, eager to see the inflammatory poster. Most were unable to believe their eyes, particularly after Principal Cage's stern warning against the use of such language. An after school fight between two boys, one Black and one White, was hastily broken up by a crossing guard. More racist graffiti appeared in the girls bathroom. Away on the first of a two day retreat for Grainsville School District principals, Braden's Principal Cage had not yet heard about the turmoil in his school.

❖ GEORGETTE AND HER MOTHER

Still seething from her confrontation with Mr. Richter earlier in the afternoon, Georgette went home that Tuesday and told her mother about the Science Fair project of Margie and Loretta. "Right in the middle of the school—right on their poster, it says we're niggers and dumb and ugly. I can't believe Margie would do such a thing! I've known her for years and we were such good friends!"

Her mother, Esther Williams, was very concerned. She immediately closed her book and removed her reading glasses. Besides being the Dean of Minority Students at WOSU, she was also a member of the university's Affirmative Action Committee. As a college undergraduate, she had been active in the civil rights movement. "We're going to need to do something right away," she said.

Georgette snapped, "Mom, I know!"

"I'll get on the phone to. . . ."

"Mom!"

Mrs. Williams stared at her daughter in disbelief. She knew that the last thing she and Georgette needed right now was a fight. "Why are you so angry?"

"I'm *not* angry!" Georgette heard the volume of her voice and calmed down—somewhat. "This is *my* battle—not yours. Will you let me handle things?"

"I *am* letting you 'handle things.'"

"No you're not! The first thing you want to do is start making phone calls."

"I'm just trying to help."

"I know. I know. But it's *my* school! *I* want to take care of this," said the headstrong teenager.

After a long pause, Mrs. Williams said, "Okay. I won't do anything right now. Just let me know what's happening, okay? This is very important."

"I know."

As her daughter ran for the stairs, Mrs. Williams called out, "I'm proud of you!"

❖ MOBILIZING FOR ACTION

Tuesday night, Georgette phoned a number of her friends and talked with them about the Science Fair project. Most of the students she called were African Americans, but she also spoke with several Whites too. Her friend Margot McCormack, a White student, said, "I support you all the way on this one, no matter what you decide to do. There's no way that poster should be displayed."

Georgette's African American friends were determined to take some sort of action—particularly Suzan, Paula, and Trent.

Suzan Parks was born in Grainsville. For nearly 15 years, her mother had worked as a staff assistant in WOSU's development office. Suzan told Georgette, "To allow that sort of stuff to be posted makes it seem like the administration supports it or something."

"We've gotta get Richter out of there," insisted Paula Winston. "I can't believe he put that thing back up, especially *after* you told him how offensive it was!" Paula was relatively new to Grainsville, her father having relocated the family from a Cleveland suburb to begin work at Heartland Technologies.

Trent Bishop was more blunt than any of the girls: "How can I go to a school with that shit?! I'm sick and tired of always getting picked on because I'm Black!" During that afternoon's gym class, Trent and Bill Spears had nearly gotten in a fight. Changing back into their street clothes, the white boy told Trent, "Man, you people sure are stinky." When Trent shoved him in the chest, several other boys had quickly interceded.

After three intense hours on the phone and numerous calls back and forth, Georgette, Suzan, Paula, and Trent made a pact to see Principal Cage first thing in the morning.

Wednesday, prior to homeroom, the four students met at Georgette's locker and then proceeded to Principal Cage's office. They asked for an appointment with the Principal. However, Mrs. Smiley, the school secretary, told them that he was attending a two day retreat for Grainsville School District principals and would be unable to meet with them. "He'll be here Thursday afternoon though. How's 3:30 right after school tomorrow? Would that work for you?"

Disappointed, the group accepted the offer and left her office.

Stepping into the hallway, Trent announced, "No way am I going to Richter's class."

"Me either," agreed Paula.

"What do you mean," said Georgette. "You're just gonna skip it?"

"Yeah," said Trent. "After what he's done, I'm not sittin' through his class. No way!"

"You'll get detention," said Suzan.

"Maybe, but I won't have to listen to some racist for an hour," rebuffed Trent.

Paula looked at Georgette and said, "You do what you want—me, I'm not going."

Georgette, an honor student, stared at her friends in disbelief. How could she not go to class? Then she remembered the Science Fair project that she and Paula had worked on together. "We're supposed to present our project in this afternoon's class."

Paula sharply answered, "You can go, girl, but I ain't! I don't want nothin' to do with Richter!"

❖ MR. RICHTER'S SCIENCE CLASS

Wednesday afternoon, Mr. Richter's eighth grade science class met in the Media Center. Over the course of Wednesday and Thursday, each team of students was scheduled to make a formal presentation of their project and defend their results. In taking attendance, Richter noticed that 6 of his 24 students were missing.

"That's funny," he thought. "I could have sworn I saw Georgette earlier today." He then realized that her partner Paula Winston was missing too. The two girls were supposed to present their project on the solar system that day. Examining his role book, it dawned on Mr. Richter that 5 of the 6 missing students were African Americans. Looking out over his collected students, he realized that *no* African Americans were present! He tried to collect himself. In the back of his mind he sensed a connection between the students' absence and the Science Fair incident.

But, the teacher had a class to run. The first team scheduled to present were John, Shawn and Eric. They studied water preservation. Second on the list was the team of Margie and Loretta. Mr. Richter noticed that, in their presentation, they were more reserved than usual; missing was their typical confidence and presence.

Reading directly from her notes, Margie said, "We found . . . uhm . . . that boys linked blacks to all sorts of . . . uh . . . athletically. . . ."

Two boys in the front row snickered. Mr. Richter immediately reprimanded them. "Margie and Loretta are presenting deeply disturbing, scientific evidence! It's not funny! They've uncovered rampant, covert racism in this school. Rather than laughing, you should all be deeply ashamed!"

The class quieted down and was more attentive. Even more shaken, Margie and Loretta continued documenting their troublesome findings.

❖ MISSED MESSAGES

Shortly before noon on Thursday, Principal Cage called in for messages. It was the final day of his retreat for Grainsville administrators. Mrs. Smiley, his secretary, said he'd had three phone calls and that Mr. Richter had set up a 3:45 appointment. She also reminded him of his afternoon meeting with Georgette, Paula, Suzan, and Trent. "Don't forget you're meeting with those Black students today at 3:30," she said.

"Yeah," he replied. "Could you reschedule that and Richter too? My daughter's got a gymnastics meet over in Wrightstown."

"Sure," said Mrs. Smiley.

"Do you know why they wanted to see me?" he asked.

Mrs. Smiley hesitated a moment and then said, "They didn't say."

Georgette, Paula, Suzan, and Trent arrived ten minutes prior to their scheduled appointment. Looking up from her typewriter, Mrs. Smiley told them, "Oh! I meant to let you know that Principal Cage will not be able to meet with you today. He's got a family conflict."

Trent was incredulous, "What?! What do you mean?! He ain't here?!"

Mrs. Smiley replied, "That's right. His daughter has a gymnastics meet today. He did ask me to reschedule though."

Georgette spun on her heels and stormed out of the office. In doing so, she nearly knocked over Mr. Richter, who was coming in for his appointment. "Oh hi, Georgette!" he said. Georgette hadn't seen the teacher in two days. She skipped class on Wednesday and Thursday's class was canceled due to a bike safety assembly.

Mr. Richter continued, "Georgette, I'd like to—." The student ignored her teacher and kept walking.

❖ MRS. WILLIAMS GETS INVOLVED

Georgette walked into her house and slammed the front door. The noise startled her mother who was working at her computer in the family room.

"How did your meeting with Mr. Cage go?" Mrs. Williams called. She watched her daughter walk angrily past the family room on her way to the cookie jar. Georgette grabbed a handful of Oreos. "Well, what did he say?" pressed the mother, looking up from her computer.

"He blew us off."

"Excuse me? He blew you off? What!?"

Georgette came to the family room and stood in the doorway. "You heard me, he blew us off! He decided he didn't have the time or something." Georgette was now on the verge of tears. Mrs. Williams rose from her desk, walked to daughter, and held her gently by the shoulders.

Mrs. Williams looked at Georgette for a moment, then said, "You want me to try?"

With tears in her eyes and cookie crumbs around her mouth, Georgette nodded and rested her head on her mother's shoulder.

❖ A TRIP TO SCHOOL

Mrs. Williams went with Georgette to school on Friday morning. Their first stop was the Media Center, where Mrs. Williams saw Margie and Loretta's controversial project for the first time. She winced as she read:

> Boys associated Blacks with: Niggers, lazy, strong, good athletes, stealing, good basketball players, can jump high, ghettoes, loud music, crime, dumb, good football players.

"Oh my god!" she said. "If that isn't the most racist thing I've seen in I-don't-know-how-long, I don't know what is!" "Mom, ssshhh. You don't have to yell," hissed Georgette. The teenager was feeling self-conscious standing next to her mother. In fact, she quickly excused herself and ran off to class. Mrs. Williams wasted no time making her way to Principal Cage's office.

Braden's secretary, Mrs. Smiley greeted her. "Hello, what can I do for you?"

"Yes, I'll like to see Mr. Cage. Now." There was an urgency in her voice.

"Is this regarding our vacant custodial positions?"

Mrs. Williams stared at her in utter disbelief. "No," she icily stated. "My name is *Dean* Esther Williams of WOSU. My daughter, Georgette, is in the eighth grade and I would like to discuss a matter with Mr. Cage."

"Oh, I'm sorry," said Mrs. Smiley. "Mr. Cage won't be in today; he's doing a site visit at Sherwood Middle School. He'll be back on Monday though. Would you like to see him then?"

"Let's just forget it." The mother left the office.

Outraged by the poster, humiliated by the school secretary, and unable to meet with Principal Cage, Mrs. Williams went straight home and called her office saying she'd be a little late. Then, she got herself comfortable and called several of her friends whose children also attended Braden Middle School. A meeting was arranged for Saturday morning in the recreation room of the First Methodist Church—Mrs. Williams' husband was on the board of the church. The parents of all African American Braden Middle School students were invited, along with other parents whom they felt would be sympathetic to their cause.

❖ A PROTEST IS ORGANIZED

On Saturday morning, approximately 100 supporters, composed of parents and children, gathered in the First Methodist Church's recreation room. Several parents who had seen Margie and Loretta's project, in addition to Mrs. Williams, described the girls' poster. Georgette, who had copied verbatim the poster's findings, read them to the congregation. As she read, she was interrupted several times by audible gasps.

The group met for three hours organizing a protest for the coming Monday morning outside of Braden Middle School. They would call for an immediate public meeting with Principal Cage, at which time they would present him with a list of demands. These included: the removal of what they viewed as a racially offensive science project; the hiring of a person-of-color as a school counselor; the study of minority cultures for four months of the school year; and, that science teacher Greg Richter be asked to resign immediately. If they were not satisfied with Principal Cage's response, the parents agreed to protest by refusing to allow their children to enter the school.

❖ MONDAY, MARCH 20

By 8:15 a.m. on Monday morning, nearly 125 parents and students had assembled in the chill air outside of Braden Middle School. Nearly a week before, Margie and Loretta's science project had first been posted. A few Caucasian students snickered as they made their way past the demonstrators and into the building. Inside the warm school, White students crowded around the windows and looked out at the gathering, while awaiting the 8:30 homeroom bell. When the crowd saw Principal Cage arrive in his blue sedan at 8:25, they began a chant.

"What do we want?"

"JUSTICE!"

"When do we want it?"

"NOW!"

As he turned into the parking lot, Principal Cage was astonished to see so many people gathered in front of the school. He took a last sip from his Styrofoam coffee cup, collected his briefcase, and shut the door to his car. He had no idea why so many people had congregated in front of the school. As he walked towards the school entrance, he noticed that most of the faces in the crowd were African Americans. Several people, including Mrs. Williams, angrily made their way towards him.

Confused, he reached out to accept a paper that was being thrust at him. Several people began shouting, "Hey-hey! Ho-ho! That racist Richter's gotta go!"

"What are you going to do?!" shouted Mrs. Williams.

"Yeah, what's your choice Cage?!" shouted another.

"We *demand* action," continued Mrs. Williams.

The throng of supporters shouted for action.

Principal Cage did his best to read the document in his hand. The crowd began their chant once again.

"What do we want?"

"JUSTICE!"

"When do we want it?"

"NOW!"

◆ ◆ ◆

Promise and Fear (A)

Debi Phillips

❖ KEVIN THOMPSON, DYS CASE WORKER

Kevin Thompson was a kind man with a large smile. His powerful physique and powerful intellect served him well in his work for the Department of Youth Services. He'd worked for the department for fifteen years; the last five in the Dixby branch, the office that served the needs of youth and families throughout the five hamlet region of Ashmont, Dixby, Carlyle, Mt. Morris, and Rosendale.

Like most DYS case workers, Kevin, a licensed social worker, wrestled with more than double the case load recommended by the Child Welfare League. But Kevin's keen sense of justice continued to fuel him when his colleagues grew dispirited and moved on to other careers. Kevin loved his work, was fully at peace, and expected to be with the Department of Youth Services for his entire career.

On this day, the case worker was in his office in Dixby. He had the Collins' file opened in front of him and had just spoken with Dalva Collins on the telephone. Dalva Collins had five children, Royal who attended Mt. Morris Middle School, Cecie and Mary who attended Harrison, a two year old and a baby at home. She sounded alright, a little reserved. It seemed that life in the family had finally settled down since he'd assisted the mother in petitioning for a restraining order against her husband earlier in the summer. The years prior to the restraining order had been difficult ones.

The initial DYS complaint against Clay Collins was placed by a neighbor who'd witnessed the father beating his eight-year-old son, Royal, in the backyard. Kevin, having been assigned to the case, learned that Royal's beating was only one of many incidents of physical and emotional abuse delivered by the troubled Clay Collins. In trying to stabilize the family, Kevin had been forced to put the children under protective supervision twice. Counseling and positive reports from supervised visitation resulted in the children being released each time back to the custody of their parents. But Clay Collins could only control his drinking for a while and then the pattern of drinking and abuse would begin anew. In the second year of Kevin's involvement with the family, the violence escalated, culminating in the restraining order.

Kevin was about to go into a "reconsideration" meeting. The Collins' case was one of the continuing cases he would bring to discuss with his supervisor. Kevin had visited the house twice since July. He observed each time that the children and mother responded well to the calm that had resulted from the father's absence. The Collins had been on a "priority one" status but Kevin was thinking about lowering their rating to a "priority two." He intended to check in once, possibly twice a month, to make sure the father hadn't returned to the home—an action that was all too common in these family abuse situations.

Kevin had considered contacting the children's schools as a safeguard, but, thought better of it. Kevin believed teachers in Mt. Morris were particularly loose lipped and knew the damaging repercussions that could result from idle gossip. He felt the family had been through enough and, for now, it was his sense that the family was safe. Kevin decided, as their case worker, to lower their priority rating and do his best to stay in touch.

❖ MT. MORRIS

Mt. Morris was one of a string of small, self-governing hamlets in a farming region interspersed with lakes and woods. Mt. Morris was the largest village with 15,000 residents. The others were Ashmont, Dixby, Carlyle and Rosendale. Historically, the villages were independent but connected by friends and relatives—established communities interested in the well being of the entire region. The local paper covered news throughout the five towns.

For many years, the inhabitants of the five villages considered the area a haven. Here, they felt free of the crime and pollution experienced by the large metropolis 60 miles to the south. Of course, they welcomed the hundreds of vacationers attracted to the lakes and woods each summer. After all, they brought important revenue to the area. For as long as many citizens could remember, the region had been a wonderland. Lately, however, it seemed the quality of life was beginning to slip.

The town was rated as the fastest growing community in the state for the third year in a row. Resolution of an old tribal lawsuit had released hundreds of acres of land, and property values were still relatively inexpensive. Many young families, willing to make a long work commute and lured by the low cost of real estate and the bucolic setting, were moving in from the metropolis to the south. About forty percent of the new population was African American or Latino. They were fast outnumbering the indigenous Native American population that had always been the region's small minority population. Mt. Morris' population was becoming increasingly diverse and racial tensions were escalating. Every weekend there seemed to be another racial disturbance between the minority groups. Whites in the area waited and watched, not willing to give up their haven, and yet, a few white families had already moved away.

❖ ERICA SUZMAN AND THE MOUNT MORRIS MIDDLE SCHOOL

Erica Suzman had grown up and spent most of her adult life in Ashmont, one of several villages in a beautiful region of a large midwestern state. She had, in fact, graduated from Ashmont High School, left the area to go to college, and returned four years later to teach at the high school. Erica had been Ashmont High's ninth grade science teacher for fourteen years.

During those years, Erica built a strong and vital science program and gained a reputation for being an exceptional teacher. She loved science. She loved learning about the world around her and loved helping others learn about it, too. She eagerly stayed abreast of her field, taking countless courses and workshops. Needless to say, her enthusiasm for the subject was contagious. Kids of all abilities seemed to thrive in her classes.

At the same time, Erica had a real interest in kids' development outside of the classroom. She worked hard to create extracurricular activities that would broaden Ashmont students and allow them to interact informally through mutual interests. Erica had created and managed a photography club, a drama club, and had made the girls' varsity soccer team a community institution. The local papers had named Erica, "Coach of the Year," five different times.

Erica was a single woman who willingly dedicated her life to her profession. But after years of teaching and encouraging adolescents in their growth, the dynamic teacher was ready for a change. She'd learned a lot about children and schools in her career and was ready to take her philosophies about children and learning out of the classroom. Erica wanted to be a principal.

The educator was promptly hired as a middle school principal in the neighboring community of Mt. Morris. Mt. Morris Middle School had just suffered under the three-year tenure of an incompetent principal. Max Christopher, the superintendent of Mt. Morris School District, habitually referred to Erica's predecessor as "the worst appointment in the history of the school system."

Max was pleased with Erica Suzman's appointment. The superintendent saw a number of strengths in the candidate right away. First, Erica was known as an exceptional teacher. The region was so connected that a teacher's success in one school district was well known in neighboring communities. Second, Max saw an enthusiasm in Erica that had been sorely lacking at the school for three years. Max pushed the school board for the appointment saying he recognized a potentially great principal and would be willing to dedicate the time necessary to guide the young principal in her first years on the job. Erica was hired.

Mt. Morris Middle School was a new building, six years old, built to meet the needs of the growing population. At the time Erica took the helm, 820 students were enrolled and 41 teachers were on staff. The school contained grades 4-8. The fourth and fifth grades were on the first floor in self contained classrooms. Grades 7 and 8 were on the second floor. The upper level students moved from classroom to classroom for their different courses. Reflective of the population changes, 250 students were enrolled in fourth grade while there were only 100 eighth graders. Currently, twenty-two percent of the students enrolled were minority. Only one minority teacher worked in the middle school, Rosa Jimenez, and she had worked in the district for seventeen years. Average faculty tenure in the middle school was 18 years.

❖ ERICA'S ENTRY

The selection process for the Mt. Morris Middle School principalship had been arduous. Erica was first interviewed by a committee of middle school teachers and John Schaeffer, the acting principal, retiring after 31 years in the district. She was one of four candidates recommended to go before the superintendent and the school board to present her ideas on education generally and for the middle school specifically. Erica spoke with this group on three different occasions. Finally, in late March, Erica was appointed principal. Her contract would begin July 1.

From the moment Erica's appointment became public knowledge, she spent as much time at the middle school as she could. First on the list of priorities was appointing an assistant principal. Harriet Clyde had been acting assistant principal while John Schaeffer, the former assistant, was acting principal. Mrs. Clyde had been a sixth grade teacher at the middle school for fifteen years and was enthusiastic about her new leadership role. She applied for the assistant's position along with seven other candidates. A committee was formed of five teachers, John Schaeffer and Erica to interview the applicants and select a final candidate for recommendation to the board for a final appointment.

Erica had immediate misgivings about Mrs. Clyde. She thought the woman was quick to jump to conclusions and her thoughts on children and schooling seemed unfocused. Erica told a friend she had reservations because the woman "seemed so excitable and old fashioned."

But Harriet Clyde was clearly the favorite candidate. Erica tried to persuade the committee to consider the strengths of the other candidates but the group was adamant. The new principal was torn. She wanted to follow her instincts but her head told her to follow the lead of those who knew the school better than she. Finally, Erica decided to trust the judgment of the committee. Harriet Clyde was appointed as assistant principal of the middle school.

Erica also worked with a group of teachers to establish the upcoming year's school budget. In fact, by the end of June, the new principal had managed to interact with about half of the school's faculty on a number of projects. Erica spent weeks in the school during the summer, as well. If teachers came into the building, she made an effort to meet them and chat about the year ahead. The new principal was convinced that dependable and constructive interactions over time were important. Harriet Clyde spent July and August at her summer home. Erica did not see her until two days before school started.

❖ THE YEAR BEGINS

Erica had spent a good deal of time preparing for her first formal interaction with her faculty. She called the usual staff meeting for the morning before the students were to arrive; her agenda was simple—to introduce herself, welcome the teachers back to school, and make it known that she was their resource and her door was always open. She also wanted the teachers to know that they'd be seeing a lot of her around the school—in the halls and in their classrooms—in an effort to get to know the school, the kids, and the teachers.

But, when Erica stood in front of the group the morning of the meeting, she felt a coldness, a sense of distrust. Every face in the room was without a smile; the prevalent mood—somber. Even the teachers she'd worked with in late spring seemed distant. Erica did her best to brighten the atmosphere but the teachers would not be budged. They listened quietly and when Erica wished them a good year, they quickly grabbed their books and papers and exited. Erica overheard one teacher, Mrs. James, say to another, "I was here years before she came and I'll be here years after she's gone. How many more times do I have to listen to, 'my door is always open?'"

❖ ROYAL COLLINS, STUDENT

It was the second day of school. Erica's head was swimming as she tried to grasp all of her responsibilities. But, she put on her warmest smile and, together with Mrs. Clyde, greeted the children as they arrived at school. When the bus pulled up to the curb and the children filed off, Erica saw Royal Collins right away. The weeping child looked so frightened. "My goodness, what's the matter?" Erica asked, kneeling down to the child. "My—my mom. She didn't do my homework," stammered Royal. Impatiently, Mrs. Clyde clucked, "Well you know better than that! Your mother's not supposed to do your homework!" "No—no, I mean . . ." began Royal. But this was too much, the child broke into more sobs.

Erica couldn't help giving Mrs. Clyde a look. It didn't take a genius to figure out what this child meant on the second day of school. "You mean your mom didn't sign your back-to-school papers?" Erica asked softly. "Yeah," replied Royal, looking up hopefully. Erica smiled, putting her arm around the boy, "Oh Honey, that's alright. Really. It's only the second day of school. You still have time to get them signed." "No-o-o-o-o!" Royal wailed, his eyes again filling with tears. "Ms. . . . My teacher say I have to *bring* them. Today! Or, or I can't have recess."

Defeated, Royal put his head in his hands and wept quietly. Erica watched the little boy. Why would a child react like this because he'd forgotten his papers? This emotion seemed rooted in something more than back-to-school nerves. Erica looked to Mrs. Clyde but she was calling to two boys riding piggy back. So, she pulled Royal away from the crush of the oncoming children and said she'd walk with him to his room and explain it all to his teacher. Erica believed his teacher needed to be alerted to the depth of this child's emotion.

❖ MRS. JAMES, TEACHER

Mrs. James, the fourth grade teacher, was in the back of the room. She was a tall, matronly woman of firm manner and strong physique. Some students had just pulled down pieces of a bulletin board display in an early morning chase and Mrs. James was overseeing the display's repair.

Lillian James loved teaching. She loved the order and the routine. But Mrs. James had also been teaching for many years and worried whether she had the fortitude to recast yet another group of wild things. And, those wild things were changing, too. No one could deny the fact. "Children are so rude and disrespectful today," she'd said in a recent phone conversation with her sister-in-law. "They used to come to me with a sense of propriety that was crude but at least malleable. Today children come to school with no values at all. And parents don't help either."

Mrs. James turned and saw Ms. Suzman walking to the back of the room with the tear-streaked Royal in tow. Oh Lord. This was all she needed this morning—the new principal inside her classroom and with Royal Collins. She already knew about Royal. His third grade records had told her everything she needed to know.

Erica watched Mrs. James walk briskly over to greet her. The look on the teacher's face made Erica instinctively send Royal to his seat.

After pleasantries, Erica related the story of Royal's arrival at school concluding with, "It just seems like more than back-to-school jitters." Mrs. James glared at the new principal and said nothing. Erica continued more tentatively, "Will you let Royal go to recess today and bring his papers tomorrow? You know they're not due in central office until next week." Mrs. James replied, "You know, Miss Suzman, I spoke to Royal's third grade teacher, Joan Becker, and she said Royal emotionally manipulated everyone and his behavior was a roller coaster. She said she never had a student who was so disruptive. I maintain standards in this classroom, Miss Suzman. I don't acquiesce to emotional misbehavior. Children are in school to learn."

Erica would not be thwarted. "Mrs. James," Erica said, "I'm asking you to trust me on this. Give me a day. I'll call the mom myself to make sure those papers come in. This is a new school for Royal. Let's let him start with a clean slate, give him the benefit of the doubt. I'll talk to Mom and see what I can find out."

Mrs. James looked at the new principal for a long moment and then smiled. "Very well, Miss Suzman," replied the teacher, "Royal can go to recess. In fact, I'll give all the children another day. I take it your door is going to be open to ten-year-olds, too."

"My door is going to be open to anyone who needs me, Mrs. James. I—I'll let you know if anything comes of my conversation with Mrs. Collins. I'm sorry I disrupted you," stammered the new principal.

"Not at all, Miss Suzman. Come in any time," responded Mrs. James.

❖ DALVA COLLINS

Erica went to her office and called Royal's mother. The conversation with Mrs. Collins was puzzling. Erica felt Mrs. Collins was pleasant but somewhat vacant. Erica did hear the mother brighten when the principal complimented Royal but when Erica tried to engage her in a conversation about how Royal spent his summer, the mother became vague and elusive.

Moreover, there was a lot of background noise as Erica and Mrs. Collins talked. To Erica it sounded as though young children were playing nearby and taking full advantage of their mother's diverted attention. The principal looked down at Royal's file during the dialogue and saw that Royal had three younger sisters and a baby brother. She also noted that Dalva Collins was twenty-six years old and her husband, Clay Collins, was twenty-eight. Erica began to remark on how busy Mrs. Collins must be with five children when she heard a few deep, muffled words directed at the mother. Mrs. Collins hastily said she was sorry but had to go. Erica could only quickly remind her about Royal's back to school papers. Mrs. Collins said, "Yes, Miss. Goodbye." Erica sat with the dial tone ringing in her ear.

❖ ERICA'S FIRST WEEKS

The days streaked by. And the new principal struggled with one challenge after another—teachers dissatisfied with room assignments; parents dissatisfied with teacher assignments; book and supply shortages; orienting new staff with no established orientation procedures; responding to faculty questions and student questions; completing the endless back-to-school forms and reports; breaking in a new secretary; and getting back—in a timely manner—to the continual inquiries from the superintendent. The administrative tasks left Erica feeling tired but satisfied. She felt like she was *almost* staying on top of it all. Staff interactions, on the other hand, left the new principal feeling very uneasy.

It had been Erica's intent to get inside the classroom of every teacher in the building by the end of September. Informally, she'd step into a room during passing times or before and after school and have a brief, friendly exchange with the teacher. Teachers were guarded but would, more often than not, inadvertently share some bit of information about their students or teaching style. Erica learned a lot in these short exchanges—good and bad. The staff was generally traditional in style but the principal sensed a professional receptivity that made her optimistic about her faculty's professional development.

Mr. Young, however, was another story. He was the seventh grade math teacher. Erica was eager to chat with him because so many of the staff seemed to respect his work. She went to his room early in the year and her visit with the teacher proved to be very positive. Mr. Young was open, courteous, and very informative. But, just when Erica was making ready to leave his room, she looked up and saw a diagram sketched on the chalk board. It was an odd design; a circle with three cones pointing into the center. Curious, Erica asked about it. Mr. Young grinned broadly and said, "Oh, that's my geometry quiz. I put it on the board and tell the kids whoever can tell me what it is gets an "A" for the day. No one ever has the answer." Erica chuckled and said, "Well, I guess I'm out of an A, too. What is it?" The teacher laughed, "It's three Ku Klux Klan members looking down a well at one of their victims!"

❖ HARRIET CLYDE, ASSISTANT PRINCIPAL

During the first week of school, Erica had requested that she and Mrs. Clyde arrange regular biweekly meetings. To Erica's surprise, the assistant principal asked why she couldn't just check in if she had a problem. Erica was adamant. She knew the meetings would be important for team building and learning about the school. She coyly reminded Mrs. Clyde that she *needed* her—needed regular access to her knowledge about the school and community.

Harriet Clyde relented but came to the meetings with an attitude of bemused detachment. Try as she might, Erica could not get the assistant principal to open up. Moreover, it wasn't long before Erica was encountering teachers in the hall or lounge who, in conversation, would allude to a point Erica had made *only* in one of her meetings with Mrs. Clyde.

Erica was furious. She confronted the assistant principal but Mrs. Clyde assured her—with a smile—that all of their conversations were held in the strictest of confidence. The meetings between the principal and assistant principal quickly degenerated into a cold review of assigned tasks and their status.

❖ ROYAL AND MRS. CLYDE

Mrs. James had been sending Royal to Mrs. Clyde regularly. The child was always guilty of one infraction after another. Erica felt Royal's offenses were minor—candy in class, talking, not coming when called at recess. She supposed that Mrs. James was trying to prove a point about the boy's incorrigibility but thought it best not to interfere. Discipline was supposed to be managed by the classroom teacher, then Mrs. Clyde, and ultimately Miss Suzman.

One day, about two weeks after school opened, Erica passed Mrs. Clyde's office and saw the assistant principal with her finger in Royal's face, screaming, "You know what you had to do!" Royal looked wretched. Erica couldn't ignore this tirade. She entered Mrs. Clyde's office and asked Royal to wait outside. When the child left the room, Erica closed the door and said, "Mrs. Clyde what did he do?" "This is the second day in a row that he came to school without his spelling test signed. He failed, of course, and Mrs. James wanted his mother to know about it." Erica was beside herself, "Mrs. Clyde, you *screamed* at a child for not returning a signed piece of paper? Isn't that a bit much?" Mrs. Clyde responded, "Joan Becker, his third grade teacher, is my neighbor, Miss Suzman, and let me tell you—this child doesn't understand anything less. Besides, we run a tight ship here at Mt. Morris. If you don't set the standards when they arrive, all hell will break loose in the seventh and eighth grades."

Erica was thunderstruck. She paused, took a deep breath and said, "Mrs. Clyde, every child in this school will be disciplined with courtesy and respect. You will not scream at children as part of their discipline. You will talk to them calmly and with reason. Maybe we need to arrange training for you to show you what this means. Meanwhile, if you see yourself losing control, as you just did with Royal, I think you'd better send that child—whoever she or he is—to me. In fact, for now, I want you to take a break from Royal. When Mrs. James sends him to the office, he'll wait with the secretary until I can see him. You're *not* to interact with him. Do you understand?" Harriet Clyde barely managed to say, "If that's what you want, fine." "It *is* what I want, Mrs. Clyde," replied Erica. It was the beginning of a daily check-in between the principal and Royal Collins.

❖ DOTTIE BAUER, JUVENILE OFFICER

Dottie Bauer was a short, broad woman with an irresistible laugh and a love for "good characters and better gossip." She'd lived in Mt. Morris throughout her life and had been hired by the police force a week after graduating from high school. She'd been in the department for 22 years, the last seven as a juvenile officer. Dottie liked to say she was glad when she was made a "juve" and could wear street clothes, "That uniform made me look like a refrigerator in military blue."

Dottie was one of two officers in the juvenile unit where the work had been increasing so much of late that the team was trying to justify hiring a third officer. Everyone believed the new population of kids coming into Mt. Morris was increasing their workload. When asked about her job, Dottie would say, "Hey, one minute I'm a law enforcer and the next, I'm a social worker. It ain't boring."

The juvenile officer was convinced that her town and its institutions needed to work together to respond to the changing needs of its citizens. To that end, she was the one officer that made the schools her responsibility. As she became aware of families impacted by criminal or civil actions, she'd make a note of it and at least twice a year, visit the five Mt. Morris schools and update the school personnel. Principals and guidance counselors always appreciated the information Dottie provided.

❖ DOTTIE VISITS MT. MORRIS MIDDLE SCHOOL

It was the third week of September. Dottie had updated her school lists throughout the summer and was ready to share what she could with school personnel. The Mt. Morris Middle School was her first stop.

Dottie Bauer sat at a table with Erica Suzman, the new middle school principal, Harriet Clyde, and Katie Downs, the guidance counselor. The juvenile officer had known Harriet and Katie for a number of years and was comfortable with both women. She liked the new principal immediately.

Dottie had brought a list of about seventeen cases that she thought the educators would want to know about. As the juvenile officer described each case, Erica listened with growing dismay. To her mind, no child should be subjected to some of what Dottie was describing. The principal was glad Katie was at the meeting. Her insights on many of the situations were helpful.

Dottie had reviewed the situations of about four families when she came to the next family on her list—the Collins family. There was a restraining order in effect against Clay Collins. The plaintiffs were Dalva Collins and her five children. Clay could not go within 100 yards of his family for a year. Erica asked, "How long has the restraining order been in effect, Dottie? Why didn't someone tell us?" "It just took effect on July 1st," answered Dottie, "I don't know why you don't know. It isn't clear whose job it was to inform you. Anyway, now you know." "And what precipitated it?" continued the principal. "Years of physical abuse. The father spent some time in prison. He's got a very serious drinking problem. When he drinks, he beats up the wife and kids," Dottie told the principal. She continued, "He's dangerous, Erica. But when the restraining order came down, he left town. Word has it, he's back in Tennessee with his mother."

Katie, the guidance counselor looked up Royal in her folder and said to Erica, "He's slated for counseling services but, we haven't been able to nail down a time to begin just yet." Erica asked, "Do you know how he got referred, Katie?" The counselor replied, "No. I don't have his file with me. I do know he's not Special Ed." "Yet," interjected Mrs. Clyde snidely. Erica flashed the assistant principal a withering look and turned to the guidance counselor, "He needs those services, Katie. Do what you can to get him started. If there's really a problem, come and see me." Katie sighed deeply and made a note in her folder. To her assistant principal, Erica said, "Mrs. Clyde, I want you to alert Mrs. James to this situation."

❖ ROYAL

By late September, Royal had been visiting Erica every day after school for two weeks. The student and principal had become friends. Together, they'd chat for about ten minutes and then Royal would run to catch his bus. Erica would invariably send him off with a piece of candy from her candy dish. This always made Royal smile.

Erica thought the check-ins had helped Royal's behavior. At least, his trips to the office during the day had lessened considerably—two trips last week; only one this week, until today. She had been alarmed when, earlier in the week, John McKay, sitting on the detention bench, had seen Royal walk by and said, "Nobody likes that kid." Erica had been standing at the front counter and asked, "Why's that, John?" John, a likable kid, said, "He's a cry-baby. And he always has his finger in his nose." John grinned slyly and added, "We call him Cootie Boy."

This morning Royal sat looking at Erica across her desk. Erica was un-nerved. She saw the same terror in the boy's eyes as she had seen the morning he got off the bus on the second day of school. The principal looked again at Mrs. James' note. It said, "Royal very meanly mocked another student. When I corrected him, he had a huge tantrum. He upset the entire class."

"Okay, Royal, what happened?" asked the principal. With tears in his eyes, the boy confirmed that he had done everything his teacher said. He con-cluded, saying, "I don't know why I'm so bad, Miss Suzman." Erica replied, "You're not bad, Royal. Something's going on inside you this morning that makes you act bad. What was it like getting ready for school this morning? Was Mom up? Did you have breakfast?"

Royal's eyes darted away from Erica's. The little boy put his hands in his pockets. He said very quietly, "She was up. We had toast." Erica was wonder-ing how to continue when she heard a crinkling noise. She asked Royal what it was. The little boy pulled a creased and rumpled piece of paper out of his pocket and handed it to his principal. Erica carefully unfolded it.

The paper held a picture of a woman. The figure was strong and brown, her hair and features bold but for the mouth. The mouth was ambivalent—in fact, a slanting, red line. The woman held two balloons. In one hand, was a red balloon with a happy face; in the other hand, was a purple balloon with a sad face. On the right side of the paper was a poem:

My Mom

I have a mom named Dalva
man, I love my mom. She hugs
me. I hug her. She mean
a lot to me.

In the bottom, left corner, was another poem:

In Your Heart

In your heart somebody
loves you. In your heart
somebody hates. But God
loves you.

Erica looked at the paper for a long moment. "Royal," she said, "this is beautiful. This picture shows me how much you love your Mom." The boy was pleased. "Did you make this in class, Royal?" Erica continued. "No, I been working on it on the bus," said Royal. "Well, I think you have a lot of artistic talent. Did Mrs. James show you how to write these poems?" asked the principal. "Yeah," said the boy. "Are you going to give this to your Mom?" queried Erica. Royal very hastily said, "No. She—no. You want it?" "Oh Royal, thank you. I'd love to have it," Erica said softly. "It's going to go right here on my wall. But, if you change your mind and want to give it to your mom, it'll be right here."

Erica taped the picture up and then, together, they agreed that Royal should return to class and apologize to the little boy.

❖ AN EXCHANGE

It was fifth period. Erica had returned to her office for a few minutes respite after her chaotic morning. She'd been on her feet responding to one crisis after another since meeting with Royal a couple of hours before. The sprinkler system had gone off in the art room. Mrs. Sullivan, the art teacher, had run into the office yelling, "We weren't supposed to do *water* colors!!" On top of that, the seventh graders had gotten out of hand under Mrs. Clyde's lunchtime watch and Erica had found herself patrolling the cafeteria after she'd called a silent lunch.

The principal had only been at her desk a moment when her eyes came to rest on Royal's poems. Erica considered showing the picture to Mrs. James and remembered that she'd often seen her in the teacher's lounge fifth period. On impulse, she pulled the picture off the wall and went to the lounge.

Mrs. James was alone at a small table grading papers. Ned Young and Howard Palmer were at the other end of the room discussing an addition Mr. Palmer was having put on his house. Erica walked over to Lillian James and said, "Hello, Mrs. James." Mrs. James looked up from her work long enough to reply, "Oh. Hello, Miss Suzman." The teacher returned to the task at hand. Erica continued, "Mrs. James, I wanted to talk to you about Royal." Mrs. James smiled, "You know, I have 28 other students, Miss Suzman." Not wanting to get caught up in that argument, Erica said, "I know you do, Mrs. James. But Royal presents some unique challenges. Mrs. Clyde told you about his father's restraining order—." "Yes, she did. Does its existence require that I lessen my expectations?" queried Mrs. James. "Well, no. Of course not," spluttered the principal. Erica continued, "You know, Royal confirmed everything you reported about this morning's tantrum." "Good," said Mrs. James, "he told you about mocking John Stebbins, the little boy with multiple sclerosis?" "Yes, he did," answered Erica, "Did he apologize as we agreed he would?" "Oh yes," asserted the teacher, relentlessly marking the papers.

Erica paused for a moment and then said, "You know, Mrs. James, you were absolutely right to send him to the office as you did. One child can't be allowed to dominate a class like that. And—I want you to know, that I'm perfectly comfortable with you sending him down any time he acts out like that. I want to support you." Mrs. James continued grading. After a moment, she said, "Thank you, Miss Suzman. I'll keep that in mind."

Erica watched the teacher make her red marks and then said, "Mrs. James, may I show you something?" "Of course," replied the teacher. Erica placed Royal's picture on top of the pile of student papers. The teacher reluctantly laid down her red pen and looked at the art work. She gazed at the wrinkled paper for a long time. Erica thought she saw something in the teacher's face soften. Finally Mrs. James said, "He asked me for help on these poems. I didn't know what they were for." "He told me he'd been working on this on the bus," said Erica. The teacher pursed her lips and nodded.

Mrs. James handed the picture back to the principal, stood up and gathered her papers, "He still comes to see you after school, Miss Suzman?" "Oh yes. Everyday. Just until it's time to catch the bus," explained the principal. Mrs. James looked intently into Erica's face for a moment and said, "Well, that's good to know." Lillian James turned and marched out of the room.

❖ A MEETING WITH THE SUPERINTENDENT

Like other principals in the district, Erica and the superintendent met bimonthly to collaborate on policy and direction. Much of their conversation focused on the direction for the troubled Mt. Morris School. This was their third meeting of the year. Each brought a list of items to discuss. It was a productive meeting. Max, and then Erica, crossed off items on their lists in short order.

One of Erica's last agenda items was staff development with regard to diversity. Erica mentioned the changing racial makeup of the school. "Demographics in this community are changing. Children of color are only going to increase in number," explained the principal. "You don't need to tell me about the town's demographics, Erica. Just get to the point," the superintendent retorted. Erica heard the edge in her boss' voice but persisted, "I think the faculty needs some sensitivity training around racial and cultural differences."

"Now hold on," said Max, "You've got a limited professional development budget. And we agreed that your teachers needed technology training." "I think we should take another look at that, Max," responded Erica. "No, Erica. No. Maybe next year. But right now you've got other priorities. Is there anything else on your list?" "Well . . . no," stammered Erica. "Good. Because there's something else I want to talk to you about," said Max.

There was a pause. Erica waited. And then Max said, "Erica, I understand you have a relationship with a fourth grader. He comes to your office every day—." Erica was astonished; how did he know about Royal? She sputtered, "I do . . . How do you know?" Max said, "It's my job to know. And, don't ever lose sight of the fact that this is *still* a small town, Erica." The superintendent paused and then continued, "Tell me what's going on."

Erica couldn't believe it but did as she was asked, recounting Royal's first few weeks, describing Mrs. Clyde's harsh discipline and concluding with a recap of Royal's daily visits. Max listened attentively and then said, "You know it's not surprising that you'd empathize with that kid, Erica. You're both out-siders, new to the school—." Erica was stunned. "But, Max . . ." she stam-mered. "No, hear me out, Erica," said the superintendent, "I understand your need to help the kid. But he needs more than you can give him. Use your re-sources, like the guidance counselor. And work on your relationship with Lil-lian James. Get yourself out of the loop, Erica. You've got a whole school of needy kids! You're a principal now, not a classroom teacher. You've got to use your head more than your heart."

Max looked at his watch. "Geez," the superintendent said, "I'm late for the rotary luncheon. Okay, Erica. Keep up the good fight. See you in a couple of weeks."

❖ A VISIT

It was a Thursday morning early in October. Third period had just begun. Er-ica was standing at the counter in the front office, signing a number of requi-sition forms—construction paper, toilet paper, paper towels. If the first month was any indication, some of her budget allocations were going to be depleted by December. Mrs. Clyde was standing at the counter, as well, preparing a week's worth of absentee lists to send to central office. The women had been laughing. Olive Simons, the new secretary, had just described how she and her husband chased a squirrel out of their attic using her grandmother's girdle and an old cooking ladle.

Erica was still smiling when she smelled the sweet stench of alcohol. She looked up from her papers and found herself facing the grim countenance of a short, wiry and intense looking man. The principal said mechanically, "Can I help you?" The voice was hushed. The principal heard the words, ". . . my son." Erica replied, "I . . . I'm sorry, sir. I don't know who your son is." "Collins," said the man. "Royal Collins?" asked Erica incredulously. The prin-cipal turned to look at Mrs. Clyde but the assistant principal had disappeared. The man made no reply, his dark eyes gave Erica the answer. She felt the pounding in her chest, "Sir, I can't let you see your son. You're not allowed to see him. In fact, I have to ask—" Before Erica could finish the man snapped, "He's my son. I have a right to see my boy."

Erica said nothing for a moment, never taking her eyes from Mr. Collins' face. Then, she turned to Mrs. Simons' desk. She took a small piece of paper from Olive's memo pad and as she wrote, the principal said, "Mrs. Simons, will you go get Royal Collins from his classroom?" The principal handed the paper to the secretary. The words on the paper said, "CALL POLICE!" Mrs. Si-mons nodded and left the office.

Erica turned again to Mr. Collins and asked if he'd like to wait for his son in her office. Clay Collins said, "I'll wait right here." Erica responded, "Of course. You can take that seat by the door if you wish." Clay Collins remained standing although a little wobbly. Erica tried to look busy at Olive's desk. The silence was chilling. Finally, Olive Simons returned to the office. She was flushed and nervous, saying, "They weren't in the classroom, Miss Suzman. Maybe they're at an elective." Mr. Collins hearing this, moved toward the women and said, "I'll get him. Where is he?" Erica replied, "Well, it'll take a few minutes to pull his schedule and find out, Mr. Collins. But I'll—" Clay Collins turned and left the office and stood in the hallway, Looking both ways as if to begin a room to room search. "Mr. Collins, wait . . . Don't!" Erica said as she moved to follow him into the corridor.

❖ CASE PREPARATION QUESTIONS

1. Erica Suzman is a new principal. Critique her entry plan and performance during the first few months of school. What would you have done differently?

2. Increasingly, multiple institutions and individuals are involved in the lives of "at risk" children. Who should be responsible for coordinating the work of these various individuals and institutions?

3. Erica Suzman worked with many individuals including her superintendent, assistant principal, and guidance counselor on the Royal Collins case. Assess these relationships and describe how she might have managed these relationships differently.

◆ ◆ ◆

Promise and Fear (B)

Debi Phillips

Six police officers entered Mt. Morris Middle School from the front door and surrounded Clay Collins as he was beginning to search for his son, Royal. Two of them drew their weapons. The father was whisked out of the building, searched and put, handcuffed, in the back of a patrol car. Within minutes, Clay Collins was on his way to the police station.

Miraculously the hall was empty when Clay Collins was apprehended. Olive Simons and Erica Suzman stood gaping at each other. The episode happened so quickly it almost seemed they had imagined it.

The two women were brought back to reality, however, when Officers Gunther and Corey walked into the building. The principal, secretary and police officers quickly moved into the main office. Officers Gunther and Corey introduced themselves and asked if Erica and Olive would answer some questions for Clay Collins' arrest report. "Of course. We'd be happy to help," replied Erica. But Mrs. Clyde interrupted, "Is he gone yet?" Only her head was inside the office door. "You might say that," quipped the principal.

Erica introduced Harriet Clyde to the officers and said, "I need the front office covered Mrs. Clyde. Olive and I are going into my office to answer some questions."

The women answered the officers' questions as truthfully as they could. Were they threatened? What kind of language did Clay Collins use? Was he inebriated? Did he touch them? The questioning lasted about twenty minutes, and then Donna Gunther said, "I think we have it." Erica countered, "Officers, I have a few questions. Can you give me a few more minutes?" Wanting to be helpful, Donna Gunther said, "Sure." The principal turned to Mrs. Simons, "Olive, you don't need to stay for this. I'll see you out front in a few minutes." The officers thanked the secretary for her help and Olive left.

Erica said, "Officers, I have a little boy at this school and I'm responsible for his well-being. Can I be certain he's safe to go home after this?" Donna Gunther replied, "Clay Collins is under mandatory arrest for violating his restraining order, Miss Suzman." Erica wanted to make sure she understood, "You mean, he's in jail? For how long?" Officer Gunther said, "Collins will be confined until he's arraigned for indictment—arraignments happen routinely, probably by tomorrow if we're lucky." "And after that?" Erica persisted. Donna Gunther looked at her partner. Ed Corey took over, "At his arraignment he'll more than likely be released." "How?" demanded the principal. "Personal recognizance. The defense attorney could make any number of arguments to have him let go."

Erica was trying to grasp the implications of what she'd just been told. Donna Gunther continued, "But, keep in mind, Miss Suzman, the restraining order is still in effect—and Mr. Collins learned this morning what happens when he violates it." "You mean that man will be back on the streets with nothing between him and his family but a piece of paper that he's ignored once already? I'm not reassured, Officer." said Erica bluntly. Donna Gunther said quietly, "Well, let's hope he's learned otherwise. Right now the law doesn't let us keep people in jail indefinitely simply because they want to see their kids."

❖ ERICA AND HARRIET CLYDE MEET

There was a lot to do around the Collins affair; people to notify. But Erica was furious. To her mind, Harriet Clyde had abandoned Olive Simons and the principal when they were possibly in real danger. When Erica returned to the office, she asked if she could speak to Mrs. Clyde alone and led the way back to her office.

"Mrs. Clyde, where did you go?" Erica demanded as she sat down behind her desk. "You mean when Mr. Collins—?" asked Mrs. Clyde. "I mean when Mr. Collins arrived," stated the principal. "Well, clearly he was angry, I thought I'd get Katie to come and reason with him," replied Mrs. Clyde. Erica was beside herself. "Mrs. Clyde, if a dangerous individual comes into the office, you contain that situation by getting the police involved. You do not bring another person into the mix. If Katie had come, you'd only have succeeded in putting her in jeopardy, as well." "Well, I couldn't find her," said the recalcitrant assistant principal, "so, no harm done." "No thanks to you," retorted Erica.

Erica was more angry than she'd been in a long time. Taking a slow, deep breath, she said, "I'm worried about damage control, Mrs. Clyde. Do you know whether anyone besides us knows about the arrest?" Harriet Clyde responded, "I was in the East wing when the police were in the parking lot with Mr. Collins." "Did you see them?" asked Erica. "Yes, and so did the classes in the art room and the band room," responded the A.P. "Terrific," groused Erica. The assistant principal continued, "The kids got to crowd around the windows." "Oh Geez," replied the beleaguered principal. "Which classes?" "Fourth and fifth grades—not Mrs. James' class," Harriet Clyde said with increasing confidence. "I know a number of people in the neighborhood who are home during the day, too," Harriet volunteered. Reading her mind, Erica said, "So, word is going to get out." "I think so," confirmed Harriet.

Erica said, "Well, I can't wait any longer. There are people who have to be alerted to this . . . Max Christopher, Lillian James, Katie Downs, Dalva Collins and Royal." Mrs. Clyde asked, "Royal? Is telling a ten-year-old boy really necessary?" Erica wasn't sure; she remembered Max Christopher's words, "It's *still* a small town." Students who witnessed the arrest might have recognized Mr. Collins. Erica felt she couldn't risk Royal hearing about it on the street.

The two women also discussed the need to tell the faculty. Harriet Clyde volunteered that if the local paper got involved, the teachers would need to know. Erica had to agree. She said, "I'll compose a memo. Olive can put it in their mailboxes. And, Mrs. Clyde, if anyone asks, you're not to mention the family name." Mrs. Clyde replied, "Well, of course not, Miss Suzman."

Erica said she would call Max Christopher and Mrs. Collins and asked Harriet Clyde to speak with Mrs. James and Katie Downs. The principal reasoned Mrs. Clyde would never learn to *act* like an assistant principal if she didn't let her *be* an assistant principal. Erica concluded the meeting saying, "I'll tell Royal once I've confirmed it with his mother. Maybe I'll get Katie involved." She picked up the phone receiver to dial Max's office and Harriet got up to go track down the people on her list. But, just as the assistant principal got to the door, she said, "So, maybe it wasn't such a bad idea that I went to look for Katie." With the receiver still at her ear, Erica watched open mouthed as the woman left her office. Suddenly it occurred to her, "Katie?! Katie's office is at the West end of the building. What the hell was Harriet doing in the East wing?"

❖ INFORMATION SPREADS

Max Christopher listened closely, asking only a few questions as Erica described the morning's events and the action plan. "Collins? Is that the father of the fourth grader you've been seeing?" inquired the superintendent. Erica felt her stomach turn, "Yes. It's the same kid." Max persisted, "And are you removing yourself from that situation?" "Not yet. Not now. In some ways I'm the one positive relationship he's got in this building. I'm not going to take that away from him now. I can spare ten minutes a day. It's why I'm in this business." There was silence on the other end of the line. Finally Max asked, "And the guidance counselor, she's in the loop? "Mrs. Clyde is informing her now. I'll touch base with Katie later in the day," Erica replied. "Make sure she's involved in a substantive way, Erica. As for the rest of the affair—sounds like you have your bases covered. Keep me informed of any new developments— especially if you get a call from the media." Erica hung up the phone and breathed a sigh of relief.

There was no answer when the principal phoned the Collins' home.

Mrs. James stood in the hallway outside her classroom listening closely as Harriet Clyde filled her in on the morning's developments. The teacher only asked if Royal was going to be informed and Mrs. Clyde told her it was their intent to tell him, but last, after all other parties were notified. Curious, Mrs. Clyde asked, "Why? Do you want to be there Lillian?" Mrs. James replied, "Oh, no. I'm sure Erica will handle it." Lillian James thanked Harriet Clyde for keeping her "in the loop" and went back to her classroom. The assistant principal went to find the guidance counselor.

With the news about Royal's dad, Katie Downs rubbed her forehead and seemed to cradle herself as she folded her arms across her chest. She said nothing. Finally, Mrs. Clyde said, "Katie? Is there anything you want to do?" Katie looked up at the A.P. and replied, "Of course! There's a hell of a lot I want to do!" Bewildered, Mrs. Clyde said, "My, everyone certainly is grumpy today." Katie sighed and said, "I'm sorry, Harriet. I guess I'm feeling a bit overwhelmed. About Royal—are you sure he's out of danger? You know, we have a responsibility to disclose.[1]" Mrs. Clyde answered, "Well, I'm not sure. I know the police took Mr. Collins away. I—." "Maybe I'd better talk to Erica myself," interrupted the guidance counselor.

❖ KATIE AND ERICA MEET

Erica was at her desk trying again to reach Mrs. Collins when Katie came in. "Oh, Katie, I'm glad to see you. We need to talk," said Erica as she hung up the receiver. "Erica," said Katie, "I need to tell you something." "What?" asked the principal. "I wouldn't know Royal Collins if I tripped over him in the hall," announced the guidance counselor. "WHAT?" asked Erica in disbelief. "I thought you were meeting with him?"

Katie told Erica everything. She said, "Erica, I started the year with thirty-seven referrals and twenty-eight carry overs. I had so many scheduling conflicts that I can't even give you a count. It's October and I still have seven messages on my desk from parents wanting a schedule change for their kids. And, now I've got to get the CAT testing scheduled in the next two weeks or we won't have comparisons to give Max Christopher in the spring. Look, I tried twice to meet with Royal!!"

Erica listened, trying to frame a constructive response. Finally she said, "Katie, why didn't you tell me you were so overwhelmed?" "It's the status quo, Erica," replied the counselor. "It may have been the status quo in the past, Katie. It can't be status quo with Royal."

The principal looked out the window, bouncing her pencil on the desk. She was angry with herself. She'd made progress interacting with her mainstream classroom teachers but hadn't thought to meet with any of her non-mainstream staff. How could she have been so stupid? She realized something had to be done about Katie's situation but wasn't sure what to do. Finally, Erica looked at the counselor and said, "Look, Katie. We have two problems here. The immediate problem is Royal's circumstance. The second problem is your workload. We've got to focus on Royal right now."

---

[1]The guidance counselor is referring to a state law that requires teachers, educational administrators, guidance or family counselors, psychologists and others to make a report to the Department of Youth Services or to the person in charge of the school, institution or facility any time there is reasonable cause to believe that a child under eighteen is suffering serious physical or emotional injury resulting from abuse, including sexual abuse, or from neglect, including malnutrition.

Wearily Katie said, "You know, we've got a responsibility to disclose." Erica looked puzzled. "Are you sure, Katie?" responded Erica, "I said the same thing to the police, but they told me that Royal was out of danger for the foreseeable future because his father was in jail awaiting arraignment." "But what about long term?" Katie asked. "The restraining order is still in effect," said Erica. "A lot of good that did him today," retorted the counselor. "All I can tell you is," Erica continued, "right now, they say he's not in danger. The safeguards are in place; whether they work, I don't know."

Katie said with a sigh, "I suppose there's nothing DYS can do now, anyway. But I've got to tell you, I may not *know* Royal but I know *about* him. That kid is really shut off." "What do you mean?" asked Erica. "I had one of my first group sessions with some other fourth graders the other day. Royal's got some real socialization issues. The kids talk about him and ostracize him. And, they claim he's stealing the desserts from their lunches." Erica shook her head, saying, "Listen Katie, wait and see what they do to him if they find out about his dad." "Why would they find out?" asked Katie. "Two elementary classes in the art and band rooms saw the father put in a police car and taken away." "Oh God," said Katie.

The conversation turned to how and when Royal should be told. Erica said, "I want to talk to him. He comes to my office everyday. He trusts me. I've tried his mother three times, but there's no answer. I think we should inform her of our intent, but if I don't reach her by 2:00 p.m., I'm going to pull him and tell him." "How?" Katie asked. "You know it's important how the message is framed. You've got to leave Royal feeling safe and knowing that we're committed to keeping him safe. And, what about the kids who might tease him?" Katie thought for a minute more and added, "Why don't I sit with you as you tell him. It's not a conversation you want to have in isolation. And, it'll establish an agenda for Royal and me to start meeting."

"Alright. It's probably a good idea to have another adult present. So, you'll hear from me between now and 2:00 p.m.," stated Erica.

❖ KATIE AND ERICA TALK TO ROYAL

By 2:00 p.m., Erica had still not reached Mrs. Collins. Time was running out if Royal was going to be told before he left the building. Erica got on the intercom to Katie's office and asked her to pull Royal from class and bring him down to her office. Katie said she'd get Royal and be right there.

When Katie and Royal arrived, Erica invited them to take the chairs in front of her desk and pulled her chair out to sit with them. The principal spoke briefly to Royal about Katie's job as a counselor and how he would start visiting her soon. And then Erica told the little boy that she had something to tell him, and she thought Mrs. Downs should be with them when they talked. Royal sensed something was wrong. His eyes were wide as he looked from one woman to the other.

Erica began, "Royal, you know your father isn't supposed to come near you or your mom or your sisters and brother, right?" Royal immediately looked at the floor. He said nothing. Erica sensed Royal's avoidance and pressed, "Royal? Do you know that your dad isn't supposed to come around?" The little boy whispered, "Yes." Erica continued, "Tell me, Royal. Why isn't he supposed to come around?" "Because he hurts us," Royal said reluctantly, still looking at the floor.

The principal took a breath and proceeded, "Royal, I have to tell you something that might frighten you but I want to say first that you're very safe. You have nothing to be afraid of. . ." Royal raised his head and looked into Erica's eyes, waiting. "Your dad came to the school today, Royal. But because he's not supposed to come near you, we called the police and they took him away," Erica declared. "Where is he now?" Royal asked. "The police put him in jail," Erica gently replied. Under his breath, Royal whispered, "They'll let him out." "What?" asked the principal. "They'll let him out," repeated the child. "Why do you say that Royal?" asked the principal. Finally, looking at Erica the child said, "They always do." Erica couldn't help but glance at Katie. She responded as best she could, "The police were very firm with him, Royal. He was arrested. If he comes near you again, he'll be arrested again."

Royal looked down at the floor once more. There was an awkward silence. Finally, he asked, "Where's my mom?" Erica answered, "We tried to call her, Royal. We didn't get any answer." The boy nodded and said nothing. The principal asked, "Royal, are you okay? Do you feel safe?" After a minute, Royal slowly nodded again.

Erica watched the boy for a moment and asked, "Royal, will you tell us if you ever see your dad? This is very important. It's our job to help you learn and to protect you, too." Something in Royal's head and shoulders stiffened again. Erica persisted, "Royal? Will you tell us? Will you tell us if you ever see your dad?" Royal hesitated and barely nodded.

As he was leaving the office, Erica gave Royal a hug and asked him to come and see her after school. The little boy was limp, he said nothing. Katie whispered to Erica that she'd talk to Royal about how to deal with kids who teased him on their way back to class. Erica had completely forgotten that part of the conversation.

Fifteen minutes later, the bell rang and Erica sat waiting for Royal. She wanted to check in with him one last time. He never came. Finally, she left her office to look for him but got caught in the hall breaking up a skirmish between two fifth graders. By the time she got out the door, she could only wave helplessly as the child's bus pulled away from the curb.

❖ DAYS PASS

Erica finally reached Mrs. Collins the next morning. The mother was as elusive as when Erica spoke to her in early September. All the principal could get from the conversation was that Mrs. Collins was aware of the arrest. Erica hung up the phone and shook her head in bewilderment.

As the week progressed, Erica grew more certain that the media hadn't gotten wind of the arrest nor had students recognized Royal's dad. Apparently Royal had not been subjected to any taunts related to his father. Some teachers had asked Erica about the affair and those exchanges had been helpful and constructive. If Mrs. Clyde didn't stir things up, Erica thought the affair might recede as quickly as it had erupted.

On Wednesday, Mrs. James actually stopped by Erica's office and reported "stellar behavior" for Royal throughout the week. Erica welcomed Mrs. James' involvement but was uncertain what the child's "stellar behavior" might be indicating. Katie met with Royal once on Monday and again on Thursday morning. The counselor stopped into Erica's office Thursday afternoon and said, "I've never seen a kid clam up like this."

Royal only visited Erica once during the week following his father's arrest.

❖ ROYAL MAKES A CALL

On Friday morning at 11:00 a.m., a week after the arrest, Erica encountered Royal in the hallway. The principal smiled and asked him where he was going. Royal said, "I have a stomach ache. I'm goin' to see the nurse." The boy looked up at her. Erica was always touched by Royal's eyes. They revealed so much. On this morning, Erica thought they revealed a fever. She patted Royal's cheek and said, "I hope you feel better, sweetheart."

Minutes later, the principal returned to her office and attacked a pile of paperwork she'd been avoiding for too many days. Time passed and Erica lost herself in a central office memorandum on custodial support. The phone rang. The principal picked up the receiver to hear Olive announcing a call from the Mt. Morris police.

An Officer Baker got on the line to say their dispatcher had just received an anonymous call from a child saying his father was in his house beating up his mother. When the dispatcher asked the father's name the child said, "Clay Collins." Erica's heart sank. Officer Baker said they were able to track the call to the pay phone at the school. The principal said, "Royal Collins, Clay Collins' oldest child, is a student here."

Erica asked Officer Baker what the police intended to do. He said a scan disclosed an existing restraining order. The police were on the way to the house to investigate. The principal snapped, "Of course there's an existing restraining order! He was arrested for violating it a week ago! Why is he out of jail?" Erica demanded, feeling out of control. Officer Baker reminded the principal that this was his first involvement in the case but he knew arraignments had been happening quickly. They were experiencing overcrowding in the cells. Erica was dumbstruck. The father had been on the streets and she had no knowledge of it. Her thoughts jumped to Royal.

"I'm very concerned. If the father is in the home when you investigate, and he figures out it was Royal who called—if not today, then someday soon this child could be in serious danger," Erica contended. Officer Baker assured the principal that the police never revealed their source of information. Erica said, "It's critical, just critical, that I be kept informed. I have to know what happens when you go into that house," Erica said. "Look, we'll do the best we can," replied the officer and hung up. Erica went to find Royal.

The child was not with the nurse. Mrs. Reynolds said, "Royal Collins? I haven't seen him all morning." Erica ran to Mrs. James' room. When she looked in the door, Royal was at his desk in the front of the room. The teacher was giving a spelling test. Erica entered and whispered, "This is urgent, Mrs. James. I have to talk to Royal." Lillian James nodded. The principal led him from the room. With the classroom door shut behind them, Erica turned to the little boy and said, "Royal, I know about the call." Tears exploded from his eyes and Royal howled, "He'll kill me! He'll kill me!"

❖ DONNA GUNTHER AND ED COREY, POLICE OFFICERS

It was noon and Donna Gunther and Ed Corey had just gotten back on the road after a lunch break when the call came on their radio. The two police officers looked at each other knowingly. They'd been in on the Collins arrest a week ago and were already getting called on him again. Ed said cynically, "Hey, a street cop's work is never done." Donna chuckled and turned the car in the direction of the Collins' house.

Having heard the patrol car pull up in the driveway, Dalva Collins stood in the door jam with the screen slightly ajar. Ed Corey said, "How are you Mrs. Collins?" "I'm fine, thank you," said Dalva. Ed continued, "Is anyone in the house with you, Mrs. Collins?" "Just my children," the mother replied. Donna Gunther watched Mrs. Collins closely and let her partner conduct the interview. The questioning continued. "Is your husband on the premises? Are you in danger? Are your children in danger?" Donna felt like she was watching a practiced game of cat and mouse. Ultimately she interrupted and asked, "Would you like us to enter the house and make sure you are safe, Mrs. Collins?" Dalva said, "Oh no. There's no need for you to come in. I've got my laundry all over the place. Everything's just fine, thank you."

Donna Gunther reminded the woman that the restraining order called for Clay Collins' immediate arrest should he come within a hundred yards of his family. "You'll call the station if you see your husband, won't you Mrs. Collins?" asked Donna. Dalva Collins replied, "Oh yes. I will." The officers wished the woman a good day and returned to their car.

The officers' report stated that Dalva Collins showed no signs of stress or abuse and there was no evidence indicating the woman was in danger. Ed Corey wrote, "No search warrant will be sought at this time." No report was made to the principal at Mt. Morris Middle School.

❖ A CALL TO DYS

It was 12:30 p.m. Erica had taken Royal immediately to Katie Downs' office. Royal was very frightened. He didn't want to face his father. The child said, "He comes and stays at our house some days. He comes and he hits us." Erica said, "Royal, the police are going to your house right now. And, until they tell me your father is gone, I'm not letting you go home." That seemed to reassure the boy but he quickly asked, "And Cecie and Mary?" "Honey, who are Cecie and Mary?" questioned Katie. "My sisters, at the Harrison School. If they go home, they're gonna get it, too," replied Royal.

Erica could have kicked herself. Royal had three younger sisters and a brother. Two were at the Harrison Elementary School and two were still at home. Of course the Harrison School needed to be alerted. "Royal, we'll call the Harrison School right away." And then the principal said, "Royal, I'm going to call Mrs. Reynolds to come and sit with you for a few minutes. There are a few things Mrs. Downs and I have to do. But we'll be back and we'll tell you exactly what's happening, okay?" "Okay," said Royal. His eyes looked haunted.

The women left Royal listening to a book tape, with Mrs. Reynolds at his side. They went to Erica's office and before the door was shut, Katie said, "We have to call DYS." "OK," said Erica. "DYS and the Harrison School. Is there anyone else?" asked the counselor. "The police, if they don't get back to me in another hour," replied the principal. Erica also considered calling Max Christopher but decided to wait until the day's events played themselves out. "Let me handle the calls to DYS and the Harrison School. I'll let you know what I find out," said Katie. "Call the school first. We have to make sure those kids stay safe," said the principal. "Right," confirmed Katie. Erica sighed, "And then we can decide what to tell Royal."

◆ ◆ ◆

Promise and Fear (C)

Debi Phillips

❖ A LOST AFTERNOON

Katie Downs' call to DYS resulted in a Friday afternoon visit by the case worker, Kevin Thompson, to the Collins' home. A short conversation with Mrs. Collins gave Kevin reason to believe that Clay Collins was on the premises. The case worker left the house and drove immediately to court to obtain a child protection warrant that would authorize him to take custody of the children.

At Kevin's request, Juvenile Officer Dottie Bauer and Officers Gunther and Corey met the case worker at the Collins home at 3:00 p.m. to escort Kevin as he presented the child protection warrant. As suspected, Clay Collins was present. Mrs. Collins, however, claimed the father had a right to be in his home with his children. She declared she was going to go to court on Monday morning and rescind the restraining order.

After some deliberation, the case worker decided not to take custody of the two children at home and police officers decided not to arrest Clay Collins. They thought such actions futile in the face of Dalva Collins' intent to rescind the restraining order. Nevertheless, the group insisted that, while the restraining order was in effect, Clay Collins should leave the premises. They watched as the father packed some belongings and left the house.

After receiving a call from Donna Gunther assuring her that Mr. Collins had left, Katie Downs requested a patrol car to pick up Royal at Mt. Morris and his sisters at Harrison at 4:00 p.m. on Friday afternoon to take them home.

❖ THE NEXT WEEK

Royal Collins attended school Monday but seemed particularly pensive. He would not talk about how he spent his weekend. Tuesday morning the child's name was on the absentee list. At 1:00 p.m. on Tuesday afternoon, Dottie Bauer called Erica and told her that Mrs. Collins had called the station to report her children missing. The mother said her husband had kidnapped her five children.

The Mt. Morris police were put on alert and descriptions of Clay Collins and his vehicle were sent to police departments throughout the region. There were no sightings of the father and children reported on Tuesday or Wednesday. On Wednesday evening, the local television station reported the disappearance and mentioned Mt. Morris and Harrison schools in passing.

Throughout the day on Thursday there were again no reported sightings. At 6:00 p.m., Erica Suzman was alone in her office when the call came. Royal Collins and his brother and sisters had been found safe and their father arrested. The juvenile officer requested that Erica come to the police station to help identify the children. The Department of Youth Services was sending them indefinitely to a foster home of undisclosed location—a safe home.

Rash Decisions (A)

Edward Barnwell and Sean Reardon

"In my opinion, Gina Neal's respiratory problems and outbreaks of hives are related to the quality of the air in her work environment at the Reynolds School. I strongly advise her to stay away from the Reynolds School until the environmental problems are addressed."

—signed, William Holt, M.D., October 12

Bill Eberly, principal of the Reynolds Elementary School, looked at the note Gina Neal had given him before she had gone home two days earlier. He wondered if her doctor was right. After the flood in five classrooms in the North wing two months ago, his teachers had initially complained about the awful odors in the carpets. But many now were reporting symptoms of respiratory ailments, skin irritations, and hives; the dust, chemicals, and flooding associated with the roofing project were all reasonable candidates for their cause. The teachers wanted to know why he hadn't gotten rid of the foul-smelling carpeting after the floods, what was causing their symptoms, and whether it was even safe for them and their students to be in the classrooms at all.

Eberly didn't know what was causing the symptoms; he had seen only one case of a rash himself, and that had been attributed by the teacher to her chocolate allergy. All the other cases had only been reported to him second hand. He knew that one of the most vocal of the teachers had a history of assorted, often complicated, and unusually rare, health problems—a history that to his mind bordered on hypochondria. Removing the carpets would mean a major disruption of school for students in five classes, something he wanted to avoid if at all possible.

Eberly's frustration increased as he studied the results of the air quality tests he had received a few days earlier from Dr. Deanna Storm, Assistant State Epidemiologist at the Maine Department of Public Health (MDPH). Dr. Storm had told him that there were any number of possible explanations for the reported symptoms. They might be, as many believed, physical reactions to residual chemical agents from the roofing project, or to microbes, bacteria, fungi, or pollen in the air; but they might also be due to some contagious viral infection that was "going around." In addition, she suggested, the symptoms might be psychogenic—the staff might be experiencing "a contagious psychosomatic illness . . . feeding off one another's certainty that they have a problem associated with the environment, eventually causing outbreaks of similar physical symptoms."

No one knew how safe the building was—not even the "experts" at MDPH. Even if he could not discover the cause of the symptoms, Eberly felt he had to take some action.

❖ THE REYNOLDS SCHOOL

The Reynolds Elementary School was a 400-student K-3 facility, one of nine neighborhood public elementary schools in Augusta, Maine. The school employed 61 adult staff members, 45 of whom worked exclusively at Reynolds, and 16 who were either part-timers or itinerant staff assigned to multiple buildings. Of the 61, four were male, including the principal, Bill Eberly. Eberly had been at Reynolds for five years. Prior to that, he had been principal for three years at Rumford Elementary School, a small K-6 school also in Augusta, but had transferred to Reynolds for the opportunity to work more exclusively with younger children.

The Reynolds School was a one-story masonry structure containing a block of classrooms built in 1948, and an annexed media center built in 1964. All classrooms and hallways were carpeted. An oil-fired hot water heating system supplied heat to the building. Heat distribution in the original building was through passive radiators while distribution in the North wing was aided by forced recirculation through unit ventilators in each classroom. Each unit drew makeup air directly from the outdoors, and passed it through fiberglass mat filters in each unit ventilator. Makeup air could be augmented in each room by opening windows. There was a central exhaust system in the North wing.

During the "oil crisis" in the 1970s, school custodians blocked external air vents to the unit ventilators in the North wing and sealed off exhaust ducts to the central exhaust system to contain heated air within the building and improve energy efficiency. The vents and ducts had remained blocked since then, in violation of local building codes. There was no regular inspection of the heating/ventilation system at Reynolds and no schedule to inspect, clean, or remove unit ventilator filters.

The school's physical layout—a large "U" with two core instructional areas, known as the North and South wings, connected by a cluster of common areas, tended to divide the staff. (See Exhibit 1 on page 83.) North and South wing teachers interacted infrequently during the school day and often did not know one another well. The staff was also divided by teaching style, with some teachers favoring traditional classrooms and pedagogies while others used newer methods. Eberly refrained from dictating teaching methods, though he tried to encourage those he favored. He stated, "My assumption is that people here are professionals and can make decisions and carry them out—my role is to encourage collaboration and provide resources when I see people with good ideas."

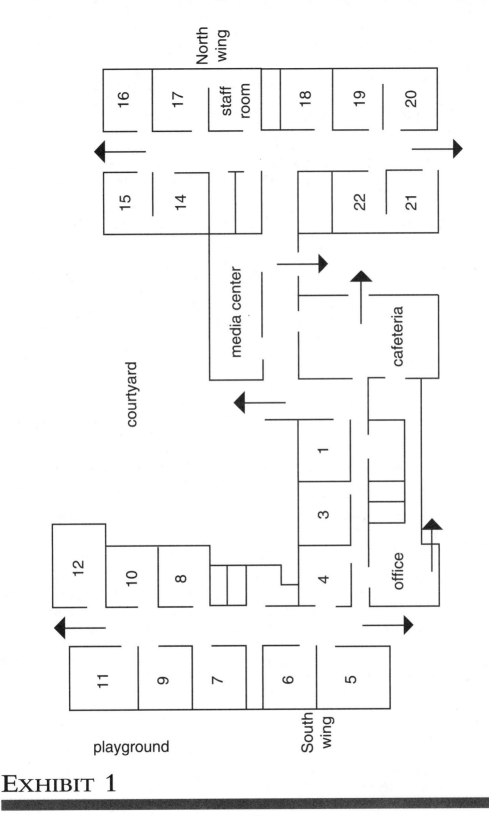

EXHIBIT 1

School staff encouraged and welcomed participation of parents as visitors, volunteers, or through the Parent-Teacher Organization (PTO). Eberly believed that communications between school and home were an important part of developing this school-home partnership. However, many Reynolds School parents were single, working, or transient, and so were not very involved in school activities. A small group of parents, led by Helen Bell, PTO president, were very active. Eberly had a good relationship with Bell.

❖ THE FLOOD

For the previous four years, the roof of Reynolds' North wing regularly leaked whenever there was a heavy rain or snow and rapid ice thawing. Buckets to collect dripping water were a common sight in North wing classrooms. To address this problem, the district contracted the previous Spring with Walker Roofing Company, a local construction firm. The roofers would remove the tar and gravel from the North wing roof and replace it with a commonly used synthetic rubber roof. The work was to be completed during the summer school vacation.

During removal of the old roof, Walker employees used jackhammers to loosen roofing materials. As workers jack-hammered the old asphalt and gravel surface, black particles sifted through the exposed tongue-in-groove ceiling boards, depositing a fine dusty film over most exposed surfaces in the North wing. In some areas, particularly the media center, these particle deposits were more substantial, leaving scattered piles of black material on shelves, computers, and floors. Some surfaces were wiped clean by school custodians, but with a daily shower of dust over six or seven days, it was futile to try to clean up until this phase of the project was completed. By August 12, many exposed surfaces had not been cleansed of the black sooty material.

On Saturday evening, August 12, a heavy thundershower swept through central Maine. The roof drains on the North wing were clogged with debris from the roofing project and several inches of water quickly backed up onto the still-exposed ceilings of classrooms 18, 19, 20, 21, and 22. No one was in the building at the time, and the water leaked through the ceiling boards throughout the night, until Sunday morning, when the Augusta Fire Department responded to an alarm at the Reynolds School apparently set off by the short-circuiting of a moistened ceiling alarm. The Fire Department notified Walter Russell, the district's director of maintenance, who then summoned school custodians and Eberly. Within minutes, all were at the school surveying the situation: several inches of standing water was in the five classrooms and the hallway, and more water was still dripping from between the ceiling boards. To make matters worse, the five teachers whose rooms were flooded had already set up their classrooms for the fall, and now almost everything in the room was damp or drenched.

"This is unbelievable, Walter, unbelievable," Eberly said. "These teachers are going to be just sick about this. I'll call them all tonight to tell them what happened. We're going to have to take up this soaked carpeting and thoroughly dry these rooms. Can we have these rooms ready by September 6th?"

"I can't replace the carpets!" claimed Walter. We've already overspent our capital improvement budget for the summer projects. This new roof was expensive! The best I can do is have the custodial crew extract the water from the carpets and bring in some fans and keep the windows open. It'll be good enough. Things will dry out by the time school starts. Don't worry."

❖ THE SCHOOL YEAR BEGINS

The five teachers in rooms 18-22 faced a daunting task. They had already put in a lot of time preparing their rooms for the upcoming year. And now they had to clean up the damage from the flood and begin anew. The flood had ruined books, paper supplies, wall displays, and shelves. The moisture even damaged materials in the closets.

The clean up was smelly, backbreaking work. As the teachers moved their furniture around, they found pockets of a now tacky black dust that ultimately had to be scraped away to be permanently removed. But despite the damage and disruption, the five teachers worked long hours through the remainder of August repairing their classrooms for the upcoming school year, all time beyond their 190-day contracted work year.

There was one gnawing problem, however. The flooded rooms reeked with a dank, locker-room odor and the teachers were insistent that something be done. Eberly responded by pushing Walter Russell to alleviate the odor. Russell, notorious in the district for his slow response to maintenance concerns, finally did, and on August 22, two weeks before school opened, Walker Roofing, after initially refusing to assume any responsibility for the odor problems, contracted Enviro Cleaning Company to steam clean the carpets in rooms 18-22. Following the steam cleaning, Enviro applied Advanced Odor-Zyme, an odor-masking agent.

Nonetheless, the odors persisted. On September 5, the day before the opening of school, Enviro returned and again cleaned and deodorized the carpets. On September 6, Eberly walked through the school checking for odors, and found none. "It's good to get back to business," he thought at the time, "maybe people will calm down now about the smell and the carpeting."

The calm did not last, however. Within the first week of school, the odors returned, more unpleasant than ever, and staff began complaining of a variety of respiratory and other ailments. Betty Durham, a first-year kindergarten teacher in room 19, showed Bill a rash on her neck, but attributed it to a possible allergy to chocolate. During the same week, a parent of a girl in room 20 called and reported her daughter was staying home with a skin rash.

As the days passed and minor physical complaints persisted, teachers began to compare notes in the staff room and they connected complaints about breathing difficulties, clogged nasal passages, as well as what they perceived to be the unusually high rate of flu symptoms, with the continuing odors in the carpet. Gina Neal, the Media Aide, had been particularly vocal in her concerns about the ubiquitous black dust in the media center after the roofing project. On the fourth day of school she called in sick, complaining of respiratory problems. When she returned after three days' absence, she told Eberly her physician thought her respiratory problems were related to the quality of the air in the school. Privately, Eberly questioned the diagnosis because Gina had always complained of respiratory ailments and allergies.

But September wore on and teachers became increasingly convinced that their health problems were related to the carpeting. They grew more anxious and conversations in the teachers' room grew more heated: "Something's down there, and it's making us sick. I think maybe it's time to notify the teachers' association about this mess. Maybe THEY can get those damn rugs out of here."

❖ EBERLY TAKES ACTION

Eberly decided this was not a problem that was simply going to go away quietly. He called Brad Mason, the Superintendent, and informed him of the situation. Eberly said, "Brad, our carpet still stinks, and now staff are sure that any and all ailments are directly linked to the odor. I think the teachers' association is preparing to file some kind of a grievance about working conditions. I can't get Walter to rip out the carpets. And I'm concerned that parents may start complaining."

"But Bill," Mason replied, "there is no money in the budget for replacing the carpets. I can't authorize an emergency expenditure until we're sure it's necessary." Eberly wasn't convinced that removing the classroom carpets was necessary, but he felt he had to do something to respond to his staff's concerns. He contacted Dr. Deanna Storm of the Bureau of Health Risk Assessment at the Maine Department of Public Health (MDPH). As he later recalled:

> I did not believe that the carpeting posed a health risk, but I knew the staff were very concerned. I brought in the people from the MDPH to let the teachers know I was doing something, but I tried to downplay it so I wouldn't validate their fears and add fuel to the fire by suggesting that this was a problem that the MDPH folks should be involved in.

Dr. Storm cautioned Eberly that it might be very difficult to determine what was causing the odor and whether it was related to the ailments reported by the Reynolds staff. She did, however, assure Eberly that MDPH would help in any way they could. On September 18, MDPH staff collected air samples from classrooms 14 (to get an ambient reading from a nearby room that had not been flooded and was odor-free), 18, 19, 20, 21, and 22. Air samples were sent to Universal Laboratory in Rockford, New Hampshire for mold and mildew analysis. The analysis would take nearly two weeks as it involved developing cultures from the air samples.

In the meantime, waiting for the air quality test results, Eberly tried to allay staff concerns about the possibility of a link between respiratory ailments and North wing odors. But staff members would not be reassured and were angry at having to wait two weeks for test results before any action would be taken, and demanded that Eberly get rid of the carpeting. The principal spent extra time talking with faculty members one-on-one and devoted time in faculty meetings to discuss and explain the carpeting issue. He said:

> I know it smells down there. But we always have a high incidence of flu and respiratory problems at this time of year. It takes a while for all of us and for the kids to get reacclimated to the germ pool inside the school. We're doing the air testing now. I asked the district nurses to compare our absentee rate with other schools and to get a sense of the relative presence of respiratory problems in district schools. They tell me that, compared to the other buildings, our absenteeism isn't that unusual. What more can I do?

❖ THE HEATING SEASON BEGINS

On the afternoon and evening of September 23 in preparation for the coming heating season, Reynolds custodians opened all the North wing heating units, removed and vacuumed the filters, and then placed them back into the vent units. New filters would have cost less than $3 each, but the district did not have the correct size in stock. The old filters had been in the heating unit system for over 7 months.

For the first time in five months, the Reynolds School heating system was turned on throughout the building the morning of Monday, October 2. By noon, Frieda Dillon (the teacher in room 21) and two kindergarten students (rooms 19 and 20) left for home complaining of irritating welts and swelling on exposed skin. After school, a Reynolds paraprofessional complained to Eberly about "an itchy sensation" on her arms. During the course of the day, her schedule had taken her into rooms 3, 4, 8, 11, 18, 19, and 20.

Eberly was made aware of more skin complaints throughout the week and began to wonder if the rashes were related to the heating system. Checking with the secretary and nurse, he discovered that there had been several more reports of skin problems among staff and students that he'd not known about. The principal decided to monitor staff and student absences over the next week, paying attention to any mention of skin irritations. He did not mention his suspicions to staff or parents. His primary concern was to avoid raising additional concern without clear evidence that there was a pattern to Reynolds illnesses that could be conclusively attributed to the school's environment.

Soon enough, however, Betty Durham came down with a skin rash. She claimed symptoms disappeared on weekends and reappeared when she returned to school on Mondays. Her doctor believed the rash was related to the school environment. When Betty told teachers in the staff lounge about her skin problems and her doctor's conclusions, four North wing staff members noted that they, too, had experienced minor welts, rashes, and skin irritations in the last week or so. One of the four, Frieda Dillon, kindergarten teacher in room 20, went to Eberly and said, "Ed, I'm worried we've got a huge problem down in our part of the school and it's much more than a smelly carpet. You've got to do something soon or the union will file a grievance. We cannot work in these conditions. Other teachers in the staff room were outraged when we all started comparing notes!"

Eberly responded by reassuring Dillon that he was doing all he could, and that they would know more when the air quality test results came back. Until then, he said, he understood the teachers' concerns, but he didn't want to disrupt classes unnecessarily. He told the kindergarten teacher, "Let's wait just a bit longer for the testing results. Do you realize how crazy it would be to clear out five classrooms to remove carpeting and install a new rugs?! You'd be out of your classroom for more than a week, and who knows where we could put you."

While a number of staff were convinced that the building was unsafe, not all Reynolds staff believed there was a problem. There had been no complaints about respiratory or skin problems in the South wing. In faculty meetings, South wing teachers expressed their annoyance at what one termed the "overreactions" of her North wing colleagues and the disruptions their "tantrums" were causing the entire school. And Walter Russell offered his unsolicited opinion, as well:

> There's nothing wrong at Reynolds, except whatever is wrong in the heads of those crazy women you've got over there—maybe they're all suffering from PMS or something! There's no reason to tear up the carpeting because of a few women's hysteria.

❖ LAB RESULTS

Universal Lab's analysis of the September 18 air sampling was forwarded to MDPH and a summary analysis was sent to Bill Eberly on October 11, more than three weeks after the samples had been taken. (See Exhibit 2 on page 90.) On October 12, Eberly called Dr. Deanna Storm, MDPH Assistant State Epidemiologist, for clarification. Eberly found the test results confusing and contradictory. Dr. Storm told Eberly that the symptoms reported by staff members at Reynolds could be attributed to one or more of four basic causes: 1) Some kind of contagious viral infection—the symptoms might not be linked to the building at all, but to some "bug" going through the population; 2) Reactions to some residual chemical agents present within the environment, possibly from the roofing project; 3) Reactions to microbiological "creatures" that had contaminated the air—bacteria, fungi, pollen, and; 4) Psychogenic phenomena—the symptoms, however real, might be caused by some kind of contagious psychosomatic illness.

She explained:

> In most cases of "sick building syndrome," you never locate a causal agent with any level of certainty. You can sometimes suspect what might be contributing

factors, but in most cases, you just never know. . . . We'd like to help, but don't get your hopes up that we'll be able to identify the "cause" of the illnesses quickly, if we ever do. In the meantime, you might think about moving kids and staff out of that part of the building. I don't think the symptoms are life-threatening. Still, you want to be careful how you handle people's anxieties.

❖ A NOTE FROM THE DOCTOR

On October 13, Gina Neal presented Eberly with a note from her physician, ordering her to stay home from school "until the environmental problems are addressed." Although, she did not spend time in the five suspect classrooms, she attributed the hives she had developed the previous day to the black dust that had accumulated in the media center during the roofing project. "Ed, I'm sorry," she said, "but I'm going home now, and I won't be back until things are cleaned up, doctor's orders."

Eberly told Neal that he understood, and that he thought she should follow the advice of her physician. Privately, however, he thought her symptoms were unrelated to the Reynolds environment:

> I was in the awkward position of having to support the opinion of another professional—her doctor—even though I didn't believe it at all. Gina is something of a hypochondriac, and she had managed to convince her doctor that the school environment was somehow to blame for her symptoms. There was nothing I could do publicly, however, except support her.

On Sunday night, October 15, two months after the flood, Eberly sat at home looking over the background material Dr. Storm had given him on air quality investigations from the Federal Centers for Disease Control, and thinking about the letter from Gina Neal's doctor. The phone rang. It was Frieda Dillon. "Ed, you're not going to believe this," she said, "I'm at school with Sue, Betty, and Elizabeth Knowles. We've been working down in our rooms (19-21). All of us have broken out with rashes."

By the time Eberly arrived at Reynolds School, the four presented no visible symptoms. They had waited for him near the office, located in the South wing. Elizabeth, a parent volunteer helping Dillon, was a nurse. She confirmed that all four had, indeed, developed hive-like symptoms. "By the way," Dillon added, "I've gotten two calls from parents this weekend, worried about their kids' recent rashes, wondering if we are aware of a possible link with this school. One parent refuses to send his daughter back until he's satisfied the place is safe. What should I tell him?"

❖ CASE PREPARATION QUESTIONS

1. Bill Eberly received information from many sources about the environment of the Reynolds Elementary School. Describe these sources and assess their reliability. How well did he manage this information?

2. What actions can a leader take when the information she or he receives is ambiguous?

3. Many decisions were made about the Reynolds School. Describe the decision making process. Do you think Eberly had the right individuals involved? Is there anyone else you would involve?

EXHIBIT 2

STATE OF MAINE
DEPARTMENT OF HEALTH AND HUMAN SERVICES
DIVISION OF PUBLIC HEALTH SERVICES

M. Mary Burford
Commissioner

Phillip T. Price, Jr., M.D., M.P.H.
Director
Division of Public Health Services

Health & Welfare Bldg.
6 Hazen Drive
Augusta, ME 03301-6527

October 11, 1994

Bill Eberly—Principal
Reynolds Elementary School
Augusta, ME 09301

Dear Mr. Eberly:

On Monday, September 18, 1994 at 7am, an air monitoring survey for mold/mildew was performed at your school, as per request by Walter Russell, Augusta School District Maintenance Superintendent. The purpose of the survey was to document the airborne levels of mold/mildew spores, which may be the result of a roof water leak.

Air samples were collected in rooms 14, 18, 19, 20, 21 and 22 to determine the level of airborne spores in the school. Analysis of the samples showed the following results:

Location	Concentration (CFU)*
Room 14	5,000 Mold
Room 18	68,000 Yeast

Room 19	180 Mold
Room 20	less than 11 Mold
Room 21	2,200 Yeast, 100 Mold
Room 22	11 Mold
Blank**	930 Yeast

These Mold/Mildew results present a confusing problem to which we have no solutions in its interpretation. Essentially, some of the rooms had low colony counts, such as rooms 19, 22, 20. Some rooms had yeast counts which we have never encountered before in our surveys. The analytical lab also said that the presence of yeast colonies in any number is a rarity in air in schools and does not necessarily indicate a pathogenicity. The lab was not confident of their interpretation of the analytical results, such as, is this an unhealthy situation?

*CFU—Colony Forming Units.
**Blank—Probably contaminated.

Therefore, the Occupational Health Program recommended a resampling of the same areas to verify the previous results. Sampling was done on Friday, October 13 at 7 am. The same rooms were sampled including Room 14 which had been cleaned extensively Saturday and Sunday using a quatanary ammonia germicide.

While there are no public health criteria levels for mold and mildew, some analytical authorities recommend a colony forming count of below 800. Other labs feel anything over 10 CFU can be a problem to people who are sensitive to mold and mildew. In either case, your levels are questionable and I feel that the re-sampling may give a clearer picture.

Relative humidity levels in the school were within the acceptable range of 35 to 65%. Higher levels can cause the advent of mold-mildew formation. Lower levels can cause dry conditions which may lead to headaches, eye irritation, sinus problems and sore throats during the heating season.

If you have any further questions, please do not hesitate to call me.

Sincerely,

Peter Bolton
Industrial Hygienist
Occupational Health Program
Division of Public Health Services

3190s/PB/bw
cc: Walter Russell

♦ ♦ ♦

Rash Decisions (B)

Edward Barnwell and Sean Reardon

Eberly decided it was time "to take strong measures to contain the problem," as he put it. Sunday night, October 15, after returning home from meeting the small group of teachers at Reynolds, Eberly called Superintendent Mason for his approval to relocate the five affected classes, all kindergartners and first graders, until a solution to the problem could be found. He also told Mason he thought it was time for a parent meeting and asked if Mason would be available Wednesday evening. The superintendent agreed to the moves and to his participation at the parent meeting.

Eberly next called Dr. Storm and asked if she'd be available for both the parent meeting and a staff meeting he was planning to call for Monday afternoon. Dr. Storm was glad to make herself available for both.

Finally, the principal called the teachers of the five classrooms to tell them of his decision. They were mostly relieved to be out of the "contaminated rooms," but also worried that the process of moving would be unsettling and confusing to the young children.

Monday morning, October 16, the five classes settled into their temporary locations—three classes in the cafeteria and two in the media center. The relocations went smoothly, with only minimal confusion. Nevertheless, the new quarters were sparsely equipped for instructional purposes, and the students' sense of adventure was not shared by the staff.

Once the five classes were settling in to their new spaces, Eberly announced the Monday afternoon staff meeting and composed a memo to parents announcing the moves and calling for a community meeting on Wednesday evening, October 18. (See Exhibit 1 on page 96.) The principal knew that news of closing part of the North wing would heighten already mounting tensions and hoped the community meeting would provide an opportunity to quell rising concern. Moreover, MDPH had taken some additional tests after the contradictory results of the previous week and Eberly had been assured that he'd have the results of the second round of tests by Tuesday, October 17. The principal thought it might be reassuring to parents to be apprised of the most up-to-date assessment of conditions in the building. Eberly also informed parents that Superintendent Mason and Dr. Storm would be available at the meeting for questions, as well. The memo was sent home Monday afternoon.

❖ THE MONDAY STAFF MEETING

Eberly, Dr. Storm, two MDPH officials, and the entire Reynolds staff met in the teacher's lounge at 2:45 p.m.

Eberly began by thanking everyone for their help making the adjustments that morning, and assured the group that two principles would guide decisions about what responses were appropriate to the situation:

1. Staff would be apprised of information just as soon as it is received.
2. Decisions would be based on the collective interpretation and recommendations of a "crisis management team," made up of Eberly and MDPH staff, in consultation with Mason. The team would base their decisions on the information available at the time.

The meeting was tense, the exchanges worried, impatient. Staff members were annoyed, tired, and defensive. Some felt their concerns were not being taken seriously by Eberly and the MDPH officials. They asked why it was taking so long to get answers, and why no one seemed overly concerned about the health of the staff and young students.

The genuine concern of the Reynolds staff convinced the crisis management team to meet again the next day to review the findings of the second round of air quality tests. The team set their meeting for 3:00 p.m. Tuesday afternoon and dispersed.

❖ A MEETING OF THE CRISIS MANAGEMENT TEAM

Eberly hoped the results of the second round of air quality tests would confirm the theory that mold or mildew in the carpets of the five classrooms was causing the symptoms and complaints. But when the lab report arrived on Tuesday afternoon, it showed "no measurable yeast count in any tested location" and "significantly reduced mold/mildew counts compared with [the] initial testing." (See Exhibit 2 on page 97.) The moldy carpet theory now seemed defunct.

In their meeting, the crisis management team began to concentrate on a chemical contaminant theory. They ordered samples taken of the carpeting, the filters, and the black dust and began an analysis of the many chemical agents that could be implicated: those used in the roof, in the ceiling insulation, and in the cleansing compounds used on the rugs.

Furthermore, the team decided to respond to reported cases of hives as if they confirmed the presence of some contaminant, even though no case to date had been verified by a physician.

The crisis management team had two concerns: 1) that all the moving around of classes might be making matters even worse by transporting suspected contaminants to other areas of the building, and 2) that the two classes now using the media center might still be at risk of contamination because the black dust from the roof had fallen so heavily in the media center. The team's last decision was to move the two classes elsewhere in the building.

❖ MORE MOVES

On Wednesday morning, the two classes in the media center were moved to share classrooms with others in the South wing, their second move in three days.

But the doubling-up of classes in the South wing proved to be so chaotic for the teachers and students that Eberly decided that afternoon that he would have to make more suitable arrangements. A flurry of calls among Eberly, Superintendent Mason and MDPH staff resulted in yet another major decision: school would be canceled for the students from rooms 18-22 for the next two days to allow staff to set up more productive, yet temporary, instructional spaces within Reynolds for Monday, October 23. The art room was appropri- . ated, a medium-sized office given to another class, and the cafeteria continued to be "home" for three classes. Eberly sent a memo home to parents that afternoon, and prepared to explain the actions to the parents that evening.

❖ THE PARENT MEETING

On Wednesday evening, October 18, nearly 125 parents and staff gathered at nearby Meadows School to listen to Eberly, Mason, and the MDPH officials report on the Reynolds School environmental health crisis. Walter Russell, the director of maintenance, sat in the audience.

The crisis management team presented information about the lab results received and pending. Eberly reviewed the decision to close the five classrooms, with those students staying home for two days while teachers prepared for the changes. Throughout the evening's discussions, parental concerns centered on the health of their children and the uncertainty of what might be the short- and long-term effects of exposure at Reynolds. The next day's *Augusta Monitor* headline captured town feeling: "School's Woes Mystery: 100 Parents Seek Answers."

❖ A RASH OF SYMPTOMS

On Thursday, following the parent meeting, staff and parent volunteers began to wash every exposed surface of all materials and furniture from the affected rooms for relocation to other areas of the building. They used a special cleansing solution prescribed by MDPH.

By Friday morning, Eberly was deluged with reports of hives and itching. A number of the reports came from students and staff from rooms 14 and

17—rooms that had not been flooded. Several staff members asked for workers' compensation forms. A delegation of teachers from rooms 14-17 came to Eberly during their lunch break. "We think that whatever was down in Rooms 18-22 has spread to our classrooms, too. No one should have to go into that part of the building at all."

In response, Eberly called an emergency lunchtime meeting of the crisis management team. The group quickly decided, and Eberly with the help of office staff told every staff member by 1:30 p.m., that the entire North wing would be closed until further notice. Over the weekend, staff and parent volunteers would be asked to assist in washing and moving materials from rooms 14-17 to other parts of the building and to the nearby Meadows School, which would host four classes. Space at Meadows was necessary because all alternative space at Reynolds was now in use. With confirmation from Superintendent Mason, the crisis management team also determined that the carpets in rooms 18-22 would be removed.

Eberly spent Friday afternoon and evening at the school, helping the teachers, staff, and parents prepare for the move. In the course of those hours, still more disturbing news came to his attention. Two parents called to report their children had hives. Helen Bell, PTO president, came to the office to see Eberly; her neck and arms were covered with red and white welts, and she was having difficulty breathing. She had been in Room 4, helping clean some materials from Room 20 that were going to be used in Room 4 during the relocation period.

At 7:00 p.m., Frieda Dillon called Eberly at school:

> Ed, I've been here sorting through some books and things I brought home over a month ago and kept in my garage. I haven't touched the stuff since, I swear. Well, within 10 minutes of looking through the box tonight, I broke out with hives again. This is my third outbreak! I'm scared. What's going on?! I feel like burning the box. Maybe it's contaminated or something. I just talked to my doctor. He thinks I'm crazy if I go back into that school. What should I do?

❖ RETHINKING PLANS

By 9:00 p.m. Friday, everyone had left Reynolds, except Eberly. He slumped in his chair, reeling from the relentless string of confounding events. For the first time he was convinced there really was a health risk. The number of reports that afternoon was overwhelming—parents, children, Frieda Dillon. And when he saw Helen Bell—who he trusted deeply—with welts and hives, he felt guilty that he'd been so skeptical for so long. Should he make a unilateral decision to stop the next day's move? Eberly was especially concerned about moving potentially contaminated materials and furniture to another school.

The principal decided to alert the superintendent and Dr. Storm. Mason was out of town overnight, and could not be reached. Eberly called Dr. Storm at her home and told her of his new concerns. The doctor cautioned Eberly that there were few cases of hives actually confirmed by medical professionals. She stated, "An itch does not make it a case of hives. Remember, there's been a lot of publicity over this situation, and more than a few stressed-out people. The symptoms are probably real, but we really don't know of more than a few confirmed cases. And in a population of that size, a few cases may be a perfectly 'normal' incidence level."

The parents and staff would gather at Reynolds to begin moving at 9:00 a.m. the next morning. Mason would not be back until 1:00 p.m. What was the principal going to do? For Bill Eberly, it was going to be a long night.

EXHIBIT 1

REYNOLDS SCHOOL
Augusta, Maine
09301-5692

Office of the Principal (207)225-0830

IMPORTANT INFORMATION FOR REYNOLDS SCHOOL PARENTS

October 16, 1994

There has been an outbreak of the hives (rash) among staff and students in one section of our building's North wing over the past week or so. We also have had a number of respiratory ailments that may or may not be related to the hives. At the moment, the cause of the rash is not known, although it seems likely that it is related to something within the four or five rooms affected.

We are taking precautions to reduce and eliminate any health risk to staff, parent volunteers, and students. Effective today and until we have a solution to the problem, students in the following classrooms will be moved to other sections of the building:

Grades 1/2	Millie Calhoun
Grades 1/2	Debbie Kurtz
Grades 1/2	Patricia Stein
Grades K	Betty Durham
Grades K	Frieda Dillon

Moreover, we will be holding an open meeting to discuss the situation on Wednesday, October 18 at 7:30 p.m. The meeting will be held in the cafeteria of the Meadows School. Superintendent Mason and officials and physicians from the Maine Division of Public Health Services will be present to answer any and all questions. We strongly encourage you to attend.

MDPH officials have been working with us to determine what might be causing the outbreak of hives, and what to do about it. We will continue to do what we can to make the programs run smoothly and successfully for Reynolds students.

In order to monitor the situation more closely, it would be helpful if you would contact the school if any child has come down with any hive-like rash this school year, regardless of what classroom they are in.

We will keep you informed as we receive more information or develop a plan to remedy the situation.

Bill Eberly

EXHIBIT 2

STATE OF MAINE
DEPARTMENT OF HEALTH AND HUMAN SERVICES
DIVISION OF PUBLIC HEALTH SERVICES

M. Mary Burford
Commissioner

Phillip T. Price, Jr., M.D., M.P.H.
Director
Division of Public Health Services

Health & Welfare Bldg.
6 Hazen Drive
Augusta, ME 03301-6527
(Te;/ (207) 271-4676

October 11, 1994

Bill Eberly—Principal
Reynolds Elementary School
Canterbury Road
Augusta, ME 09301

Dear Mr. Eberly:

On Monday, September 18, 1994 at 7am, an air monitoring survey for mold/mildew was performed at your school, as per request by Walter Russell, Augusta School District Director of Maintenance. The purpose of the survey was to document the airborne levels of mold/mildew spores, which may be the result of a roof water leak in August. Air samples were collected in rooms 14, 18, 19, 20, 21 and 22. Repeat sampling was done on October 13 also at 7 am. A complete cleaning of room 14 using a quatanary ammonia germicide had been done on October 7 & 8. This room had not been flooded in August however it had water damage on the walls from previous leaks.

Location	Concentration (CFU)*	
	9/18/89	10/9/89
Room 14	5,000 Mold	less than 14 Mold
Room 18	68,000 Yeast	less than 14 "
Room 19	180 Mold	69 "
Room 20	less than 11 Mold	14 "
Room 21	2,200 Yeast, 100 Mold	300 "
Room 22	11 Mold	58 "
Blank**	930 Yeast	less than 14 "
Outside air	———	14 "

* CFU—Colony Forming Units.

** Blank—Probably contaminated.

While there are no public health criteria levels for mold and mildew, some analytical authorities recommend a colony forming count of below 800. Other labs feel anything over 10 CFU can be a problem to people who are sensitive to mold and mildew. The chemist performing the analysis believes that yeast present on 9/18 was a result of a contaminated sample. This is why yeast was found on the blank. Airborne yeast is unusual and is typically found in food establishments.

Relative humidity levels in the school were within the acceptable range of 35 to 65%. Higher levels can cause the advent of mold-mildew formation.

Lower levels can cause dry conditions which may lead to headaches, eye irritation, sinus problems and sore throats during the heating season.

If you have any further questions, please do not hesitate to call me at 271-4676.

Sincerely,

Fran Thomas
Industrial Hygienist
Occupational Health Program
Division of Public Health Services

3190s/FB/bw

GOVERNANCE

Making decisions and taking action in public education today is a complicated matter. Public education rings with a cacophony of voices, each expressing their personal views about the role of schools and schooling in our society. Dilemmas and tensions in the area of governance now are endemic to the role of the educational administrator. Fundamentally the question is one of balance—how does an educational leader mediate between the opinions of the stakeholders and the opinions of the professionals? With the growing emphasis on shared decision making and site-based administration, the position of the administrator as the top-down hierarchical authority is no longer valid. Cases in this section explore how administrators make decisions while developing consensus with parents and other stakeholders in the educational enterprise.

❖ AN APPLE FOR THE TEACHER

At the request of the school board, Superintendent Paula James and her Administrative Council explore school-based management (SBM), an innovation about which she is enthusiastic. The Council agrees that the schools will implement SBM in the areas of personnel, staff development, and expenditures of the school equipment funds. Trouble emerges when Mark Meisel, principal of West Middle School, and his site-based council enact plans that differ from those of the rest of the district.

❖ WHO GOES?

Tom Andrews is the K-8 principal of Northam, a closely knit, well-regarded "neighborhood" school which for the last five years has housed a special-needs preschool program. The school is overcrowded; one group of students must be moved next year to another neighborhood elementary school, which has a reputation for being more like a "boot camp." The preschool program and the third grade seem the most "moveable" groups.

❖ THE ALLEN SCHOOL

Trouble erupts for Sandra Harris, the new interim principal of a well-regarded Chicago magnet K-6 school, when two members of the newly constituted Local School Council (LSC) chastise her publicly at one of their first meetings. In developing a survey instrument to begin a complete school-wide evaluation, Harris had consulted her Professional Personnel Advisory Council (PPAC) before the LSC. Many of the "new guard" members remind Harris that they are the governing body of the school, not the PPAC.

❖ AUGUSTA COUNTY—BEECH MOUNTAIN INSTITUTE

Superintendent David Myers' plan for school reform includes both curricular and organizational changes, as well as a consolidation of high schools. Some residents have resisted other attempts to consolidate the county's schools. Mark and Jessica Garvin-Leeds, co-founders of the Beech Mountain Institute, a nonprofit outdoor educational organization in the county, issue their own plans for reform and are met with hostility from the superintendent, school board members, and the many local residents.

Suggested Readings

Badaracco, J. and Ellsworth, R. (1989). *Leadership and the quest for integrity.* Boston: Harvard Business School Press.

Elmore, R. (1987). Reform and the culture of authority in schools. *Educational Administration Quarterly, 23,* 60–78.

Malen, B., Ogawa, R., and Krany, J. (1989). What do we know about school-based management: A case study of the literature—a call for research. In W. Clune and J. Witte (Eds.), *The practice of choice: Decentralization and school restrictions* (pp. 289–342). Philadelphia: Falmer Press.

Tichy, N. and Devanna, M. (1986). *The transformational leader.* New York: Wiley & Sons.

Weiss, C. (1993). Shared decision making about what? A comparison of schools with and without teacher participation. *Teachers College Record, 95,* 69–92.

An Apple for the Teacher

Katherine K. Merseth and Jeffrey Young

Superintendent Paula James put down the phone and gazed out the window at the bleak March day. The sky was gray, the ground a depressing brown. The wind kicked a few tired leaves across the parking lot. Eric Hodges, Riverside's K-12 computer coordinator, had stormed out of Paula's office minutes earlier. And she had just had a brief and heated telephone exchange with Mark Meisel, Principal of the West Middle School. Paula sighed, still staring at the brittle leaves being tossed about outside, until it hit her—she was going to be kicked and tossed by the district's political winds if she wasn't smart about her next move. The seasoned Superintendent pulled out a pad of paper and began scribbling some notes.

❖ RIVERSIDE PUBLIC SCHOOLS AND SUPERINTENDENT JAMES

Riverside was a relatively homogeneous city of 28,000 residents in a large midwestern state. The district had nearly 7,000 students enrolled in 5 elementary schools (grades K-6), 2 middle schools (grades 7-8) and one high school. Most residents in Riverside were professionals who commuted to a large metropolitan area 18 miles to the north. In the 1980s, Riverside had experienced declining enrollments and a shrinking tax base. Unlike other towns with similar declines, however, the Riverside School Board and the City Finance Committee remained supportive of education. In the three most recent years, the school budget had grown at a rate of 4.5, 3.7 and 4.8 percent. The political base for the schools was quite solid. In fact, many of Riverside's citizens elected to live in Riverside because of the excellent reputation of the schools.

Community support of the schools was one factor that had attracted James to the Superintendent's position nearly three and one-half years before, when Steve Maloney retired after 17 years as Superintendent. She suspected that the Riverside parents would be supportive of any carefully designed programs to put the city at the cutting edge of education. During her interviews, the board had been impressed with her vision of education and her insights into various reform efforts, such as school-based management and portfolio assessments. When they made a site visit to her district, colleagues, parents and school board members emphasized her skills in leadership and her ability to make everyone feel part of the system. James managed through consensus, though she was also known to take direct and swift action when the situation warranted. The members of the Riverside School Board voted 5-0 to hire her.

❖ SCHOOL REFORM IN RIVERSIDE

In June, at the request of the School Board, Superintendent James and her administrative team began exploring school-based management (SBM). The Board was particularly supportive of the idea of SBM as a way to increase community involvement in the schools. Two businessmen on the Board persuaded the other members that decision-making by those closest to the implementation of the decision represented effective management practice. Though she had no formal experience or training in school-based management, James had always felt that teachers and parents should have more of a voice in the delivery of education. As a leader who valued collaboration and enjoyed people, the notion of sharing decisions did not threaten her. In fact, she saw this as an opportunity to try out some ideas that she had been reading about in educational journals. SBM, she believed, was an issue that many talked about, but few tried. She joined the School Board in their enthusiasm to implement SBM.

The Administrative Council of the Riverside Public Schools included the eight principals, the Assistant Superintendent for Curriculum and Instruction, the Director of Personnel and the business manager. During the school year, the Council met once every two weeks for three hours. Each member reported on the deliberations of the Council when they met with their building staff, or, in the case of the Assistant Superintendent for Curriculum and Instruction, with the six K-12 curriculum coordinators.

At the final Administrative Council meeting in late June, most of the Council members were enthusiastic about the idea of SBM, though some with less certainty than the Superintendent. Since there were no Council meetings in the summer, it was not until September that the Council began to discuss ways to implement SBM. Everyone seemed to believe that sharing decisions was a good direction in which to move, but some, including most of the principals, recognized that it would require a significant change in culture in the schools. A few principals urged that the district begin slowly. After some discussion, the Council agreed that, in this first year, school-based management would be implemented in three areas: personnel, staff development, and expenditures of the school equipment funds.

The Council then spent time determining the composition of the school-based "site councils." After much debate, they decided that the council at each school would include parents, teachers, and the principal. The specific workings of the site councils were left up to the individual schools to define. While most of the schools accepted the general guidelines for their local councils, at least three councils assumed the additional responsibilities of developing long-range plans for their school and articulating guiding principles of education for their building.

One of the most enthusiastic supporters of school-based management was the principal of West Middle School, Mark Meisel. Meisel was in his second year at West. Previously he had served as a junior high principal in a neighboring community for four years. Meisel was eager to assert his leadership in a school system that valued education and often told his colleagues that this was why he had applied for appointment at Riverside.

❖ SCHOOL–BASED MANAGEMENT AT WEST MIDDLE SCHOOL

Consulting with the co-presidents of the PTO and the teachers' building representative, Meisel quickly organized a plan for the West Middle School site council. Elections were held among the parents and teachers; six parents and six teachers were chosen to join Meisel on the council. Meetings were held on the third Tuesday of each month. While it was rare to have full attendance, a small core of teachers and parents was always there. Two of the teachers who regularly attended had been particularly critical of Meisel and his management of the school during his first year in Riverside. Despite their earlier criticisms of him, Meisel found their views generally constructive and helpful. Though Meisel had hoped that the council would explore long-range plans and develop guiding principles, the council members didn't seem ready to commit to this kind of planning. And because the council seemed to be functioning extremely well with many positive comments coming from parents and staff, the principal decided not to push it.

One of the first concerns the council tackled was a personnel issue created by the long-term absence of a seventh grade teacher due to an extended illness. The council examined the issue thoroughly and professionally, keeping the rights of the teacher and the needs of the students clearly in mind. A subcommittee of the council interviewed long-term substitute candidates, and through the council, forwarded a recommendation to Superintendent James and the Assistant Superintendent for Personnel. The council was also instrumental in the creation of a staff development program that identified and addressed the needs of the faculty at West. The newly designed program even included a parent education component. Both Superintendent James and Meisel were optimistic about SBM at West Middle School. As the year progressed, parents and staff expressed a positive interest in the council and its activities, as well.

The third area of responsibility designated by the Administrative Council—expenditures of equipment funds—also produced a consensus decision by the West site council. There were several competing candidates for this money, including tumbling mats for the gym and special tape recorders for the language program, but the council decided that the money should be used to purchase computers for the instructional program. The council voted to purchase several Apple IIe personal computers and printers with their equipment budget of $20,000.

The decision about which computers to buy had not been an easy one. During the discussion, Meisel noted that the district's computer coordinator, Eric Hodges, in his report to the School Board the prior spring, had recommended that the entire system, K-12, use Macintosh computers, because future applications and software were likely to be written for this machine. However, the teachers on the West site council voiced strong support for the IIe's. "Why should we change, Mark?" one teacher challenged. "We all know how the IIe's work, and we already have software at West for the IIe." Meisel mentioned that he thought the high school and two of the elementary schools were already moving toward using the Macintosh. That brought a sharp response from Ellen Large, a seventh grade teacher on the council and one of Meisel's harshest critics. "Look, Mark! Can't you see that the teachers are the ones who have to use these machines? Not you! If we change to a new line of computers, this will be just one more example of the administration adding more work for the teachers without adequate compensation! No way, Jose!" Eliot Lucas, an eighth grade teacher whose bass voice was invariably heeded, then said, "I think this is our opportunity to experiment with SBM. We are professionals, we need to take responsibility for making decisions about our school. Let's vote!" Parents, looking uncomfortable, said nothing. A third teacher moved that the council approve the purchase of the IIe's. When the vote was taken, all six teachers and two of the parents voted for the motion, and three parents voted against it. Meisel abstained.

❖ COMPUTER COORDINATOR GETS WORD

When Paula James returned from her luncheon with the Board of Realtors, she noticed Eric Hodges sitting in her outer office. "Paula, I've got to talk to you!" Hodges blurted out.

James motioned him into her office. "What's up, Eric?"

He tossed a purchase order onto her desk. "Look at this!" he exclaimed. "What the hell does Meisel think he's doing ordering Apple IIe's? We've got a K-12 policy to change over to Macintoshes, don't we?" he shouted.

Stunned, James asked, "Have you talked with Jim (the Assistant Superintendent for Curriculum and Instruction) about this?"

"No, he's out of town this week and won't be back until next Tuesday," Hodges responded. "Listen, that decision was made from both a financial and an instructional perspective. Meisel just can't—"

"Calm down, Eric," said Paula. "I'll call Mark and find out what's going on and I'll let you know what I find out. Don't worry. We're all aware of the K-12 policy. This has got to be some kind of a misunderstanding." The Superintendent continued trying to reassure the irate computer coordinator but he would have none of it. He left Paula's office saying, "You know the right thing to do, Paula, so do it! You're in charge of this school system!"

❖ THE TELEPHONE CONVERSATION

When Paula James reached Mark Meisel they exchanged a few pleasantries and then Paula got right to the point, "Mark, Eric Hodges brought me your purchase order requesting Apple IIe's. What's going on? Everyone on the Administration Council approved Eric's K-12 policy to change over to Macintoshes last spring. I thought you agreed that it would be advantageous for the students to have consistency in their instruction? And what about the cost benefit of all schools ordering the same hardware from one vendor? Certainly the town Finance Committee would like to see us do that!"

Meisel responded that those were certainly valid concerns and explained to the Superintendent that he had raised the issue of K-12 curricular consistency when the SBM council at West was making their decision. "Paula, we talked about all of that," he said," but the teachers were adamant. They didn't want to learn a whole new system when the one we have works just fine."

Frustrated, James replied, "But Mark, you know that the middle schools have been criticized for their inflexibility. This will add more fuel for the fire."

Meisel shot back: "I'm sorry, Paula. The SBM council gave careful consideration to this issue and determined that the Apple IIe is the best match for West Middle School staff and students. The council was given the responsibility for making this decision and it acted appropriately. The vote was 8-3 in favor of the Apple IIe. What do you want me to do? Reverse the decision?"

Paula hung up the phone and chided herself for putting Meisel on the defensive. It never ceased to amaze her how quickly the tide could turn in her job. The Board of Realtors luncheon had gone so smoothly and now this. The Superintendent sat for a moment, staring at the profusion of papers on her desk, and then turned to the view out her window as she began to grapple with her newest dilemma.

❖ CASE PREPARATION QUESTIONS

1. What skills are necessary for parents, teacher, principals, central office personnel, and superintendents to operate effectively in a system moving toward school-based management?

2. School-based management is often seen as a vehicle to influence relationships among staff, to renew school organizations, and to enhance children's learning. Do you see any evidence of this in Riverside?

Who Goes?

Edward Barnwell

Tom Andrews bent over the keyboard of his home computer on a late and chilly January night, as his fingers clicked out the final words of a letter to

January 9
Dear Northam Parents and Faculty,

   Over the past few months, there has been a vigorous discussion about next school year. Because of increasing enrollment, Northam School won't be large enough to house its special preschool program and the K-3 population after this year. Of course, the great debate has been, "Who goes?"

   The most logical choices are sending either the third graders or the preschool program to nearby McKenna School. Both programs are Northam's most "moveable": the third grade because it could attach to McKenna's present grade 4-6 population; the preschool program because it is largely self-contained, and draws special needs children from around the district. These children eventually attend their own neighborhood elementary schools, so many leave Northam.

   After careful consideration of the options, issues, and concerns, I have decided to recommend to Superintendent Bishop and the school board that Northam's third grade move to McKenna, starting next Fall. McKenna would be a 3-6 grade school instead of beginning with fourth grade, as it does presently. . . .

   There are MANY strong opinions about this issue and I don't presume to have the only perspective on the situation. It is important to me that you continue to let me, Superintendent Bishop, and the school board know how you feel about the space and relocation issues, whether you agree with us or not. Despite rumors to the contrary, the school board has NOT yet decided how to resolve our problems, so please speak up!

   Sincerely,

   Tom Andrews, Principal

staff and parents of the Northam Elementary School. Northam had 240 students, preschool through third grade and was set in the small New Hampshire city of Abingdon. Andrews looked at the finished product.

❖ DECISION MAKING IN ABINGDON

Which class would go was up to Andrews. Although the school board technically had final say over all decisions in the district—and had sometimes overruled principals in the Abingdon school system—principals were usually granted autonomy, on the grounds that they knew their schools better than anyone else. Andrews had come to his decision weeks earlier. He had not gone public in the hope that continued debate at faculty and PTO meetings would let all sides feel they were getting a fair hearing.

But even as Andrews re-read the letter, his mind strayed to a conversation months earlier with Ginny Urbanski, his assistant principal and chief confidant over his past twelve months of deliberations.

"We're going to get hammered on this one, Ginny. It's an unpopular decision," Andrews concluded, as he and Ginny walked along a snow-covered path near the school.

"Yeah, but there comes a time when you've got to base decisions on what's good for the kids and then stick to that principle," she had said.

Andrews also recalled a recent conversation with Urbanski, about decision making and setting policy at Northam. He had told her, "I don't want parents and staff to feel outside the process. I don't want them to keep quiet. I really think that if, as a community, we keep airing it all out and help people talk about it, they'll support my recommendation. They'll come around."

As Andrews pursued his philosophy of full expression of beliefs by community members, he began to worry about the way he was perceived as Northam's leader. He saw his most immediate priority as gaining the support of the vast majority of Northam parents and teachers. But what if they didn't support his recommendation? What then? Whose school was it?

❖ TOM ANDREWS

Tom Andrews, at almost six feet tall and with a reddish beard, was nearing forty and had spent his collegiate and professional career in New England. He had played football while studying Economics at Dartmouth, and he still jogged regularly. His career as an educator also had something of the rugged individualist to it. Andrews began his career as a fourth and fifth grade teacher in a "one room schoolhouse" in Vermont and Andrews later became a teaching principal in a small K-6 elementary school in northern Vermont. Since the district superintendent had to cover seven towns, Andrews had been left to run his school as he saw fit. He came to Abingdon to head the K-6 Worthington Elementary School before requesting a transfer, five years ago, to Northam because of its smaller size.

At Northam, Andrews tried to build a sense of community. Although he lived in a different neighborhood, he arranged for his own children to attend Northam. At a meeting of the school's Parent Teacher Organization, one parent with several children at Northam observed, "He isn't a controlling-type person. Some PTO's are run by the principal, but not Tom. He's here to be informational and to make sure we see all sides of each issue." Among his small faculty, Andrews was known for letting individual teachers experiment within their classrooms. For instance, when one third grade teacher had proposed setting up a "town administration" in his class to better illustrate civic responsibilities, Andrews enthusiastically supported him.

Not that life as Northam's principal was always pleasant and harmonious. Andrews had already had to make his share of controversial decisions, most recently in what he called "an environmental air quality fiasco," that ultimately involved relocating the entire student body to other sites for almost six weeks. Students as well as some teachers had developed skin rashes and breathing difficulties, and as the department of public health tried to diagnose the cause, the Northam parents became increasingly alarmed. Then Andrews called community forums. "There are no secrets," he had said. He made every effort to share information with the parents, sending out updates daily. He was proud of the fact that staff and parents knew what he knew, as soon as he knew it.

"I was inclined to keeping us in the building, but when it became clear that there was a groundswell of support from parents and staff to move out, I became convinced that the only thing to do was to do that.

"But that situation was unfolding day by day, sometimes hour by hour, and it called for immediate responses. It was a different kind of crisis than Northam's overcrowding problems, where we had more than a year—almost too much time—to figure out solutions."

❖ NORTHAM SCHOOL AND THE PRESCHOOL PROGRAM

Northam School filled a building dating back to the 1930s, as well as an extension constructed in the 1960s. The smaller red bricks of the old schoolhouse merged into the larger, brightly painted concrete blocks of the newer addition. There were signs that the school was having trouble accommodating its approximately 40 preschoolers and 200 students in kindergarten through third grade. The auditorium had been converted to classrooms, leaving a two-foot wide piece of stage and the remnants of the stage curtain. Those classrooms, as well as most of the other rooms in the old part of the building, were hard pressed to hold the twenty to twenty-five students that had come to populate each. Andrews and Urbanski were not immune from the crowded conditions and had moved to makeshift offices located at the end of a hallway and separated from the rest of the school by a five-foot-high partition.

Northam was considered very much a neighborhood school by parents and teachers alike. Although it belonged to the city of Abingdon, Northam Village had a long tradition of being a distinct, close-knit neighborhood with its own sense of identity. Residents were loyal to the notion of "community," and parents of Northam students considered the school safe, comfortable, and "good." Northam parents were very active within the school and frequently dropped by to visit or help out. The building itself was used regularly for community functions. In fact, Tom often joked, "Who doesn't have a key to the school?" Northam's dozen teachers, for their part, felt like they were part of an extended family: they had a comfortable relationship with parents and easy access to Andrews.

The preschool program had come to Northam five years earlier, at the same time as Andrews. Called the Abingdon Development Preschool (ADP), it was established by the Abingdon School Committee eight years ago and was designed for handicapped students from all over the city. It included its own staff: two teachers, two speech and language therapists, an occupational therapist, and the administrator, Ginny Urbanski. Previously, ADP had been housed at Eastham, another K-3 school, which had also become overcrowded. Five years ago, the school board had declared ADP's transfer to Northam "temporary" until a permanent home could be found or constructed.

The preschool and the K-3 program in Northam Elementary School enjoyed an amicable relationship. Children in the kindergarten classes would come over to the preschool for cooperative play sessions. Sometimes the older students helped the preschoolers with science projects; and once, when the second grade and the preschool were studying insects, they met outdoors for a joint picnic and some firsthand observation. For parents, the relationship was not so close. Many of Northam's social activities occurred on Fridays when the preschool was not in session. ADP parents were rarely involved in Northam activities; they tended to maintain greater connections with their own neighborhood elementary schools, where their children, when they finished the ADP program, would return for kindergarten.

The ADP program occupied the school's two largest classrooms in the newer wing. These were the most handicapped-accessible rooms in the building. There were some grumblings that ADP was using the school's prime property for its smaller numbers while the K-3 children and their teachers were getting squeezed. Certainly, Northam was not an ideal facility for the preschool. The library and assembly areas were downstairs and, according to Urbanski, "it was like a field trip" to transport the preschoolers, even though a special handrail was added to help the less mobile.

❖ GINNY URBANSKI

Urbanski, who was in her late thirties, had been involved with the preschool program for all its eight years and had accompanied it to Northam as its administrator. She was very experienced in special education and often helped Andrews understand the special needs and requirements of these children.

While Andrews worried about the politics of who should go, Urbanski offered educational arguments about why ADP should stay: "The age gap between the preschoolers and the kids at McKenna is going to take away all the chances for contact they have with the kindergarten," she said. "And the facilities at McKenna just don't fit preschool children. The learning materials in the library are all geared towards a higher educational level, and my kids won't even be able to reach some of the playground equipment."

❖ "THE INCUBATION PERIOD"

Northam's crowded conditions had caught the attention of the larger community in the Fall, four months before Andrews sat down to write his letter. The *Abingdon Free Press* published a series of articles with accompanying photographs detailing the overcrowding, and quoted a few concerned parents. The Abingdon Fire Department issued citations of code violations and asked for immediate compliance.

Andrews had been meeting regularly with Abingdon's School Superintendent David Bishop to discuss space issues for nearly a year. The principal liked to refer to this strategizing time as "the incubation period." The first meetings with Bishop confirmed that some of Northam's students would have to move to another school, and that the only available site for Northam's overflow was McKenna, which had just constructed a new, mostly vacant million-dollar wing.

In the meantime, Bishop assured Andrews, the district would be building a new and larger elementary school to replace Northam and it would comfortably accommodate the preschoolers and older children alike. Andrews and Bishop even walked the wooded perimeter of the proposed site with the new school's architects. Their plan was to construct and occupy the new school in two years.

In their on-going discussions, Bishop, a silver-haired veteran of more than twenty years in Abingdon's central office, cast the first vote for moving Northam's third grade. Bishop was familiar with space issues. Two years ago, he tried to reconfigure the district's entire school system, proposing the replacement of the three-year high school with a larger four-year complex. The district's middle schools would serve grades 6-8, freeing up 500 spaces in the elementary schools formerly occupied by sixth graders. The elementary schools would in turn be reorganized to solve overcrowding problems, mainly by changing schools for grades 4-6 to grades 3-5. The school board, however, had voted down the twenty million dollar high school proposal, leaving Bishop without the desired change. Still he had no objection to reconfiguring individual schools.

For Andrews, moving the third graders—or any students—to McKenna was not that simple. Recently, Vera Maxwell, the head of the PTO, had cornered him after visiting her daughter's second grade classroom at Northam, saying that she was uncomfortable with conditions at McKenna. She told him what he already knew: there was a demerit system for misbehavior; parents weren't invited into the school; the children weren't even allowed to have snack in their classrooms. "I'm not all that pleased with how our oldest daughter is coping at McKenna and she's the 'tough nut' in our family," the mother had said. There's no way my youngest will ever survive there next year as a third grader—she's too fragile and sensitive."

Andrews shared these and other parent concerns in a meeting with Bishop, in October. Bishop wasn't sympathetic. Smiling at Andrews across his desk, he said, "McKenna's not a bad place. Those yuppies at your school are making a big deal out of nothing. They're pampering the kids, just trying to throw their own weight around."

"These parents have real and potentially legitimate concerns about a learning environment for their kids," Andrews replied, with a slight edge to his voice. "They aren't making things up. A lot of our parents are parents at McKenna, too. They aren't made to feel like partners in the educational process. And McKenna does run more like a junior high school, even though it's grades four through six. I worry that the staff there may expect third graders to be more like sixth graders."

"That's ridiculous! We've got K-6 schools that work fine," Bishop answered. "There's nothing inherently wrong with having third and sixth graders based in the same facility. If you have a K-6 building or a 3-6 building, you're going to get a school culture that's responsive to that age range."

"But what about Ed Williams?" Andrews added, stopping short of criticizing McKenna's principal, who was well known in Abingdon for his almost militaristic strictness. Bishop coldly shot back, "What about him?" Andrews quickly realized Bishop wasn't willing to discuss the topic and said nothing further. The rest of the meeting passed uneventfully.

Andrews had been open about Williams with Northam's parents and staff. In a conversation some time before, PTO head Maxwell said to Andrews, "Who do they think they are, at McKenna, the Army?" Andrews answered, "McKenna does run like a boot camp." That remark had made the rounds of the PTO. In Northam's faculty meetings, Andrews had often condoned criticism of McKenna's rules and regulations and was sometimes heard to say, "We just do business differently than Ed does." Now that McKenna was the ordained location for some of Northam's students, Andrews wondered if he had helped stir up concerns.

Andrews left the October meeting without a clear picture of what to do. "I had a natural affinity to be an advocate for the preschoolers," Andrews later recalled. "Before coming to Northam, I had chaired a committee in Abingdon that looked into special needs programs throughout the district and became committed to giving the ADP kids a permanent home instead of just passing them along.

❖ MORE CONTENTION

That same October, different groups within Northam School had begun to galvanize and express views of their own. The PTO sent out a letter to Northam parents, arguing that ADP would be the easier program to move, saying, in part:

> ADP is a preschool. Although many children attend preschool before entering kindergarten, most (if not all) preschools are situated in locations independent from any other school program. The average child in preschool, we believe, does not suffer in any way from this lack of contact with other close-in-age youngsters.

A contrasting view came in a letter from the ADP staff (minus Ginny Urbanski) and focused on the lack of appropriate facilities at McKenna—such as handicapped-accessible closets, bathrooms, and playground equipment. In addition, the staff noted:

> Our program also relies on the greater school environment for additional interaction and modeling opportunities. These interactions become much less meaningful as the differences in age increase. Further, moving our children out would only be a temporary solution to a long-term problem, said one of the parents. We feel very strongly that the program should stay here at Northam until the district can find a permanent location, and one that's developmentally appropriate.

Andrews found even stronger feelings in his K-3 faculty meetings. Urbanski had told him that she had seen some of the ADP teachers in tears over confrontations with their K-3 counterparts. "There's already a feeling that ADP doesn't belong here, and I'm afraid that people are going to take it out on the preschoolers. In a late November faculty meeting, the entire K-3 faculty surprised Andrews by issuing a joint statement read by veteran third grade teacher Ted Nutley.

> We are in favor of moving the ADP program because we believe that will have the least adverse impact on students, parents, programs, facilities, and staff. Northam School is an acceptable facility as a K-3 school. It is not an acceptable facility for the preschool program because it is not all on the same level. It is illegal for students in wheelchairs to have to manipulate stairs. McKenna is an acceptable facility for ADP as it is all on one level.

Andrews received the statement with a nod of his head and a glance around the room.

"Well, Tom, are you in favor of the ADP going to McKenna?" the teacher pressed.

"I could make a case either way," Andrews had responded, trying to hold the neutral ground he had staked out for the past eleven months.

"Why don't you just tell us which side you're on?" Nutley rejoined, with exasperation in his voice. Andrews looked around the room again and inferred from the silent expressions of the dozen or so other faculty that they had the same question.

Andrews felt his stomach tighten. He knew he could only buy so much time before he would have to show his cards. "At some point," he thought to himself, "you have to make a stand as a manager. I don't want to be seen as someone who doesn't have an opinion." However, he said nothing more in the meeting.

❖ ANDREWS' TURNING POINT

Andrews remembered the afternoon in early December when he became clear about his position. For what seemed like the umpteenth time, he had told Ginny, "There's no getting around my being principal of the K-3 program. If we send off the third graders, it's going to shake the relationship I've been trying to build with those parents and staff. They'll say that my loyalties were misplaced, and they might just be right."

"McKenna wouldn't make sense for the kids in ADP," Urbanski asserted. "It's a place designed for older kids. So what if the K-3 folks react, is it really that big a deal?"

"Is McKenna *that* detrimental to the educational needs of your kids," Andrews countered, "that it's worth the risk of alienating most of my K-3 parents? Even if sending the third graders is the right thing to do, is advocating for the right thing always the right thing? We're going to get hammered on this one, Ginny."

"Yeah, but there comes a time to base decisions on what's good for the kids and to stick to that principle."

❖ CASE PREPARATION QUESTIONS

1. Describe how Tom Andrews mediates between the opinions of the stakeholders at Northam Elementary and his own professional views.

2. Describe Tom Andrews' strategy in making the decision. Would your strategy differ, and if so, how?

3. When is it appropriate for a principal to share decision making and when is it not?

◆ ◆ ◆

The Allen School

*Darryl Ford, principal co-author, assisted
by Paula Kleine-Kracht, Roger Shouse,
and Susan Ryan*

Located in one of Chicago's most historic neighborhoods, the Allen Magnet School prided itself on providing individual attention to its 170 students in grades kindergarten through six. Allen, a public school, emphasized the classics in literature, offered a strenuous mathematics program, and encouraged the development of critical thinking skills. Students took foreign language classes, participated in a music program that taught theory as well as performance, and studied art history as well as studio art. The library and computer facilities supported the basic academic programs and enriched the curriculum. Allen boasted a full-day kindergarten and a photography club, published a student newspaper, and sent its students on field trips to recitals, operas, and museums. Students in grades three through six learned to program computers, and all of the students participated in career days.

Because of its special programs, the Allen School attracted students from all over the city. Eighty-two percent of the students were Black, fifteen percent were White, and the remaining three percent were Hispanic. Fewer than one-quarter of Allen's students came from low income homes, compared to one-third in the city as a whole. Very few of Allen's students lived in the lower middle class neighborhood surrounding the school. Most of the students were bused to school, but Allen's attendance rate was over 97%, almost 10 percentage points higher than the district average. The school's student turnover rate was less than 10%, compared to a district average of about 35%. The school had no chronically truant students.

With a small and selective enrollment, special programs, dedicated parents, a stable student population, and an experienced faculty, the Allen School's students excelled. On standardized tests, they always performed well, usually better than district, state, and national averages. In recent examinations, over 60% of Allen's third graders and 78% of the school's sixth graders scored in the top quartile on 21 nationally normed reading assessments, far exceeding district and state averages.

❖ LOCAL SCHOOL COUNCILS

In 1989, a state-mandated restructuring of leadership in the Chicago public schools took effect. The plan established Local School Councils (LSCs) for each of the more than 500 Chicago schools. LSCs were to set the educational policy of the school, approve the school improvement plan (another legislated reform), approve the school budget, and hire or fire the school principal. The LSCs entitled parents to an unprecedented level of decision making power in the schools, giving them the majority of seats on the councils. LSCs were to include six parents, two community members, two teachers, the school principal, and, at the high school level, one student.

Elections for the LSCs were held simultaneously throughout the city. The Allen LSC election process exhibited all the diversity and strength that had built the school's reputation. Over a hundred parents and community members attended a forum to hear the positions of the Allen LSC candidates. The parent candidates included an Illinois Bell employee, a volunteer with the city's Police Youth Division, a bank administrator, current and former PTA presidents, an attorney, a professional storyteller, a legal stenographer, and a Lutheran pastor. Community candidates included a community activist employed by a local bank, a police officer, an employee of the city department of streets and sanitation, a former teacher, and another past PTA president.

Forum observers were impressed with the candidates' knowledge and their apparent commitment to the continued success of the school. Unfortunately, however, the council aspirants were not so sanguine about each other. Two of the candidates were particularly concerned about the competition. Sarah Jenkins, a parent, and Arnold Smith, a community candidate, had long been active in the affairs of the Allen School. Both had previously served as PTA presidents and Jenkins was then serving as the president of the Local School Improvement Council (which was to disband with the creation of the new Local School Council). Jenkins and Smith each noted that they had worked "long and hard" for Allen, while many of the other candidates had never before participated in the life of the school. Jenkins remarked, "Our work laid the groundwork for the power we have today. We *earned* our authority."

Jenkins and Smith won seats on the council, as did the new PTA president and parent, attorney Bill Johnson. He was later elected president of the LSC, as well. The additional Allen parents elected were, Frank Howard, Rachel Brown, Lelia Gomez and Sam Shelby. Art Happs was elected as a community representative who had no prior connection to the school. The two teacher members appointed to the council were Mildred Hawkins and Jerry O'Hara. Principal Sandra Harris rounded out the body.

❖ SANDRA HARRIS, PRINCIPAL

Allen's principal, Sandra Harris, was appointed on an interim basis shortly before the opening of the academic year. Prior to her appointment, Harris had been the fifth grade teacher at the Allen School for six years. She had worked in the district a total of seventeen years. Unlike some principals in the district, Harris possessed all the formal credentials—she had earned a degree in administration, passed the principal's examination, and was not "grandfathered" into the position. Over the years, Harris had earned the respect of her school community, working in some instances with a number of the new council members.

The previous Allen principal, Harold Jameson, had simultaneously managed the Allen School and a second elementary school. This arrangement had lasted four years. When school reform legislation made it difficult to continue in both positions, Mr. Jameson left Allen to continue in a full-time capacity at the other school. The second school was larger and suffered from most of the disadvantages that plague inner city schools. Harold Jameson wanted to help the school overcome those challenges. Sandra Harris was then appointed by the superintendent as acting principal of the Allen School, with the understanding that the Allen LSC would have to approve her permanent appointment at the end of the academic year. Teachers, parents, and members of the community had recommended Harris for the interim position and gave her their full support as she started her work.

When asked, Harris was gracious in acknowledging Harold Jameson's part-time stewardship of the Allen. She always credited Mr. Jameson's contribution to establishing the school's excellent reputation. At the same time, she would remind the listener that under Harold's part-time leadership there had been no significant change in policy or test scores either. Harris thought it was time to breathe new life into the school.

One day, early in the Fall, Harris had stopped in the teachers room and encountered a few of her colleagues. The group sat comfortably for a few moments and talked openly about the change in leadership. Mildred Hawkins, a ten year veteran of the school said, "Jameson's part-time status didn't cause any difficulty at Allen because of the teachers. With the faculty we have, I think this school could run by itself." Sandra Harris said nothing in reply, assenting to the caliber of her staff, but wondered if her full-time involvement might eventually cause some discord.

Harris was commencing her first principalship on three weeks notice, concurrently with the broadest school reforms ever legislated in Chicago history. The novice principal would be leading a mature faculty with established curricula and procedures and would be sharing power with a new body—the Allen LSC—that had yet to fashion itself into a cohesive working unit. This was an unsettling proposition, to say the least.

❖ THE PRINCIPAL'S WORK BEGINS

Despite the professional culture and performance of the school, Harris was convinced improvements could be made. An important innovation, she thought, would be changing the perception of the principal's role. Harris wanted the Allen faculty and students to perceive her as a "principal teacher." She wanted them to see her consistently supporting their learning and teaching. For that reason, Harris instituted a policy change that required teachers to submit a weekly lesson plan. She believed receiving weekly lesson plans would allow her to make suggestions and serve as a resource person. She was, of course, concerned the faculty might view the new requirement as intrusive but thought the benefits would outweigh the liabilities. Moreover, she thought she could mitigate those liabilities through individual consultation and assurance. In the end, only John Simon, the sixth grade teacher, made public his dissatisfaction with the policy and Harris easily won him over. She made a point of looking closely at his plans each week and offering encouragement and aid, "I like your ideas about the M.L. King unit, John. Would you like to use my Martin Luther King board game?"

Harris also wanted to update and expand Allen's procedures for evaluating teachers and assessing their classroom needs. At the same time, the new reform legislation required that Harris conduct an assessment of the school as a basis for developing a three-year school improvement plan. Harris quickly realized she could use the school improvement plan as a vehicle to refine Allen's evaluation procedures. In consultation with her PPAC (Professional Personnel Advisory Council), she developed a series of survey instruments to begin a complete school-wide evaluation. Surveys were devised for a number of constituencies—teachers, students, parents, graduates, and high school teachers of Allen graduates.

However, Harris' aim to innovate was not always compatible with the legislated reforms. In fact, the principal's desire to implement change specific to the needs of Allen teachers and students was often challenged by the demands of Chicago's reform requirements. After coordinating the LSC candidates' forum, and the election, Harris had to schedule LSC meetings and contend with the myriad tasks that evolved from them—writing bylaws, forming subcommittees and gathering requested information—all in addition to performing her normal duties as principal.

❖ THE PROFESSIONAL PERSONNEL ADVISORY COUNCIL

Versions of the Local School Councils and the Professional Personnel Advisory Councils existed in Chicago schools prior to the reform laws. The new laws mandated the functions and configurations of both groups. Although, unlike the LSCs, the PPACs were loosely defined and allowed to vary from school to school. PPACs were to be comprised of building teachers and had no formal decision making power. Their role was solely to advise the principal on issues related to the running of the school.

Before the reform laws, The Allen School's version of the PPAC was a small but influential body. Many credited it for steering the school successfully during the four years of part-time administration. Three teachers served on the Allen PPAC and membership rotated annually. Sandra Harris had served on Allen's PPAC and was comfortable with the collegial nature of the group. With the introduction of the reform laws, some members of the Allen school community questioned whether teachers should serve on both the LSC and the PPAC. After some discussion, the Allen faculty decided it was in the best interest of communication to allow one teacher to serve on both councils.

❖ AN EARLY LSC MEETING

The meeting began uneventfully. The minutes from the last meeting were approved, old business was completed, and then new business was addressed. Harris described the assessment that was to precede the school's three-year improvement plan. She presented the evaluation questionnaires and explained that she had consulted with members of the PPAC and prepared the questionnaires herself.

Council members, Jenkins and Smith, were outraged that Harris had consulted the PPAC and not the council in developing the survey. The other council members, including President Johnson, expressed no displeasure and, in fact, seemed pleased with the content of the surveys. However, the "old guard" was not appeased. Both argued that Harris should have consulted the LSC earlier, since the school improvement plan was supposed to be formulated under the council's auspices.

Harris responded that she would gladly make any changes that the council deemed necessary, but Jenkins and Smith said they needed more time to study them in order to make constructive recommendations. Jenkins wanted the council to take copies home and suggested that they be considered for approval at the next council meeting. Smith also recommended that a conversation around issues of "proper procedure" be scheduled. Jenkins and Smith continued to convey their misgivings about being "side-stepped" and their reprimands grew more and more heated. Finally, a parent in the audience interrupted the "tirade," saying Jenkins' and Smith's behavior was "rude and non-productive."

In her defense, Harris told the group that, in the interest of time, there were some actions she had to initiate on her own. She told the council if she were forced to wait for their input on every action, she would get nothing accomplished. Perturbed by Smith's and Jenkins' increasingly intense attack, Harris finally remarked, "I have been reprimanded sufficiently," and said she would keep the incident in mind. Harris then excused herself to make copies of her assessment instruments so, as requested, council members could take them home to "study."

Nonetheless, while Harris was out of the room, a second confrontation occurred. The meeting had already lasted two hours, and council president, Bill Johnson, made a motion to adjourn. Arnold Smith interrupted, saying, "Hold on there, Bill. I have another item I'd like to discuss." Smith then informed the group that he'd been told by an associate that an educational consultant named Gregory Sherman had recently made a lengthy presentation to the

PPAC. Smith wanted Sherman to give the same presentation to the LSC and deliver it "exactly" as he had at the PPAC meeting.

Mildred Hawkins was beside herself. The teacher-member of both the LSC and the PPAC, said, "Arnold, I don't know who you've been talking to but, Gregory Sherman was a candidate for about thirty school councils. He's a salesman for crying out loud! He wanted council membership in order to position himself to sell his company's school products. He gave the PPAC a sales pitch—for curriculum material that wasn't worth the paper it was printed on!!" Mildred told Arnold that she would not waste her time attending any LSC meeting that Sherman addressed.

Nevertheless, Arnold Smith made a motion to invite Gregory Sherman to make his presentation for the LSC. The motion was rejected. Bill Johnson adjourned the meeting in spite of Sarah Jenkins' efforts to raise another issue. As council members gathered up their belongings, Arnold Smith fumed, "I put Sandra Harris in that principal position, and I can remove her from it when the time comes."

❖ REFLECTIONS

Later, when asked about consulting the PPAC before the LSC, Harris concluded that Jenkins and Smith were reacting less to her interaction with the PPAC, and more to her presence in the school. Harris thought parents and community members had previously taken an active role in running the Allen School and many people were inclined to view the new administrator with suspicion. In addition, many distrusted the PPAC, because it was comprised of teachers and was seen as the "arm of the union." Harris, however, suggested that she found the PPAC, a body of "professional educators" and a helpful source of advice and input.

Still reckoning with the "newness of it all," Harris wanted to deal fairly with various factions in the school while working for the benefit of the children. She was savvy enough to know that a variety of perspectives could benefit Allen students and was willing to draw on the different perspectives that confronted her. At the same time, she felt that the LSC had to get beyond factionalism. She knew she and the LSC had to work together in a way that would best serve the children. "But I can't wait for the LSC to act in order to run the school," she remarked. "You want to make sure you're following the law, the spirit of the law, but at the same time, you want to get things done. You want to lead."

❖ CASE PREPARATION QUESTIONS

1. When new governance structures are introduced, ambiguity often results. Describe the ambiguity in the Allen School. If you were Sandra Harris, what would you do to clarify this ambiguity?

2. How does one exert leadership while building consensus?

◆ ◆ ◆

Augusta County—Beech Mountain Institute

Sean F. Reardon

❖ A SPECIAL SCHOOL BOARD MEETING

On Tuesday evening, January 21, the Augusta County School Board held a special public meeting. The Board president, Alvin Geidt, had called the meeting to discuss a proposal for school reform that had been circulating through the county since the 16th in a document titled "Description of an Alternative School System," sponsored by a local non-profit organization called Beech Mountain Institute. The meeting was called with only five days notice, because the proposals contained in the Beech Mountain document would require the Virginia State Legislature to waive some state curriculum requirements for Augusta County, and the deadline for submitting waiver requests to the Legislature was February 1.

The Beech Mountain document suggested a number of school reforms, including:

◆ replacing report cards with assessment by exhibition;
◆ replacing age-grading with multi-age, multi-ability grouping;
◆ replacing textbooks with hands-on learning;
◆ basing teaching on a "brain-based learning theory";
◆ replacing the subject-based curriculum with an integrated theme-based curriculum.

Jessica Garvin-Leeds, one of the principal authors of the "Description of an Alternative School System," later explained some of the thinking behind the document, "We were trying to find ways to take the best ideas for rural schools from around the country and apply them to Augusta County. The idea was to redesign our schools around these ideas, to change the pedagogies of the schools."

❖ AUGUSTA COUNTY

With only 8,000 residents in its 646 square miles, Augusta County was the least densely populated county in the Eastern United States. The county, situated in the Potomac highlands of western Virginia, was divided by ridges into two long valleys, each named after the tributary to the Potomac which ran through it. Sanford, the county seat and largest town, was located in the central valley, known as South Fork Valley. Newberry was the largest town in North Fork Valley, which, with only 25% of the county's population, was the least populated area of the county. Only one two-lane road wound up and over Beech Mountain, the steep ridge between the North Fork and South Fork, and in good weather the fifteen-mile drive from Newberry to Sanford took thirty minutes; in snow, the road was sometimes dangerous and impassable.

Agriculture was the main industry in Augusta County, with some retail trade, infrastructure development, and tourism contributing to the local economy. On the south side of the county was a Navy communications base, home to several hundred families. In 1991, the per capita income in the county was $10,064, fifty-seven percent of the U.S. average. The county budget, excluding education costs, was $815,000 annually, of which about $500,000 was raised annually from property taxes. The remainder came from a variety of sources, predominately coal severance funds and federal payments in lieu of taxes for the twenty-nine percent of the county that was federally-owned national forest.

People in the county described a tension between the North and South Fork valleys, dating back to the Civil War and before. The North–South divide was evident during the Civil War, when the county became a battleground. North Fork residents sided with the Union, while the South Fork residents fought for the Confederacy. After the war, the South Fork prospered and a middle class affluence grew in the area, further widening the divide between the North and South Valleys. Augusta County's relative isolation in past and present times contributed to a continuity and cultural strength, but also helped perpetuate the intra-county division.

As in many rural communities, newcomers to Augusta County found the community difficult to join. Those not born in the county were considered outsiders, "come here's," as they were referred to locally—often after living in the area for 20 or 30 years. As one local resident put it:

> Well, when I was a kid, somebody from Pittsburgh was about like somebody from Mars. You know, you just never saw anybody except the people you were raised with. . . . There wasn't any tourism, and people just didn't come in here that much. Of course now, it's different. But what does it take to overcome being an outsider? In my opinion, you don't. I mean, you can be friends. You can have friends and everything, but you've still got a brand.

❖ AUGUSTA COUNTY SCHOOLS

Augusta County had three K-6 schools, one K-12 school in Newberry, and one 7-12 school in Sanford. Sanford High School enrolled roughly 300 students from the South Fork. Total enrollment at the Newberry School was 350 students, 100 enrolled in grades 9-12. The county had an annual education budget of $6 million; 4.7 million from state aid, 1 million from federal sources, and $300,000 raised locally. With roughly 1,500 students, the county averaged $4,000 per pupil expenditures. Because of the small number of high school students enrolled at Newberry School, however, the county spent $1,000 more per high school pupil in Newberry than in Sanford. Moreover, the county spent more per pupil on transportation than any other county in the state.

Consolidation of the high schools had long been an issue in the county. Depending on the climate of local and state politics, proposals to consolidate the two high schools had been on and off the school board agenda for decades. Two years ago, then superintendent William Bauer proposed a school consolidation plan and the school board—with a 4-1 South Fork majority—approved it. Consequently, the state was in line to give Augusta County $11 million for the construction of a new comprehensive high school in Sanford. The existing high schools in Sanford and Newberry were to be closed.

However, in Newberry, the local high school was a point of pride. Many in the North Fork feared that consolidation would mean the end of the sense of community. An additional concern about consolidation was the danger of busing students over Beech Mountain in the winter. North Fork residents, who drove to Sanford far more often than South Fork residents drove in the opposite direction, feared the mountain road, sometimes choosing to stay overnight in Sanford with relatives when the weather was particularly bad.

Before the state awarded Augusta County the money under Bauer's consolidation proposal, school board elections were planned and held. A group of North Fork residents opposed to consolidation, the Augusta Citizens for Community Schools, worked aggressively to elect North Fork representatives to the Board. They registered every eligible North Fork resident to vote, and called each of them on election day, offering rides to the polls. South Fork residents, content that the consolidation plan had already been approved, turned out in low numbers. Two new North Fork representatives—Alvin Geidt and Terry Lewis—joined Jerry Laing, until then the lone North Fork Board member, giving North Fork a 3–2 majority on the School Board, despite the fact that they represented only 25% of the county population. The terms of all three North Fork Board members were scheduled to last four years.

At their first meeting, the new Board elected Alvin Geidt as its new president and withdrew the consolidation plan approved by the previous board. They willingly forfeited the $11 million for a new school in favor of keeping the two local high schools open.

Feeling obstructed by the make-up of the new Board, William Bauers left the district within months of the election. A year later, the Board voted unanimously to appoint David Myers as Superintendent. Myers came to Augusta

County from a job as Assistant Superintendent in Stevens County, Virginia. Prior to that he had been with the Virginia State Department of Education for twenty-one years serving in a variety of positions. At the time he was hired, Myers made clear that he believed the consolidation decision belonged to the Board. He commented:

> My feeling has always been that we need a consolidated high school. But when I was hired, I took the attitude that I'm going to do what the Board directs me to do. I told them I would study the issue and make my recommendation, but if they don't want to consolidate the high schools, they will not be consolidated.

❖ THE SUPERINTENDENT'S REFORM PLAN

Four months after his appointment, Myers proposed a school reform plan for Augusta County at a public meeting of the School Board held on November 21. In his extensive speech, Myers described his vision of a school environment characterized by "multi-age, multi-ability classrooms, authentic assessment, qualitative reporting methods, professional team work, and significant parental involvement. (See Exhibit 1 on page 132.) A program demonstrating these characteristics," he argued, "will provide a safe, caring, stimulating environment where students grow and learning flourishes."

Myers later explained that his proposal was driven by what he saw as the changing educational needs of the community:

> I think generally the folks here think of quality education as meaning that kids can read, write, compute numbers, and get a high school diploma. And years ago, that may have been true. But today that's not true enough. I want to give the students of Augusta County a comprehensive education that prepares them to be productive citizens in today's world. I want them to have access to an education that meets everyone's needs—college bound students and vocational students.

In addition to curricular and organizational changes within the schools, his plan included a proposal to build three new schools—two consolidated K-8 complexes, one on either side of Beech Mountain, and a single consolidated high school in the South Fork Valley. Myers told the assembly that he believed consolidation would mean fiscal savings and a higher quality education for Augusta County children.

Superintendent Myers did not ask the School Board to vote on the proposal at the November meeting. Instead, following the November meeting, he spoke at every school in Augusta County, describing his plan and asking for feedback and support. Whenever he described his plan, he always invited other proposals. One resident recalled him saying, "if this plan doesn't suit you, please come to me and offer other suggestions."

A month later, having spoken at all the schools in the county, Myers held a referendum on the facilities/consolidation portion of the plan. He said he would only present his proposal to the Board if it received 60% support from voters. Sixty percent support, he later stated, would have demonstrated a clear majority in support of the facilities/consolidation proposal. Moreover, it was common in Virginia to require a 60% approval for bond issues, rather than a simple majority. The referendum gathered 59% of the vote, and Myers did not ask the School Board to vote to approve the facilities/consolidation proposal.

❖ BEECH MOUNTAIN INSTITUTE

In 1972, starting with "$200 and a pickup," Mark and Jessica Garvin-Leeds moved to Augusta County and established Beech Mountain Institute to run outdoor education programs. Mark had just received his doctorate in Education and Jessica had just completed a Master's degree in Divinity. Both were highly committed to serving children. Located within an easy day's drive of the East Coast's major population centers, the Institute primarily assisted student groups from many of the private schools along the East Coast.

Beech Mountain's original mission focused on outdoor education programs. Over the years, however, the Institute broadened its focus to include a variety of other programs, including an alternative technology center and a community health center. A small but influential program was the Virginia Scholars Program. It was started with a $5,000 donation from Virginia insurance executive Dwaine Arnold. Its aim was to help high-achieving high school students statewide get into competitive colleges and universities.

Beech Mountain's budget grew steadily over the years, tripling in the late '80s from $500,000 to almost $1,500,000. Funding sources for the non-profit organization varied—individuals donations, foundation support, the governments of Canada, Nepal, the Netherlands, Sweden, and Tibet, as well as the U.S. Government's Appalachian Regional Commission and USAID. Along the way, the Institute was able to purchase 400 acres of wooded land near the peak of Beech Knob, the highest point along the ridge of Beech Mountain between the North and South Fork valleys.

Many in Augusta County did not trust the Garvin-Leeds and Beech Mountain Institute. No one seemed to know exactly what they did up on Beech Knob and rumors abounded. Some thought they were communists; others thought the rock-climbing courses they taught were a front for a CIA survival-training operation; and the 30-foot diameter yurt they had built on the mountain was rumored to be a missile silo. More commonly, they were considered by many to be "hippies," involved in drug use and inappropriate sexual behavior.

Beech Mountain's non-profit, grant-dependent financial status also angered and confused many in the community. The Institute hired more outsiders than local people, and did not pay taxes because of its non-profit status. Mark and Jessica "didn't work," but "lived off of grants," in the words of a number of county residents. Freddie Watson, a South Fork resident and 20-year member of the School Board, had long been suspicious of Beech Mountain's motives:

If you were my neighbor, and you moved in, bought the next farm up here to me, I would look at you more for what you did than at where you came from. And I think if you weren't a hostile neighbor, that if you were a nice person, if you wanted to get along, in 20 years you would definitely have been accepted. And that's the thing. Beech Mountain has been subversive. They haven't been up front. They haven't been square. They've been underhanded in their dealings, and they're looked on with suspicion.

Other residents, however, thought that the suspicion of Mark and Jessica was unfounded. Rose Carpenter, a Virginia native who married an Augusta County resident and worked as a teacher at Newberry School, thought that county residents were suspicious because they did not understand what Beech Mountain was trying to do. She said, "Knowing Mark and Jessica, I'd have to say that a lot of people have false perceptions. When they came to the community and set up the Institute, they tried to involve local children. But people around here are reluctant to let the children go out to camps and such."

Sam Bryant, a local ophthalmologist who had gone away to get his own college education, argued that people were particularly suspicious of Mark and Jessica because they were educated:

They haven't been accepted by natives, local people. A few of us have made friendships with them, but the vast majority haven't. I think the easiest way to explain that is that people here are suspicious of education. And small towns fear outsiders. I think that's why they're so wary of Mark and Jessica. They have two strikes against them. But me . . . you know, they watched me play football; they saw me soap windows. You know, I'm just little Sammie Bryant. The fact I went away and got an education, that don't scare them a bit.

❖ THE BEECH MOUNTAIN DOCUMENT

In 1989, former insurance executive and then Governor, Dwaine Arnold, asked Mark and Jessica to organize a Governor's Summit on education. Beech Mountain raised money for the summit through grants and invited several nationally-prominent educators to attend. Because of her involvement in the Summit, Jessica became interested in education issues on the state level. At that time, consolidation was high on the state's agenda, with the state offering financial incentives for districts to consolidate their schools. Jessica believed that, all other things being equal, community schools were preferable to consolidated schools, and she found evidence in the literature to support her belief.

Because of Jessica's new interest, Beech Mountain Institute, in 1990, launched a new initiative, the Community Schools Program. The program began by producing a Community Schools Handbook, written as "a tool for school reform and community regeneration . . . to answer the question, 'What do citizens need to know to make informed decisions about their rural community schools?'" The Handbook, written by Jessica and Beech Mountain staff member Hank Sorenson and titled *Your Choice*, was published in the spring of 1991, prior to Myers' arrival in the county. The previous superintendent, William Bauer, and Alvin Geidt both served on the committee that reviewed a draft of the book prior to its publication.

Following its publication, Mark and Jessica distributed the handbook to schools throughout the county and met with local residents. They felt that there was real community interest for some of the ideas in *Your Choice*. The North Fork residents were passionate about saving their high school, and residents in the South Fork seemed genuinely interested in reform. Jessica came to be an opponent of consolidation and wanted to find other, and better, ways to organize the schools: "Instead of arguing about consolidation, I hoped we could talk about what we really want out of our schools, and work on that."

In January 1992, responding to continued interest from several people in the county, including School Board president Alvin Geidt, Jessica and Hank Sorenson wrote a nine-page "Description of an Alternative School System." (See Exhibit 2 on page 139.) Jessica described the paper as a "talking paper." She said, "It was never intended to be a *plan*—it was too sketchy. We meant it as a document to raise ideas, to get people talking, to see what kind of ideas might be used as levers to change the system."

On Tuesday evening, January 14, Jessica was in the Beech Mountain office finishing the paper. She gave a copy to Alvin Geidt's daughter, who worked at Beech Mountain, and asked her to take it to her father. She also gave a copy to Rose Carpenter, a friend, whose opinion she trusted.

That same day, Mark was in Richmond meeting with Governor Dwaine Arnold to discuss the Virginia Scholars Program. The two had known one another for years, and when the Governor asked Mark for some information about the merits of a 4-day school week, Mark suggested some of the ideas contained in the talking paper. The Governor was interested, and Mark suggested making one school a pilot school to demonstrate such ideas—a "break-the-mold school," he said. The Governor said that such a school would need legislative waivers, and he called State Senator Dorothy Evans, Chair of the Senate Education Committee, and asked her to speak with Mark about possibilities.

The following day, Wednesday, January 15, Mark met with Senator Evans in Richmond. She listened attentively to Mark's ideas and grew increasingly enthusiastic. The Senator asked Mark which Augusta County school site he was intending to use. Mark said the Institute had developed a positive working relationship with educators at the Newberry School and thought he'd like to try to arrange a collaboration on that site. Senator Evans told Mark that if the state received a formal request for waivers by February 1, she thought she would be able to get the waivers approved for the following fall.

After speaking with Mark, Senator Evans ran into Senator Arlene Cassett, who represented Augusta County and faced a difficult reelection campaign. Evans told her that Augusta County was considering a proposal for waivers to start a pilot school program, and that there was a good chance they would be approved. Cassett immediately tried to call Superintendent Myers to congratulate him. She did not reach him until the following morning.

Meanwhile, Mark arrived home in Sanford on Wednesday night, excited by the Governor's and Senator's interest in the ideas. Mark, Jessica, and Hank Sorenson talked Wednesday night about when and how they should let Myers know of the developments. They decided to wait and call him in the morning.

On Thursday morning, January 16, Superintendent Myers received a call from State Senator Arlene Cassett. "Congratulations, Al," she said, "it looks like your new plan is going to move right through the legislature. The chair of the Education subcommittee seems very supportive. I think you'll get the waivers you need to start a pilot program at Newberry next fall."

Myers thanked Cassett warmly, though he had no idea what plan she was referring to. He hung up the phone without asking any questions, wondering if maybe it was a plan the district had proposed before he began as superintendent six months earlier. He immediately called John Hargood, principal of Newberry School, and asked him if he knew what this was about. Hargood figured that he must be referring to the Beech Mountain "Description of an Alternative School System" that Rose Carpenter had shown him earlier in the week. John Hargood had a copy sent to the Superintendent within the hour.

Myers had mixed feelings about what he read in the paper. Some ideas he supported, some he did not. At the same time, Myers was furious that he had not been briefed about the plan. He said, "I wouldn't have known about it if Cassett hadn't called to congratulate me. I'm the Superintendent of Schools and here's an outside group going to the legislature without informing me or the Board of Education. And this plan could significantly influence education in the district."

Later that morning, Mark Garvin-Leeds called Superintendent Myers in his office. He explained that the county would have to make a request to the legislature for waivers within two weeks if they were interested in trying to create an alternative school. Myers was cordial with Mark, and suggested a special School Board meeting to discuss the possibility; he told Mark that he would talk to Alvin Geidt to set it up. Later that day, Alvin Geidt agreed to the special meeting.

In the next few days, Augusta County residents began to hear about the Beech Mountain document and Mark's visit with the Governor. According to Myers, his phone rang off the hook with calls from people demanding to know about the plan. He gave copies of the "talking paper" to any and all who asked for it, and soon every photocopier in the county was churning out copies. A memo from Myers announcing the special School Board meeting appeared in store windows throughout the county. Scrawled across many of the announcements were handwritten warnings urging residents to attend the meeting: "Be There! Last Chance!" they urged; "Wake Up!" (See Exhibit 3 on page 147.)

On Tuesday evening, January 21, the road across Beech Mountain to Newberry High School where the meeting was to be held was lit up by an endless stream of headlights. By 7:00 p.m., when the meeting began, some 600 people from all over the county were crowded into the school's gymnasium for the special meeting. Sitting at the front of the gym were Alvin Geidt and the other four members of the School Board, Superintendent David Myers, Mark and Jessica Garvin-Leeds, and Hank Sorenson.

❖ JANUARY 21: THE SPECIAL SCHOOL BOARD MEETING

School Board President Alvin Geidt began the meeting by reminding those present about the November School Board meeting when Superintendent Myers' proposal was discussed. An invitation, he said, was extended at that time to any citizen or group of citizens who wanted to submit an alternative plan. Beech Mountain had apparently done so, he said, and the purpose of tonight's meeting was to discuss that plan.

Jessica was the first speaker. She began by identifying herself as a long-time resident of Augusta County and a parent of children enrolled in Augusta County schools. She then apologized to the School Board, Dr. Myers, and the rest of the county for the way the "talking paper" had come to their attention.

> The various events took off in a way that we didn't intend. I know that many of you have been rudely shocked and distressed by the way this information has come forward and I offer you my apology. I would like to make a particular apology to the Board because it is certainly their place to hear and know about these things, and most particularly, to Dr. Myers, our Superintendent. I have apologized to him repeatedly in private. He has been very gentlemanly but I feel that he deserves a public apology from the Institute.
>
> I do not view this document that is circulating as a plan. It doesn't have the necessary detail or features of a plan. It is a "talking paper" and it was written for the purpose of continuing the discussion that I had been involved in with many people. It is not an application to anybody for anything. It was not a request to anybody for money.

Mark spoke next, and described his meeting with Governor Arnold on the 14th. He apologized to Myers for not calling him immediately from Richmond to let him know about the meeting. He concluded by explaining the official position of Beech Mountain on the issue. Beech Mountain, he said, would like to be part of a team effort to improve the schools in Augusta County; such an effort would include the input of the county's professional educators, the input of citizens, and the input of outside experts.

Hank Sorenson, speaking next, emphasized as well the importance of community involvement in successful rural education. The three speakers from Beech Mountain received no applause. In contrast, when South Fork School Board member Freddie Watson spoke, he was interrupted repeatedly with loud cheers. "It takes a lot of gall and a lot of arrogance," he said, "to go to the Governor and the chair of the Senate Education Committee to propose as radical a change in education as Beech Mountain has, without the knowledge of the School Board and Superintendent." Watson called on the Superintendent for his views. Myers was greeted with applause.

Myers began by asking why, when the county had rejected his reform plan only two months before, they should now discuss another plan. Though he had put four months into preparing his plan, the School Board Meeting in November had spent only 10 minutes discussing the curriculum reform portions of it; the rest of the time had been devoted to a debate about its consolidation proposals. He had no more time, he said, to discuss such plans; he had to get on with the business of managing the schools. But if the North Fork wanted to adopt Beech Mountain's proposal, he suggested, the School Board could sell the Newberry School to the highest bidder, who could then contract with Beech Mountain to write grants and run the school. He then stated, "Then I can get on with the business of working with them on the kind of curriculum and instruction they want. I do not feel, however, that county funds ought to be put into this program in Newberry if you are going to go with a curriculum different from the rest of the county. The money should come from grants and private investment."

The crowd responded with cheers and applause. Those from the South Fork cheered at the opportunity to rid themselves of responsibility for paying for education in Newberry. Someone from the North Fork shouted out that they would rather privatize than consolidate.

Following Myers' remarks, Alvin Geidt opened the floor to comment from the audience. Twenty-one people spoke; twenty of them opposed the idea of seeking waivers for the kinds of ideas contained in the "talking paper." All but one of those who spoke in opposition were from the South Fork. Some were opposed to the suggested reforms saying the same ideas had been tried in the 1960s and failed. They also expressed concern that students would not be prepared for college, and college entrance requirements would not be met. One South Fork resident said he didn't want his children to be "guinea pigs."

Others were more opposed to Beech Mountain and the steps Mark and Jessica had taken than to the ideas in the paper itself. Several people suggested that a few of the ideas in the paper were useful, such as a course in human relations, but that, overall, the plan was too radical. Others resented what they perceived as Beech Mountain Institute trying to tell them what to do. Donnie Caitlin, Mayor of Sanford, argued this point:

> We have elected the school board who in turn have employed what would seem to me at this point a very capable superintendent of schools. . . . It is not right that we be kept in the dark about this grandiose plan on how our schools might be managed by an outside entity. We have a school board and we have a superintendent. . . . I've grown up here, with the exception of my military service, and went to school here. And it's a darn good place to live. And I'm not ready to relinquish the administration of my county to the Beech Mountain Institute!

Mark and Jessica were not the only ones mistrusted. One person said he came to the meeting not only because he didn't like the plan, but because he did not trust the three Board members from the North Fork. When Alvin Geidt turned down requests by Freddie Watson and others for a meeting the following week to reconsider Myers's plan, members of the audience criticized the Board for failing to act:

> You wonder why we don't trust you! The School Board doesn't want to consider any solution that looks like it might lead to consolidation. We'll fiddle while Rome burns, and Richmond will come in and tell us what to do.

Only Rose Carpenter spoke in favor of the ideas and of Beech Mountain:

It bothers me that we attack the people who care. We have the Governor's ear. There are good things in the plan; we have an opportunity to make a difference in the schools. Don't let hate hold us back. We have been doing nothing but tearing each other down this evening; instead, let's take the good ideas in this paper and build on them. This could be a positive opportunity.

Toward the end of the five-hour meeting, Jessica Garvin-Leeds formally withdrew the paper from consideration.

This was never intended as a plan; I wish to formally withdraw it from discussion. I feel the purpose of writing this plan has been accomplished if we can fill a room as large as this and all talk about education. I hope every school now has another meeting to discuss their particular problems.

❖ CASE PREPARATION QUESTIONS

1. What roles do the history and geography of the region play in this case?
2. David Myers presented his vision for the Augusta County schools, while the Beech Mountain Institute offered a "talking paper" suggesting certain reforms. Assess each statement.
3. Do you think K-12 education in Augusta County is in need of reform? How would you decide? Whose decision is it?

EXHIBIT 1

SPEECH ON SCHOOL REFORM
presented by
Dr. David Myers
November 21, 1991

Board Members and Guests attending this evening,

We have been blessed in Augusta County with beautiful mountains, great fall colors, an abundance of wildlife, clear streams, two wonderful river valleys, and healthy people to live in the valleys, hollows, and mountains. But we are cursed by a mountain range which divides our county culturally and often makes travel difficult and sometimes dangerous. Our county is further troubled by the area it covers being the fourth largest county in Virginia in square miles, and the second in least population per square mile. Our low population and low tax base creates a financial nightmare. All of which makes decisions affecting our schools most difficult.

What we will be talking about tonight is a vision, but not just a vision, but a "shared vision." Without a "shared vision" all of us will have no idea of what we are trying to accomplish by improving the school system as a whole. We will make little progress toward providing the education so needed by our children and youth.

To create fundamental change in our school district involves struggles with an educational system that is clearly outdated. The academic program and most facilities no longer serve us or the children we are educating. System-wide failure threatens the very existence of our school system and the future of all children under our charge.

In order to have a cost efficient, academically productive, and quality school system we must engineer fundamental reform and develop a plan for educational excellence. We must redefine our role and function as the board and caretaker of the school district. We must present to the people of Augusta County a united vision that focuses on children and youth, that will give our students an opportunity for a well-balanced life, academically, socially, physically, ethically and morally. This plan must be well thought out and meet with the approval of most of the citizens of the county. This is an awesome responsibility for each of us and as a board.

We must now begin to fix our county school system. We need to quit blaming people for problems or to look to others to fix it for us, and start fixing our school system ourselves. Parents blame teachers, teachers blame administrators, administrators blame board members or teachers, board members blame the state, and the cycle goes on and on. Remember, however, when you point a finger at someone, three fingers could be pointing back at the real problem.

We need to have a vision and explain that vision, mission, and goal statements that are credible and worthy. We need to quit our internal bickering and get on with the task of teaching kids.

With these thoughts in mind, I present for your consideration this plan for school reform in Augusta County. From this we can begin to discuss and create a plan which will consider all of the public concerns in developing a school system which will assure a quality education for all children in the future. Let's begin by creating a vision for our educational program. What will our educational program be like three years from now?

You will see the Augusta County School Program nurturing the continuing growth of student's knowledge and understanding of themselves and their world. The school environment will be characterized by appropriate practices; multi-age, multi-ability classrooms, continuous progress, authentic assessment, qualitative reporting methods, professional team work, and positive parent involvement. A program demonstrating these characteristics will provide a safe, caring, stimulating environment where students grow and learning flourishes.

Our classrooms will be non-competitive and encourage students to learn from one another as well as from their teachers. Diversity of skills and knowledge will be accepted and accommodated by grouping and regrouping students for an effective instructional program.

The program will grow naturally from level to level and exhibit developmentally appropriate practices. These practices will allow for the broad range of student's needs, learning styles, knowledge, experience, and interests. Continuous learning will be enhanced through a coordinated and integrated curriculum incorporating a variety of instructional strategies and resources.

The school program will view authentic assessment and qualitative reporting methods as integral components of the teaching-learning process. Continuous assessment will support the student's learning and assist the teachers in making appropriate educational decisions.

Augusta County Schools will value and welcome teachers, parents, and students as partners in education. Teachers will regularly collaborate, plan, consult, and involve parents and students in developing a climate of respect and success for lifelong learning.

In order to achieve this philosophy we must provide a curriculum for Augusta County Schools that reflects the values and expectations of the Augusta County community. We must reaffirm our faith in the worth and dignity of each individual and create in the Augusta County School System a place where students receive a quality education in an environment which promotes individual growth and initiative. In the true spirit of community schools, our employees will work with the family as well as the community to foster intellectual, physical, social, moral, and ethical development consistent with the needs of productive citizens. Our mission then will direct several goals:

1. to sustain a school climate where academic achievement is valued, acknowledged, and advanced by the staff and pursued with vigor by the students;

2. to prepare a well-qualified school staff whose role, central to the education of the children, is recognized and respected, and whose productive service will be acknowledged through continued support, fair compensation, and appreciation;

3. to teach a curriculum of basic studies in the elementary schools with increasing differentiation occurring in the middle and high schools to accommodate diverse personal and vocational interests;

4. to maintain a physical and social environment which is conducive to the learning process;

5. to recognize the differing needs and interests of individual students and to provide appropriate topics of study and instructional activities which will enhance and stimulate each student's growth and development;

6. to ensure that the learning environment is one which gives students ample opportunity to develop critical thinking and problem-solving skills;

7. to create a school climate which promotes strong positive self-concepts and generates interventions to ensure the continued personal growth of each student;

8. to instill in each student those common values necessary for living and working together as responsible citizens in a democratic society; and

9. to foster a broader understanding and appreciation of the school system in the community.

In order to achieve these stated goals the following curriculum objectives will be incorporated into the curriculum:

Learning experiences will not only meet the general needs of the students, but also the specialized needs of individual students such as advanced academic programs, special education, specialized vocational training, and remedial assistance.

A variety of student activities will be devised and be consistent with the purposes and objectives of the schools such as, in addition to current organizations, we will include thespians, newspaper, foreign language and academic clubs, as examples.

Provisions will be made for experimentation with new instructional materials, procedures, and programs such as computer-assisted instruction, resource computer room, distance learning utilization, team teaching, interdisciplinary learning teams, exploratory studies, and independent studies.

There will be a provision of opportunities for students and teachers to participate appropriately in decision-making through student government, curriculum councils, faculty senates, school improvement committees, and effective schools implementation teams.

A balanced and comprehensive program of student services will become available for all students. The schools will strive to meet both the special and exceptional needs of all students.

Our schools will be organized to encourage participation and innovation. They will be designed to improve the educational operation and to help the schools adapt to changing conditions. This process shall allow the principal, staff, students and community to build upon school strengths and to correct or compensate for its weaknesses.

Computer-assisted design programs will be utilized by a committee of staff, students, and community to actually design facilities. This will be completed in cooperation with the school architects in order to provide the basic needs for the new facilities.

An organizational structure, developed by the school staff, will also be designed. This pattern may include innovative organization patterns in site-based management, administrative services design, differentiated staffing, alternative instructional schedules, and academic coordinating teachers.

The utilization of community resources will be expected. This would include mentorships, school-business partnerships, community services credit for students, academic boosters clubs, and community resource teachers.

As a result of an identified curriculum and operations plan, a new instructional learning plan will be available. This will result in quality programs accessible for all students. With totally new facilities, staffing plans, and curriculum organization, the instructional program will be focused on the educational needs of students to successfully compete in a highly technical environment with an emphasis on the essential skills of critical thinking and adaptability. Now let us look at instruction. What should we expect?

Our instructional plan will utilize the following program components:

The high school will have its emphasis on a core curriculum of basic skills. The core curriculum shall consist of those courses required by both state and county policy:

◆ Communications (Reading/English/Speech/Writing)

◆ Thinking and Learning (Critical Thinking/Integrated Studies)

◆ Life Management (Science/Health/Vocational)

◆ Humanities (Arts/Social Sciences/Languages/Literature)

◆ Sciences (Computer Application/Sciences/Mathematics)

Electives will include but not be limited to: Computer Sciences, Computer Programming, Advanced Mathematics, Advanced Sciences, Physical Science, Biological Sciences, Technology Applications, Business Education, Cooperative Education, Drivers Education, Home Economics, Health, Vocational Education, English/Language Arts, Social Sciences, Advanced History, Performing Arts, Fine Arts, Music, Foreign Languages, Speech and Drama.

The total school facility and each instructional area will be wired for utilization by computers and distance learning. Computer labs will be established; one may be utilized for computer applications and a separate lab, manned by a resource teacher, for use by different classes and for individual student work.

The use of these program components and the availability of additional staff will result in advanced honors classes and advanced placement classes. Some of which are: mentorships, independent studies, community services, geometry, trigonometry, calculus, computer math, technical math, biology 2, physiology, physics 1, physics 2, chemistry 1, chemistry 2, special topics, speech and communications, advanced literature, media, conversational foreign language, twentieth century studies, art 3, art 4, advanced techniques in art, commercial art, music appreciation, advanced choir/band, drama, adult roles and functions, special topics in home economics, agribusiness, mechanics, horticulture, and special topics in agriculture.

Additional classes will be available through the utilization of distance learning facilities. As the schools have available distance learning facilities, full utilization of available programming will occur. Please note that I have purposely omitted remarks about athletics but will cover those offerings later in the presentation.

An ambitious vision for curriculum and instruction, maybe, but it is a vision that is within our grasp. All we need to do is reach out and take it, dream it, then make the dream come true for the sake of our children and youth in Augusta County.

Let us now discuss personnel. If we are to reach our dream three years from now, it is necessary to have a highly competent, well-trained and innovative school staff—a staff who is capable of making decisions about teaching and learning, a staff who helps to build our school system not tear it down, a staff that works as a team and is not concerned about what's in it for me.

During the next two years we have to be concerned also with efficiency of services. We cannot continue to operate over formula and survive as a school district. As our plan unfolds and efficiency increases staff will be added back into the system to achieve our ultimate goal of providing for the wide range of needs and interests of all students.

What should we expect three years from now for our professional staff? I believe we must allow staff time for training during the regular work week. Excellent teachers need the extra time the most. We cannot expect people to work longer, we must help them to work smarter and give them time to do it. To provide release time for staff training, we will utilize community people to teach the students such informative lifestyle skills as personal hygiene, career guidance, poultry and timber industry issues, and the sciences, math, literature, music, art, and traditional customs so that they are never lost or forgotten.

The real power of school reform in Augusta County will come from teaming. The major mission of this team will be to ensure the success of students by shared planning, shared placement of students, and shared responsibilities for student discipline. The teams will provide support for our teachers as they put knowledge into practice.

We will begin this effort with a teachers academy beginning in the 1994–95 school year and begin to work regionally with other counties to provide the best staff development opportunities available to our teachers.

Our service staff will complement and serve our system in ways never dreamed of before. They will also be trained, highly skilled and be teachers themselves. All employees will be teachers regardless of their position within the system. Instruction will begin on the busses with taped lessons, stories, and critical thinking problems. Instruction will continue in our kitchens and hallways and classrooms by cooks, custodians, and teacher aides well versed in child development. The school secretary will become highly technical through the use of an integrated computer report and message system that will tie in all schools in our county, the RESA, and State Department of Education.

Our school principals will become managers, skilled in interpersonal relations, group processing, crisis management, and public relations. Staff development for principals will be focused on all levels of management skills.

Our central office staff will be support staff dedicated to serving the needs of schools and teachers. They will continue to deal with administrative functions such as transportation, maintenance, and food service, but focus on servicing and improving our schools and the teaching and learning process.

Ambitious again, you bet! But necessary if we are to provide an exemplary education to our children and youth. I have struggled, since coming to Augusta County, with the problem of not losing staff, and even adding staff in the future, with our existing deficit. The answer was given to me at Newberry High School on October 30th by a gentleman attending the meeting. I'll discuss this solution later in the presentation.

Lastly, in order to live our dream three years from now we need an environment that students, parents, and employees are proud of and an environment geared to teaching and learning. The plan I am proposing now has been developed with much input and discussion and takes into account every concern parents, teachers, and students have in regard to the children. What I am now ready to present is a fair compromise, and the plan essential for school reform in Augusta County.

I propose we begin by changing the basic structure of our school organization. I propose that we have three levels of educational opportunities. Elementary schools housing grade K-5, middle schools housing grades 6-8, and a high school housing grades 9-12.

With this facilities plan no child, grades K-8, will ever have to cross any mountain, and only six percent of our students or approximately 100 students will be transported over a mountain that they have not crossed before. A new transportation communication system, state road priorities, and genuine concern for the health and safety of all of our children should relieve the concerns of parents. I am pleased now to present the last dream in our vision. A dream for facilities that will be unmatched in the state of Virginia. A dream that is a fair compromise for educating our children. Let me begin with our elementary/middle school plans:

❖ DEMONSTRATION/PRESENTATION

Highlights: New Structure (Elementary, Middle, High School)

- ◆ K-8 North Fork Educational Complex
- ◆ Current J.H.S. to be Middle School
- ◆ New Brandywine School
- ◆ New Sanford Elementary/Upper Tract School
- ◆ New single high school outside of Sanford
- ◆ Need to only purchase two sites for schools
- ◆ Move Central Office to Middle School
- ◆ Sell McCoy House and old Central Office to pay for school sites
- ◆ No cost to county for facilities or land
- ◆ More innovative academic programs
- ◆ More athletic opportunities for boys and girls

- Athletic buses
- Evening opportunities for adults
- Health wing at North Fork Middle and new high school for evening and weekend health care for citizens
- Athletic contests to be alternated between Sanford and Newberry so no student needs to travel a long distance each week
- Using existing athletic facilities to save enough money for exemplary academic facilities
- Radio station at the high school
- TV station at the high school
- County school system newsletter done by students at the high school
- Outdoor wood burning heating system saving $10,000 a month
- Only approximately 99 students to cross mountain
- No child grades K-8 will cross mountain

EXHIBIT 2

Description of an Alternative School System

◆ SYSTEM STRUCTURE

The proposed system is divided into four Academies. These parallel the twelve years of schooling we now have, taking roughly three years each, although it is recognized that children will move through the system at different rates.

◆ EVALUATION AND PROMOTION THROUGH THE SYSTEM

Passage from one Academy to the other occurs through Exhibitions, in which students demonstrate to a school and community panel their mastery of different aspects of the curriculum. Report cards are eliminated. Ongoing assessment occurs through: mini-exhibitions, the teacher carefully observing each student at work, and development of portfolios. Teachers have learned how to "test" students' growth without relying on paper examinations. They do this constantly, in order to make adjustments in what they offer that student.

◆ CURRICULUM

The curriculum is based in modern knowledge of how the human brain grows and functions. It is an integrated, thematic curriculum, structured so that teachers are clear about what they are trying to achieve with their students, but open-ended so far as how they get there. It reflects theories of multiple intelligences and personality types. Textbooks are used only as resources, and do not dictate curriculum in any way.

The curriculum has been created by the teachers with the help of experts during the course of the teacher training program. Over a period of several years, teachers have been trained in the skills but also the theories and scientific knowledge on which the system is based. They have become "learning experts"—they work comfortably in a variety of teaching modes, flexibly applying a wide range of skills because they understand the forces at play in human learning and brain development. They work with the children to design learning tasks that are inherently meaningful and that cut across multiple learning styles and subject matter.

◆ LEARNING GROUPS

Students are arranged in multi-age, multi-ability clusters spanning several years of age. Each teacher is Advisor for about twenty students, and may stay with the group for three years. As Advisor, the teacher takes particular responsibility for following the development of that child and for communicating with the family.

Teachers are clustered into teams with a ratio of roughly one teacher to twenty students. The teacher teams work closely together, playing on one another's strengths. (See attached sheet from *Guide to School Change*.) All children in a group work on the same thematic material, though they may do varying activities related to it. The age groupings overlap each other enough to provide options for student placement. For example, one teacher has a K-2 group, another a 2–4 group. (Grade groupings are *not* used to dictate curriculum—the grade groupings simply help dovetail this system with other parts of the larger public school system, such as statewide testing and placing students who transfer in or out.)

◆ TEACHING METHODS

As learning needs dictate, a variety of student-centered teaching methods are used. Teachers have become knowledgeable about brain-based learning theory. They are familiar with the ideas of multiple intelligences, diverse learning and personality styles, and the relationship between a student's experiences and the development of the person's brain. Furthermore, the teachers have been trained in teaching methods compatible with this modern knowledge about the human brain. Training has included working with cooperative classroom groupings, the process approach to skills such as writing, the Foxfire approach, and Paideia seminar facilitation skills. Teachers make extensive use of peer tutoring.

The teachers have expanded their skill at integrating all subjects into a theme and incorporating outside resources into the learning experience. Students' dependency on teachers as the sole conduit of learning is reduced as students learn to draw on other people, the resource rooms, and most of all on the resources available in the community and the natural world around their school. In contrast to a conventional school, there is a great deal of movement in and out of the school building—students going out, visitors coming in, computer modems and telephones in use to gather information.

◆ TEACHER SUPPORTS

Each teacher meets regularly with a professional support group. These groups serve as "mirrors" for their members—providing objective feedback, helping teachers create professional development plans for themselves, and providing for shared information and ideas. They are the heart of the teacher evaluation system. Through the Faculty Senates of the Academies, these support groups create staff development plans that respond to the work-based needs of the teachers.

The Fourth Academy differs from the others in that the entire school is laid out as a resource center. There are no courses or classes as we know them now. The program is still thematic, with students drawing on the different resource centers and teachers for the help they need. In other words, the whole Academy now works the way one classroom worked at a lower level.

◆ SPECIAL SUPPORTING FEATURES OF THE PROGRAM

Health Center which is both a provider of medical services and also a learning resource center akin to the art, science and music labs.

Four-day school week as a means of cutting operating costs; major employers following a daily schedule that accommodates the school day in support of family needs.

Bus system that serves the entire county population rather than just students.

Public library that pointedly accommodates school needs.

A strong entrepreneurial component in the Fourth Academy; throughout the system, a wide variety of linkages between local government and business and the activities of the students. Examples include apprenticeships by students in businesses, students doing research for the Development Authority, grade schoolers "Adopting a Business," etc.

Constant and wide spread use of community members to enrich the exposure of students to adults with local history to share, stories to tell, skills or information to communicate, and insights to offer into the world of adult work.

Student work is displayed everywhere—books, videotapes and audiotapes in the library, projects and art work in store fronts and throughout the school buildings. Students are regular contributors to local and regional newspapers, serve on community committees, and provide community service.

An Advisory Program in which each student is part of an advisory group under teacher guidance. In the higher academies, the Advisory Group replaces Homeroom. It is the primary group identification for students. Advisors track their students' work, offer needed advice, put them in touch with assistance when needed, and report on their work to parents. Advisors stay with the same group of students for several years, getting to know them well so as to be of the greatest assistance to them.

A pre-school program available to all children, and all children in the same program. This is paid for in part by a sliding fee schedule, in part by Head Start monies, in part by Special Education money. (Waivers will probably be required to implement such a program.) This program will be philosophically the same as the rest of the system, accommodating individual styles and abilities without tracking. Older students are frequent helpers/visitors to younger groups.

A variety of options bring community members into the schools. For a fee, adults can sign up on a monthly basis to eat lunch in the cafeteria with the students. They receive color coded meal cards for the days they plan to eat. A room in the school has been set aside as a senior center so senior citizens can hang out at school. Adults in the community are invited to take part in tutorials that would be useful to them. Some tutorials are offered in the evening, providing students with extra flexibility for getting help. Occasionally, non-teacher adults offer tutorials in their area of expertise.

◆ Features of the High School Program

To graduate, every student completes a project in three out of five areas. One of these is a major project, usually consuming much of the final year of school.

Project Areas

1. An autobiographical thesis, *Who Am I?*

   Chapters would include such topics as an examination of personal religious beliefs, a blueprint of the student's dream house, a portrait (written or otherwise) of an important person in the student's life, a family genealogy, and a political analysis of the student's home town, community, or county.

2. Life in the Real World

   Projects could include producing a realistic Business Plan, preparing a solid research paper on potential careers for that student and how the student would prepare for them, achieving journeyman status in a trade. (These may not be exactly equivalent—remember, for some students this would be their major, for others a minor.)

3. Design

Projects might include preparing a one-person art show, designing a unique building, or designing and creating a piece of furniture.

4. Performance

Putting on a recital, directing a play, choreographing and performing a dance.

5. Exploration

Conducting scientific research and presenting the results through multiple media (e.g., a written paper and a slide show), preparing a research paper on a new field of scientific inquiry, setting up a computer system to serve a particular need.

Very important: Projects are presented to a real audience, including non-teachers capable of judging the quality of the performance. Students select their project ideas with the help of their advisors and key teachers; ideas are approved by a teacher panel.

Students still take courses, as well. However, they do not qualify to graduate by accumulating course credits. Courses are of two types; integrated explorations of themes, and tutorials.

◆ INTEGRATED, THEME-BASED COURSES

An example: Change in Augusta County, from prehistoric time until now. This course would examine local geology, find out what evidence we have of prehistoric life here, look at waves of human occupation, consider the different cultures and economies that have existed here, and constantly pursue essential questions about why and how things change. Students would gain insight into the important roles of different disciplines of study, an understanding of what they involve, and would acquire a new perspective on their home.

Another example: How Does Our Town Work? Students would examine all the different systems, human, physical, and natural, that make up the life of a town. How do these systems affect each other? Where, beyond the town, do the systems lead?

Other theme examples: Personal Responsibility in Today's World; The Ideals of the Declaration of Independence Two Centuries Later; News and World Affairs; Good Health.

The thematic courses serve several purposes:

1. They are inherently meaningful;

2. They help students understand what they need to know and why;

3. They challenge students in many ways at once;

4. They tie together knowledge from many sources, as do most of the demands of adult life.

To elaborate this part of the curriculum we will need some expert assistance from the national associations for the teaching of the various fields.

◆ TUTORIALS

Tutorials are more like our traditional courses. They are planned by the upper level teachers in support of the thematic courses. They ensure that everyone is comfortable that the core material of central fields has been mastered. Teaching methods accent coaching, peer tutoring, and small group work and make use of technological aids where possible. Where appropriate, certain topics and issues are dealt with in large lectures, possibly followed by small group discussions, as many courses are managed at the college level.

Naturally, every field has key material that must be covered. However, teaching style in these tutorials emphasizes the process by which a student learns to think like an adult in that field, rather than *focusing* on coverage.

◆ NOTES TO ALTERNATIVE SCHOOL PLAN

This program is fanciful—reaching for the stars. Nonetheless, almost every element in it is being done somewhere today. Knowledgeable assistance is available to help local staff fill in the details.

This is clearly not a fully worked out plan. It is a beginning, based on three principles. First, designing a school system, especially an innovative, modern system, should be a collaborative effort. Experts have their role, bringing in modern knowledge about learning, curriculum, school finance, and teacher training. But experts are not enough. Designing a new school is a team process where teachers, parents, administrators, citizens, and students all bring special knowledge and distinct priorities.

Second, we are morally obligated to provide our children with a flexible, useful, and rigorous education—one that provides them with choices in the future. However, the way we go about that may differ significantly from the way that suits, let us say, a school in Richmond.

Third, designing a new learning program should be based on modern knowledge of how the learning organ—the brain—grows and develops. Modern research clarifies that the brain's natural function is to make sense out of a flood of sensory experience. It literally, physically, grows and diversifies by creating mental order out of chaos. To produce growth and learning, each brain must do this work for itself. Furthermore, each brain is unique, and becomes more so the more it learns. Thus, experiential richness and diversity must be hallmarks of an effective educational environment.

This piece is not directly aimed at solving financial problems currently facing Augusta County. However, the following features could contribute to improving that picture:

1. Regrouping teachers and students, cutting some positions;
2. Serious consideration of the four-day school week;

3. Elimination of certain assumed costs such as textbooks, to be replaced by everyday resources;

4. Teaming up with other service providers, such as a collaboration with the county library on purchasing the books needed for student reading.

It is hoped that outside funding sources will find aspects of this effort sufficiently appealing to support it. The planning process can also be profoundly cost conscious, seeking cuts where possible.

As school consolidation discussions have gone forward, two groups of students are often pointed to—the achievers, whose parents fear they will not get the necessary higher courses required for college, and the non-achievers, who are at risk to drop out of school. Often the discussion seems to pit the needs of these two groups against each other. The kind of program outlined here is likely to meet the needs of the at-risk student much more fully than they can now be met, simply because it is a less linear, more flexible approach. Exactly how the program dovetails with the current vocational program will require some tinkering and thought.

As for the college bound, this program takes seriously the motto of the Coalition of Essential Schools, "less is more," when it comes to course proliferation. Sadly, while college bound students seek course credits, research can't show much linkage between what students have taken and what they actually learn. If you think otherwise, why are colleges wailing about the unprepared students they are receiving from high schools that have been adding courses for years? A much greater need than more courses is a program that guarantees that students are indeed mastering essential thought processes. Students from this program may require help explaining their high school experience to the colleges they wish to attend. But they will be able to demonstrate their ability to use their minds constructively in real life.

◆ HOW TO BEGIN?

We must recognize that this fanciful piece jumps forward an entire generation. What are the stages along the way? Here are guiding comments—far from a total plan.

1. All teachers, as soon as possible, need to receive training in some of the fundamentals employed here, such as working with cooperative learning groups.

2. Teachers must learn the fundamentals of brain-compatible curriculum design and learning theory. This should be done through someone who can work with the group over time, rather than through independent workshops.

3. Representatives from the school community should visit a functioning school program that models brain-compatible approaches.

4. New programs are often phased in from the bottom up, or imposed system-wide. These may not be the best or only choices. It might be better to have several things going on at once—the most interested and prepared teachers

at all levels should be able to start applying what they know. Some teachers can begin to work together to create themes around which to organize their work with students. Teachers who are really nervous about all this may need time to watch, while taking an introductory, related class.

5. One way to start is to create a school within a school. This then becomes a lab for teaching other teachers and parents how it works. It also becomes a place for ironing out some wrinkles.

6. Parents and the general community need to be informed about the principles on which change is based. They need repeated contact, lots of opportunity to ask questions. Some parents should probably be included in teacher training so they can help explain to other parents.

7. The very first step is for a significant group of people within the school community to decide to act together to move in this general direction. It can grow from there.

◆ WHAT CAN BEECH MOUNTAIN OFFER?

Beech Mountain's staff are skilled at gathering information, locating and assessing resources, and writing grant applications. They are also trained in facilitating collaborative meetings. They have a broad background in modern educational issues and current trends in educational thought. They have specific knowledge about a large number of innovative programs around the country. Beech Mountain staff will work for you if you decide to make fundamental change. But the school community must drive the effort. Beech Mountain has one piece of the puzzle. Other people hold other pieces; the teachers and principal hold the most important pieces of all. Nothing significant can be done without support of the community.

Some contrasting characteristics of conventional and restructured classrooms follow:

CONVENTIONAL CLASSROOMS

Based on subjects, broken into teachable increments.

Students divided into age groups.

Curriculum divided into separate subject areas.

Subjects taught sequentially.

Textbooks as curriculum guides.

Main information sources are teacher and textbooks.

Computers as teaching machines or subjects of study.

Evaluation based on tests.

Teacher schedule based on coverage of material.

Students stay in school all day, mainly with teacher.

Outcomes based on subject coverage.

RESTRUCTURED CLASSROOMS

Based on research about how the human brain works and grows best.

Students work in multi-age, multi-ability groups.

Curriculum integrated around themes.

Subject material learned as it arises in thematic context.

Textbooks as resources.

Information comes from a wide range of real life sources.

Computers as learning tools, data processors, information gatherers.

Evaluation based on portfolios, exhibitions, and teacher observation.

Teacher schedule responsive to individual student need.

Students do a lot of work outside school walls, often guided by community resource people.

Outcomes based on students' useful capabilities.

EXHIBIT 3

SUPERINTENDENT OF SCHOOLS
David Myers, Ed.D.
DIRECTOR OF ADMINISTRATIVE PROGRAMS
George Lee
DIRECTOR OF STUDENT PROGRAMS/
CERTIFICATION
M. Jackson Powers

BOARD OF EDUCATION
Alvin Geidt, Ph.D., President
Daniel A. Smith
Frederick T. Watson, D.V.M.
Jerome C. Laing
Terence M. Lewis

P.O. Drawer 888, Sanford, Virginia 12345
Telephone Area Code 703-555-1234
and 555-5678
Fax Number: 703-555-9876

TO: Principals and Others

FROM: David Myers, Ed.D., Superintendent

SUBJECT: Special Board Meeting

DATE: January 21, 1992

A special meeting of the Augusta County Board of Education has been called for the purpose of discussing an alternative educational system for Augusta County by Beech Mountain Institute.

This meeting will be held at Newberry High School on Tuesday, January 21, 1992 at 7:00 p.m. The public is invited to attend this meeting.

AC:djn

ORGANIZATIONAL DESIGN

Educational administrators design and manage the structures and systems that deliver education to children. How these organizations are structured has an important and lasting effect on the quality of education available in the organization. For example, the grouping of students in schools or classrooms, the assignment of teachers to students, and the allocation of time to learning are all administrative decisions that profoundly influence student educational outcomes. Frequently, decisions about organizational design involve an assessment of human, fiscal, and physical capacity of the system and the ability and willingness of the organization to undertake significant change. The following cases offer an opportunity to explore these issues.

❖ DANTE ALIGHIERI HIGH SCHOOL A AND B

A restructuring effort at a large urban public high school with a diverse community results in a redefinition of the five houses within it and the implementation of heterogeneous groupings in all classes (including math and science), team teaching, and cooperative learning. Some teachers, especially in math, resist the idea of heterogeneous groupings and communicate this to students in their classes.

❖ OTTAWA HIGH SCHOOL

Jim Henderson, principal of Ottawa High School, leads his staff in the consideration of revamping the daily schedule of the 1600-student high school. While some teachers think it is a good idea, others, including those in the Performing Arts department, see the changes as a threat to their programs.

❖ WHAT'S YOUR PLAN, MR. SOMMERS?

Monroe, a small town in Massachusetts, is experiencing declining enrollments and dwindling budgets. In response, a regionalization initiative is proposed to merge Monroe with a neighboring district but the proposal loses in a public vote. Mr Sommers, an experienced superintendent in a larger and more affluent district, is applying for the Monroe superintendency. As part of the interview process, he must present a five-year strategic plan.

Suggested Readings

Anyon, J. (1981). Social class and school knowledge. *Curriculum Inquiry, 11,* 3–42.

Cohen, E. (1988). *Designing groupwork.* New York: Teachers College Press.

Elmore, R. (1990). Introduction: On changing the structure of public schools. In R. Elmore (ed.), *Restructuring schools: The next generation of educational reform* (pp. 1–28). San Francisco: Jossey-Bass.

Kane, C. (1994). *Prisoners of time research.* Washington, DC: National Education Commission on Time and Learning.

Oakes, J. (1986). Keeping track, part 1: The policy and practice of curriculum inequality. *Phi Delta Kappan, 68,* 12–17.

Oakes, J. (1986). Keeping track, part 2: Curriculum inequality and school reform. *Phi Delta Kappan, 68,* 148–154.

◆ ◆ ◆
Dante Alighieri High School (A)

Edward Miller

Felecia Jackson, a bright African-American ninth grader at Dante Alighieri High School in the city of Bridgeharbor, was good at math. Math was Felecia's favorite subject. She was in an honors level Algebra I class, taught by Preston Lowell. Math and Music Theory were the high points of Felecia's school day.

Today Mr. Lowell seemed to be in an especially good mood. He was passing back the tests they had taken two days before.

"Ladies and gentlemen," he intoned, "I must congratulate you on your performance on the last test. The average grade of this group was 86. Very impressive."

Felecia reached for her paper as Mr. Lowell passed her desk and held it out to her. Her grade was a 92. "Yes!" she said, making a fist. "Mr. Lowell?" Felecia waved her hand at him. "Are we going to make it all the way through the book by the end of the year?"

"I have no doubt about it," he said. "We're considerably ahead of schedule. We'll be starting Chapter 15 tomorrow."

"The Algebra Project class is only on Chapter 6," said Felecia.

"Yes, I know that," said Mr. Lowell. "And to be perfectly frank with you, I'm not at all surprised. Putting students with different ability levels in the same math class just doesn't work. I told them that. I've been teaching Algebra for seventeen years, and I've had every kind of class—good and bad. Heterogeneous classes just penalize the smart students. Aren't you glad you're in a group like this one?"

Most of the students, including Felecia, looked around at each other and nodded happily.

❖ THE SCHOOLS WITHIN A SCHOOL

The Bridgeharbor Public Schools were committed to a system of "controlled choice" in which students and their families, in the spring of the eighth-grade year, expressed their preferences among five "schools within a school" at Dante Alighieri, the only public high school in the city. The five choices included three larger mainstream programs—Achiever House, Bulldog House,

---

and Success House (formerly named House A, House B, and House C, respectively)—and two smaller, alternative programs called Summit Academy and the Blackstone School of Technical Arts (see Exhibit 1 on page 157).

❖ FELECIA JACKSON

Felecia Jackson liked Preston Lowell, her Algebra teacher, and she enjoyed her small Music Theory and Harmony class. She had been playing the piano and synthesizer since she was five years old and liked to write music. But in other ways Felecia's first year at Dante Alighieri had not been a happy one.

Felecia had gone to one of the better K-8 schools in the city and done well academically, although her teachers had noted some behavior problems. "Felecia is extremely bright," her eighth-grade language arts teacher had written in a team guidance report, "but her enthusiasm sometimes causes her to use bad judgment. At times she talks out in class without thinking. She is very competitive, and excels when we have games and contests as part of the lesson, but she can also be impatient and even hurtful in her comments to other students. She has a tendency to scapegoat others when things go wrong in cooperative or team situations. With improvement in her social skills, Felecia will be an outstanding student."

Felecia and her mother, a software sales executive, had had their hearts set on Summit Academy, the most prestigious and sought after of the five schools within a school at Dante Alighieri. Its reputation was tops: the best teachers and the best record of college admissions. Their second choice had been Achiever House. Almost twice as large as Summit Academy, it was said to be more impersonal and less stimulating, but still had a strong reputation for academics and success in college admissions. Achiever House was the second most popular of the five houses. The Jacksons' unenthusiastic third choice had been Bulldog House, with its reputation for tough discipline, team spirit, and a no-nonsense administration and staff. It was popular with some athletes and cheerleaders and with certain parents who believed that the other programs were too "permissive."

Much to the Jacksons' dismay, Felecia had been assigned to Success House even though it had not been among their top three choices. Success House was the newest and least popular program at the high school.

The school administration advertised it as a "priority" that all incoming students be assigned to their first or second choice program at the high school. It was an "equal priority," according to the school, to balance the programs' populations by race and academic ability. At the same time, the administration maintained that the different programs provided equal opportunities for all students. There were, however, glaring disparities in the public perception, and therefore in the popularity, of the five programs.

The wildly popular Summit Academy had been the first choice of 253 of Felecia Jackson's 500 classmates but had space for only about 60 of them. Those 60 were chosen by lottery, with an effort to balance the group demographically. The ones not chosen were eventually distributed among the other programs (see Exhibit 2 on page 160).

Achiever House, with spaces for 120 incoming ninth graders, had been the first choice of 131. Again, the lottery system determined the winners, so that almost none of the students who were closed out of Summit were assigned to Achiever House.

Only 44 of the incoming ninth graders had named Bulldog House as their first choice, but it was the second choice of more than 100 students. There were 125 places for freshmen in this house. Because of the priority on giving students their first or second choice, those who named Bulldog House as third choice were unlikely to get it.

The Blackstone School, the vocational-technical program at Dante Alighieri, had been the top choice of 47 ninth graders, with space for 75.

That left Success House as the first choice of only 25 of the 500 incoming ninth grade students, and the second choice of another 39. With spaces for 135, Success House ended up taking in a fairly large number of students who didn't want to be there at all—Felecia Jackson among them.

❖ HOUSE C BECOMES SUCCESS HOUSE

The administrator of Success House was Carlos Arriaga, a cultured and dignified Cuban-born educator who had been trained as a clinical psychologist and worked as a guidance counselor before becoming the head of House C—Success House's previous incarnation—ten years ago. Carlos spoke French, Italian, and Portuguese as well as English and Spanish, which came in very handy in dealing with the high school's ESL students, most of whom were assigned to his house. Carlos believed the presence of an increasing number of black Haitian immigrants in Bridgeharbor was part of House C's image problem. "It's simple prejudice, that's all," he told his friends on the faculty. "Almost all of the Haitian kids are assigned to our house. And I've overheard kids in the halls referring to House C as 'The Island.'"

In the public's perception of Dante Alighieri's house system, Summit Academy and Achiever House were predominantly white and Asian, while Success House and the Blackstone School were predominantly black. (See Figure 1 for actual enrollment figures.)

The growing perception of House C as the "reject house" was creating a serious problem for the school administration. As a result, the superintendent and principal had put increasing pressure on Carlos to make his program more competitive.

	Summit Academy A	Achiever (House A)	Bulldog (House B)	Success (House C)	Blackstone School of T.A.	School Total
White	132 (53.0%)	263 (55.3%)	262 (52.3%)	236 (49.7%)	151 (50.3%)	1044 (52.20%)
Black	87 (34.9%)	144 (30.3%)	169 (33.7%)	171 (36.0%)	103 (34.3%)	674 (33.7%)
Hispanic White	13 (5.2%)	36 (7.6%)	37 (7.4%)	34 (7.2%)	26 (8.7%)	146 (7.3%)
Asian	13 (5.2%)	28 (5.9%)	22 (4.4%)	23 (4.8%)	9 (3.0%)	95 (4.7%)
Hispanic Black	3 (1.2%)	5 (1.1%)	10 (2.0%)	9 (1.9%)	10 (3.3%)	37 (1.8%)
Native American	1 (0.4%)	0 (0.0%)	1 (0.2%)	2 (0.4%)	1 (0.3%)	5 (0.02%)
Total	249	476	501	475	300	2001

FIGURE 1

Various ideas for redefining the house structure of the school were circulated. The school board favored a plan in which the three larger houses would have been given new identities along curricular lines: there would be a math and science house, a humanities house, and a performing arts house. But the faculty had rejected this idea as likely to exacerbate racial divisions; whites and Asians were already heavily overrepresented in upper-level math and science courses.

Carlos was deeply committed to the principle of equal access to educational opportunity and to the goal of lessening the racial inequities that had been revealed by a four year old survey of enrollment patterns in upper-level courses at the high school (see Exhibit 3 on page 161). He had read much of the research on tracking and believed that it was largely responsible for the low level of achievement of minority students. And he was determined to do something about it.

A year before Felecia's arrival at Dante Alighieri, Carlos began working with a core group of like-minded teachers. Together they hammered out a proposal for a new vision of House C at Dante Alighieri—a program where every student would be encouraged to reach his or her full potential, where heterogeneous classes, team teaching, cooperative learning, and mutual caring and encouragement would empower every student to succeed. They would call it Success House.

Part of the plan was a core curriculum for all ninth and tenth grade students in the house, with heterogeneous classes in language arts and social studies. The teachers in those departments were eager to go along with his plan. Carlos thought the math and science classes should be untracked as well, but he knew there would be resistance from the teachers. So he agreed to the math and science departments' insistence on ability grouping for Success House ninth and tenth grade core classes in those subjects. Still, he felt very strongly that every student should be expected to learn algebra as a matter of basic mathematical literacy. He disapproved of the math department's willingness to let students graduate from D.A.H.S. with just two years of math for "dummies"—the lowest track general math and pre-algebra courses.

As a result, Carlos persuaded a young math teacher, Ms. Bregenza, to take on what he called the Algebra Project: a two-year course designed to get even the least skilled incoming ninth graders through Algebra I by the end of tenth grade. Students entering Success House wouldn't be allowed to choose general math or pre-algebra. "Higher achievement for the students starts with higher expectations by the teachers," said Carlos.

Carlos' plan was accepted by the superintendent and the school board and House C officially became Success House the September Felecia entered ninth grade. At the same time, House A was renamed Achiever House and House B became Bulldog House. (The school's athletic teams were nicknamed "The Bulldogs.")

Most of the math teachers were skeptical about the Algebra Project. "What does he know about teaching math?" they said of Carlos in the department workroom. Some, who had been assigned to bridge two houses against their will and teach core classes, worried that they would end up having to teach untracked classes, or teach "algebra" to students who simply didn't have the background or the arithmetic skills to learn it. Preston Lowell was among this group.

Carlos had insisted that even the upper-level Algebra I and Geometry classes offered as part of Success House's core curriculum not be designated as "honors" sections. Unfortunately, although Carlos got to write the description of his core curriculum for the school course catalogue, he didn't have any control over the scheduling process. That was the department heads' job, together with the assistant principal for management. When the students' schedules arrived in September, Carlos found that only some of his requests had been granted. All of his Success House ninth graders were assigned to heterogeneous core classes in language arts and social studies, but the math and science program was a mess. Nearly half of the ninth graders were assigned to math or science sections in other houses because of schedule conflicts.

Felecia Jackson, for example, was in an Algebra I Honors class in Achiever House because there was apparently no way the computer could schedule her into Music Theory and Harmony and also put her in a Success House math section. Carlos couldn't prove it, but he strongly suspected that the math scheduling hadn't worked because the department head hadn't wanted it to work.

❖ FELECIA REACTS

After Mr. Lowell's math class, Felecia went to Language Arts, taught by Paula Petrie. For the first half of the class period students were to work in groups of three, discussing and preparing a written analysis of the book they had just finished reading, *Black Like Me*. Ms. Petrie had put Felecia together with Adelle Onoba, a quiet Haitian girl who had been in the United States for just one year, and Joe Blocker, a motivated but struggling white boy who was having a hard time focusing on his schoolwork because his father was dying of cancer. Adelle was probably the hardest-working student in the class; her mother had called Ms. Petrie to tell her Adelle got up at four every morning to prepare for school. Adelle's mother begged Ms. Petrie for advice on how to persuade Adelle that she needed more sleep. Adelle's English was still not good enough for her to do well in writing, in spite of her intense effort.

Ms. Petrie moved around the room, stopping to listen to the discussion in each group and coach her students. When she got to Felecia's group she found Adelle and Joe were writing silently on their own, while Felecia sat scowling with her arms folded.

"What's happening here?" asked the teacher. "Why aren't you working on this assignment together?"

No one said anything.

"Well?" she persisted. "Felecia?"

"I can't work with these two dummies!" Felecia exploded. "I shouldn't have to! This one," she pointed to Adelle, "can't even speak English, and the other one's in Algebra Project. They're not on my level. How can I do decent work when I have to work with stupid people!"

"Felecia," said Ms. Petrie, struggling to control her anger, "you will apologize to Adelle and Joe immediately. They are not stupid."

"They *are* stupid! And *you're* racist! You put me with these two dumbbells because you think I must be as stupid as they are! Go ahead—call my mother! I don't care! She said she's going to get me out of stupid Success House anyway because it doesn't work! Success House is a joke!"

Felecia picked up her books and stormed from the room. The only sound was Adelle's quiet sobbing.

❖ CASE PREPARATION QUESTIONS

1. What problem was the house system at Dante Alighieri High School intended to solve? Did it?

2. Dante Alighieri High School illustrates a mismatch between perceptions and realities. How would you resolve this situation if you were an administrator at the school?

3. Carlos Arriaga, a middle manager, appears to have more responsibility than authority. How might he change this?

4. What influence does organizational structure have on teaching and learning?

EXHIBIT 1

Welcome to Dante Alighieri High School!

Dante Alighieri, the only public high school in Bridgeharbor, a city of about 95,000, serves approximately 2000 students from 29 nations of origin. Its diversity of race, culture, academic ability, and socio-economic class is prized by this high school renowned for its achievements in academics, fine and dramatic arts, and athletics.

Over the years, D.A.H.S. has developed a tradition of establishing programs of choice which (1) create smaller communities within the larger school, and (2) attempt to cater to the individual needs of our students. There are five such programs to which ninth graders can belong:

Summit Academy: Located on the fourth floor, Summit Academy is the oldest alternative high school program within D.A.H.S. The 250 Summit students (grades 9–12) have been selected randomly from an applicant pool to insure a representative cross-section of the student body with respect to racial/ethnic background, gender, and geographic district.

Unique features of the Academy are: heterogeneity of classes; close student-teacher relationships; shared decision-making; and leadership and communication.

Summit Academy graduated its first class in June 1973; its graduates are consistently placed in many of the top institutions of higher learning in the country.

Achiever House (formerly House A): Located on the third floor of the D.A.H.S. building, Achiever House oversees the academic growth of 475 students. The House is characterized by a focus on the specific individualized needs and concerns of each student. The program recognizes the rich diversity of the City of Bridgeharbor and of the student body.

To achieve these goals, commitment to the following concepts and services is emphasized:

◆ The constant pursuit of academic excellence

◆ The concern for educational quality and equity

◆ Strong parental involvement and support aimed at the development and reinforcement of a positive environment and community among Achiever House students, parents, and staff

◆ Active and ongoing student support teams/groups to offer continuous assistance and counseling to all students in need

◆ A Core Curriculum for 9th and 10th grade students (English, Math, Social Studies, and Science)

Study Skills instruction for all Achiever House students to increase their proficiency in the areas of critical thinking, reading, and content-oriented study skills.

As ninth graders Achiever House students choose basic, intermediate, or advanced-paced versions of the core curriculum.

Bulldog House (formerly House B): Bulldog House, with approximately 500 students, is located on the second floor of the D.A.H.S. building. The program stresses academic challenge and student accountability in an atmosphere of group spirit, dedication to the goal, and respect for self and others. We enlist parental involvement and support in reinforcing the discipline code. Bulldog House emphasizes the basics of education in a setting that focuses on the disciplines of learning and the development of high standards of achievement, manner, and dress. Students take the courses prescribed in the fundamental Bulldog House core curriculum, which provides a solid foundation in grammar and literature, mathematics, history, science, foreign language, and study skills.

Success House (formerly House C): Success House is a new and exciting response to the needs and aspirations of students, parents, and faculty. Located on the first floor of the D.A.H.S. building, it serves 475 students and is guided by the following statement of its mission:

> Success House is committed to providing a quality education to ALL students by continually raising their academic, social, and personal skills to their optimum level through the efforts of the student, home, school, and community; where ALL are empowered to create a "community" dedicated to the education of the whole student, the establishment of a democratic decision-making process, the participation in community service, and the recognition and appreciation of individual differences.

All students in this house are being prepared for college. If students choose not to attend college they will be well-prepared for the workforce. Students in grades 9 and 10 take the core curriculum in teams within the house. The math and science courses are leveled; English and social studies courses, in grades 9 and 10, are unleveled.

Fundamental to the Success House philosophy are these specialties: cooperative learning; team teaching; democratic decision-making; diversity and cross-cultural education; and a strong sense of community.

Blackstone School of Technical Arts: Established in 1888, the Blackstone School is the second oldest vocational program in the United States. In our program, students learn to use both their hands and their minds well. As a result, they develop an understanding of technology and its role in our economic and social history.

Our learning environment values physical and artistic expression: students show their learning through products and actions in addition to written work. They gain skills for immediate employment and build a strong foundation for further education and future careers.

Students major or take an elective in one of the following shops, each of which is part of an industry-wide cluster: computers, electronics, graphic arts, culinary/baking, teaching careers, health careers, automotive/autobody, carpentry, contracting, drafting, electrical, metal work, and environmental technology/landscaping.

The Blackstone School of Technical Arts serves 300 students and is located in the basement level of the D.A.H.S. building.

It is a priority at D.A.H.S. to have all students enrolled in programs they have selected as their first or second choices. It is an equal priority to have the population of each program, to the extent possible, represent the demographics, aspirations, and ability levels of the student body as a whole. Programs of choice may differ in theme, emphasis, and management. However, they provide equal opportunities for students.

In conclusion, for ninth graders, the Schools-Within-A-School model creates the advantages of a home base, the opportunity for close monitoring of student progress, and a stronger, more personal relationship between families and the school. At the same time, it provides student access to the widespread resources of a large, comprehensive high school.

EXHIBIT 2

Dante Alighieri High School

Ninth Grade Placement Process

The number of openings in each house/program will be determined by the high school administration. If any house or program has a number of applications greater than the number of openings, then a lottery will be conducted with the house or programs that are oversubscribed. This primary lottery is only done with students who have selected first choices and an applicant may only be in one primary lottery.

This primary lottery seeks to place students according to three criteria: geographic district, gender, and the ethnic/racial code. The final distribution pattern should closely represent the existing eighth grade pattern with respect to the three criteria.

Once the students are placed in these houses, applications of those students who have not been placed are redistributed to their next viable choice (i.e., one that has not already filled its openings).

At this point if a house or program with its first and next viable choice combined is greater than the number of openings a secondary lottery is conducted to assume a reasonable distribution of those remaining, according to geographic district, gender, and ethnic/racial code.

This process continues until all students have been placed into a house or program.

During the entire process, we also keep an eye on several other balancing concerns: elementary school, ability levels (as indicated by course request data), and students receiving special education services.

No student is guaranteed his/her first choice, except students who apply to the Blackstone School of Technical Arts.

EXHIBIT 3

Summary and Statistical Abstract of an Enrollment Study of Minority Academic Achievement at Dante Alighieri High School

The Concerned Black Staff of Dante Alighieri High School recently met to discuss the low numbers of black students who received awards for academic achievement in various subjects. During that meeting, preliminary results were presented indicating the underrepresentation of black students in certain upper-level and honors classes. In addition, much discussion centered on the small numbers of blacks being inducted into the D.A.H.S. National Honor Society and the quality of guidance services provided to black students.

As a result of this discussion, an enrollment study examining the academic achievement of black students was conducted.

The results of the study suggest that at the highest levels of academic achievement at Dante Alighieri High School there currently exists two separate populations of students. One population, composed primarily of white and Asian students, progresses into upper-level courses in high percentages. The second population, composed primarily of black and Hispanic students, does not progress in equitable percentages into upper-level courses and is grossly underrepresented in such courses.

TABLE 1

ETHNIC GROUPS AT D.A.H.S. (GRADES 9–12)

	Number of Students	Percent
White	1337	52.5%
Black	872	34.2%
Hispanic White	180	7.1%
Asian	117	4.6%
Hispanic Black	39	1.5%
Native American	4	0.2%
Total	2549	100%

TABLE 2

ENROLLMENT IN UPPER-LEVEL MATH COURSES

	Number of Students	Percent of Total Enrolled	Percent of Ethnic Group
White	153	63.8%	11.4%
Black	32	13.3%	3.7%
Hispanic White	2	1.9%	1.1%
Asian	53	22.1%	45.3%
Hispanic Black	0	0%	0%
Total	240	100%	9.4%*

*Percentage of all students taking upper-level math

TABLE 3

ENROLLMENT IN UPPER-LEVEL SCIENCE COURSES

	Number of Students	Percent of Total Enrolled	Percent of Ethnic Group
White	254	68.6%	19.0%
Black	65	17.6%	7.5%
Hispanic White	5	1.4%	2.8%
Asian	46	12.4%	39.3%
Hispanic Black	0	0%	0%
Total	370	100%	14.5%*

*Percentage of all students taking upper-level science

TABLE 4

ENROLLMENT IN UPPER-LEVEL ENGLISH COURSES

	Number of Students	Percent of Total Enrolled	Percent of Ethnic Group
White	220	68.8%	16.5%
Black	73	22.8%	8.4%
Hispanic White	4	1.3%	2.2%
Asian	21	6.6%	18.0%
Hispanic Black	2	0.6%	5.1%
Total	320	100%	12.6%*

*Percentage of all students taking upper-level English

TABLE 5

NUMBER OF JUNIORS INDUCTED INTO NATIONAL HONOR SOCIETY, BY HOUSE

	Summit	House A	House B	House C	Blackstone	Total
White	15	9	6	4	0	34
Black	3	0	0	0	0	3
Hispanic White	0	0	0	0	0	0
Asian	1	3	2	0	0	6
Hispanic Black	0	0	0	0	0	0
Total	19	12	8	4	0	43

◆ ◆ ◆

Dante Alighieri High School (B)

Edward Miller

Paula Petrie, the young language arts teacher, immediately called a meeting for early the next morning with Felecia Jackson and her mother, Marcia. She wanted to discuss Felecia's outburst in class against Adelle and Joe. Paula was deeply upset by the incident. She was one of the core group of teachers who, working with Carlos Arriaga, had developed the philosophy and plan for Success House, and she was committed to making heterogeneous classes work for all of her students. It particularly disturbed her that Felecia thought there was a racist motive in Paula's assigning her to work with Adelle and Joe. Paula believed that detracking classes was essential to raising the level of minority students' achievement.

When Felecia and Marcia Jackson arrived, Paula invited them to sit down and went straight to the issue at hand. She said, "Felecia, what you said in class yesterday about Adelle Onoba and Joe Blocker made me feel bad—and I'm sure made them feel terrible, too. Adelle may not be able to speak and write in English as well as you can, but she's certainly not stupid. And neither is Joe."

Felecia stared at her shoes and made no reply.

"Ms. Petrie," said Mrs. Jackson, "that was wrong of Felecia to say those things in front of the other kids and hurt their feelings. She has promised to apologize to them. But I feel that Felecia has been hurt as well, by being assigned to such a low level English class. She is an extremely bright student, and she simply is not being challenged in English. I think the real problem is she's bored."

"Mrs. Jackson," said Paula, "one of the most important things we're trying to do in Success House is to get away from the practice of labeling students and classes as 'high' or 'low' ability. There's a very large body of research showing that this hurts children, defining them as winners and losers in the education system, and keeping them from fulfilling their potential as learners."

"I sympathize with your motives," Mrs. Jackson replied, "but experience shows that mixing ability levels in the same classroom just isn't fair. It's fine for the slow learners, I'm sure, because they're under pressure to keep up. But it just holds the quicker ones back. Students like Felecia learn better when they're in a class with others of similar ability."

"It doesn't have to work that way, Mrs. Jackson. I have another class this year just like Felecia's, with just as wide a range of students, and I feel that it

---

works beautifully. Everyone is learning because everyone is working together. Yes, the less advanced students benefit by exposure to the more advanced ones, but it works the other way, too. I feel that it's important for Felecia to learn not just literature and poetry and math but also how to value and respect others who may not be as mentally agile or have the same background as she but who nevertheless have a great deal to offer as human beings."

"I admire your values, Ms. Petrie, but I must question your methods. For the sake of your social values, you are willing to sacrifice my daughter's education. The fact is, she is learning three times as much in her honors math class this year than she is in her mixed-ability English and social studies classes put together. I've talked to Mr. Burnside, the head of the math department, and he agrees that this idea of detracking won't work. He said to me, 'Mixed ability grouping is fine in elementary and middle school, but somewhere you have to draw the line. After all, they don't *all* go on to medical school.'" Mrs. Jackson paused to collect her thoughts and then continued, "I'm just talking about common sense, Ms. Petrie. And there are quite a few other parents in Success House who feel as I do. We are prepared to insist that our children be transferred to other programs unless you place them in honors-level classes next year, and we're writing a letter to Mr. Arriaga telling him just that."

Ottawa High School

Michelle Bauerly under the supervision of John Mauriel, Bush Educators Program

The sturdy pillars of Ottawa High School (OHS) were symbolic of the tradition and stability in the Ottawa community. A small town, in a northern midwestern state, Ottawa had a population of 19,740 residents. It sheltered 755 farms and more than 500 retail, wholesale and professional firms. Industry played a significant role in the support of education in Ottawa. *Jameson's Feed*, for example, provided musical instruments, marketing, and consulting to OHS' accredited performing arts programs. The community took pride in the school's outstanding performing arts programs as well as the school's commitment to academic excellence.

Special programs at Ottawa High School included a strong choral, orchestra, and band program, the International Baccalaureate Diploma program, an advanced placement program (IB), the Arts Magnet School, and a tech prep and youth apprenticeship program called T.O.P. Team. The T.O.P. Team (Together Ottawa Prospers) was a school-to-work program that combined "school-based and work-based learning to create a smooth transition from school to work" through partnerships with industry. Juniors and seniors admitted to the program followed a specific set of courses.

The current student population of 1,375 was expected to increase to 1,450 in the next year, with an annual growth rate of nearly 1.8% expected for the next four years. Projected enrollment for the year 2000 was 1,750. Currently, 46.8% of OHS graduates attended a four-year college, 11% attended a two-year college, and 16% attended a technical college. On the PSAT, juniors averaged 54.9 (78th percentile) in math and 44.9 (65th percentile) in the verbal test. The annual drop-out rate was approximately 1.9% for the past three years (see Exhibit 1 on page 174 for graduation statistics).

Two years earlier, the school building had undergone extensive remodeling that provided new music facilities, a career counseling resource area, and a student commons area.

❖ THE WINDS OF CHANGE

For as long as anyone could remember, OHS offered a 6-period day with an early bird period in the morning (see Figure 1 on page 176). The early bird was an optional forty-five minute period before the regular school day. Many of the students who used the early bird option were in the International Baccalaureate program, and wanted to fit in performing arts classes along with their IB classes. Because of the excellence and tradition of the programs in the arts, many students chose to take two performing arts courses, which caused particular difficulty in fitting other elective courses into the regular 6-period schedule. (Course enrollment trends are shown in Exhibit 2 on page 177.)

Three years ago, however, during a time of discussion about changing to an eight period day, Alden Torsen, the industrial arts teacher, commented that perhaps OHS ought to look at "going the other way," meaning four periods a day. It made sense to Torsen—class periods would last longer, giving teachers more time to teach; teachers would teach the same number of hours, and students would have more choice. Torsen wrote down his ideas and talked with the principal, Dr. Sidney Kraus, a thirty year veteran of Ottawa schools. Dr. Kraus, however, was an avid believer in a seven period day and the idea was not given much consideration.

Torsen let the idea sit for a while, but continued to talk with other faculty about his beliefs. He also persisted in his research and even visited several schools during his school vacations.

❖ JOHN HENNING AND HIS VISION

Prior to John Henning's move to Ottawa, he was assistant principal in a suburban school in Illinois. In one of his interviews with the Ottawa School Board, John articulated a vision for OHS. He vowed to work to create:

◆ a "family-like atmosphere"
◆ a school focused on students' needs
◆ teachers who think interdisciplinary rather than departmentally
◆ real evidence of people collaborating to develop a direction for the school
◆ greater staff, student, and community involvement
◆ an environment in which people perceive that others genuinely are interested in their well being and want them to succeed

John Henning was hired and began his tenure at OHS in September, 1991. One of the first initiatives the principal wanted to bring to OHS was a more responsive schedule. During the fall of his first year at Ottawa, John researched and discussed the idea of this structural change with various staff, including Torsen. Torsen was very supportive and told Henning what he knew about a 4-

period schedule. Henning liked what he heard. The teacher and principal spent many hours discussing the advantages of implementing such a change.

Henning even offered these ideas in a written report that he prepared as part of a professional development program at a local college. In his essay entitled "Creating an Efficient Curriculum Delivery System," John wrote: "Meaningful change in secondary education involves consideration in the following zones:

1. Curriculum content (including the desired outcomes)
2. Appropriate teaching methodology
3. Suitability of the curriculum delivery system (the schedule)"

Later in the same report he stated: "A change in the delivery system that improves student access to the menu and permits our staff to deal with a smaller and more manageable number of students each day is very important to children's learning. Working on the delivery systems piece at this time might lead to the most significant simultaneous advancement of these three essential areas. To this end, Ottawa High School is considering a four period block schedule, but we will be open to adjustments and other variations."

❖ HENNING'S SCHEDULE

John Henning promoted a schedule that consisted of a 4-period day. Periods lasted ninety minutes. Courses lasted ninety school days (one semester). To Henning's mind, such a schedule had a number of advantages. Students would have more time to dedicate to mastering a subject in depth and would have fewer learning and behavior expectations to know. Teachers would have fewer classes and fewer students at any given time, permitting them to attend to individual learning needs and plan more effective lessons. Inherent in such a schedule would be the ability to offer an eight-course, in-depth sequence of study rather than the traditional four courses offered over two semesters (see Figure 2 on page 184).

Henning kept copies of this schedule always within easy reach:

TABLE 1

Daily Schedule	
First Bell	8:05
First Block	8:15 to 9:45
Second Block	9:55 to 11:25
Lunch	11:30 to 12:15
Third Block	12:20 to 1:50
Fourth Block	2:00 to 3:30
Student Dismissal	3:30

❖ INVOLVING THE FACULTY

Henning knew that a change in the schedule went far beyond the clock. It really was a vehicle for changes in the curriculum, teaching methodology, and assessments. John used an analogy to convey his point: "You can't rearrange the chairs on a ship and hope that it goes in a different direction."

Henning worked hard to plant seeds around the schedule change issue. He provided opportunities during staff meetings for teachers to discuss journal articles on the four period structure. He also encouraged staff members to visit other schools operating under such a system. His attention to staff input gained John Henning faculty respect. Several teachers commented that he was "never dictatorial" and generally very supportive. Many, it seemed, were beginning to embrace John's view of the new schedule. Veteran history teacher, Hank Simmons said, "I have confidence that John will get the job done."

In reflecting on the process, Henning observed that "change isn't easy . . . it's a continuous process, it's not just something you do once." He said that to lead change effectively, "You can't use a hammer. You have to get everyone to work together."

❖ CURRICULUM DELIVERY SYSTEMS COMMITTEE

John Henning created the Curriculum Delivery Systems Committee (CDS) in the summer of 1992. One of its functions was the formal consideration of changes in the schedule. The committee was made up of 2 parents, 2 students, 2 board members, 6 teachers, and 2 administrators. Alden Torsen was a teacher member of the committee. Torsen said that the committee appointment was the first time he "felt hope" that a real change could actually happen. He believed a change in the structure would "have a positive effect on what we're working toward: the education benefits far outweigh the immediate inconveniences."

The group actively asked questions, made visits to other schools, and evaluated strengths and weaknesses of various forms of block scheduling. The intensity of the effort varied over the next year. Over time, some of the teacher committee members thought the schedule change issue was a "frustrating topic," because it "was being talked to death."

However, in July, 1993, one year after it was formed, the committee informally established the following time-line for implementation of the 4-period block schedule:

◆ July/August, 1993—inform and ask for support of new superintendent

◆ 1993–94 School Year—educate the community and gain staff acceptance

◆ October/November, 1993—present a proposal to the school board

◆ January, 1994—students register for the 1994–95 school year with new system

◆ Summer, 1994—faculty involved in extensive in-service/staff development

◆ Fall, 1994—implement the structural change

◆ Future—modify as necessary

One member of the committee, Alice Jensen, an English teacher, said at the end of the summer meeting, "We may not have examined everything thoroughly enough, but something needs to be done . . . Let's get at it! Sometimes you just know when it is right." Yet, not everyone on the committee was as comfortable as Jensen. Some committee members—particularly parents and board members—were concerned about the uncertainty of the cost of the change and felt that there was still a great deal to iron out.

❖ FOCUS GROUPS

Throughout the process, Henning was committed to supporting the work of the CDS Committee and fostering effective communication. To these ends, Henning organized focus group interviews and staff meetings to cultivate support for the 4-period schedule. The focus groups were made up of 5–6 teachers and students of the OHS community and were led by a member of the Curriculum Delivery System Committee. Each group was asked to meet three times to discuss constituent points of view on the proposed change. The following is a summary of the comments that were presented during the interviews.

❖ OHS STAFF RESPONSE

OHS had a stable and mature "veteran faculty." Teachers considered themselves highly qualified and innovative but the larger Ottawa community thought the high school teachers were particularly conservative in their teaching approach. Alden Torsen announced more than once that the past several years at the high school had been a period of "stagnation." Recently, however, OHS saw a turnover of 1/3 of its faculty, due largely to retirements. In fact, thirteen "new" staff members were added in the fall of 1993. They became a part of a faculty of 80 full-time certified staff, of whom 19 were women.

The CDS Committee formally distributed information about a four-period schedule to OHS faculty in the summer of 1993. (See Exhibit 3 on page 185.) By the time the 1993 school year began, veteran teachers were divided into various stages of acceptance: those adamantly against any possible change, those happy with the status quo, and those enthusiastic about the idea. History Department Chair John Hansen said, "People are conducive to change here. In fact, this is a staff that wants to educate children and wants to do it better. If people feel the schedule change will help kids learn, even if they don't like it, they'll do it."

TABLE 2

CDS FOCUS GROUP DATA

Benefits	Concerns
good for lab classes	absenteeism
allow variety of activities	less time (30%)
allow for depth discussion	top down decision
more guided study	course sequence-retention
departmental flexibility	too much too fast/we're pushing it
more hands-on activity	loss of teacher cooperation
advanced students may gain	stability of block classes
increase course offerings	channel one: announcements when?
increase graduation requirements	music
more community-based training	lower ability students fall behind
smaller classes	public reaction to teachers teaching less
team teaching	teacher training
change is good	do we have enough dollars??
tie between OBE & 4-period day	number of preps
"drip vs. splash"	staffing–student ratio–loss of jobs

Suggestions	
need curriculum writing time	"skinnies" (shorter) for low ability kids
more teachers trained for IB	do not rush
last two years of an IB course should be back to back	guarantee smaller classes
bring in teachers from schools currently using it	construct reinforcement for staff/students
visit more school sites	need to mandate interdisciplinary work
good contract settlement to boost morale and attitude	make sure it is the right thing
hear department by department reaction	grad. requirements must be increased
more information given to staff teacher involvement beyond the few who worked on proposal	staff support & increased communication

English teacher Ed Johnson commented, "It's essential that teachers be made thoroughly aware that this will require as much a change in their delivery of instruction as it'll demand of the school and students. Doing more of what they're doing in longer periods will not be acceptable."

In late September 1993, a group of teachers in the staff room were discussing the proposed change in schedule. Bill Dixon, an eleventh grade math teacher, stated, "A student may take a foreign language in the fall semester and then not have another course in that language until the following fall. If we have a gap between courses, the lapses will be detrimental to long term learning. I don't know if this is going to work."

"That's true, but we could look for new ways to take care of those kinds of problems. Like, we could have a review seminar between courses," responded Tom Hammond, a 12th grade English teacher. "The really exciting part is," Tom continued, "that we could add courses that we've always wanted to teach."

"Yes, it really would give students more electives and choices," chimed in Jane Anderson. Jane was a special education teacher. She added, "There could be a lot more variety in the offerings. Also, longer class periods would save a lot of wasted set-up and tear down time. But, has anyone really thought about the cost of implementing this system? For example, we'd really need some curriculum writing time. I'm not doing that for free."

"Yeah," added Bill Dixon, "our department would need new materials and textbooks. Students would have the time to do more collaborative, hands on learning. Our current equipment won't support longer class times. And how will this schedule change impact the number of staff we need?"

"Absolutely right. We don't want any staff cuts around here," said Jane.

"Well, if you took a vote today, I think a majority would be in favor of it," responded Bill. The others nodded in agreement. "That's probably true," said Rob, the administrator of the T.O.P. Team program, "but there are still a number of teachers, especially in the arts, who need to be convinced."

❖ PERFORMING ARTS

Many performing arts faculty worried that the new 4-period schedule would damage the success of their programs. The band director, Justin Thurston, cited student schedule simulations that had been done. Band and music students were left with less contact time with performing arts courses. Thurston told whoever would listen, "Fewer periods will reduce the likelihood of a student taking two performing arts classes because two classes would constitute 25% of the student's schedule (2 of 8 courses). With the current schedule, two performing arts classes are only 16% of a student's schedule (2 of 12 courses). Why did we build this program to see it destroyed by this schedule change?"

When he heard Justin Thurston's argument against the schedule change, Alden Torsen said, "Right now, music is the tail that's wagging the dog. Music should have to work it out with music. No other department should have to work it out for them."

❖ THE STAFF AND THE COMMUNITY

Several teachers raised another concern related to the relationship between the high school and the district office and community. Bill Dixon, the math teacher, summarized the feelings as, "A lack of trust between what goes on at the district office and what goes on up here at the high school . . . I don't think the teachers will support the 4-period schedule if we're not given the funds needed to make it work. I'd need some assurance, and I guess it boils down to that trust, that the School Board and Central Office are going to fund it and support us in our efforts. You know what Sidney Kraus, the former principal used to say, 'This community and school board wants to drive a Cadillac on a Chevrolet budget. They want a first class operation, but they don't want to pay for it.' I think that sums it up pretty well." Sarah Campbell, a French teacher, who lived in Ottawa all her life, said, "If the community is informed, it won't be a problem, but if not, residents will find all the negatives."

Prior to the end of the summer of 1993, the only information forwarded to Ottawa residents had been a short article in the school newsletter. No other mechanism was in place to gather community views.

❖ THE OTTAWA SCHOOL BOARD AND SUPERINTENDENT

The School Board and Superintendent had not been deeply involved in the discussion about the 4-period schedule change. Harry Boxford and Frank Barsamian, two board members who had an understanding of the structural alternatives, retired from the board at the end of June, 1993. The 4-period schedule change had not been discussed or debated during the election and the feelings of the two new board members were unknown. Superintendent Dr. Richard Fish also retired with Harry Boxford and Frank Barsamian. John Henning had introduced his plans to the new superintendent, James Bauck, in the summer of 1993 and felt that Dr. Bauck was supportive of the idea of a schedule change.

❖ THE BUDGET

The cost of the new schedule was a concern for those involved in the decision making. Several people believed that cost would be the "show stopper." While the exact costs were unknown, Henning estimated that an additional 7–10 staff members would be needed to cover additional courses. This meant an increase in costs of approximately $300,000.

Ottawa School District had operated with a deficit balance over the past several years in order to avoid program reductions. During the 1991–92 school year, revenues in the general fund totaled $18,522,208 (an increase from 1990–91 of 2.72%), while expenditures totaled $19,336,975 (an increase of 6.38%).

❖ NEXT STEPS

According to the timeline set forth by the Curriculum Delivery Systems Committee, Henning should present his 4-period block schedule proposal to the School Board in October, 1993. In the fall of 1993, many faculty members supported Henning and his belief that "the schedule is at the heart of school reform," while others were disquieted by the proposed change. The 1993–94 school year could be the last year of the 6-period day. Should Principal Henning follow the proposed timeline or make a different plan?

❖ CASE PREPARATION QUESTIONS

1. What problem was John Henning trying to solve?
2. There are a number of different constituent groups who stand to be affected by the proposed schedule change. Describe who they are and how they see the change. What argument would you put forth to the Ottawa school board that describes the proposed changes?
3. To what degree does changing the organizational structure of a school influence teaching and learning?

EXHIBIT 1

Graduate Profile

Summary	1991	1992	1993
In-State Public Four-Year Colleges	25.56%	22.3%	22.9%
In-State Private Four-Year Colleges	10%	10.1%	10.5%
Out-of-State Four-Year Colleges	15.08%	14.4%	13.4%
Total Four-Year Colleges	**50.74%**	**46.4%**	**46.8%**
In-State Public Community Colleges	11.85%	12.6%	11.6%
Out-of-State Two-Year or Tech. Colleges	1.11%	1.1%	.4%
Total Two-Year Colleges	**12.96%**	**13.7%**	**12.0%**
In-State Public Technical Colleges	8.52%	11.9%	13.4%

Summary	1991	1992	1993
In-State Private Technical Colleges	3.33%	0.4%	2.8%
Total Technical Colleges	**11.85%**	**15.9%**	**16.1%**
Total percentage attending post-secondary institutions	**75.55%**	**76%**	**74.9%**
Other:			
Employment	20.37%	18.3%	18.0%
Military Service	4.07%	4.3%	4.6%
Returning to OHS	——	.7%	——
Post-Secondary Option	——	.3%	——
Undecided	——	——	2.5%

DROP OUT RATES

Grade	1990–91	1991–92	1992–93
Grade 9	2	—	2
Grade 10	8	2	7
Grade 11	5	8	4
Grade 12	8	6	12
Total number of students:	**23**	**16**	**25**
Percentage: (of students)	**1.9%**	**1.3%**	**1.9%**

OTTAWA SENIOR HIGH SCHOOL

Early Bird 7:15–8:05	Period 1 8:10–9:03	Period 2 9:08–10:01	Period 3 10:06–10:18 10:18–10:23 10:23–11:16	Period 4 A Lunch 11:16–11:51 B Lunch 11:48–12:18 C Lunch 12:14–12:44	Period 5 12:49–1:42	Period 6 1:47–2:40
	Structured Program 1 335 Math 311	Refresher Math 311	Algebra 9 311	A Lunch Refresher Math 311	Algebra 9 311	Prep
	Wood 2,3,4 205	Wood 2,3,4 205	Wood 1 205 Plastics 205	C Lunch T & I 212	T & I Out	Prep
	Basic Algebra	IB Higher Alg 10	Basic Math Topics	A Lunch Basic Math Topics	IB Higher Alg 10	Prep
	Resource	Resource	Resource	C Lunch Resource	Resource	ESL
				B Lunch French 1 365	French 1 365	Resource
IB Eng 10	Prep	Eng 10	Eng 10	B Lunch Speech 1	IB Eng 10	
	SLD	Speech 1	Eng 10	Eng 10	SLD	
	Level 5	SLD	SLD	C Lunch SLD	Level 5	Prep
	Adv Wr	Level 5	Level 5	C Lunch Level 5	Prep	Level 5
	Eng 10 Mod	Eng 9	Eng 9	B Lunch Eng 10 Mod Prep	Adv Wr	Eng 9

FIGURE 1

EXHIBIT 2

COURSE ENROLLMENT

English	1991–92	1992–93	1993–94
English 9	217	254	234
English 9 Mod	36	39	44
* *IB* English 9	48	61	62
English 10	207	221	249
Speech I	246	269	294
English 10 Mod	44	37	42
* *IB* English 10	52	52	64
AOM Am Lit	19	18	26
Adv Wr	126	138	128
AM Lit	196	217	226
Ap Comm 1			26
App Comm 2			26
Basic Writing	107	119	126
Best	137	178	190
British Lit	13	18	19
Drama	31	21	32
Journalism	31	15	17
Popular Lit	111	127	86
Commun/Speech 2	139	76	58
World Lit	46	48	73
Publications	25	31	18
* *IB* English 1	42	42	47
* *IB* English 2	20	29	29

Social Studies	1991–92	1992–93	1993–94
AM Studies 9	264	302	289
* *IB* AM Studies 9	55	58	63
AM Studies 10	262	274	306
* *IB* AM Studies 10	46	49	59
Eastern World	68	27	
Early Civilizations	169	184	
World Religions	24	49	
Modern West. Civilization	113	88	
Peace Quest	148	188	
Great Decisions			61
International Studies			218
Sociology			189
World Culture			97
* *IB* Mod European 1	46	41	54
Polit. Science	219	212	219
Economics	222	214	220
* *IB* Mod European 2	23	37	32
* *IB* Theory of Knowledge		12	11

Mathematics	1991–92	1992–93	1993–94
* *IB* Geometry 9	42	53	58
Geometry 9	13		8
Algebra 9	127	149	123
Pre-Algebra	53	57	28
Math 9	37	23	27
* *IB* Higher Algebra 10	31	39	39
Higher Algebra 10	21	13	15
Geometry 10	138	120	132
Basic Algebra	96	128	165

Mathematics	1991–92	1992–93	1993–94
Basic Geometry	64	81	101
Applied Math 1			47
* *IB* Pre-Calc 11	21	19	28
Pre-Calc	27	28	20
Higher Algebra 11	74	80	109
Basic Higher Algebra	54	55	64
Pre-Calc 12	18	26	22
Refresher Math	35	43	34
* *IB* Calc 12	15	11	12
Trig 12	22	22	22
Math Topics	33	43	
Basic Calc			46
Structured Prog 1	17	13	27
Structured Prog 2			14

Science	1991–92	1992–93	1993–94
Gen. Science 9	177	216	213
Intro Phys. Science 9	135	140	137
Gen. Biology	218	241	264
Human Biology	70	54	62
* *IB* Biology		19	11
Field Biology	51	41	62
Practical Chem	49	57	59
Gen. Chem	62	105	80
* *IB* Chem	24	16	22
Physics	58	58	73
* *IB* Physics	46	47	70

PE & Health	1991–92	1992–93	1993–94
PE 9	308	344	350
PE 10	196	199	211

PE & Health	1991–92	1992–93	1993–94
PE 2	23	10	23
PE 3	24	28	22
Fitness 1	21	20	41
Fitness 2	19		14
Aerobics	31	34	18
Modified PE	28	28	23
Health	214	189	268

Music	1991–92	1992–93	1993–94
Choir 9	147	143	140
Varsity Choir	100	95	113
Concert Choir	86	90	89
Orchestra 9	24	33	36
Symphony Orchestra	53	52	43
Band 9	63	57	65
Concert Band	69	75	79

Business Ed	1991–92	1992–93	1993–94
Keyboard 1	51	100	146
Typing	55	17	
Keyboard 2	48	45	44
Business Math	10		
Word Processing 1	64	66	147
Word Processing 2	27	35	89
Accounting 1	56	44	62
Accounting 2	13		
Intro to Business	25	28	52
Business Law	56	54	71
Office Procedures	22	36	18
Business Seminar	13	11	16
Business work study	13	11	16
Computer Accounting 1			7

Foreign Language	1991–92	1992–93	1993–94
Spanish 1	137	163	172
Spanish 2	111	115	128
* *IB* Spanish 3	48	33	44
* *IB* Spanish 4	15	15	13
French 1	50	69	67
French 2	57	36	65
* *IB* French 3	17	37	19
* *IB* French 4	9	9	20
German 1	46	50	33
German 2	38	36	39
* *IB* German 3	19	21	17
* *IB* German 4	2	15	8

Personal & Family Science	1991–92	1992–93	1993–94
Better you	23		
Life Management			19
Interior Design	25	10	10
Sports Foods	23	18	22
Foods 1	70	54	23
Foods 2	42	29	14
Commercial Foods			3
Child/Parent	16	29	16
Fashion	25	24	10
Human Relations	31	44	38
Succeed on your Own	15	27	29

Industrial Technology	1991–92	1992–93	1993–94
Weld 1	38	53	35
Weld 2	16	14	17

Industrial Technology	1991–92	1992–93	1993–94
Metal 1	18		
Wood 1	29	16	33
Wood 2	26	16	33
Wood 3	26	26	17
Wood 4	11	8	14
Electricity	1	4	5
Electronics 1	59	47	39
Electronics 2	15	16	23
Intro to Drafting	1	4	3
Arch Drafting 1	30	30	32
Arch Drafting 2	16	9	12
Arch Drafting 3	2	5	4
Tech. Drafting 1	11	12	6
Tech. Drafting 2	8	3	3
Tech. Drafting 3	4		2
Auto 1	49	48	71
Auto 2	24	18	15
Vocat. Machine Shop	12	10	15
T & I work study	22	18	14
Technology		15	28
Plastics	16	18	

Agriculture	1991–92	1992–93	1993–94
Ag 1	19	20	19
Ag 2	19	14	19
Natural Resources	27	36	17
Small Animals	49	44	43

Agriculture	1991–92	1992–93	1993–94
Small Engines	46	52	66
Ag Mechanics	27	11	7

Art	1991–92	1992–93	1993–94
Art 1	91	84	72
Art 2	46	45	37
Art 3	26	37	36
Art 4	37	25	22
Art 5	8	33	27

Arts Magnet	1991–92	1992–93	1993–94
Music Theory		25	
Theory of Knowledge		13	
Theatre Art		10	
Humanities			16
Communications			16
Visual Arts	11		

Year Long Course = one semester
Semester Course = one quarter

Sample Schedules of Teacher and Student

Teacher A

	Quarter 1	Quarter 2	Quarter 3	Quarter 4
Period 1	English 10	Amer. Lit	Amer. Lit	English 10
Period 2	English 10	English 10		
Period 3			IB English 10	IB English 10
Period 4	Amer. Lit	Amer. Lit	IB English 10	IB English 10

Teacher B

	Quarter 1	Quarter 2	Quarter 3	Quarter 4
Period 1	Gen. Physics	Gen. Physics	IB Physics	IB Physics
Period 2	Gen. Physics	Gen. Physics		
Period 3			Gen. Physics	Gen. Physics
Period 4	IB Physics	IB Physics	Gen. Physics	Gen. Physics

Grade 12
Student A

	Quarter 1	Quarter 2	Quarter 3	Quarter 4
Period 1	Band/Orch <hr> IB Physics	Band/Orch <hr> IB Physics	Band/Orch <hr> IB Physics	Band/Orch <hr> IB Physics
Period 2	German	German	Calculus	Calculus
Period 3	IB Mod Eur 2	IB Mod Eur 2	Newspaper	Newspaper
Period 4	Open	Art 4	Art Draft	Phy Ed 3

Grade 10
Student B

	Quarter 1	Quarter 2	Quarter 3	Quarter 4
Period 1	Am. Studies 10	Am. Studies 10	English 10	Word Proc.
Period 2	French 2	French 2	Basic Algebra	Basic Algebra
Period 3	Gen. Biol. 10	Gen. Biol. 10	Phy Ed	Health
Period 4	Speech	Small Animals	Foods 1	Art 2

FIGURE 2

EXHIBIT 3

Material Distributed to OHS Staff

I.   ISSUE OF CONCERN

Creating an Efficient Curriculum Delivery System

Meaningful change in secondary education involves consideration in the following zones

1. Curriculum content (including the desired outcomes and fitting assessment processes)—what is really important to learn?
2. Appropriate teaching methodology.
3. Suitability of the curriculum delivery system—the schedule.

Two of the areas, the curriculum, and teaching methodology, have been evolving to some degree, but not nearly at the pace necessary to keep up with preparing our students for life beyond their secondary education. A change in the delivery system will improve student access to the curriculum and permit our staff to deal with more manageable numbers of students each day. Working on our delivery system at this time will lead to significant simultaneous advancement of these three essential areas. To this end Ottawa Senior High School's faculty recommends a four period block schedule. Continual modifications will be made as identified and deemed necessary.

II.   OUR PRESENT STRUCTURE

a. Students attend 5 days a week 179 days a year.
b. Six period day with Early Bird option. Classes are 53 minutes in length with 5 minutes passing time.
c. Teachers teach 5 periods each day.
d. Teachers have 130–160 students per day.
e. Students attend 5 to 7 classes each day.
f. 20-$\frac{1}{2}$ credits are required for graduation.

III.   PROPOSED STRUCTURE

a. Students attend 5 days a week 179 days a year.
b. 4 period day: Classes are 90 minutes in length.

    c. Teachers teach 3 of 4 periods a day.

    d. Teachers have 75–90 students per day.

    e. Students attend 4 classes per day (this number may be smaller dependent upon financial support).

    f. A faculty committee will need to work on increasing the credit and graduation requirements, keeping the state's new graduation rule in mind. (Transition time will be needed.)

    g. Wednesday's classes will be 70 minutes in length to accommodate a 54 minute advisement period for all students.

    h. Year-long courses under a traditional system (179 meetings in 53 minute classes) are condensed into a single semester (approximately 90 meetings in 90 minute classes).

    i. Semester-length courses under a traditional system will be offered in quarter-length classes (nine weeks in duration). Students change these classes at the end of each nine-week term.

IV. WHY CHANGE?

    a. Rejuvenate the institution.

    b. Increase student access to the curriculum.

    c. Allow time for teachers to work together.

    d. Reduce stress for students and staff.

    e. Allow for individual student accessibility to teacher.

    f. Raise student performance.

    g. Provide an expanded curriculum.

    h. Provide an opportunity to review graduation requirements and the state graduation rules.

    i. More efficient use of time (we presently stop and start 12–14 times a day).

    j. Reduces student/teacher ratio.

    k. Increase student contact time with teachers.

    l. Promote sanctity of the classroom by reducing interruptions.

    m. Provide implementation of innovative teaching methodologies.

    n. Promote interdisciplinary study.

V. WHAT HAS BEEN DONE?

    a. Board set a goal to improve curriculum in the mid-1980's.

    b. The Curriculum Delivery System Committee has been exploring options for the past two years.

        1. School visits have taken place.

        2. We have networked with other schools.

     3. Research continues.

  c. The following groups have been met with:

     1. Department Coordinators

     2. Student Council

     3. Full OHS Faculty

     4. Board of Education

VI. **WHAT NEEDS TO BE DONE?**

  a. Make a clear statement to staff on 4 period day changes.

  b. Expand base with:

     1. Additional school visits

     2. Continued research

  c. Meet with Board of Education

     1. to update on progress.

     2. Maintain support—$.

     3. Seek approval for continuing implementation.

  d. Continue to inform and include:

     1. Parents

     2. Students

     3. Staff

     4. Board Members

     5. General Public

  e. Staff communications.

     1. Meet with staff in small focus groups to listen to and inform of progress.

     2. Access outside consultants to talk with staff.

     3. Continue site visits and communicate with other teachers presently involved in a similar program.

     4. Continue discussion at staff meetings.

     5. Develop a clear time schedule.

  f. Establish new graduation requirements.

  g. Seek board approval.

  h. Establish and seek approval for staff in-service time through summer work and/or temporary decrease in student days.

  i. Draft new course proposals and registration guide.

  j. Register students. Develop master schedule. Involve total faculty in extensive in-service/staff development. Implementation—January–September 1994.

◆ ◆ ◆

What's Your Plan, Mr. Sommers?

Claudia Johnson

The Monroe school board was lobbying hard to persuade Jack Sommers to leave his job as superintendent of Elgin schools and move over to the superintendent's slot in Monroe. From what Sommers had heard through the grapevine, many people in Monroe schools were in a state of shock since Tony Perez, the last superintendent, had left unexpectedly for a "dream job" with a private-sector educational consulting firm. It was the third time in six years that Monroe had lost its superintendent. Perez was popular, and few could believe he would leave Monroe during such a crisis.

Perez had been working for over a year in support of a proposed regionalization of Monroe and Harris schools. Perez and most of the Monroe school board saw regionalization as a sensible response to Monroe's continuing declining enrollments and dwindling budgets. Surprisingly, Perez had left a month before the final vote on regionalization. While the merger proposal had passed in Monroe by a very small margin, it was strongly rejected by Harris voters. School officials in Monroe and Harris were unprepared for the negative outcome. No one was prepared to run Monroe schools as an independent district. "The high school had only 250 students in a building designed for 700. At this rate, how long could it survive?" Perez remarked later.

Perez, whom Sommers had known for several years, had called to urge Sommers to consider the job. "I know it might not be the best-known district around," Perez told Sommers, "but they've got a good group of teachers working there. I've even heard rumors that Harris might re-consider regionalization with Monroe a year or two down the road. I would feel a lot better having left if I knew someone qualified was going to lead Monroe through the next few years."

When Tony Perez announced his departure to the Monroe School Committee, a veteran member had said, "Most people wouldn't touch a situation like Monroe's with a ten foot pole. It's too volatile for most people's blood, with too many variables that could affect the schools' future. No money, no students, minimal community support—not exactly a recipe for success. On the other hand, Monroe could present a fascinating challenge for an experienced superintendent."

❖ JACK SOMMERS

Jack Sommers' whole career had been in public education: and he had worked his way up through the ranks from history teacher to superintendent, earning a Harvard Ed.D. along the way. Over the years, he felt lucky to have worked in affluent communities such as Watley and Elgin. And Sommers had to admit that as pleasant as life was in the Elgin system, he wasn't feeling challenged as a superintendent. The work of building up the district was done, his assistant superintendent and principals took care of most of the routine work. Monroe would be a lot of work at this point in his career, but maybe he could feel productive again. "I have time for one more district in my career," he thought, "maybe my last district can be my best."

Sommers agreed to interview for the Monroe superintendency. As part of the interview process, the Monroe School Committee required candidates to present a five-year strategic plan for Monroe schools. The school board was brand new, since most of the former members had resigned after the regionalization effort they spearheaded had collapsed. The new board was taking no chances and they wanted no surprises. They wanted a superintendent who would stay put. "Most important," remarked one committee member, "we want someone who believes in Monroe." The new school year was about to begin, and the board was under pressure to fill the superintendent's slot as quickly as possible.

To prepare his strategic plan, Sommers began to wade through piles of reports that detailed the recent history of Monroe schools. He also arranged a number of phone calls with Perez. Personally, he needed to be sure that Monroe had the resources that would allow him to implement a plan that would deliver a quality education to all Monroe school children. He also needed to ensure that he could deliver on what he was going to sell the school committee.

❖ THE TOWNS OF MONROE AND HARRIS

Monroe was a small town, 20 miles south of a major urban center. It had a population of 10,400 residents. Historically, its citizens tended to be farmers or tradespeople, and many families had lived in the community for generations. People in neighboring towns often described Monroe residents as "working class." Town pride ran high in Monroe, and "Go Tigers" signs celebrating the high school football team were often seen along main routes into town.

To the north, east, and south, Monroe was ringed by six of the state's wealthiest communities: Harris, Melville, Preston, Rochester, Birmingham, and Watley. Harris was the closest, only two miles down the road from Monroe. Some people said that being surrounded by such affluent communities had given Monroe an inferiority complex. Over twelve percent of Monroe's population was over 65, and school-aged children comprised fifteen percent of the town residents. Median family income in Monroe was approximately

$50,000, and the average value of a single family home was $166,000. Realtors trying to attract newcomers to Monroe focused on a quiet, safe environment, affordable housing, and small schools.

Like many of its affluent neighbors, Harris had benefited from the rise of the high technology industry in the region. Harris had become a popular home site for many young professionals flocking to the industry, and had a population of over 18,000, growing over fifty percent in the last decade. The vast majority of Harris residents were between the ages of 18 and 64, and more than half of them were employed as managers and professionals; only six percent of the town's population was over 65. Median family income was over $70,000 and the average value of a single family home topped $240,000. In Harris, realtors typically highlighted the nationally-acclaimed schools, the high percentage of residents with college degrees, and rising property values.

❖ MONROE AND HARRIS SCHOOLS

Monroe maintained a complete K-12 district, with three public schools housing 1,140 students—one elementary school with 610 students, one middle school with 293 students, and the remaining students in the high school. The current school budget was $7.1 million. Average per pupil expenditure was $4,700 across all grades, and $7,200 at the high school level. Each year, approximately 40–45 Monroe eighth graders transferred to the Muskegon Valley Vocational School. Typically, seventy percent of Monroe graduating seniors went on to college. SAT scores for the district were now on par with state and national averages. Two years ago, however, twelfth grade Educational Assessment Profile scores were the second highest in the state.

Harris maintained its own K-6 district, with four elementary schools that housed 2,125 students. Over the past six years, enrollment in Harris kindergarten classes increased fifty percent. Another 1,500 students in grades 7–12 attended a regionalized Harris-Sumner district, a partnership established in 1955. The combined budget for Harris' K-6 schools, and for Harris' share of the regionalized 7–12 schools, was currently over $21 million. Average per pupil expenditure across all grades was $5,616; per pupil costs at the high school topped $7,000. Only 2.5% of Harris students chose to attend schools other than Harris public schools.

Harris schools had an excellent reputation in the area, and one had won the "National Flag of Excellence" from the U.S. Department of Education. Harris SAT scores were generally over one hundred points above state and national averages. Qualified high school students were permitted to take courses at nearby colleges and universities in lieu of high school courses. Ninety-three percent of Harris graduating seniors attended four year colleges.

❖ MONROE AND HARRIS SCHOOL FINANCES

In his study of the Monroe district, Sommers learned that the regionalization effort with Harris had started two years earlier, and people on both sides of the issue waved the banner of "quality education for Monroe youth." But Sommers had been in the business long enough to know what the regionalization initiative was really about: declining enrollments and budgets.

Enrollment rates had been falling in both Monroe and Harris for over 15 years, particularly at the high school level. Between 1973 and 1990, Monroe High School enrollment had dropped from 675 to 250. During the same period in Harris-Sumner, high school enrollment dropped from 1600 to 1050. And even though kindergarten enrollment in Harris was expanding, Sumner was a more mature community and its elementary school enrollment was static. Administrators of the regionalized district were reluctant to predict long-term enrollment growth. As officials in both Monroe and Harris saw it, empty classroom seats meant higher costs—costs that no town could afford for very long. Between the effects of a law to limit property taxation and dwindling state aid to schools, the picture was now very bleak.[1]

And while student enrollment rates in Monroe and Harris remained an area of concern, school budgets continued to rise, and at rates well beyond the growth rate of 2.5% stipulated for local town budgets under the tax laws. Monroe school budgets, for example, showed an average annual increase of 7.1% from FY 1983 to FY 1987, buttressed by ED-2 state aid.

Toward the end of the decade, however, the state aid available to schools decreased in the face of the declining state economy. In Monroe, ED-2 aid (as a percentage of the total school budget) decreased from 31% to 17%. As a result, Monroe's school budget increases in FY 1988 through FY 1990 were 1.9%, 2.1%, and 0.2%, respectively. As fixed costs in Monroe's town budget continued to rise in the late 1980's, Monroe's finance committee allocated a decreasing share of the overall town budget to schools. Whereas school budgets

---

[1]*Property Taxation Limitation:*
In this state, local city budgets were traditionally funded primarily from levies on residential and commercial property taxes. But in 1980, in response to what was perceived as the ballooning costs of local government, state residents launched a referendum to limit property taxation, and to "cut the fat" from local town budgets. Schools were seen as prime abusers of public funds, since they often represented the largest portion of a town's budget, and were exempted from line item vetoes in town meetings. The new law capped property taxes at current levels, and limited growth of local government budgets to 2.5% per year. The legislation did make provision for towns to vote to override property taxation limitation in order to provide increased funding. If a general override was voted in by a majority of voters, then that amount would become part of the base used to calculate future local tax levies.

represented 48% of the town budget in FY 1983, this percentage shifted to 42.6% by FY 1990. At this point, a tax override for education had never been attempted in Monroe.

Max Lyne, a member of Monroe's School Committee (and later State Under-Secretary of Education) first sounded the alarm in the Monroe community in 1986. As head of the Monroe Taskforce on Declining Enrollments—a volunteer group of school committee members, school officials, teachers, and parents—Lyne warned the town that:

> Larger schools will still be able to preserve most of their programs during this period of declining enrollments, whereas schools as small as Monroe High School have many courses and programs that may not be able to be carried at all due to insufficient numbers. Can a small high school provide the academic offerings to keep its students competitive for post-secondary education? If fiscal resources are limited, what is the most equitable division of resources between a small high school (with inherently high costs) and a burgeoning elementary program (with increasing costs)? . . . Should cost alone dictate these issues?

In Harris, between FY 1986 and FY 1990, school budgets rose at an average annual rate of 6.5%. As Harris' superintendent Alan Kramer wrote in the town's 1989 annual report, "doing better than average . . . carries a price." As state aid declined, Harris officials looked more and more to override the property taxation limitation law to shore up dwindling revenues available for schools. Between 1989 and 1991, Harris voters approved three overrides for education.

Monroe was forced to make numerous staff cuts. Most of the cuts were made in administrative staff, since Monroe's contract with the local teachers union was in place until 1992 and prohibited layoffs. Harris, too, avoided teacher layoffs, but it did negotiate an agreement with the teacher's union to freeze teachers' salaries for 1991.

❖ MONROE AND HARRIS SCHOOL CURRICULA

Graduation requirements for high school students in Monroe totaled 100 credits which included 8 semesters–English; 4 semesters–math; 4 semesters–science; 1 semester–freshman history; 1 semester–social studies; 2 semesters–U.S. history; 6 semesters–P.E. (completed by junior year); and 1 semester–typing/keyboarding. Graduation requirements in Harris-Sumner totaled 80 credits: 8 semesters–English; 6 semesters–social studies; 4 semesters–math; 4 semesters–science (1 must be biology); and 4 semesters–P.E.

"No matter how small the budget gets, there is only so far you can cut high school curriculum offerings before you threaten courses needed for state graduation requirements," Sommers thought as he analyzed the Monroe documentation. By 1990, Monroe had cut most of its athletic programs. Extra-curricular offerings and electives were slashed. High-end and low-end sections of core courses were also cut. Monroe High School offered only one advanced placement course, in U.S. history.

In contrast, through Superintendent Kramer's efforts, and with the support of tax overrides, Harris was able to maintain its curricular offerings at the high school. Harris-Sumner offered 120 high school courses, in comparison with 69 in Monroe; of these, 14 were AP courses. In addition, Harris offered over 75 extra-curricular activities.

Sommers had been told by Tony Perez that Monroe town selectmen blamed the school budget crisis mainly on rising salary and benefit costs for school staff, mandated costs for special education, and costs for building repairs and upgrades. Selectmen were becoming increasingly concerned that these perceived "entitlements" were restricting a quality education for all Monroe children, particularly at the high school.

"When the town started looking at curricula in other towns, particularly Harris, we had a hard time convincing the board that Monroe's high school curriculum was broad enough to provide students a good education. The numbers were against us," Perez told Sommers.

❖ REGIONALIZATION

In 1990, Monroe's town selectmen initiated their own plan to solve the town's school problems. Selectmen chair Charles Rodney "invited" Superintendent Perez to a meeting with Superintendent Alan Kramer and two Harris selectmen. The purpose of the meeting was to discuss the possible regionalization of Monroe and Harris schools.

This was not the first time the subject of regionalization had surfaced in Monroe. In 1959, when high school enrollments were on the rise, and Monroe lacked the funds to build a new school, a proposal circulated to combine Monroe and Melville high schools in a regionalized district. The proposal soon failed because Monroe voters made it clear they wanted their own K-12 district. Again in the 1970's, Monroe school officials briefly considered regionalizing with another district, but the idea was dropped due to lack of community support.

Harris' Kramer made no secret of his interest in regionalization: money. "We have a common problem here. In a tight financial climate, how are we going to maintain the quality of education for our kids?" Kramer asked. If Monroe and Harris were to regionalize at all grade levels, Kramer believed that the districts could receive an additional $2.2 million in regional state aid. That money, combined with the considerable savings available through more efficient operations, staff reductions, and fuller classrooms, could reduce the need for property tax limit overrides. Moreover, Harris' selectmen had long been interested in Monroe's waste treatment plant, and hoped that regionalizing educational services might be the first step in sharing other services, as well. It was a productive meeting and all parties agreed to take the prospect of regionalization back to their electorates.

In the Spring, town meetings were held in Monroe and Harris. Both were marked by low attendance yet each meeting resulted in a vote to pursue regionalization plans with the other town. The finalized plan called for regionalization combining Monroe with Harris for grades K–6, and with Harris-Sumner for grades 7–12. This plan would have to be approved by voters in Monroe, Harris and Sumner.

Both Superintendent Perez and Superintendent Kramer publicly asserted that, in the first year of regionalization alone, Monroe could save over $500,000 through the increased state aid benefits offered to regionalized districts and by reducing per pupil expenditure costs at the high school level. Further savings could be realized by selling empty school properties in Monroe (Fuller Middle School and Monroe High School). Perez also told Monroe's town selectmen that more budget savings were possible under regionalization through proposed staff reductions; that regionalization could provide a "motivating sense of competition among teachers that would improve morale and thus, help improve Monroe education." (In actuality, union contracts stipulated that tenured teaching staff—which accounted for most of the faculty in both towns—could not be laid off.)

Superintendent Perez tried to sell regionalization to Monroe residents in a town forum. He announced, "By providing a larger pool of students, a regionalized district can offer more programs at varying levels, and we can increase the scope and quality of extra-curricular offerings. If we join with Harris, our students are assured a top-notch education at a relatively low cost to Monroe." He then explained the financial implications telling the group that Monroe would have to pay its share of any regional district expenses. In addition to regular operating expenses, the regionalization proposal with Harris-Sumner stipulated that Monroe would have to pay $1.66 million to Harris and Sumner to offset Monroe's share of construction costs for the regional high school facility already built in Harris. The sum would be paid out over 20 years. Tony Perez said, "Harris Superintendent, Alan Kramer, has insisted that buy-in assistance from the state would reimburse Monroe for all but $233,000 of total regionalization buy-in costs."

❖ REGIONALIZATION: THE DEBATE

Judging from the newspaper articles Sommers read, Monroe had virtually divided itself into two factions over the issue of regionalization. The situation was equally divided in Harris. Superintendent Kramer and other school officials were working furiously to win over voters who were unimpressed by the prospect of their children going to school with Monroe students. (Specific details of the regionalization plan are presented in Exhibit 1 on page 199.)

In Monroe, the pro-regionalization group SHARE included among its members town selectman Bob Royal, most members of the school committee, and many younger parents. In interviews, SHARE proponent and Monroe School Committee Chairman Herb Greene reminded voters that "Harris-Sumner has a lot of things that Monroe needs and does not have, such as a business manager, a personnel manager, and a curriculum director."

At a local cable television debate over the regionalization issue, Joe Carmen, a member of SHARE and a candidate for the Monroe School Committee, stated that "as a very small, independent district, we have no room for error. Absolutely none. If you want to have a small district, and you want to pay big bucks, then we can go it alone. But, one way or the other, you're going to have to pay for education. And with inflation running at 4–6%, and tax revenues running at only a 2.5% increase, the money is going to come out of your pockets. Unless, of course, we regionalize. Efficiency comes with large size."

Meanwhile, the Monroe S.O.S. (Save Our Schools) was a group established to lead the fight *against* regionalization. One of the group's key figures, William Greafe, who was also on the Monroe Finance Committee, wrote an impassioned plea to Monroe residents to "stop selling ourselves short. We must not allow ourselves to slip into a false mindset that we cannot put forth a strong, productive, progressive, and therefore, top educational system of our own. We must stop thinking that 'others' are the only ones who can achieve excellence."

Carol Phillips, the sole Monroe School Committee member to oppose regionalization, reminded Monroe voters that the savings available through state funding for regionalization, as touted by Kramer and Perez, were subject to appropriation. "This year, the reimbursements on transportation costs for regionalized districts were cut from 100% to 86%, and for local districts from 43% to 39%. It should be obvious to everyone by now that the state is cutting the amount of aid it is giving out. There is no guarantee of this reimbursement, whether we are a region or not. Ultimately, the regional aid could be as low as the local aid, and in the meantime we have added buses and increased our expenses."

In interviews, Phillips also noted that, according to state regulations for regionalized school districts, the consolidated district would be governed by a combined school board, weighted according to the town's relative populations. Under the proposed merger with Harris and Sumner, Harris would have 57% control, Monroe 33%, and Sumner 10%. Although each member of the school committee would have one vote, the votes would be weighted by the population of each town.

Soon, Monroe teachers and students were embroiled in the debate. Art Stewart, a Monroe high school teacher said, "Regionalization's so-called economy of scale is advantageous if you're talking about paper clips, but it's a disaster if you're talking about human needs. I'm convinced that as enrollment goes up and parents get involved, there will be a restructuring of the budget. I fear for Monroe's cultural identity if it regionalizes." Eileen Garven, a first grade teacher, commented, "We are doing a great job of educating the youth of Monroe. Just come and see. But no matter how great a job we do, we're guilty through our association with Monroe. This town does not promote itself well, so people think we have a bad program. If this elementary program were in another town, you would think it was amazing."

Student members of S.O.S. held a televised rally in front of the Monroe High School, shouting "No, no, we won't go!" Senior class president Teresa Myshinksi said, "I know everyone in my school. It would be weird for me to go to a school where I don't know everyone. Harris-Sumner is too big."

Similar rifts developed among Harris residents over the regionalization issue. Superintendent Kramer lobbied hard among Harris voters, proposing regionalization as the antidote for further tax overrides. "Harris is facing a school budget deficit of $900,000. Overrides were needed in the past three years. Overrides will not maintain what we have in Harris-Sumner. They'll mean cuts in current services even though we got the override. This last override represents an 8.5% increase in the tax base for the residents of Harris, at a time when things have been very difficult for everyone. The advantage of pooling our resources is to be able to provide not less than what we have, but at least what we have now and perhaps more. The thing you have to ask yourself is that since you will increase your costs of education under either plan, which one is likely to keep that cost increase lower? If we don't regionalize, Harris will have to pass a $3 million tax override to maintain its current school staffing, and the average Harris homeowner can expect to pay $300 to $400 more in property taxes."

Business Director Ryan Park offered a sobering view of the financial future for Harris schools. "We're at a point where it is much more costly for a town to maintain the same level of educational services now than it used to be. There isn't any sugar daddy out there that's going to solve problems for local schools right now. To maintain their educational services, towns will either have to raise taxes or find efficiency, at least until there's some structural change at the state level."

Tom Berger, a member of the anti-regionalization group, Harris Citizens for Harris Schools, warned, "The quest for the almighty dollar is not worth jeopardizing the school's excellence and the town's property values." Harris resident Donald Fein objected to the Harris School Committee's presentation of the regionalization agreement. "They present it like a business deal. Many people don't look at the schools that way."

Some Harris residents seemed worried that the social class differences between Monroe and Harris students would create problems. Harris School Committee Chairwoman, Lynn Smythe, acknowledged these concerns at a school committee meeting, "There's a perception of a traditional class difference between Monroe and Harris." She went on to explain that some Harris parents were concerned that a merger with Monroe would bring a bad element into Harris and would escalate problems with drugs or violence in the schools.

The *Harris Spectator*, a newspaper published by students at Harris-Sumner High School, offered the following report on regionalization,

"Monroe High School: These words alone are enough to raise little hairs on the necks of most Harris-Sumner students and draw comments about '*those* Monroe people.' No one can quite pin down where this attitude came from or why it exists, but it's there, and it applies to a good portion of the student body."

❖ REGIONALIZATION: THE VOTE

One month before the Harris and Monroe regionalization votes were scheduled to occur, two tax overrides for education, one in the amount of $350,000 and the other for $850,000, failed in Monroe. The smaller override was defeated by a margin of 1417 votes to 1170 votes; the larger override was defeated by 1731 votes to 833 votes. The failure meant seventeen school positions would have to be cut before summer. Athletics, transportation, and special education programs would also need to be cut.

At about the same time, Tony Perez resigned the Monroe superintendency and public reaction to the development was to rally around their schools. Public opinion seemed to coalesce around the cry that Monroe town government lacked faith in Monroe schools. Three weeks prior to the vote, both the Monroe Board of Selectmen and the Town Finance Committee reversed their pro-regionalization stance, and voted unanimously not to endorse regionalization with Harris-Sumner. (Bob Royale was no longer a selectman.) Selectman Bernard Arnold said, "I do not believe the majority of the Monroe student population would benefit from the merger. The honor students may benefit, but seventy-five to eighty percent of our children will be adversely affected."

On June 11, 1991, in the midst of a violent rainstorm that kept many voters home, Monroe approved regionalizing grades K-6 with Harris, and grades 7–12 with Harris-Sumner. The final vote count was 984–930. By 155 to 117, Sumner residents approved allowing Monroe into the current 7–12 Harris-Sumner regional district.

Six days later, Harris voters defeated by a margin of 2–1 the proposal to merge grades K-6, and Harris-Sumner grades 7–12 with Monroe. The final vote was 1,460 votes to 724. Harris school committee members were stunned, and wondered how they could have so misread the town's attitudes. Local papers reported that Lynn Smythe, Harris School Committee Chairwoman, was "overwhelmed by the defeat, and tears spilled down her cheeks as voters filed out." Commenting on the outcome, one elderly Harris resident said "I think people are basically afraid of change."

One Harris resident, who refused to identify himself to reporters, said, "There is a smugness in this town. Many of these people came here from working class neighborhoods twenty or twenty-five years ago. Now they don't even want to look at a place like Monroe. It reminds them of home." At a press conference, Harris School Business Manager Ryan Park summed it up: "The issue wasn't regionalization, the issue was Monroe."

❖ THE AFTERSHOCK: SCHOOL CHOICE

Just a month after the Monroe-Harris regionalization vote, in July, 1991, Harris became one of the first three communities in the state to establish an inter-district school choice program.[2] Superintendent Kramer created a new brochure highlighting Harris-Sumner schools, and took out ads in area papers advertising available student slots in the Harris system.

In the final stages of research on Monroe schools, Jack Sommers discovered the impact Harris' school choice program was having on Monroe schools. Nineteen high school students, and thirty-five elementary and middle school students were leaving Monroe for Harris schools in September. Within these numbers were the children of four Monroe School Committee members. They thought strongly enough about Harris schools that they were willing to resign their positions to let their children benefit.

Sommers also learned that along with the departing students, Monroe would have to send Harris $321,000. Of that total, only $40,500 would come from state aid. The rest would have to come from local tax levies.

Jack Sommers sat in his office mulling over the history of Monroe schools. He wondered what his strategic plan could be for the children of Monroe. Could the town afford to maintain its own district? Could it afford not to? Whatever his plan, it was clear it would impact a lot of lives.

❖ CASE PREPARATION QUESTIONS

1. What problem was Mr. Sommers trying to address in his statement to the school board?

---

[2]As part of his "Millennium" educational reform package, the state governor signed legislation to create a voluntary, state-wide school choice program in the spring of 1991. Pilot implementation was slated for the following fall. The school choice law provided for both intra- and inter-district programs. Each city and town would make its own decision about whether it would accept students from other communities. The law made no provision for transportation of students between home and receiving districts.

As originally enacted, school choice law stated that if a parent chose to send his/her child outside the home district, the home district must reimburse the receiving school district for the cost of educating the child. This reimbursement was to be equal to the full per pupil expenditure rate spent by the receiving district. That reimbursement would be deducted from state educational aid to the student's home district. If the amount due exceeded the limit of per pupil state aid available to the home district, then the home district must make up the difference out of local tax levies.

The funding formula for school choice was altered in the second year of implementation. The revision stated that the home district would pay only 75% of the receiving district's per pupil costs, up to a ceiling of $5,000.

2. In an era of declining support for public education, what concrete actions can administrators take to reverse the trend?
3. Offer your strategic plan for the Monroe Public Schools.

Exhibit 1

Proposed Merger Plan for Monroe, Harris and Sumner Public Schools

Monroe would regionalize grades K-6 with Harris, and with Harris-Sumner for grades 7-12.

School Board:

The regionalized school committee would be made up of 5 Harris members, 4 Monroe members, and 3 Sumner members (voting would be weighted according to town population). An interim school committee would be made up of members currently on school committees in each community. Those members would remain until their current terms expired.

Busing:

No children in K-3 would be required to attend school outside their home community, except in the case of a special needs students, with an Individual Educational Plan, and with the parents' approval. Students in grades 4-6 would also be educated in their home communities, except if a) a special needs student required specialized services not offered in the home community schools; b) a parent requested that the student be educated in another district school (as long as there was room and it was approved by the school board); c) when the school committee felt there was either overcrowding or underutilization of schools in a grade level in one town.

Personnel:

During first year of transition, all local school systems would remain intact. Tenured teachers would be protected under Chapter 71, Section 42B of State General Laws. If positions in local districts were eliminated due to regionalization, current staff would be given preferential consideration for similar positions in the regionalized district.

Buildings:

Each town would have at least one elementary school. No town may build a new elementary school unless it is approved at town meetings in each of the three towns in the regionalized district.

The regionalized district would continue to rent current school facilities in all three towns, with the exception of the Atlantis Middle School and Hoover Elementary School in Monroe. These facilities would be returned to the town of Monroe.

Budget Process:

The regional school committee would first approve a tentative budget. An annual budget hearing would then be held. Adoption of a final budget would require both 2/3 of school committee members and 2/3 of total weighted votes. The budget must also be approved by two of the towns with the majority of the student population (either Munroe/Harris or Harris/Sumner). If not approved, the budget would be revised and resubmitted. If not approved by two of the towns on this second try, the school committee could call a meeting of all registered voters from all three towns. A simple majority of eligible voters present at this combined meeting would be sufficient to approve the budget.

Cost Sharing:

1. Construction—construction costs for facilities for junior and senior high students would be apportioned: 70% to Harris, 25% to Monroe, 5% to Sumner. Construction costs for elementary schools would be apportioned according to the student population in those grades in each town.

2. Operating costs—determined on the basis of student population. The student population in grades K-12 in each town would be totaled for the last three years. The apportionment to each town would be the ratio that each town's three-year total bears to the regional total for those years. Operating costs would include transportation costs.

3. Capital costs (buy-in provision)—Monroe's share of capital costs of the district (junior/senior high) schools, after depreciation, amounts to $1.66 million. This would be paid at the rate of $83,000 per year for 20 years. The buy-in money would go to the towns of Harris and Sumner at the same ratio they paid for the construction.

Apportionment of Revenue:

Each year, the district would determine the amount of revenue to be used to reduce assessments to individual towns. It would then apportion it to the communities according to student population in each town. Chapter 70 state aid to local towns would go to the region to reduce local assessments at the same rate that they would have received it as a local community (i.e. each town would receive an amount equal to the amount of Chapter 70 state aid it received in FY 1992).

Addition of Other Towns:

Would have to be approved by member towns.

Withdrawal of Any Town:

A town may petition to withdraw from regionalized district, provided it has paid its share of operating costs. The town would remain liable for construction costs incurred while it was part of regionalized district. A withdrawal amendment must be approved by all three towns.

CURRICULUM AND ASSESSMENT

Educational administrators must possess deep knowledge and understanding of curriculum and assessment. Defining the relationship between curriculum, assessment, and standards is an essential role of the educational administrator. In addition, educational leaders must be familiar with a wide range of curricula, instructional approaches, and methods of assessment (including those related to special needs and other "at-risk" students). Cases in this section offer an opportunity to manage dilemmas that are fundamental to creation of effective learning communities for students and adults.

❖ JOE FERNANDEZ AND THE *CHILDREN OF THE RAINBOW* GUIDE (A AND B)

Joseph Fernandez, former superintendent of Dade County Public Schools, became chancellor of New York City Public Schools in January 1990. He has an agenda for reform and begins initiating those changes shortly after becoming chancellor. The case takes a close look at Fernandez' initiatives and gives particular emphasis to the implementation of an elementary curriculum guide called *Children of the Rainbow*.

❖ IMAGINING THE WORLD

Graham Pendray, Chairman of the history department at the Wilson School, wants his department to create and institute a new world history course for all freshman and sophomores. He believes the course will better prepare students for participation in the global society. Course proponents discover there is serious resistance within the community from an influential alumnus, members of the school's Curriculum Committee, and some members of the history department.

❖ LAKE WOBEGON WEST HIGH

George Larson, the hands-off principal of Lake Wobegon West High School, is disturbed by the inordinate number of A's and B's that are awarded in the fine and performing arts classes. His management style has won him both loyal supporters and detractors. The disparity among teachers' grading policies has resulted in inequities in class standings which are very important to both the students and their parents. The arts courses are given the same weight as math and science classes.

❖ WHO KNOWS BEST?

Carol Jenkins is one of the most sought after third-grade teachers at Fairview Elementary School because she is able to teach students of all abilities. Katie Shea is one of Carol's new students. Carol learns that the previous year Katie's mother requested that the school assess Katie's eligibility for special education services. The evaluation determined that Katie did not require special services. Mrs. Shea was outraged and arranged for an independent evaluation of her child; the independent evaluation recommended special education services for the child.

Suggested Readings

Fullan, M. (1991). *The new meaning of educational change.* New York: Teachers College Press.

Graham, P. (1984). Schools: Cacophony about practice, silence about purpose. *Daedalus, 113,* 29–57.

Herman, J., Aschbacher, P., and Winters, L. (1992). *A practical guide to alternative assessment.* Alexandria, VA: Association of Supervision and Curriculum Development.

Mitchell, R. (1992). *Testing for learning: How many new approaches to evaluation can improve American schools.* New York: Free Press.

Uyterhoeven, H. (1989). General managers in the middle. *Harvard Business Review, 67,* 136–145.

Wiggins, G. (1993). Assessment: Authenticity, context, and validity. *Phi Delta Kappan, 75,* 200–214.

Joe Fernandez and the *Children of the Rainbow* Guide (A)

Ed Kirby

❖ RAINBOW STRIFE

New York City Schools Chancellor Joseph Fernandez considered the fax that he had just received from Community School Board 24's President Mary Cummins on November 26, 1992. The message was "No," School Board 24 would not represent itself at a conciliation meeting that Fernandez had scheduled for November 30th. Fernandez had demanded the meeting in the hope of settling the public contest of wills that had been raging between himself and School Board 24. His showdown with School Board 24 had become one of the hottest issues in the New York media. Since the Spring, Mary Cummins and her school board had publicly rejected the New York City Board of Education's curriculum guide titled *Children of the Rainbow,* a first grade teacher's resource addressing the need for tolerance of all peoples in New York's multicultural community.

The curriculum guide resulted from a policy commitment by the New York City Board of Education in 1989. The policy was prompted by the riots that hit the city in the wake of the murder of a black youth, Yusef Hawkins, in the white neighborhood of Bensonhurst. As the Board of Education's policy directed:

> New York City is composed of a culturally diverse population; if its schools are to accept cultural diversity as a valuable resource, then school personnel, parents and students must be able to recognize biased attitudes and actions, both subtle and blatant, that lead to discrimination on the basis of race, color, religion, national origin, gender, age, sexual orientation and/or handicapping condition.

In the Fall of 1991, Chancellor Fernandez had distributed the curriculum guide to districts and had advised the community school boards to review the *Children of the Rainbow* before using it. He had further directed any community school board to come to his staff with an alternative if it was dissatisfied with the guide. While the New York City Board of Education has the authority to set policy guidelines for curriculum in the system's 32 community school districts, the local community school boards have direct authority over the actual curriculum taught in the district.

Community School Board 24, however, was refusing to cooperate. At a public hearing in March led by President Mary Cummins, the nine member school board had voted unanimously, and without protest from the audience, to reject *Children of the Rainbow* because it offended the moral values of many families in the district. In April, Cummins had launched a letter writing campaign urging the rejection of *Children of the Rainbow* throughout New York City. In retrospect, some observers of the controversy suggested that the curriculum guide may never have become a public issue had it not been for Cummins' vocal opposition.

Community School District 24 covers an area of Queens that includes the sections of Maspeth, Glendale, Middle Village, Corona and Elmhurst. The district is primarily working and middle class and has a large Catholic population. At the time of the controversy, the district was made up of 27,000 students, with a diverse student body that was 49% Hispanic, 27% White, 18% Asian, and 6% African American. The school board was entirely White.

School Board 24 was particularly opposed to the 3 or 4 pages of the curriculum guide that stressed the need for tolerance of gays and lesbians. The "Theme B: Families" section of the guide instructed teachers "that classes should include references to lesbian/gay people in all curricular areas and should avoid exclusionary practices by presuming a person's sexual orientation, reinforcing stereotypes, or speaking of lesbians/gays as 'they' or 'other.'" The section also stated that "[C]hildren need actual experiences via creative play, books, visitors etc. in order for them to view lesbians/gays as real people to be respected and appreciated." The curriculum guide, in its "Families at Home" bibliography listed, among other books, *Heather Has Two Mommies*, *Gloria Goes to Gay Pride*, and *Daddy's Roommate* as possible books for teachers to read to their students.

❖ THE *CHILDREN OF THE RAINBOW* CURRICULUM GUIDE

In 1990, just months after Joe Fernandez had become the Chancellor of New York City schools, gay and lesbian activists began meeting with Fernandez' staff to encourage them to comply with the Board of Education's multicultural policy which had, since its inception in 1989, received little attention. While Fernandez had not brought a specific agenda for a "tolerance curriculum" from his former job as superintendent in Dade County, Florida, he began to listen intently to proponents of "multicultural" curricula and of initiatives to promote tolerance of gays and lesbians. In April of 1991, Elissa Weindling, one of the members of the Gay and Lesbian Teachers Association which had approached Fernandez, was assigned by the Chancellor's staff to develop the section of the curriculum that would address families headed by gay and lesbian parents. Fernandez' staff completed a first draft of the first grade curriculum guide, including Weindling's section, in the early Fall of 1991.

This draft was reviewed by, among others, the Chancellor's Multicultural Advisory Board, the Chancellor's Central Committee on Multicultural Education, and a panel of more than a dozen academics. After reviewing the draft, members of Fernandez' Multicultural Advisory Board urged that the Fernandez staff drop *Heather Has Two Mommies* and *Gloria Goes to Gay Pride* from the bibliography. Even gay and lesbian advocates who reviewed the curriculum guide suggested that the two books were inappropriate for first graders. Nevertheless, when the first draft of *Children of the Rainbow* was released to the 32 community school districts later in the Fall of 1991, the books remained cited in the bibliography.

Despite the process of review at the Central Board of Education, *Children of the Rainbow* had been developed without input from the community school districts. As Stan Karp reported in the publication *Rethinking Schools* article "Trouble Over the Rainbow":

> The Central Office process that produced *Children of the Rainbow* had excluded most district board members, parents and teachers. Chancellor Fernandez' 25-member advisory board and the review process at the Board's Brooklyn headquarters were no substitute for an inclusive debate that might have created support for the curriculum before it arrived in the mail from 110 Livingston Street. Even gay activists later acknowledged that they had relied too heavily on lobbying central board personnel while Catholic, Pentecostal, and other church groups were mobilizing anti-gay sentiment in the boroughs.[1]

The *Children of the Rainbow* Curriculum Guide was a teacher's resource guide. The reality of the Board of Education's teacher guides, according to many in the system, was that they usually ended up "on the shelf" and did not affect what happened in New York's classrooms in any substantive way. In fact, it was not even clear that the distribution of the Guide throughout the school system was consistent from district to district or school to school.

The deadline for submitting alternative plans to the *Children of the Rainbow* guide was October 31, 1992. One year after the distribution of the first draft, School Board 24 rejected the deadline. Fernandez responded on November 9th by issuing a letter to President Mary Cummins demanding that her board submit an alternative teaching guide. Four other community school districts also ignored the October 31st deadline but Fernandez and his staff were negotiating successfully with these boards to come to a compromise plan.

School Board 24, however, had not responded to any encouragement for compromise. They were rejecting the entire guide outright and were offering no alternatives for the Chancellor's review.

---

[1]*Rethinking Schools*, Spring, 1993.

In his letter, Fernandez warned Mary Cummins that he would "not allow School Board 24 or any community school board simply to refuse to implement a Board of Education policy," and commented that he would "do everything in [his] power pursuant to law to ensure the Board of Education Policy is complied with."[2] Fernandez offered a new deadline of November 13th for submission of an alternative plan.

On Friday, November 13th, Mary Cummins responded to Fernandez' ultimatum by sending him a three volume alternative curriculum along with a letter highlighting Board 24's rejection of the *Children of the Rainbow*, stating:

> . . . [w]e are not going to make any use of your teaching guide entitled *Children of the Rainbow—First Grade* because it is shot through with dangerously misleading homosexual/lesbian propaganda.

On Tuesday, November 17th, Fernandez informed Board 24 that while the alternative curriculum did "respond to the need to recognize the heritage of our students' diversity," it did not comply with the board's requirement to address sexual orientation. Fernandez also informed Board 24 that he had directed his deputy for instruction to help the district to develop an acceptable curriculum.

Within one hour after receiving Fernandez' letter, Cummins responded with another letter claiming that Board 24 was in full compliance with the Board of Education policy and wrote, "[we] therefore reject your suggestion that it needs to be expanded to include material aimed at promoting acceptance of sodomy."

On November 26th, Fernandez summoned the members of Board 24 to a November 30th "conciliation" meeting, required by the state's decentralization law before the chancellor can take action against a local board. Cummins responded quickly and, again, in writing: "You have no right to summon us to your office for a conciliation meeting, because there has been absolutely no misconduct by this board that justifies your intervention."

❖ JOE FERNANDEZ

Fernandez began his career as an educator in Florida, in Dade County Schools, the fourth largest school system in the nation. Between his first teaching job at Miami Coral Park High School and his appointment as superintendent of the Dade County school system twenty-four years later, Fernandez assumed greater and greater levels of leadership in many diverse positions.

Perhaps the defining step of Fernandez' early career was in his first and last job as a school principal. Central High School was a city school of 4,600 students plagued by racial tension, violence, vandalism, difficult learning con-

---

[2]The quotes of Joseph Fernandez and Mary Cummins have been taken from the press coverage of the conflict. Original press clippings from which the quotes are taken are on file with the author.

ditions, and an apprehensive staff. Fernandez' tenure at Central was identified from day one by change. At an aggressive pace, Fernandez made sharp changes in the school: instituting a new discipline code; setting new expectations for the behavior and performance of the entire school community; and making over the appearance of the school by cleaning and painting buildings and renovating the school's grounds.

Throughout his career in Dade County, Fernandez recognized and capitalized on opportunities for initiating systemic change. As an Assistant Superintendent, Fernandez developed previously untapped resources in Dade County—support from businesses, community, and parents. Among his accomplishments, Fernandez often cited the creation of the county's first *strategic plan,* an outline for future improvement in the district that addressed the upcoming five years; the *Dade Partners Program* which united nearly 1,000 individual schools with local businesses; and the *Attendance Boundaries Committees* (ABC), which was a strategy to include community (especially parents) in the design of re-zoned geographical boundaries for greater racial balance in Dade County.

❖ THE DADE COUNTY SUPERINTENDENT AND SCHOOL BASED MANAGEMENT

When Joe Fernandez succeeded Leonard Britton as Superintendent of Dade County by a unanimous vote of the school board, he was given a clear political mandate to wield the kinds of influence he had made manifest as a teacher, assistant principal, principal and assistant superintendent in the district. Given the geographically and culturally diverse nature of Dade County,[3] Fernandez felt that he had to identify a mission for Dade that would encourage innovation and improvement in all of the schools, no matter how diverse their student populations. In two years as superintendent, Fernandez implemented several reforms. He "professionalized" the status of teachers and principals, elevating salaries at all levels and elevating the status of primary and middle school principals to the same level as high school principals. He promoted Satellite schools, a program that elicited business support to start public schools within work sites, thus enabling parents to be closer to their children and to make use of the support of the host business. He engineered a record setting $980,000,000 bond issue, the biggest school bond ever raised in the nation's history.

Fernandez also launched a program that he would later call "a battle plan for the ages," School Based Management. Fernandez was the first nationally recognized superintendent to implement School Based Management (SBM)

---

[3] 2,100 square miles encompassing a range of communities from inner city to wealthy suburbs to poor rural towns, and many races: Whites, African Americans, Hispanics, Cubans, constant immigration from Central America and the Caribbean.

aggressively and it soon became synonymous with Dade County and the name "Joe Fernandez."

In its design, Dade County's form of SBM allowed an individual school to be run by a "cadre" made up by the principal and representatives of the teachers, parents and other staff of a school community. The cadre would have influence on almost all aspects of the school's operation, including the management of the budget and the appointment of staff. While the principal would have the power to veto the cadre's proposals, the Superintendent's office could overrule a principal's veto if the principal was seen to be obstructing the progress of the school.

Perhaps more interesting in the evolution of Dade County's SBM than Fernandez' success in signing on 155 out of 273 schools, was the process by which he introduced the initiative to the district. Fernandez distributed a manual addressing "the beginnings of school based management" throughout the district and developed resource libraries of current writing about educational change in all of the district's school clusters.

Teaming up with union head Pat Tornillo, Fernandez held a conference that brought union leaders and school principals together to discuss the possibilities for SBM. Under Tornillo, the union would soon become a cooperative sponsor of the plan. Fernandez and Tornillo even broadcast a TV show to address questions for the public about SBM. As the process of implementing SBM neared, the pair ran several "dog and pony shows" around the county eliciting support at a grassroots level. In the first applications for SBM status, 57 schools submitted proposals.

❖ NEW YORK CITY PUBLIC SCHOOLS

When Joe Fernandez began in 1989 to entertain the prospect of being the Chancellor of the New York City School System, he was considering a system that is unique among school systems in the United States, not only for its size and diversity but also for its funding and governance structures. In terms of size, New York City's school system is the biggest in the nation, with roughly 1,000 schools, 1 million students, a $7 billion budget and 120,000 employees, more than 5,000 of whom worked for the New York City Board of Education, known as "110 Livingston Street," in the borough of Brooklyn.

New York's school system is unique in its funding structure. Neither the Board of Education nor the chancellor has control or authority over the amount of money directed to the system. Rather, the mayor's office oversees the roughly $7 billion per year schools' budget. The mayor, in a sense, is a gatekeeper for all money entering New York City Schools, and it is the mayor who has the responsibility to keep a balanced budget for the city. The school system has no power to demand funding increases and must negotiate yearly with the mayor.

New York's school system is also unique in its governance structure. The system underwent "decentralization" as mandated by the *Decentralization Act of 1969* of the New York State legislature. Much of the political leverage for decentralization originated in the African American and Hispanic communities who felt that the centralized school system had failed in its attempts to achieve quality of education for their communities.

While the central Board of Education had previously held responsibility for administration of all of the city's schools, decentralization passed much of that authority to the city's 32 community school districts, each of which set up its own community school board, superintendent, and district staff. Given that decentralization was a series of compromises fought out between those who would maintain centralization versus those who would abolish it, the resulting governance structure was far from clear. Though the city now had 32 decentralized districts, its central bureaucracy did not disappear; rather its powers were modified. The situation was ambiguous at best.

As a result of decentralization, the New York City Board of Education has seven members. Five of those are appointed by the elected presidents of the city's five boroughs.[4] Two are appointed by the mayor. The Board is responsible for appointing the chancellor and for setting policy for the school system. The chancellor directs the Board of Education's "110 Livingston Street" staff and has direct administrative authority for the city's high schools and special education programs. In addition to running the city's high schools, the chancellor has broad oversight authority over the city's community school boards.

The 32 community school boards are responsible for appointing a community school superintendent and for setting policy for their district. The community board and superintendent have direct control over elementary and middle schools, but no policy or administrative control over high schools.

The chancellor's role in relation to the community school boards is not clearly defined. As Fernandez commented:

> The chancellor implements the budget, with all that implies. He has direct control over the 124 high schools and the citywide special education programs involving 125,000 kids and has an overseer's limited power over the 32 community school boards. How much power he can exert to correct mistakes in the districts and bring about reform is just enough in doubt to make it imperative that he have a strong working relationship with his boss, the school board—the Board of Education.[5]

❖ CHANCELLOR FERNANDEZ

Joe Fernandez signed on as the New York City Chancellor on January 1, 1990 for a salary of $195,000 a year, making him the highest paid public official in

---

[4]Brooklyn, Manhattan, Staten Island, Queens, the Bronx.
[5]This and proceeding quotes of Joseph Fernandez appear with his permission and, unless explicitly cited from other sources, have been taken from his autobiography: Fernandez, Joseph A. with Underwood, John. *Tales Out of School*, New York, Little Brown and Company. 1993.

the history of both the city and the state. Although Fernandez officially began work on January 1st, he had actually started working in September of 1989, while still superintendent in Dade County, attending weekend meetings with representatives from all areas of the New York system. From the beginning it was clear that Fernandez had a clear agenda for the New York City schools. He had two basic priorities with regard to the reform of governance: 1) the ability to have input into the selection of the thirty-two district superintendents; and 2) the ability to intercede whenever things went wrong (or were already wrong) anywhere in the system.

Within weeks of beginning the job, Fernandez went after the corruption that had become commonplace in many of the community school districts since 1969, one third of which were under investigation by former Chancellor Green's office when Fernandez took over. To address mismanagement and corruption systematically, Fernandez developed a monitoring office as a "watchdog committee" that would oversee the governance of community school boards and superintendents and report to Fernandez when it spotted questionable practices. In addition to increased oversight, Fernandez also issued a system wide "circular" clarifying his prerogative to evaluate and reject nominees for community school district superintendent positions.

Fernandez also moved to abolish "building tenure" for principals, the policy that allowed a principal to have a permanent position at a school after five years. Through a deftly handled strategy of rallying New York's editorial boards against building tenure while developing a cooperative relationship with the union leadership, Fernandez managed to start a wave of support for his motion. His lobbying persuaded the New York State legislature to pass an agreement into law that granted the chancellor the right to remove incompetent principals and to transfer principals against their will.

Fernandez acknowledged the apparent contradiction that he, a proponent of decentralization, was going after the "heart" of decentralization, community school governance. But he argued that the seeming contradiction was a superficial one:

> The measures I took against the district boards were a contradiction only if you could say decentralization in New York City stood for responsible leadership and meaningful distribution of power, and not a means of getting greedy fingers into the till or perpetuating a dismal status quo. Centralized or decentralized, no authority is good if it is not accountable.

Fernandez also confronted what he considered illegitimate centralized power in the system. He led the dissolution of the Board of Examiners, a bureaucratic agency within the school system that controlled the certification and hiring of teachers, that had been historically criticized for preferential hiring and systematic exclusion of certain minority groups. Simultaneously he attacked his own staff, a 5,000 position bureaucracy at 110 Livingston Street, headquarters for the Board of Education. 110 Livingston Street had been a favorite and continual target for New Yorkers who point to bureaucratic waste and incompetence in the school system. By identifying and eliminating certain departments and by demanding more efficiency of departments, Fernandez and his staff continually "downsized" the central bureaucracy. Eventually he would cut the central staff from roughly 5,000 to a reported 3,500 positions.

❖ A SHIFT OF CLIMATE: A NEW BOARD TAKES OVER AT 110 LIVINGSTON STREET

Fernandez' early work was accomplished with a Board of Education that had enthusiastically hired him and had worked collaboratively to help him build a reform agenda. By July, 1990, however, Fernandez was working with a new board that had neither hired him nor had any particular allegiance to his reform agenda; only two of the seven members were holdovers from the previous board. Conspicuously absent on the new board was former President Robert Wagner, a lifelong public servant in New York City who had, by most accounts, worked quietly behind the scenes to forge strong consensus among board members.

The new Board that took office in 1990 was appointed by the five borough presidents and by Mayor David Dinkins. It was ethnically diverse, with two Hispanics, two African Americans, and three Whites.

As soon as the new Board took office, they were confronted with the worst budget crisis to hit the city and its schools since 1976. In preparing for the 1990–91 school year alone, the Dinkins administration asked the school system to absorb $190 million of cuts. Between 1990 and 1992 the cuts absorbed by the New York City Schools amounted to three quarters of a billion dollars of its $7 billion budget. Many observers of 110 Livingston Street (including Fernandez and members of the Board) pointed to the severe budget cuts as a major source of strain that negatively affected relationships among Board members and between the Board and Fernandez—in addition to the relationship of both parties to the Dinkins administration.

❖ A DIVISIVE BOARD OF EDUCATION

Fernandez characterized the board that took office in 1990 as adversarial and "micro-managing," one that inappropriately crossed the line between setting policy and administering policy. Fernandez claimed that the board members constantly hamstrung his staff with memos requesting detailed reports on just about every aspect of his administration. According to Fernandez, this prevented his staff from getting reform initiatives implemented. He also criticized the board members for waging their own individual political agendas and derailing attempts by his staff to test new ideas. Fernandez grew to see his Board as meddlesome, divisive, and counterproductive, placing individual politics before doing what was best for students.

James Vlasto, who served as the Chancellor's Press Secretary, confirmed many of Fernandez' perceptions. He said, "The board members believed in some ways that they were each the Chancellor."

While the sentiment against the Board of Education was strongly held by Fernandez' staff and the editorial boards of the city's newspapers, the view from the Board itself was different. Dr. Luis Reyes, who came on to the Board in July of 1990 and was one of Fernandez' most consistent supporters, believed that the Chancellor and his staff may have been largely responsible for the tensions. He said:

> Joe felt that the Board was picking at him, micro-managing, but Joe and his staff wanted to tell us as little as possible and at the same time put the positive spin on everything . . . minimize actual problems and maximize the perception of positive change . . . always this self protection of giving the good news and minimizing the bad news. Joe was not a consensus builder. He often stood on the battle line and was unwilling to compromise.

Moreover, many felt that Fernandez and his staff attempted to introduce reforms in the system without including people in the community school districts in the process of building reform. Many felt that this perception considerably damaged Fernandez' potential for developing his reforms. At the community level, some would challenge reforms not so much for their substance, but because they felt that they were without a role in the whole process.

❖ THE NEW BOARD AND THE CONDOM WAR

In 1990, shortly after he became Chancellor, Joe Fernandez took up the cause of implementing a more aggressive curriculum in the schools to educate kids about and keep them safe from the risk of HIV-AIDS. Prompted first by proposals from the City's HIV-AIDS Advisory Council and by statistics suggesting that 50–80% of the systems high school students were sexually active and that as many as 29% of AIDS cases in the city may have resulted from infections as teenagers, Fernandez expanded the HIV-AIDS Advisory Council. He directed his staff to develop a plan of action, and publicly announced his proposal for the *HIV/AIDS Education Program with Condom Availability* in a Board of Education meeting. The program was intended for high school students. Fernandez was required to go to the Board to pass the condom proposal because a previous board had, in 1985, banned condom distribution in the city's schools.

Nearly all parties would point to the battles over the *HIV-AIDS Education Program with Condom Availability* as one of the first and clearest examples of the bitter divisions that plagued the Board of Education and Fernandez. In this case, the division was played out not only in the halls of 110 Livingston Street, but in the city as a whole. Community leaders, advocacy groups, churches, editorial boards and parents all rallied to either side of the debate.

Fernandez felt that the school system had a responsibility to its children. He and other proponents of the plan believed that the program was an appropriate response to a growing threat and that condom distribution was the correct response to the HIV-AIDS epidemic. Opponents of the plan leveled two criticisms: 1) that the content of the plan was immoral and undercut the right of parents to take responsibility for teaching children about HIV-AIDS and its causes; and 2) that parents and the communities had been left out of the process of developing the program.

Opposition to the Chancellor's plan was centered in a campaign by the New York City Catholic Archdiocese and an interdenominational group of religious representatives called Concerned Clergy (later called, Concerned Clergy and Parents). Concerned Clergy had demanded, under former Chancellor Green, that a formal review process be in place for any HIV-AIDS instruction so that the community would have a voice in the planning of any curriculum. While Green had developed such a process, the New York City Catholic Archdiocese and Concerned Clergy felt that the Fernandez plan had neglected to include parents and community organizations in the drafting of the plan. The New York City Catholic Archdiocese, with a parish system that spread across the five boroughs, was in a very powerful position to influence social policy in the region.

The pending vote by the Board of Education on *HIV-AIDS Education Program with Condom Availability* was in doubt as the meeting to cast the vote began. Carol Gresser, Westina Matthews and Irene Impellizzeri were expected to follow the lead of conservative Michael Petrides in opposing the proposed plan. Gwendolyn Baker, Luis Reyes, and Ninfa Segarra were expected to vote for it. In the end, however, Westina Matthews voted for the program, possibly due to pressure from Mayor Dinkins, who supported the program. In a narrow 4–3 vote, the *HIV-AIDS Education Program with Condom Availability* passed on February 27, 1991.

❖ BOARD DETERIORATION

At about the same time that Mary Cummins and Community School Board 24 began to publicly protest the *Children of the Rainbow* curriculum guide in April, 1992, relationships in and around the New York City Board of Education began to deteriorate rapidly. Months earlier, in July of 1991, President Gwendolyn Baker had resigned from the Board and was replaced by another mayoral appointee, H. Carl McCall, an African American Citibank executive who had been active in Harlem politics. Mayor Dinkins hoped that McCall would bring a new sense of leadership to the Board and would be able to forge consensus among the divided board members.

Rather than attaining consensus, however, the Board grew further divided, and by the Spring of 1992, the *New York Times* described the status of the Board in an article titled the "Board of Frustration." It stated that Fernandez' initiatives were "being hobbled by the tensions on the Board," and that the incessant queries from the Board to Fernandez' staff were distracting.

Relationships among board members were not the only ones to deteriorate. The relationship between the Chancellor and the Mayor grew publicly strained when in May 1992, the two began a standoff over potential funding. The clash followed the proposal by the New York Municipal Assistance Corporation Director Felix Rohatyn to spend a $200 million surplus on school programs. While the Mayor had the technical authority to designate the funds, both Rohatyn and New York Governor Mario Cuomo supported the use of the funds for schools. Dinkins would not be able to direct the funds elsewhere without the endorsement of the Governor. Dinkin's plan for spending differed considerably from the plan envisioned by Fernandez. Dinkins and his staff felt that the funds should be used on services as well as education. The clash illuminated the tensions between the Chancellor and the Mayor and the endorsement of Cuomo and Rohatyn for the schools marked what would appear to be an erosion of the Mayor's power.

Dinkins began to lobby for new legislation that would reconstitute the Board of Education, giving the Mayor authority to appoint a six member majority of an eleven member Board of Education instead of the current power to appoint five of seven. Dinkins felt that such reconstitution would allow him and future mayors to construct a collaborative board that would be free of the political infighting visible on the current board.

❖ THE GANG OF FOUR

On May 27, 1992 four board members passed a resolution that would severely restrict all HIV-AIDS instruction by requiring that it more aggressively stress abstinence from sex. One board member, who had voted to pass the *HIV-AIDS Education Program with Condom Availability* in 1991, joined what was now perceived to be the "conservative" voting bloc within the Board. With this resolution, the bloc of four, soon to be known publicly as the "Gang of Four," were hindering the Chancellor's efforts for implementation of *HIV-AIDS Education Program with Condom Availability.*

In June, immediately following the resolution to stress abstinence, the Board experienced private and public strife as it debated whether or not to revise the existing HIV-AIDS curriculum for K-6 students, a curriculum that, by state law, required five lessons per year addressing the topic of HIV-AIDS for children in grades K-6. (This curriculum was distinct from the Chancellor's *HIV-AIDS Education Program with Condom Availability.*) Opponents criticized the K-6 curriculum because it instructed students in the 4th and 5th grades about the use of condoms and taught the methods of transmitting the AIDS virus, with explicit naming of vaginal, oral and anal intercourse. A meeting on June 15, 1992, of the Board of Education and representatives from 19 of the 32 community school boards, elicited strong voices both supporting and opposing the curriculum guide. The opposition felt that the curriculum contained details that were not "age-appropriate" and that the guide did not adequately stress abstinence.

Days later, on June 19th, a public Board of Education meeting erupted into a verbal clash among board members over the K-6 curriculum, with the Gang of Four rallying against the curriculum. President Carl McCall eventually adjourned the meeting after it reached a stalemate with little willingness by either side to compromise. In response, on June 23rd, Fernandez presented a revised curriculum to the Board which postponed the descriptions of the transmission of HIV-AIDS until later grades and which placed greater emphasis on abstinence. The next day the Board passed the guide with five supporting votes. Two Board members abstained.

A day after this vote, Fernandez announced publicly that the scores of nearly all of the community school districts in the system had declined in reading and math. This was the first time during his tenure that the system had experienced an aggregate decline in test scores. During his first two and a half years as Chancellor, Fernandez had noted gains in test scores, especially in math. The Chancellor attributed the declines to growing class sizes and massive teacher turnover due to the severe cuts that the system had suffered.

On August 19th, against the wishes of Fernandez, the Gang of Four proposed an addition to the abstinence resolution they had passed in May. With Fernandez and two Board members on vacation, the Gang of Four overpowered the President's sole dissenting vote to pass an "Abstinence Oath" resolution that would require all consultant HIV-AIDS educators to formally pledge to stress abstinence in their presentations in the city's schools.

❖ FERNANDEZ AND THE BOARD UNDER FIRE

A day later, on August 20th, Mayor Dinkins came out in public support of the Chancellor, criticizing the Abstinence Oath and warning that Fernandez was "unhappy" in his position and that further strife and lack of support for Fernandez might drive him from the job. "I have a sense that the Chancellor is very unhappy. He is considered by many to be the best educator in the land, and he's got to feel frustrated by the inability to operate with the way that the Board works," said Dinkins. While the Mayor may have intended to foster collaboration with this statement, elements of the press characterized Dinkin's move as an attempt to build support for his proposed legislation to reconstitute the Board with a majority of mayoral appointees.

On September 7, 1992, the beginning of Fernandez' third full school year as Chancellor, a *New York Times* article titled "Educational Virtuoso or Villain," attempted to assess the Fernandez administration and noted that Fernandez no longer had an unquestioned image as a successful reformer. The article also suggested that, while there was still strong support for Fernandez, questions about his effectiveness were multiplying. The article cited critics who found that Fernandez' most popular successes, such as SBM in Miami, were merely superficial changes and that in a system like New York, driven by bureaucracy and regulations, SBM councils had relatively little ability to effect change in schools.

Despite the negative slant in the press, Fernandez repeatedly defended his administration and pointed to many positive achievements, among them: School Based Management in 250 schools; a decrease in the dropout rate systemwide; less violence; more efficient special education services; and an increase in private sector investment in the system.

On November 21st, amidst the growing clash between Fernandez and Community School Board 24, Fernandez denied a report by the *Daily News* suggesting that he had decided to leave New York after his contract expired in June 1993. Fernandez did state, however, that he wanted greater support from the Board than a 4–3 split when it voted in the coming Winter on the renewal of his contract.

It was in this climate that Joe Fernandez faced a decision of how to respond to Community School Board 24's refusal to attend a conciliation meeting to negotiate the *Children of the Rainbow*. Since School Board 24 had first publicly rejected the *Children of the Rainbow* in April, the issue had become a heated public controversy. The conservative forces that had worked with the Catholic Archdiocese to oppose the *HIV-AIDS Education Program with Condom Availability* had, since April, rallied against *Children of the Rainbow* with similar fervor.

Meanwhile, the Board of Education had taken no formal stance on the Community School Board 24's opposition and had not advised Fernandez of its stance. James Vlasto explained:

> They gave him no guidance on School Board 24. They never said 'pull back the curriculum guide.' They could have said: 'We saw this simmering since April. Stop it. Revise it. We'll look at it and vote on it.' Instead they took a walk because they knew the guide was well within the policy and had the full support of health and educational professionals; it was long overdue. They micro-managed on every issue. They could have micro-managed on this critical issue but deliberately avoided taking a stance. Instead they stood back.

Without a clear mandate from either the Board of Education or the Mayor, Chancellor Fernandez had to decide how to respond to Community School Board 24 and its adamant opposition to his authority.

❖ CASE PREPARATION QUESTIONS

1. What are the main issues that Joe Fernandez faces as he tries to implement the *Rainbow* curriculum? What strategies does he have? What advice would you give him?

2. School Board 24 challenges the superintendency of Joe Fernandez. How would you respond to such a challenge? What is the appropriate balance between local control and centralized leadership in this instance?

3. What is the role of the local community in curricular decisions?

Joe Fernandez and the *Children of the Rainbow* Guide (B)

Ed Kirby

❖ SUSPENSION

On December 1, 1992 in response to Community School Board 24's refusal to accept the *Children of the Rainbow* curriculum guide, Schools Chancellor Joe Fernandez suspended School Board 24, marking the first suspension of a community school board over a curricular matter in New York City's two decade history of school decentralization.

The next day, Fernandez assigned three members of his executive staff to take over the headquarters of School District 24 and to take charge of the suspended board's responsibilities, setting policy for the school district. Fernandez left the superintendent of District 24 and his authority intact.

On the same day, at a meeting of the Board of Education, Fernandez accused the conservative voting bloc of the Board of overburdening him and his staff with "nit-picking" requests that were undermining their ability to get their job done. The confrontation, primarily between Fernandez and Board member Michael Petrides, was prompted by an item that Petrides had placed on the agenda entitled: "Micro-management: Reality or Perception." Fernandez was quoted as saying: "You have the right to ask for reports. But this is a major, major burden on my staff to get these things prepared." When another Board member asked Fernandez if he thought the Board micro-managed, Fernandez replied: "Yes, it makes our work very difficult."

On December 5th, only four days after Fernandez' suspension of School Board 24, the New York press devoted considerable attention to a pre-publication release of Fernandez' autobiography *Tales Out of School*, a book that traced Fernandez' life from birth through the first two years of his tenure in New York. The press seized on Fernandez' revelations about drug use in his youth and his candid criticisms of political players in New York City, including the Governor, the Mayor, and members of the Board of Education.

Meanwhile, the Mayor's proposal to reconstitute the make-up of the Board of Education was receiving considerable attention in the state legislature in Albany. Given the public concerns about the governance of the city's schools, it appeared that the proposal would pass the State Assembly but would face a tougher challenge by the largely Republican Senate. At the same time, Board President Carl McCall began lobbying within the city and the state legislature for support for Fernandez' contract renewal. The Board would be voting on the issue in late January or early February.

❖ SUSPENSION OVERRULED

On December 10th, addressing an appeal by Community School Board 24 for reinstatement, the Board of Education voted to overrule Fernandez' suspension and reinstated Board 24 on the condition that Fernandez could supersede Board 24 if it failed to cooperate in moves for conciliation. Both mayoral appointees to the Board sided with the majority Gang of Four to overrule Fernandez. One Board member abstained. Fernandez characterized the Board's vote as "disappointing," but said he would give Board 24 a chance to once again mediate the dispute.

A day later Mary Cummins, President of Community School Board 24, again rejected a directive by the Chancellor to meet with him at the Board of Education, calling Fernandez' order a "totally unauthorized ultimatum" and accusing Fernandez of having a "serious misunderstanding of what mediation entails." Cummins did, however, offer an invitation for the Chancellor to meet with her three days later in *her* offices. While Fernandez agreed to allow Board 24 more time to expand their alternative curriculum guide to address sexual orientation, he still called for the meeting in *his* office.

While the back and forth communication continued to no avail through the next week, the public debate over *Children of the Rainbow* reached its most heated intensity. At a public meeting of the Board of Education on December 16th, President Carl McCall had to clear the meeting room at 110 Livingston Street because shouting and shoving matches were erupting in the audience.

On December 17th, President McCall publicly criticized the Chancellor's staff for its development of the *Rainbow* guide. McCall questioned the competence of the staff that had developed the guide, saying: "The problem I had from the beginning is that I don't think we had specialists well grounded in education dealing with multiculturalism." In a memo to his fellow board members, McCall would also say that "[t]his issue has become bogged down with deliberate distortions, misunderstandings and poor communications from all sides. People are acting out of fear and misinformation, and, as a result, extremists dominate the debate." Fernandez also issued a public statement, calling for the "temperature of the debate" to be lowered.

Weeks later on January 26, 1993, Fernandez offered revisions for the *Rainbow* guide, softening elements in the text that had met with the most opposition. For example, gay and lesbian couples would henceforth be referred to as "same gender parents," and the bibliography would no longer contain *Heather Has Two Mommies*. One supportive Board member commented on the revisions: "It indicates that he does want to participate in the process. If he was walking away and had no desire for a [renewed] contract, he might very well not be forthcoming." Officials in Community School Board 24 were reported by the *New York Times* as saying that the changes were meaningless and that they would still reject the document.

❖ THE CHANCELLOR'S FATE

On February 3rd the Board met with the Chancellor to discuss the renewal of his contract. Assessments by the press following the Chancellor's suspension of Community School Board 24 suggested that the Board was split over whether or not to renew Fernandez' contract. Some assessments concluded that four members would oppose renewal, while other assessments suggested that four would support renewal. Carol Gresser of Queens, who had initially voiced support for Fernandez, now indicated that she might not support Fernandez because of dissatisfaction with the Chancellor and pressure from Claire Schulman, the Queens Borough President.

Despite intense lobbying efforts by many influential supporters of Fernandez (most notably Board President Carl McCall and Mayor Dinkins), the Board of Education voted on February 10th not to renew Joe Fernandez' contract. Fernandez would have to resign the Chancellor position at the end of June, 1993. No member of the Gang of Four was swayed. In a solid bloc, they opposed renewal. Three Board members voted unsuccessfully to renew.

In a written public statement issued after the Board's vote, Fernandez wrote:

> This is not the end of the school year. Our children have months of instruction left. Our city needs to wage a vigorous fight for resources in Albany and Washington, and I look forward to budget negotiations with the Mayor as well . . . I intend to devote 100 percent of my efforts in the days ahead to building a brighter future for our kids. Our children need a strong advocate, and I continue to be one.

Joe Fernandez, in an afterword to a later edition of his autobiography *Tales Out of School,* reflected on the controversies surrounding his last year in office as the Chancellor of New York City Schools:

> If I was too strident, too strong, too outspoken, I'm sorry; I didn't intend to bite the hand that fed me. Yes, I made mistakes, dozens of them by my standards, although you probably didn't see most of them in the papers. I wish I hadn't made them. I wish, for example, that I'd gone right to the Board on the *Children of the Rainbow* flap and said, "OK, ladies and gentlemen, I'm trying to implement your resolution. If you don't want it implemented as written, then change it." Pride probably got in my way, and I'm sorry it did.

◆ ◆ ◆

Imagining the World

David Beare

The tension was palpable as the members of the history department and their guest sat down for lunch in the private, wood-paneled dining room overlooking the quadrangle. Surrounded by portraits of the school's founders, the gentlemen and gentlewomen chatted about the comings and goings of the students, their current courses, and the upcoming football showdown with "that rival school to the north." Although many of the faculty members would have preferred to be elsewhere in the school, they felt a strong desire to respond vigorously to the "charges" of "politically correct misdirection" that their elegantly bow-tied visitor was there to make.

Mr. Peter Armington, the uncle of a current student at the Wilson School and himself a wealthy Wilson alumnus, had read in his nephew's copy of *Voice*, the official school newspaper, that the history department was considering instituting a new required course in world history for freshmen and sophomore students. He immediately called Graham Pendray, chair of the history department, to express his opposition to this new development, saying it was "ridiculous that students at the Wilson School should be required to take *world* history but not explore the roots of their *own* culture." The conversation, however, left Mr. Armington feeling Pendray was not taking his concern seriously so Armington wrote a detailed letter, outlining his specific objections to a world history requirement, and mailed it to Pendray, the headmaster, the dean of faculty, the director of admissions and the director of development. It was this letter that hastened the lunch meeting.

Shortly after the soup, Pendray decided to break the tension and invite Mr. Armington to present his objections to the proposed curriculum change. Armington obliged with relish:

"I don't like things the way they stand now, let alone a situation in which students would be *required* to take world history. Currently, freshmen and sophomores have to take either classical history, European history, Anglo-American political history or that crazy global studies course. At least under this system, *most* of the students are taking appropriate courses centered on our shared European heritage before they get to their junior year and take U.S. History. Your proposal would force kids out of these valuable courses, into a faddish world history *boutique* course. Personally, I just can't believe a student can graduate from the Wilson School without having had at least a survey course in European history! If we want our kids to get into Harvard, Yale, and Princeton, and take their place as culturally literate citizens and leaders of the United States, we owe our students a foundation in the history and traditions of the West. Let them take the P.C. stuff in college, or even as senior electives at Wilson—that's icing on the cake. But let's make sure the students have the cake first."

Members of the history department listened to Mr. Armington patiently— they had been primed for his particular point of view—and began to raise their own points in defense of the proposal. Graham Pendray said:

"The world history requirement doesn't preclude a student taking European or classical history. We'll still offer those courses to freshmen and sophomores. If parents think it is appropriate, a student could take world history in the freshman year, and European history in the sophomore year. Indeed, they could continue taking specific European history electives in their senior year. What we want to do with this world history course is to begin to develop in all our kids the skills and attitudes they'll need to be responsible, tolerant global citizens of the twenty-first century. The times, as one poet put it, *they are a changin'*. We have to embrace that fact."

Mr. Armington was not impressed with this rationale, one he fully expected. At the end of the lunch meeting—having progressed to cookies, tea and coffee—Armington let his hand show:

"I feel very strongly about this matter. You know very well, Mr. Pendray, that students at Wilson—with all their requirements for math, science, English, foreign language, philosophy and religion, as well as history—generally do not have space in their schedules to take three and four years of history. Your evasiveness on this issue, both on the telephone and in this meeting, indicates to me your desire to continue with this project despite my objections. I must tell you this: I don't think you clearly understand who your constituents are at this school, and the desire on the part of most parents and alumni to see the school adhere to a high standard of college preparatory excellence. I have a copy of the alumni directory. I can easily obtain a list of current parents. And believe me, I am prepared to send a copy of my letter to each and every one of them to see what kind of collective action we can take to counter your department's lack of clear and sober vision."

By the end of the lunch, there was no mistaking the potentially explosive nature of the disagreement.

❖ THE WILSON SCHOOL

Located in Wilson, Massachusetts, outside of Boston, the Wilson School was founded in the late nineteenth century by a group of New York and Boston industrialists who wished to remove their young progeny from the "evils of city life" and provide a "robust atmosphere in which young boys might learn." In the twentieth century, many changes forced their way onto the idyllic country life of the great academy. Boston itself expanded, farmland gave way to suburbs and the city became connected to its surrounding populations by commuter rail and public transportation. Girls were brought to the campus in the early seventies in a contentious move which merged a nearby, struggling girl's academy with Wilson. The endowment, sufficient in the early part of the century to provide tuition free of charge to all qualified students, had been poorly managed during the decades of the fifties and sixties, leaving the school relatively under endowed. There had been similar neglect of the alumni. It was not until the late seventies that the school began to aggressively cultivate its development potential among those men and women who had gone through the Wilson School in years past. As the school entered the decade of the nineties, it was generally regarded as a very good "five day" boarding school, even an "up-and-coming" school. Wilson was not in the absolute upper tier of independent schools populated by institutions such as Andover, Exeter and St. Paul's, but it was certainly within the 10 or so schools which constituted an unspoken "ivy league" of prep schools.

The sheer beauty of Wilson's campus rivaled that of any of its competitors. The school was oriented around a stately cluster of buildings in the "campus gothic" style, which provided a central focus for both the social and academic life of the school. This was markedly different from the sprawling campuses of other schools. Indeed, families that visited the school said the "feel" of the Wilson School was much different from that of the other schools they'd visited—more "friendly" and "comfortable." Wilson prided itself on its reputation of being a "caring" institution. This designation did not come without a price, however. Academics at Wilson, while solid, were not considered quite up to the level of the other prestigious boarding schools. In fact, the presence of a large number of day students and lack of a "full boarding experience" at Wilson were factors which tended to diminish Wilson's reputation among elite schools. The image of a demanding, rigorous boarding school, set apart from the city in splendid, intense isolation, remained the preferred model for many families.

The school's endowment did not compare favorably with its competitors, a fact which had profound consequences for the school's ability to attract and retain qualified applicants, the school's lifeblood. While an endowment of $31 million was healthy, the presence of 100 and 200 million dollar endowments among its competitors meant that Wilson was forced to charge a higher tuition than those schools and provide less financial aid. This was of particular concern to Linda Hawkins, director of both minority recruitment and financial aid. Hawkins was quoted in the *Voice* article as supporting the history department's proposal of a new world history requirement. "It's a strong selling point for minority applicants," Hawkins said. "It's definitely a signal that the school is beginning to take seriously the idea of multiculturalism and is beginning to move away from a damaging and distorting Eurocentrism."

Others in the admissions office were not so convinced. Sally Dunbar, a longtime admissions associate, believed that less attention should be paid to attracting minority candidates, particularly those who needed financial aid. "We need to attract full-pay kids, the nice kids who will do well at Wilson and who we can look to provide financial support when they graduate. If we get too many of the scholarship students, kids like Sarah Briggs, that popular student from Shaker Heights, Ohio, might not apply." When asked in confidence about the new world history course, Dunbar admitted that she thought it was a mistake: "I know I'm not supposed to say this, and the liberal history department would probably throw a fit, but what the families *want*—what they're looking for—is a solid, traditional education for their kids. Wilson is already viewed as a second tier school academically, we can't afford to let our program slip like that, particularly in history, which is *supposed* to be nicely musty. It gives character and weight to the school. We need that."

❖ GRAHAM PENDRAY

There was no question that the driving force behind the history department's proposal was its chairman, Graham Pendray. Graham had been with the Wilson School since 1975, joining the history faculty after he graduated with a B.A. degree in history from Williams College. Subsequently, he had found the time between teaching and coaching to gain an M.A. degree from Boston College, as well as take a number of trips to Eastern Europe to do research for his senior elective courses on the former Soviet Union and Eastern Orthodox Christianity. Graham was a highly respected coach of boy's lacrosse—his teams were perennial contenders for the league championship—and won the New England championship last season, beating nearby rival Middlesex School in a close match. In an interview with the *Boston Globe*, Pendray proclaimed a love for the sport grounded in the "creative flow of the game. The best players are ones who can see ahead two, three, even four passes. Its that quality of imagination that separates good players from great ones."

These were qualities that Pendray attempted to foster among his students and colleagues, as well. In his courses, Pendray relied heavily on document based learning, insisting that the students themselves become the historians, the interpreters of the past. Not a fan of rote memorization, Pendray impressed upon the kids the necessity of employing the historical imagination in considering past events. If historical study was to be meaningful to students, the historian must make history "come alive." He constantly pressed his kids to identify and call into question their own assumptions about the nature of society. Likewise, he consistently urged his colleagues in the history department to think critically about their own pedagogical points of view, and routinely enlisted their help in his grand, costumed role-plays of illuminating events of the past. In keeping with his own personal dynamism, and boundless energy, Pendray attempted to keep fresh the teaching and learning of history at the Wilson School.

❖ THE HISTORY DEPARTMENT

Although they banded together to face what they considered to be a meddling adversary in Peter Armington, the members of the history department themselves were rather divided over the necessity of such a radical change in departmental offerings. At a follow-up meeting to the lunch with Armington, some members of the department registered their reservations.

David Brewster said, "I don't know, Graham. While I think Armington's presentation is extreme, I share some aspects of his point of view. I mean, are kids going to be well enough prepared for the study of U.S. History, or am I going to have to start with square one when we get to the revolution and the constitution? I don't want to get too far off the Western track, this is important stuff."

Walker Stewart, an old timer at Wilson, added, "Well, what I want to know is what is going to happen to my course on the classical world. I've spent 20 of my 37 years at this institution developing, refining and teaching that course, and the kids love it. *I* love it. Armington's right when he says that far fewer kids will have the space in their schedules to take some of these freshman and sophomore offerings that we've spent a good deal of time and energy developing. And look at European history, we've got 4 sections of that course alone!"

Alison Bailey let out a deep sigh and turned to Graham. "I'm sorry to bring this up, Graham, but we also have to think about *how* and *who* is going to develop this course, and *when* we plan to implement it. I'm all for the idea of world history in principle, but to do it in a year course at this skill level seems almost absurd. We are really going to have to be careful about clearly defining our objectives if the course is to fly. I don't know about you, but this isn't anything that I'm prepared to take on during weekends and evenings. We are going to need some release time and summer work to get this thing up and running, and don't forget I'm going on sabbatical year after next!"

Of course, Pendray had anticipated many of these objections even before he began the process of convincing the department to support the idea of the new world history requirement. In keeping with his pedagogical and personal style, however, Graham was content to let people bring their own concerns to the fore and begin to hash them out with minimal direction from the chairman of the department. Pendray was quite confident that the diverse members of the history department would, in the end, come on board.

❖ THE CURRICULUM COMMITTEE

One of the largest formal hurdles that Pendray's proposal would have to vault was the school's Curriculum Committee. Composed of the chairs of all the academic departments at Wilson School, as well as the dean of faculty, and assistant headmaster, the Curriculum Committee had final authority to recommend a change in curriculum be adopted or rejected, a recommendation to which the headmaster almost always assented.

Support in the Curriculum Committee for a new world history requirement was far from unanimous. Many of the members shared a general perception, present among the faculty at large, that the history department really wanted to expand its way into a three year requirement. Lunch table grumblings were fairly consistent from some quarters:

"I don't ask to take my kids out of history class. I can't quite understand why the history department needs to keep taking those frivolous trips to Sturbridge Village and Ellis Island. They are always taking the kids somewhere, and its always during my class. Besides, Pendray is always at the copy machine, cranking out more homework for the kids. By the time they get through all that stuff for U.S. History, the kids don't have time to do their homework for *my* class!"

A particularly vocal opponent of the plan was Howard Mallory, chair of the visual arts department. Mallory said:

"Look, I don't need to remind you that we just built a new 7 million dollar performing arts building, a facility most universities would drool over. If this committee allows the history department to require kids to take a world history course, knowing that many of those same kids are going to turn right around and take European or classical history *and* take the U.S. requirement, space in that building is going to go unused. My introduction to theater arts course will be decimated. We've got a new state-of-the-art stage, lighting equipment, and acoustics 'to die for.' That's over a million dollars worth of equipment, and its all going to go to waste—not to mention the fact that kids will be denied the chance to let their creative energies emerge!"

Other members of the Curriculum Committee knew Howard could exaggerate and took his comments with a grain of salt. Nonetheless, it was clear that, while there was a moderate level of general support for the history department's proposal, passage through the Curriculum Committee was far from guaranteed.

❖ WITH THE HEADMASTER

The morning after the fateful lunch with Armington, Pendray received a phone call from the headmaster's secretary, summoning him politely to the headmaster's office. Pendray knew, by the direct wording of the request, that this was not a meeting he could put off to another time, "Robert would like to see you at 1:45."

Dr. Robert Craddock had been headmaster of the Wilson School since 1976. A former University Provost and Professor of Medieval and Early Modern European Studies at Middlebury College, Craddock brought to the school tremendous organizational and strategic planning skills. Although his brooding demeanor prevented him from being beloved by parents and alumni, he was still considered one of the top independent school heads in the nation, and was largely responsible for rehabilitating Wilson's semi-tarnished image, leftover from the school's growing pains in the early 70's. Under Craddock's leadership, the school had expanded its physical plant, increased its boarding population, doubled its endowment, and had reclaimed its place among the elite institutions of the Northeast.

As Pendray entered the headmaster's office, Craddock nodded his head in the direction of his colleague, and—in his usual manner—launched directly into the topic at hand:

"How was the lunch meeting with Peter Armington?"

"Rough, Robert. To say the least."

"Indeed. I have three messages from him just this morning. It seems he is rather *upset*."

"Yes, and he threatened to send that letter of his to current parents and alumni, trying to drum up a backlash."

"I anticipated as much. Well, that is more my problem than yours at the moment, Graham. I don't think the course of studies at the Wilson School should be set by Mr. Armington and his activities. I do want you to know, though, that a copy of Armington's letter has been circulated among the trustees, who have taken a keen interest in its contents."

"Good grief, Armington knows his politics!"

"At any rate, the trustees are scheduled to meet early next month. The head of the education subcommittee would like the history department to make a presentation to the full board on the rationale and parameters for the new course. I would like you and the department to comply with their request. You understand, Graham, that I am four square behind the proposal. Nonetheless, I have a delicate line to walk with the trustees. If the world history project is to fly, the nature and quality of your preparation for the meeting is crucial."

"Of course, Robert."

The wheels in Pendray's head were spinning. The headmaster went on to his next meeting, and Pendray stepped out of Craddock's office into the afternoon sunshine. As he crossed the school's main lawn, heading to his apartment to get ready for lacrosse practice, Pendray was thinking he only had a month until the trustee's meeting—four weeks to make sure the new world history course would become a reality. "The success of the enterprise is all a matter of creativity and strategy," thought Graham. "The question is, do I have the imagination to think three or four passes ahead?"

❖ CASE PREPARATION QUESTIONS

1. Describe Graham Pendray's motivation and strategy for introducing changes in the history curriculum at the Wilson School.

2. Does the role of parents' participation in curricular decisions differ when the school is private rather public?

3. Both Pendray and Robert Craddock are managers in the middle. Assess their performance.

Lake Wobegon West High

Edward Miller with the assistance of Susan Leong

George Larson winced as he paused outside the band room on his morning stroll around the school. It was B Block—the wind ensemble was rehearsing. Something was very wrong, he knew, and it wasn't just the sour notes coming out of the saxophone section. Every term, more than 90 percent of the music grades were A's or B's. All the children in Lake Wobegon might be above average, but George knew in his gut that this wind ensemble had a long way to go before they'd be making superior sounds. "Are these kids really being challenged to do their best?" he asked himself.

The dilemma of the grades in all the arts courses was beginning to drive Larson crazy. And this morning, the soft-spoken, reflective principal of Lake Wobegon High had to admit that his gentle proddings were getting him nowhere. The band wasn't playing better and the performing and fine arts grades were simply too high compared with other departments' grades. It was clearly inequitable. But what could George do about it?

❖ TRAPPINGS OF SUCCESS

Lake Wobegon was a relatively affluent suburb of a large midwestern city. Many of the residents were professionals and academics, with high aspirations for their children. There were two public high schools; Lake Wobegon High, which at one time served the whole community; and Lake Wobegon West High, built in the 1960s to accommodate the rapidly growing tree-lined subdivisions on the west side of town.

The rest of the school system included eight elementary schools and two middle schools, Parker and Winston. The middle schools matched the high school: all of the students graduating from Parker Middle School were assigned to Lake Wobegon High, and all of the Winston graduates went to Lake Wobegon West.

Very few minority families lived in town, but about forty African American students, in a voluntary program, were bused in from the city daily to attend each of the high schools. A significant minority of Lake Wobegonians were Jewish.

The Lake Wobegon Public Schools were known all over the country for their excellence, and Lake Wobegon West High was especially considered an academic powerhouse. (See Exhibits 1 and 2 on page 235.) Of the 261 Lake Wobegon West graduates in the Class of 1991, 90 percent went on to further education, with 84 percent attending four-year colleges. Two-hundred thirty-two of those graduates took the S.A.T.; their mean scores were 498 on the verbal test and 567 on the math, well above the national averages.

"I think of Lake Wobegon as a really good place to work," said Dana Oliver, who taught theater and playwriting courses at the high school for twelve years. "The town is very proud of its schools, very invested in their quality, although I'm frequently suspicious that we are riding on our reputation more than on reality. I don't think we are as outstanding as we are cracked up to be. Lake Wobegon is a very driven community in terms of the outward trappings of success. The students have the sense that it's critical to get into the best colleges. It's really not okay in terms of social status if they don't go on to higher education."

❖ THE HANDS–OFF ADMINISTRATOR

George Larson had been principal of Lake Wobegon West High for eighteen years. A researcher from the University of Wisconsin who spent time observing the inner workings of the school in the late 1980s was struck by Larson's "belief in decision-making by consensus, his aversion to hierarchies, and his defense of both teacher and school autonomy. Where other administrators may resort to directives, Larson prefers to solicit voluntary compliance."

"I do not consider faculty members 'my staff,'" George told the researcher. "'Staff' is a bureaucratic term which is used by the military, businesses, and central offices."

The faculty, in turn, was fiercely loyal to Larson. "George is a superb principal for this school," said Oswald Livermore, chair of the math department. "One of the axioms of this school system is autonomy. They believe in hiring the best people and letting them do their job. The superintendent says to the principal, 'You run your school, and I'm going to support you.' The principal says the same to his department heads. George accepts the fact that there may be differences between departments—say, in the way they grade. This is an active decision, not laissez-faire management. He endorses the notion of people operating in their own ways. If there are differences, there are differences. There's no top-down interference here."

Not everyone was so enthusiastic about the principal's leadership. "George is the extreme of the hands-off administrator," said Lynn Feldman, a parent representative on the School Improvement Council. "He literally does not get involved in anything going on in the classrooms, for better or worse. He protects the teachers at all costs. And that's fine when the teacher is good. It's terrible when the teacher is incompetent. In my opinion, the school is mediocre."

"George is not a mover or a shaker," said Ben Schmidt, a Lake Wobegon father and a university professor. "He doesn't have exciting ideas. Nothing original has come out of that school in years."

Larson considered himself close to classroom issues of curriculum and assessment, and he taught one social studies class every semester. He was known as a tough grader, who gave few A's. He was also willing to champion unpopular causes—for example, supporting the student council's request for condom machines in the bathrooms in the face of strong opposition from the school board and superintendent.

In recent years, Larson had been under pressure to cut his budget because of a combination of declining enrollments and recession in the local economy. Partly because Lake Wobegon West High was considered such a good place to work, there had been virtually no turnover in the staff. George struggled to apportion the cuts evenly among the departments, though there was pressure to cut "frills" like arts programs from various quarters in the community.

❖ **"YOU'RE JUST TOO SOFT-HEARTED"**

Back in his office, George pulled a fat sheaf of computer printouts off the shelf. They contained summaries of the grades for the entire school from the first marking period, which had ended a couple of weeks ago, and were broken down by department and by individual teacher (see Exhibit 3 on page 236).

He looked up Fred Morton, the stentorian band director and longtime head of the music department. A quick scan of the numbers confirmed what George already knew: almost all of Fred's students had gotten A's and B's, and the majority of the grades—more than 70 percent—were A's. The figures for Mrs. Biddle, the other music teacher, were pretty much the same.

George had been having a friendly but frustrating argument with Fred about his grading for two years now. "Your grades are too high," he would say to him. "You're just too soft-hearted. You want to praise everybody all the time."

"Yes, I do," Fred would reply with defiant pride, staring at George through the lower halves of his horn-rimmed bifocals. "Yes, I do." And they would both laugh. But George wasn't laughing now. He was gritting his teeth. He thought back to last spring's end-of-year band concert. It's not that the band was all that bad. It was okay, but it wasn't great. And given the kind of town that Lake Wobegon was, the level of talent and energy and drive that Lake Wobegon kids typically showed in every kind of performance, George suspected that the music program could produce better results.

He also knew that it wouldn't be easy to get Fred to change. He had been teaching music in Lake Wobegon for 25 years, and he was as tenacious in sticking up for his program and his methods as he was soft-hearted at report-card time. "Now, George," he would say in his too-loud voice, "how can you say that my students aren't working hard enough? Just look at all they've accomplished."

"Fred, you know how much I value your program," George would say. "Don't I come to every single performance? But what kind of message are you sending when you give almost all A's and B's? Can you honestly tell me that three-fourths of your students have achieved excellence? That they are all producing absolutely superior work?"

"Well, George," Fred would reply, as if talking to a nine-year-old, "you're probably right. But I'm not willing to grade that way."

❖ A QUESTION OF EQUITY

Talking to Fred privately about his grades hadn't had any effect, so George considered other options, such as raising the issue at a department heads meeting. After all, there was the question of equity—of the fairness of grading policies among the different departments. Everyone knew that teachers of arts courses at Lake Wobegon West were easy graders in general, compared with the academic subjects. But, because of the community's—and George's—strong support of the arts, performing and fine arts courses were weighted as Group 1 courses (see Exhibit 4 on page 237) in the calculation of students' grade-point averages and class rank. This meant that music and art courses got equal weight with trigonometry, physics, and other high-powered academic courses. It wasn't fair. And class ranking mattered enormously to Lake Wobegon West students and their families.

A quick check of the grade distributions in the other performing and fine arts courses confirmed George's impression. In the art department, whose new acting head was Bill Pillsbury, the young ceramics and sculpture teacher, 87 percent of the grades were A's or B's. Dana Oliver, the theater arts teacher, had given 85 percent of her students A's or B's. The math department, by contrast, gave only 56 percent A's and B's. The science department was at 58 percent.

George had had a few conversations about grading with Dana, whom he found bright and eager to listen. Dana sympathized with George's argument about equity, and she generally agreed with George that A's should be given only to students who demonstrated real mastery, but in the end she seemed no more willing to change her grading system than Fred.

"Theater is an elective," Dana had pointed out. "It's clear to me that when kids get C's and D's they don't come back. Nobody's required to take my courses. So if I graded as stringently as the math department, I wouldn't have a program. Maybe I wouldn't have a job. I've often thought that I'd like to teach the theater courses pass-fail, but I'm always aggressively talked out of it by the other teachers. 'Don't do it,' they say. 'You'll get students who are there for reasons that have nothing to do with their interest in the course.' And I worry that if we make arts courses ungraded, we send the kids a message saying the arts don't matter."

❖ THE NEXT WEEK

Realizing that the issue of fairness in grading was really beginning to bother him, George Larson decided to call a meeting of the art department chairs.

"I've been looking at the grade reports from first term," said George when Fred Morton, Bill Pillsbury, and Dana Oliver were assembled in his office, "and it's clear that grades in your arts courses are highly inflated, compared with the rest of the school. Each of you is giving an A or B to more than 85 percent of your students. That is simply going to have to change."

The three teachers stared at George in stunned silence. George went on. "I'm very concerned that some kids may be taking arts courses simply to get an easy A or B in order to raise their class ranking. It has long been the policy here to give the grades in arts courses equal weight with Group 1 academic courses as a way of demonstrating our belief in the importance of artistic pursuits. But we are being unfair to students who take a lot of math and science courses when they have to work so much harder to achieve the same class rank as those who take lots of arts courses."

Fred could no longer contain himself. "We've gone over this before, George. It's not right to compare what we do with math and science and history. We work with kids who often have never tried these things before—never risked being on a stage, never risked throwing a pot, or, in my case, never sung in a four-part harmony choir. Suddenly they come in and they're willing to try to learn to read music, to sing the harmony, to listen to the other kids' parts. You want me to give those kids C's? I'm sorry. I'm not going to do it."

"But Fred," George argued, "if that kid who gets an A or B from you is really a C student, and his class rank is artificially inflated, can't you see how that might affect his ability to perform well later in college?"

"We in the arts," Fred replied heatedly, "are teaching something that these kids need to know. If that kid has done really well in the arts courses, and okay in English and math and so on, he's probably a pretty good risk for college, and in fact might be a hell of a lot more interesting human being when he grows up. This bothers me, that maybe all this concern over grading is about the grade-point averages. If that's the reason, then our educational philosophy is really off the mark."

"I agree," said Dana. "What I'm trying to foster, particularly in a course like Voice, Movement, and Improvisation, is courage, risktaking, a willingness to drop all the crap and take the plunge. I'm trying to bolster self-confidence. Suddenly, a kid comes offstage and I say, 'Good job—C.' That's a mixed message."

George turned to the young art teacher. "What do you say, Bill?" "I don't know," Bill answered slowly. "I could be a little tougher on the kids, I guess, but I don't like the idea. I grade on the basis of individual progress. If I see a kid has gotten somewhere during the semester, if there is a little bit of growth—I reward that. I'd say 95 percent of my kids are trying hard, doing the best they can. To me, a C is a negative reinforcement. It says, 'You're not that good.' And that kid isn't going to try."

"It sounds like you're trying to get us to grade the product," said Dana, "but the arts don't work that way. We're encouraging process. What's the point of education, anyway? Is it to make sure the kids 'get it right'? Or is it to motivate the kids to try?"

"In most math and science classes," said Bill, "the kids are all at the same grade and ability level. They're all pigeonholed. In my classes, I have kids from grades nine to twelve. Some have learning disabilities. Some are at the top of their class. I have such a wide spectrum of kids that I can't say, 'This is what I expect of you—this is how much you have to get done this semester to get an A.' I can't say, 'Okay, you are the best in my class. You are an A student, you are talented. And you are a D student, you are not talented.' If the person is not talented, it's not their fault. Why should I slap them in the face with a D?"

"I'm willing to acknowledge, George," said Dana, "that there may be some problem, some kind of screwball message that we're sending kids because different departments have different ideas of what A's and B's mean. Maybe we need to have a school-wide policy about what grades mean. But we don't need to tell the arts to grade harder. Now, if you'll excuse me, I've got a parent whose been waiting for me for ten minutes." And, with some flurry, Dana picked up her papers and left.

❖ THE AFTERMATH

Nothing was resolved in the meeting. In fact, the department chairs grew more firm in their position while George grew more confused. But George couldn't let go of his feeling that grading inequities existed at Lake Wobegon West. As the principal straightened his desk and made ready to go to his next meeting at Central Office, he quietly mouthed his abiding principle, "There is a solution to every problem." And, as he flipped off the lights, he wondered what the heck it was going to be.

❖ CASE PREPARATION QUESTIONS

1. What, if anything, is problematical about the current grading practices at Lake Wobegon West High School?

2. George Larson calls the teachers into his office to discuss their assessment criteria. Describe the argument made by each teacher.

3. How would you handle the situation if you were the principal of Lake Wobegon West?

EXHIBIT 1

"School Philosophy"

We are part of a larger credentialing system that requires us to rank our students. While we help to prepare them for the world of work or for further formal education, we should try to maintain a balance between the pressures of the next stage in their lives and our desire to have them experience the discipline and satisfaction of mastering the task at hand, however modest or demanding. In evaluating our students' performance, we must find criteria which promote growth and development rather than stereotype individuals or reduce their self-esteem. Because adolescents are experiencing important physical, emotional, and social changes, we need to provide them with opportunities to gain self-acceptance and self-respect, as well as to develop the skills to work or play with others. Cooperation and service, honor, compassion, and joy should also engage our attention as essential qualities of the human spirit that lend a sense of purpose and meaning to the entire enterprise. High school should be a rewarding experience as well as a means to the future.

EXHIBIT 2

The college certifying marks are C and above. A and B are honor marks.

A = Excellent
B = Above Average
C = Average
D = Below Average
F = Failure

Exhibit 3

Grade Distribution Summary—First Term 1991–1992 Lake Wobegon West High School

DEPARTMENT	GRADE BY PERCENTAGE						
	A	**B**	**C**	**D**	**F/N**	**A + B**	**Avg.**
Art	29.5	57.8	7.5	1.5	3.6	87.3	3.08
Business	35.4	46.8	8.9	0	8.9	82.3	3.00
English	14.8	55.3	20.8	5.8	3.2	70.1	2.73
Foreign Lang.	28.5	48.1	16.9	4.3	2.3	76.6	2.96
History	24.0	46.4	21.0	5.4	3.1	70.4	2.83
Home Ec. & Ind. Arts	30.7	45.0	13.8	4.1	6.4	75.7	2.89
Math	18.9	37.6	26.2	11.2	6.0	56.5	2.52
Music	72.6	23.6	2.8	0	.8	96.2	3.67
Science	18.9	39.5	29.4	8.8	3.3	58.4	2.62
Theater	8.3	76.7	11.7	0	3.3	85.0	2.87
SCHOOL TOTAL	25.2	43.2	19.4	6.0	6.2	68.4	2.75

Notes: N = Failing grade based on attendance
Grades of I (Incomplete), P (Pass), W (Withdrawn), etc. are not included in the calculation of these percentages
Avg. = Average grade, with A = 4, B = 3, C = 2, D = 1, F/N = 0
Figures for English do not include Theater, which is otherwise considered part of the English department

Exhibit 4

Students' rank in class is determined on the basis of cumulative weighted average of grades A through F and N, and is computed twice: at the end of the junior year from the final marks for Grades 10 and 11; in the middle of the senior year from adding proportionally the marks for the first two terms of the senior year to the weighted average for Grades 10 and 11. Courses taken in ninth grade are not counted for purposes of class rank. Each course in which a student received a letter grade, with the exception of the pass-fail courses, is weighted in one of three groups. Each grade in each group is assigned a point value, is multiplied by the appropriate course credits, is added and then is averaged by dividing that sum by the total credits attempted. This number is the student's weighted average. The points assigned to the three groups are as follows:

Honors		Group 1		Group 2	
A	33	A	30	A	24
A −	31	A −	28	A −	22
B +	29	B +	26	B +	20
B	27	B	24	B	18
B −	25	B −	22	B −	16
C +	23	C +	20	C +	14
C	21	C	18	C	12
C −	19	C −	16	C −	10
D +	17	D +	14	D +	8
D	15	D	12	D	6
D −	13	D −	10	D −	4
F	0	F	0	F	0
N	0	N	0	N	0

Who Knows Best?

Claudia Johnson

❖ CAROL JENKINS

Carol Jenkins was in her third year of teaching. She entered the field leaving behind a budding career in advertising to follow her dream of working with young children. After two years of study and student teaching, she received her Ed.M. in early childhood education. Certified to teach K-3, her main interest was teaching third grade.

After obtaining her degree, Carol received several job offers from area schools. She turned down one offer from the highly regarded elementary school where she completed her student teaching. "Their curriculum and instruction is too buttoned-down for me," she told astonished friends. "The principal says the parents want to see their children use elementary school to get ahead of the game. He keeps pushing workbooks, workbooks, and more workbooks. There's a lot of performance pressure there—for kids and for teachers."

❖ THE FAIRVIEW ELEMENTARY SCHOOL

Instead, Carol chose to work at the Fairview Elementary School in Harrison. Fairview was a showplace school designed for grades K-4. Occupying over 90,000 square feet, the school had 35 classrooms with special facilities for art, music, computers, and science. Six hundred and ten students were enrolled at Fairview.

Carol was actually surprised to find such a beautiful facility in Harrison because the district had such a mediocre reputation. Her classmates described it as a blue-collar town that began as a farming and milling community. The average per pupil expenditure rate in the district was about $4,000. The school system was fairly small, with 1200 students in an elementary, middle and high school. One of Carol's friends, who taught in a neighboring, more affluent town, said that Harrison residents were notoriously unwilling to spend money on their schools.

None of this really interested Carol. The novice teacher was attracted to the new facility and to the commitment of the teachers and administrators. Everyone worked toward creating a supportive learning environment for the students. During her first interview, Frank Howard, Fairview's principal, seemed less interested in the scope of her graduate course work than how she interacted with children, even bringing a few students in to meet her at the end of the meeting. Ed Ronan, the assistant principal and director of instruction, told her that his goal was to let teachers be self-directed, giving them freedom to try new curricula and teaching approaches. "If the children are learning well, and the parents are happy we're doing our job," he told her.

It didn't take long for Carol to believe that she found her niche in Fairview. She was happy in her school community and worked hard over the next two years to learn her craft and support her third graders in their learning. Some of Carol's older colleagues still relied heavily on worksheets and teacher-centered instruction but she was heartened that many of her younger colleagues were dedicated to student-centered learning. Carol experimented with aspects of both approaches, eventually finding her place somewhere between the two philosophies. While she applauded the developmental approach used by many of the K-2 teachers, where instruction is geared to the emerging needs of each student, she believed that third grade should provide children with a slightly different experience. "They are old enough now that they understand that their teacher has general expectations for them and that they should try to meet those expectations in their work. They've been exposed to all sorts of new experiences during K-2, and now it's time to perfect what they've learned. It's time for them to start learning accountability."

Fairview parents liked the results Carol achieved with her students and by the end of her second year she was the most sought-after third grade teacher in the school—for children of all abilities. Several parents with children in Fairview's Chapter 1 program thought their children made excellent progress in math and reading in Carol's class.[1] One parent remarked to Frank Howard, "Carol really seems to want to help them come off Chapter 1. Other teachers want them to stay in it because the program gives them more time with other, more advanced children."

Thinking back to her career in advertising, Carol knew how important client service was and tried hard to build a good rapport with parents. She kept her parents informed about their child's progress and listened to their concerns. Privately, she wished some parents would interfere less and rely on her professional knowledge more, but she consoled herself by thinking those

---

[1]Chapter 1 is a federally-funded program designed to help elementary students that are approximately six months behind grade level in reading and math. For a child to receive Chapter 1 services, his/her teacher refers the child to the school's Chapter 1 teaching staff, who then obtain parental permission to test the child. Based on those tests results, the child will receive varying levels of in-class assistance from a Chapter 1 teacher.

parents at least cared enough to get involved. And she felt most parents believed Fairview teachers were working in good faith and in the best interests of their children.

Entering Fairview after her summer vacation, Carol was confident and eager to begin the school year. She sat with the second grade teachers to review her class list. And the insights they gave her about her kids confirmed her hunch that she had a good group. As usual, her 23 children included a few in the school's Chapter 1 and special education programs.

❖ KATIE SHEA

Attached to Carol's new class list was a note about one of her students, Katie Shea. The note was from the school's special education administrator, Sue Gardner, and explained that Katie was a Chapter 1 student who would receive special help for language arts. She also wrote that Katie's parents had placed her on Ritalin during the preceding summer. Sue suggested that she and Carol meet to discuss Katie's case before beginning the school year.

Talking with Sue, Carol learned that Katie had been placed in the Chapter 1 program last year. Katie's second grade teacher, who used a developmental approach in her teaching, described Katie as a sweet and cheerful child who was making good progress with the special assistance available through the Chapter 1 intervention.

However, Katie's mother, Brenda Shea, was a nurse who strongly believed her daughter needed additional special education services. Mrs. Shea had requested, as was her right under the provisions of Massachusetts Chapter 766 regulations on special education, that the school conduct a TEAM assessment to determine the child's eligibility for special education services.[2]

The Sheas had lost their first child, a son, during infancy. Katie was born a few years later, and then two younger girls were born about five years after Katie. Mrs. Shea told Fairview staff that she was very worried about Katie, and wondered whether a "family history of depression and learning disabilities" was showing up in her daughter. She repeatedly told whoever would lis-

---

[2]Chapter 766 is the Massachusetts legislation overseeing provision of special education services to public school children. The legislation specifically addresses the rights of parents in issues of needs assessment and referral.

TEAM assessments are the in-depth evaluations completed to assess whether a child needs special education services, and, if so, what services are appropriate. Before 1978 in Massachusetts (when special education laws were re-written), these evaluations were called CORE assessments. Initial TEAM assessments are generally completed by the school, and an educational plan for the child is drafted for parent approval. Should the parent disagree with the results of the evaluation, or refuse to sign the educational plan, Chapter 766 allows parents to seek a second, independent evaluation. If such evaluation is completed at a state-recognized evaluation center (such as a hospital), then the school district must bear all costs.

ten that Katie was hard to control and quick to lose her temper. Sue Gardner recounted how last year, near tears, Mrs. Shea had said, "Katie is up my butt all the time, and I just can't handle it. Getting Katie ready for school in the morning is like trying to win World War II!"

Mrs. Shea also complained that in the afternoon Katie would get off the bus crying and had trouble completing her assignments at home. Although Katie's second grade teacher saw no sign of such behavior during the school day and explained this to Katie's mother on several occasions, Mrs. Shea insisted there was a problem, and demanded that the school complete a TEAM assessment on Katie.

The evaluation was conducted by a member of the Harrison district special education staff, the school psychologist, and Katie's teacher. It included assessment of Katie's academic progress since kindergarten and an analysis of her behavioral abilities along a developmental continuum. This latter analysis evaluated Katie's behavioral adjustment, attention capacity, motor coordination, activity levels and patterns, communication skills, memory, and social relations with groups, peers, and adults. Katie's physical and mental health were also assessed. Although Chapter 766 guidelines included provisions for a home visit to glean more information on a child, Katie's parents had refused.

After completion of the TEAM assessment, Harrison's director of special education determined that while Katie did demonstrate some weaknesses in her language and reading skills, she did not require special services beyond those available under Chapter 1. The study did find that Katie exhibited some difficulty getting along with children on the playground, but Fairview staff believed they could work with Katie in her regular classroom setting to improve her relations with other students.

The evaluation team met with the Sheas to discuss their findings and to ask Mr. and Mrs. Shea to sign off on Katie's educational plan—a result of the TEAM assessment. Mrs. Shea refused. She was convinced her daughter had cognitive and affective disorders that Harrison's evaluation had failed to identify. Mrs. Shea yelled, "You just don't want to take the trouble to find out what's wrong. You keep telling me Katie 'just needs time.' I think you don't want to spend the money to really help her!" Mr. Shea sat silently and seemed to shrink in his chair as the decibel level rose in the room. Mrs. Shea knew her rights, and rejected the educational plan offered by the school. She announced that she would seek an independent TEAM evaluation for Katie and left the meeting, her husband in tow.

Just before the start of the new school year, Mrs. Shea called the school to alert them that Katie's pediatrician had placed her on the drug Ritalin. The school was required to dispense two dosages to Katie during the course of the school day. She also informed Frank Howard that an independent TEAM evaluation was being conducted for Katie by the learning disability clinic at nearby Jesuit Hospital. Katie was being tested by members of the speech and language clinic department. The head of this department, Dr. Reynolds, had gained local publicity for her new theories on attention deficit disorder (ADD) in children.

❖ SPECIAL SERVICES AT FAIRVIEW

Carol knew 15% of elementary students in the district received some sort of special services. Most of these children were identified early, usually in kindergarten or first grade. The school system was fully equipped to handle the educational needs of special students. Along with special resource classes for language, reading, and math, Fairview offered services in speech, occupational therapy, physical therapy, counseling, and adaptive physical education.

Carol and some of her younger colleagues felt Fairview's reliance on pull-out programs for special education students was obsolete. They believed most special education services should take place in the child's primary classroom and were discouraged that Fairview resource room teachers were reluctant to try more inclusionary learning models. "I think it has more to do with territory than it does children's needs. It's that 'power of the resource room.' They only want to teach on their own turf." Carol also wondered how hard the children really worked in the resource room. Special education students got candy and toys, and when Carol walked by, she often saw more students playing computer games than working.

But the new teacher did realize that some circumstances merited additional services that she didn't feel qualified to provide. In two years of teaching, Carol recommended special pull-out services twice—once for counseling, and once for speech.

❖ KATIE IN THE THIRD GRADE

Carol watched Katie closely over the first few days of the school year. She found the child to be happy and friendly, walking into the classroom each day with a big smile. Carol was unsure how the Ritalin was affecting Katie's mood and couldn't help wondering if it was even necessary. She did not see any indication of the temperamental, disorganized behavior that Mrs. Shea complained about the previous year. "She doesn't strike me as an extraordinary child, one way or the other. She's just a nice, sweet girl," thought Carol.

Later, Carol remarked, "Katie isn't a great student, there's no doubt about that. She sometimes has trouble writing her thoughts. But this isn't an unusual problem for third graders. Typically, they are much better speakers than they are writers. She isn't able to formulate sentences easily, and her punctuation is poor. But Katie is certainly not the only child with these difficulties. Right now, I have six students challenged the same way."

A few weeks into the semester, Carol received a note from Mrs. Shea, "thanking you in advance for your troubles with Katie." Carol was struck by Mrs. Shea's handwriting, words were highlighted and double-lined. Some phrases made no sense. Carol guessed it must have taken over an hour to prepare the note with all its special inks and notations. Carol's reaction to the note was one of surprise and mild apprehension. She hadn't experienced any problems at all with Katie. "It's like Mrs. Shea is asking for my help and warning me at the same time." Carol didn't know what to do with the note and in the end did not respond.

Spurred by the note, Carol decided to ask if any other teachers had had any dealings with Mrs. Shea. Since Harrison was a small community and many Fairview teachers lived in the area, she thought someone might know the mother. Unfortunately, her uneasiness was confirmed. The woman was considered an "oddball." Teachers shared their suspicions that heavy drinking was occurring at the Shea's house. They also told Carol that Mrs. Shea often sent Katie off to play at neighbors' homes for hours at a time, without first asking permission. In fact, Katie's second grade teacher lived near the Sheas and told Carol that Katie showed up on her doorstep regularly and often seemed eager to stay for dinner. Feeling sorry for the child, the teacher would always let Katie stay and play with her own children. After a few hours she would hear Mrs. Shea yelling for Katie to come home and the child would thank her teacher and return to her house.

Carol tried not to listen to the teachers' room "gossip" but began to wonder about the Sheas' parenting skills. She became even more concerned when she heard that Mrs. Shea distributed pamphlets about ADD to all the parents at one of Katie's soccer matches. One parent told Carol that Mrs. Shea warned her, "Make sure the school isn't ignoring your kids' needs. Remember, the law is on our side!"

It wasn't long into the school year that Carol began receiving requests for information about Katie from Jesuit Hospital. It was required for the independent TEAM evaluation. "They keep sending me charts to fill out about Katie, asking me if Katie is focused, can she stay on task, even questions asking if she keeps her desk clean. I write back that I don't see any behavior problems and then they want an update on how she's doing in each of her subjects, asking me to provide quantitative and qualitative assessments of her progress. Katie's file is already inches thick."

During a brief, unplanned meeting after school in November, Mrs. Shea asked Carol to complete a daily progress report on Katie's behavior and academic skills. She handed Carol a handmade chart that she also wanted Carol to fill out. Carol refused. "This is not appropriate. Katie is doing fine," Carol told Mrs. Shea. The mother became irate, accused Carol of failing to do her job and left the classroom just as abruptly as she'd entered it.

Carol told a colleague, "I truly believe Brenda Shea wants her daughter to be treated like someone with pervasive difficulties, like someone who is handicapped. Katie shows some weaknesses but I still maintain she is doing fine. She's doing third grade work! It's still too early to send Katie to special education. A lot of kids will turn around during the course of the year and do much better work in April and May. They may need constant supervision but they can do it."

Later Carol said, "Sometimes, if I see kids with weaknesses who fall outside what is normal, I will refer those students to special services. But I just don't see it in Katie. You get a sense of who is a resource room child, and who isn't. Katie is just not resource room material. Besides, once a child goes to the resource room, they never graduate back to the regular class. Too often, they're SPED for life."

Mrs. Shea continued to send notes to Carol. They described Katie's misbehavior at home, asked for progress reports. Once Carol was sure the mother sent her the same ADD pamphlet she'd distributed at the soccer match. There was no question her classroom gave Katie the organized, stable environment the pamphlets stated ADD children required. Once Mrs. Shea came for a parent-teacher conference with her two younger daughters in tow. "She let them run amok in the room. The husband arrived a few minutes later, but he never spoke, not once," Carol said. "In their relationship it seems like Mrs. Shea has total charge of anything relating to the children. And that's not much!"

Carol was also sensitive to Katie's feelings. She knew Katie was aware of the commotion going on around her. The teacher's heart went out to the child when Katie announced one day, out of the blue: "I don't think I need to be in Chapter 1 anymore, I want to work with the regular kids." Carol also wondered how Katie was feeling about being put under the microscope at Jesuit Hospital twice every month. She knew it was a full day of testing every time. But she didn't ask.

❖ THE INDEPENDENT TEAM EVALUATION MEETING

The independent TEAM evaluation was finally completed in early spring, and a meeting was called at Fairview Elementary to review the findings and make a determination regarding Katie's educational plan. Attending the meeting were: Carol, Harrison's director of special education, Fairview's school psychologist, the two resource room teachers, Katie's parents, a staff person from Jesuit Hospital, and a child advocate hired by Mrs. Shea.

The TEAM assessment completed by staff at Jesuit Hospital found that Katie had many needs that would qualify her for special education services. One of the major findings was that Katie suffered from "executive skill dysfunction." The representative from Jesuit Hospital explained that this was a new term, used by Dr. Reynolds at Jesuit to describe a condition in which children suffer from a lack of cognitive organizational skills including "vigilance, sustaining, shifting sets, initiation, inhibiting, planning, organizing, and strategizing." According to Jesuit Hospital researchers, these skills occurred naturally and functioned automatically in most children. Children lacking such cognitive skills would need to be taught them or be at significant risk as content became more difficult and demands on their executive skills increased. The staff member from Jesuit offered a dim view of Katie's future. "She might look all right now," he said, "but, academically, the bottom will probably drop out a few years from now. Katie will fall apart."

None of the Harrison staff, the resource room teachers, school psychologist, and the director of special education for the district, had ever heard of "executive skill dysfunction." All were certified special education specialists, some had advanced training in human development, and all were unfamiliar with the term.

The school's hands were tied. Now that the independent evaluator determined that Katie had problems, the Sheas felt they had a case that the school must address. If the school, after reviewing the material, concluded that Katie still did not need special education services, Mr. and Mrs. Shea could appeal to the State Bureau of Special Education. The child advocate also reminded the group that should the Sheas not find satisfaction through that appeal, they could make a further appeal to the State Advisory Commission.

Throughout the meeting Mrs. Shea seemed very agitated. She nodded her head emphatically whenever the Jesuit Hospital staff member described Katie's "condition" in medical jargon. She fidgeted in her chair. But the mother said little until the presentation of the results was complete and then she puffed out her chest and demanded that Katie be placed immediately in resource room services for language retrieval, reading, and speech and that Harrison provide, at the district's expense, a private, full-time tutor during the summer to make up for what she believed Katie had missed during the year. Mrs. Shea also insisted that Katie receive individual assistance in all areas. Unless this level of support was given to Katie, Mrs. Shea announced she would refuse to sign the educational plan offered by Harrison, and would "raise a major stink" at the state level. "And what's more, there are a lot of special education parents in this town who would be *very* interested in knowing what's happening to my child in this school."

She then turned toward Carol and yelled, "You only worry about what's happening this year, in your class! What about next year or the year after that? Isn't that your problem? You teachers think you know everything. You just decide which children you want to help and which ones you don't. Have you decided that Katie isn't worth the trouble? What does it take to get you people to pay attention? My child needs help and you aren't lifting a finger!" At this point, the mother had to stop. She couldn't speak through her emotion. Pulling her husband behind her, she left the meeting.

When Harrison's special education director read the Jesuit TEAM report after the meeting, he found several inaccuracies. For instance, the report indicated that Katie did not know place values in math. Carol told the director that she had not yet taught that concept to her students. Carol also provided a tape of Katie reading a standard third grade basal reader, which demonstrated that Katie was reading on grade level, without any mistakes. This too was contrary to the findings of the independent TEAM evaluation.

The next week a meeting was held to decide Harrison's course of action. During the conference, Frank Howard insisted he didn't want the Sheas setting precedent at Fairview. "Deal with this," was his order to the team, and specifically, to Carol. Carol threw up her hands. "What do you want me to do? Katie's mother will not believe Katie is a beautiful, normal, healthy kid! And besides, I *do* deal with the here and now of my third graders. I don't worry about what happens three or four years down the road! I give them the skills they need today to learn the skills they need tomorrow. That's all I can do."

The room was silent as everyone weighed Carol's words and wrestled with the district's predicament. Carol watched her colleagues in their deliberations and thought about Katie. One thing was clear to the teacher—doing what was best for Katie today or tomorrow was going to be a long and messy affair.

❖ CASE PREPARATION QUESTIONS

1. A conflict has surfaced between the perceptions of Mrs. Shea and Carol Jenkins about the learning needs of Katie Shea. How can this conflict be resolved? Who should participate?

2. Laws require that public schools meet the needs of special education students. Do you feel that Katie Shea's needs are being met in her current program? Justify your answer.

PERSONNEL AND LABOR

Managing people and working effectively within an environment frequently defined by contracts and personnel policies requires skills of negotiation, communication, and problem solving. Often administrators need advice from professionals such as lawyers, doctors, or social workers. Administrators must know what questions to ask of the specialists and determine whether they are receiving appropriate advice. Cases in this section help examine the role of teachers' professional associations and external influences that help shape personnel and contractual policies.

❖ ON THE CUTTING EDGE OF EDUCATION REFORM

Susan Gleason, newly hired principal of the Lawton Elementary School, senses that teachers want to change the way students are assessed. Working with her faculty, Gleason encourages the teachers to implement new assessment strategies and cuts back on standardized achievement testing. Gleason also encourages a reform of the reporting system and the format for parent–teacher conferences. However, some parents don't appreciate these reforms.

❖ THE CASE OF BERNICE DEMOVSKY

Bernice Demovsky, an employee of the Mt. Hope Museum of Fine Arts, has had great success working with students in public schools. Consequently, she is given a two-year, full-time appointment to the Denver Public School System to teach art and art history. At the end of her first year in the public school system, many principals ask that she be reassigned because of her use of class time to advocate for women's rights rather than to teach art. Demovsky continues to advocate about women's issues; the museum director seeks advice from his attorney about dismissal.

❖ ASCOT SCHOOL DISTRICT A AND B

James Roeske, a relatively new and very successful superintendent of the Ascot School District considers the recommendations of his director of personnel about a high school teacher who allegedly has had sexual relations with three of his female students in the past year. The recommendations allow the teacher to resign immediately with substantial early retirement and severance benefits. Despite his relief that the matter might be confidentially settled for all involved, this does not occur.

❖ THE CASE OF JACK BUICK

Katrina Quinn, mathematics curriculum coordinator for the Hudson Public Schools, is reallocating teachers and resources to provide smaller classes next year for the below average mathematics students. As part of her job she observes that Jack Buick, a veteran teacher, doesn't teach the lower students well. Buick reacts rudely to Quinn's observations and is given a written reprimand from his principal and the director of personnel. Quinn wonders whether she should pressure Buick into resigning, allow the status quo to continue, or try to work with Buick.

❖ SUPPORTING TEACHERS AT SOMERSET HIGH

Richard Dargon, principal of Somerset High School, is awakened late one night and told that his teachers have decided to implement a "work-to-rule" provision the following day in protest for not having a contract. Dargon must decide how to support the teachers while following the wishes of the superintendent and the School Committee. Everyone—parents, teachers, and fellow administrators—is watching him.

Suggested Readings

Jackson. P. (1977). Lonely at the top: Observations on the genesis of administrative isolation. *School Review, 85,* 425–432.

Kerchner, C. and Koppich, J. (1993). *A union of professionals: Labor relations and educational reform.* New York: Teachers College Press.

Kotter, J. and Schlesinger, L. (1979). Choosing strategies for change. *Harvard Business Review, 57,* 106–114.

Kuechle, D. (1985). Negotiating with an angry public: Advice to corporate leaders. *Negotiation Journal, 1,* 317–30.

Mintzburg, H. (1990). The manager's job: Folklore and fact. *Harvard Business Review, 90,* 163–176.

Mitchell, D. (1989). Alternative approaches to labor–management relations for public school teachers and administrators. In J. Hannaway and R. Crowson (Eds.), *The politics of reforming school administration.* New York: Falmer Press.

On the Cutting Edge of Education Reform

Michele M. Pahl

Susan Gleason, principal of the Lawton School, prided herself on "being on the cutting edge" of reform. Throughout her career, she had been known to search out and access opportunities for her own professional growth. As a classroom teacher, she served on curriculum committees in her school system, took advantage of staff development opportunities during the summer months, served as recording secretary for a networking group of literacy educators, and coordinated a professional reading group that met after school. During her first year of teaching, she had enrolled in a graduate program at a local university and continued her studies on a part-time basis until she received a doctorate in educational administration at the age of thirty-four.

Doctorate in hand, Susan submitted her name as a candidate for several principalships and looked forward to her first interviews as learning opportunities. And, as her interactions with principal search committees in various towns ensued, she began to refine her views on the purpose of education and to develop priorities for site-based educational reform. Susan was honest about these issues in her interviews with school committees, parents, and teachers. It was important to her that she obtain a position in a school system that articulated a philosophy aligned with her own because she wanted her initial efforts as principal to be supported by the various stakeholder groups in the community. When, ultimately, Susan was offered the principalship of the Lawton School in Weatherfield, she felt her preparation had resulted in an ideal opportunity for her and she eagerly anticipated the beginning of the school year.

❖ THE WEATHERFIELD PUBLIC SCHOOLS

Weatherfield was a suburb in the metropolitan Boston area. The community was often characterized in the local press as "upper-middle class and professional." In racial background, the student population was relatively homogeneous; ninety-three percent of the youngsters were white, five percent were

African-American, and two percent were Asian, Latino, and "Other." Eighteen hundred students attended the Weatherfield Public Schools; students were housed in two early childhood centers (Preschool-Grade 1), two elementary schools (Grades 2-5), a middle school (Grades 6-8), and a high school (Grades 9-12). Approximately ninety-three percent of Weatherfield High School graduates went on to attend four-year colleges and universities. Special education services were provided to eighteen percent of the students, and three percent of the students received ESL support. The year Susan was appointed principal at Lawton, the average per-pupil expenditures exceeded $7,100.

❖ THE LAWTON SCHOOL

The Lawton School was an elementary school (Grades 2-5) in Weatherfield. The school was staffed by eighteen classroom teachers and eight specialists. Due to an early retirement initiative in the school system the previous year, several positions opened up at the Lawton School and new teachers had been hired to fill these vacancies. Because Susan was hired in the Spring, she was able to participate in many of these hiring decisions. In fact, her recommendations prevailed in six out of eight of the new appointments. The result was a balanced faculty representation of veteran and new teachers.

Prior to taking advantage of the early retirement initiative, Gary Thorton had spent his entire career in the Weatherfield school system, twenty-seven of them as principal of the Lawton School. Thorton was openly described by members of the school committee, parents, and teachers as a "benevolent dictator" and his tenure as principal was described by various factions in the community as "stable," "successful," and "conservative" in orientation.

Not surprisingly, Susan Gleason was hired under a "mandate for change." The superintendent and school committee wanted a principal capable of "restructuring" the Lawton School. Parents and teachers on the search committee indicated that there was a need for "curricular and instructional reform" at the elementary school level. During her interviews, Susan recognized a strong foundation of support for change but also sensed a lack of focus around the nature of change. Although she felt that this situation gave her tremendous flexibility for goal-setting and experimentation, she was concerned that the development of consensus around the focus of reform might prove challenging.

❖ FACULTY CONVERSATIONS

Soon after she arrived at Lawton, Susan initiated a series of conversations with the Lawton faculty in an effort to involve them in establishing an agenda for reform. On a personal level, she was excited about the thoughtfulness of this dialogue and was sure that the faculty enjoyed the stimulation. Susan was, herself, inspired by the conscientiousness and dedication of the staff. She was particularly pleased with the energy and involvement of the new staff members. Everyone seemed genuinely eager to do what was best for the students.

❖ THE FOCUS OF REFORM

During these conversations, one theme continually emerged as a priority for teachers. They reported that the current assessment program in the Weatherfield district provided inadequate information for instructional purposes and did not reflect the extent to which students were achieving the instructional goals in many curriculum areas. The district's assessment program was grounded in a series of standardized tests. For several years, students in all grades had consistently scored above national averages on standardized achievement tests and had performed better than neighboring communities on the state "Basic Skills" test. During the last round of the statewide "Assessment of Educational Progress," Weatherfield had been one of the state's top-scoring communities; in addition, students sampled during the last round had outperformed those sampled in previous years in the areas of language and mathematics.

Susan wanted to act on her teachers' concern but needed more information. She asked her staff to help her conduct a review of the existing assessment program. In a questionnaire that Susan developed, she asked her teachers to describe what they thought worked well with the existing program and what needed to be changed. Lawton teachers readily complied and soon Susan had a stack of detailed responses to study. The questionnaires confirmed the earlier discussions. There was underwhelming support for the state tests. Teachers felt the single response multiple choice test couldn't reflect a student's abilities in a dimensional way. At the same time, few could suggest an alternative to the standardized tests. Some mentioned "portfolios" or "authentic assessments" but Susan could tell these teachers had no substantive knowledge of these reforms. Susan thought both innovations were very promising but knew that implementing such systems would be a difficult endeavor. Nonetheless, the energy of the staff to undertake reform—almost any reform—was palpable. So Susan approached the superintendent and requested that Lawton be allowed to suspend standardized testing practices and to implement an alternative assessment program utilizing a portfolio approach.

❖ ENDORSEMENT

The superintendent's response was both supportive and cautious. Although he would not allow Susan to suspend standardized testing altogether, he agreed to a cutback in the administration of standardized achievement tests. Instead of using these tests in each grade at both the beginning and end of the year, he approved a cutback so that only students in Grades 2 and 5 would be tested and only once at the end of the school year. He felt that this would provide information on group performance and would discourage the use of standardized achievement tests as a means of assessing individual student performance. Since participation in the state "Basic Skills" testing program and the annual statewide "Assessment of Educational Progress" was mandatory, the superintendent reminded Susan that these sampling programs would need to remain in place. As a result, students in Grade 3 would be sampled for "Basic Skills" testing and students in Grade 4 would participate in the "Assessment of Educational Progress."

In addition, the superintendent allocated funds for Susan to spend on the development of an alternative program at the Lawton School. "We can't really supplant standardized testing until we're able to put something in its place," he said. "I think, for the time being, we should explore the portfolio approach as a supplement to the existing testing program."

❖ PROGRESS

Susan invested a great deal of the superintendent's funding in staff development; she expended her own time and energy in this area as well. She arranged to have consultants conduct staff development sessions on alternative methods of student assessment, she released teachers to participate in these sessions, she purchased several of the newest books on the subject, and she actively supported teacher efforts to implement new assessment strategies. Susan found that her new hires had a much better sense of the concept of alternative assessment than did the veteran teachers. At the same time, the younger teachers were overwhelmed developing their new curriculums and lesson plans. Implementing a new assessment program was almost too much to ask of the new teachers and too perplexing for the veteran teachers.

Nevertheless, a number of more experienced teachers began to experiment, and many targeted the current reporting system as another priority for reform. They believed the lack of alignment among curriculum, assessment, and methods for reporting student progress to parents was problematic. They wanted to change the report card and restructure parent conferences, in order to align these with the assessment strategies they were beginning to implement.

In her continuing conversations with the superintendent around these issues, Susan became a major advocate for and catalyst behind the development of a district-wide committee to look into these reforms. Because this process would take considerable time, Susan gave the teachers in her school permission to utilize a variety of assessment strategies as a means of evaluating student progress. She knew it was important for the teachers to develop a sense of ownership of the reform. She also suggested that they experiment with the existing report card and "play around with" formats for the parent-teacher conference. As a result, teachers were using varied approaches to report student progress during the first round of fall parent–teacher conferences. Susan was pleased with the diversity and variance in practice; she thought it would result in valuable learning for all of those involved.

❖ REACTION

The first scheduled parent–teacher conferences were held in November. During a lull in the Thursday evening sessions, Susan took advantage of a few spare moments alone in her office to reflect on the feedback about the conferences she had been receiving throughout the week. In general, the teachers seemed to feel that parents had been receptive and positive during the early conferences. Susan thought about her new teachers and how it must be a scary time for them. She remembered her first years in the classroom and how nervous she was when facing a parent. Acting on impulse, the principal went to her computer and began to compose a memo to the teachers. She wanted to reinforce their efforts and encourage them to continue.

But Susan wasn't able to write much of her memo. She was interrupted by Kathy Williams, the mother of second grader Lori Williams. The mother had just spent the past fifteen minutes engaged in a conference with Lori's teacher, Ms. Rogers, and was apparently dissatisfied with the information she had received about her daughter.

Susan had met Kathy Williams twice before, once at a PTO meeting and another time as Lori's class was departing on a field trip to the Aquarium. A small woman of Asian descent, Mrs. Williams was well dressed and behaved very professionally. It was clear she had high expectations for her daughter, Lori.

"I'm just not sure where my daughter stands anymore," said Mrs. Williams. "I kept asking Ms. Rogers how well she was doing compared to the other kids. With Lori's older brother, I always knew exactly where he stood in relation to the rest of the class. Reading, for example, I knew where Robert placed in reading—the high, middle or low group—and that was based upon the score he got on his reading tests. I understood that, and I think it's a more reliable system. Oh, I appreciate all the comments that Ms. Rogers made and I'm sure it took a lot of time, but I don't have enough background to know if Lori is doing better or worse than the other kids. And Ms. Rogers keeps telling me that this doesn't matter anymore!!! That grades are just a 'snapshot' of Lori's progress and that this 'portfolio' idea is more like a motion picture. Hah! I'll use that with the admissions officers at the colleges Lori's going to apply to."

"Please, Mrs. Williams. May I speak?" Susan tried to project a calm demeanor that she didn't feel at all. "The teachers here are providing you with some of the best information about your child that you're ever going to receive. By collecting and interpreting the work your child is doing in class on a regular basis, Ms. Rogers is able to understand Lori much better than she would be able to with only a standardized test score to go on. And, Ms. Rogers uses this information to inform her instruction. She can make better decisions about how to support Lori's learning when she knows more about her as a learner.

Susan quickly thought about Elaine Rogers. She was a new teacher, had a graduate degree in elementary education from Mt. Auburn University and had been very impressive in her interviews. Susan also knew that Ms. Rogers was being challenged—as are all new teachers—determining and establishing a positive and productive classroom environment. "They just wiggle so much," the new teacher once sighed. Susan had asked Elaine to work more closely with Mary Jacobs, another second grade teacher. Mary was a master in the classroom. While rather traditional in her approach and not particularly enthusiastic about implementing a "whole new assessment system," Mary was a kind individual who would give Elaine all the help and guidance she needed.

After considering Elaine Rogers, Susan continued, "Mrs. Williams, I know Ms. Rogers isn't satisfied with standardized testing as a tool for evaluating student progress and I agree with her. Moreover, I think we can trust that she knows how best to assess Lori's performance and that she is sharing accurate information with you. She studied these new ideas in her graduate program."

"Well, that's pretty much what Ms. Rogers said. Must be the party line," said Mrs. Williams. "She said you were on the forefront in this area; that other school systems were visiting Lawton School in order to observe the assessment program in action. I wonder if they'd like to hear what a parent thinks about this new approach! I have a stake in what happens to my children in this school and the only way I know how they're doing is through report cards, test scores, and conferences. How can you just change all of that? Have you tested this approach at all? Do you have any research studies that show how well it works? You're treating my daughter like a guinea pig and I don't like it. She'll get to high school, bomb on the SATs, and you'll apologize when it's too late!"

Susan Gleason was at a loss for words. "I'm not sure what you'd like me to do about this, Mrs. Williams. How can I respond to your concerns?"

"Well, for starters," Mrs. Williams replied, "I'm going to put this issue on the agenda for the next PTO meeting. And, I want to sit down with both you and Ms. Rogers so I can really know what's going on with Lori. Can Lori be given the reading test that she was given in the first grade? I need to set my mind at ease."

"Why don't you let me speak with Ms. Rogers and we'll get back to you tomorrow?" As the principal escorted Mrs. Williams from her office, the mother said she would expect a phone call the next morning. Susan Gleason could only wonder how best to proceed.

Kathy Williams hadn't reached her car in the parking lot when Susan Gleason plugged into the intercom in Room 8 and began speaking, "Elaine, are you available for a couple of moments? I need to speak with you about a matter that has just been brought to my attention. . . ."

❖ CASE PREPARATION QUESTIONS

1. What issues did the teachers hope to address with a change in assessment practices and reporting procedures? Did they achieve their purpose?
2. What should Susan Gleason do at the end of the case?
3. Do changes in assessment procedures affect teaching and learning?

◆ ◆ ◆

The Case of Bernice Demovsky

David Kuechle

Bernice Demovsky was a fine teacher and a well-respected art historian. She joined the curatorial staff at the Mt. Hope, Colorado Museum of Fine Arts after completing requirements for a Ph.D. in Art History at the University of Wisconsin in Madison. While working on her Ph.D., Ms. Demovsky served as a part-time instructor teaching courses in painting, sculpture and art history. She had hoped for appointment to the full-time faculty at Wisconsin upon completion of her Ph.D. but severe budget cutbacks had taken place and she was told by her dean that there was no hope of such appointment. Thus, Ms. Demovsky searched elsewhere—contacting selected colleges and universities throughout the United States and Canada.

It soon became evident that there would not likely be positions on faculties in places where Bernice Demovsky wished to locate, but in the process of her search she met Jerome Glatzner, Director of the Museum of Fine Arts in Mt. Hope, Colorado, and became intrigued with an opportunity offered by Mr. Glatzner.

❖ MT. HOPE MUSEUM OF FINE ARTS

The Mt. Hope Museum came into being in 1970 as a result of bequests amounting to $62 million from two leading Denver citizens. The Museum was conceived as an architectural showpiece in the foothills of the Rockies where outstanding American art would be featured. The building itself would have a small auditorium, several seminar rooms, two large classrooms (all of these equipped with modern audio-visual apparati), an extensive library and food facilities. About half of the collection would be permanent and would represent the best obtainable American art. The other half of the Museum's exhibit space would consist of traveling exhibits arranged for in cooperation with other museums in America and abroad.

Jerome Glatzner participated in the planning of the Museum and had served as director since the building was opened. Just before Demovsky was hired the Museum had a full-time work force of 67 people including one associate director, one personnel director, several curators, catalogers, accountants, guards, secretaries and custodians. Aside from its function as a building for display purposes, Mr. Glatzner believed the Museum had an even larger role in the community: to provide research facilities for nearby colleges and universities, to work with the Denver and suburban school systems to develop greater appreciation of the visual arts and art history and to train young artists. Members of the curatorial staff spent a considerable part of their time teaching, both in the Museum itself and in the city's schools. Two of the assistant curators spent nearly all of their working time on loan to the Denver school system, teaching courses in drawing, painting, sculpture, art history and art appreciation, and working with teachers in the schools to help them develop skills in these areas.

Demovsky's hiring was precipitated by Mr. Glatzner's hope to expand the Museum's teaching services to the community. Armed with a $129,000 grant from the Colorado Arts Council, he went looking for three additional persons to join his curatorial staff. These three would spend their early years on loan to the school system. They would be employees of the Museum and would be trained at the Museum; but upon assignment to the schools the Museum would be reimbursed for their services by the Denver School Board on a contract basis.

Bernice Demovsky heard about Mr. Glatzner's opening from a close friend, Margot Glatzner Harrington, Jerome's sister. Harrington arranged a meeting between Demovsky and her brother, and the two met and discussed the position. After a visit to the Mt. Hope facility, Demovsky agreed to join the Museum's staff. She would be paid $39,500 as an Associate Curator, the top of the rate range for this classification of work. Glatzner justified this rate of pay because Demovsky not only had a Ph.D. in Art History but had also taught for five years in various museum schools.

In her first three years Demovsky divided her time about 50–50 between the Museum and the Denver public schools. The Museum was reimbursed for her and two others who were hired at the same time according to a formula obliging the city to pay one-half of her salary and all of her fringe benefits. The fringe benefit package was the same as that offered to the public school teachers under their Union, Local 57 of the American Federation of Teachers. In fact, Ms. Demovsky and the other two curators who were assigned to the school system in similar fashion were listed on the school system rolls as members of the teaching staff, and their positions were included in the definition of the bargaining unit for the school system issued by the Colorado Labor Relations Board.

❖ THE AMERICAN FEDERATION OF TEACHERS

In the late 80's the American Federation of Teachers (AFT) reported 750,000 members in 2,200 locals around the country.[1] AFT was one of three principal

---

[1] The 750,000 AFT members included 90,000 college and university professors.

unions representing teachers and college and university faculty members in the country. The other two were the National Education Association (NEA) and the American Association of University Professors (AAUP). Of the three, only AFT was affiliated with the AFL-CIO, but the three together had engaged in vigorous membership drives in the past five years—increasing their total membership by over 25 percent during that time.

The Denver local, Local 57, represented 3,250 teachers in its various public schools for the purpose of bargaining with the Denver School Board. Their certificate of representation defined the bargaining unit as follows:

> All teaching positions (full and part-time) in the Denver, Colorado public school system except principals and those above the rank of principal.

The union-security provision in Local 57's contract called for maintenance of membership. All teachers who were members of the union at the time of certification would remain members as a condition of employment; those who subsequently joined would similarly remain members, as would all newly-hired teachers.

The most recent collective bargaining agreement signed by Local 57 with the Denver School Board was a three-year agreement retroactive to September 1 of the same year. The contract called for minimum salaries of $24,225 and a maximum of $52,000 plus a generous fringe package estimated at 23.5 percent of the salaries. Salaries would increase at the rate of 4.2 percent each year. The contract contained a non-discrimination provision regarding hires, promotions, pay raises, demotions and layoffs. It also provided for discipline and discharge for "just and proper cause," subject to approval by the Superintendent of Schools. Aggrieved teachers could take their grievances, with the aid of their union representatives, through a four-step grievance procedure. The terminal step of the grievance procedure, Step 4, provided for final and binding arbitration by a person mutually agreeable to the parties or, in absence of agreement, by a person chosen according to procedures of the American Arbitration Association (AAA).

After three years of employment, Bernice Demovsky was not a member of the union. Nor were other employees of the Museum. However, in July of her third year with the Museum Demovsky was assigned full-time to the school system—on loan from the Museum for a two-year period. She would be responsible for training high school teachers in art education and would, herself, rotate among the city's high schools instructing high school art students. With the full-time appointment came a letter from the president of Local 57 saying she was required to join the union as a condition of employment. She promptly consulted the Assistant Superintendent of Schools, Stephen Shatkin, who said that since she was officially an employee of the Museum she had no obligation to join. Shatkin, in turn, passed this information on to the Local 57 president. It was not until a year later that Demovsky had further communications with the union, then initiating the approach herself.

❖ DEMOVSKY'S WORK RECORD

Bernice Demovsky had an outstanding work record during her first three years with the Museum. Her particular specialty was Asiatic Art, and she had been personally responsible for arranging two major exhibitions at the Mt. Hope Museum featuring Chinese, Taiwanese and Philippine art works. She won considerable critical acclaim for these and managed to publish two books based on promotional and educational material she had written to accompany the exhibits. Nearly all of Denver's high school students and teachers attended the exhibits and heard Demovsky's accompanying lectures in the Museum's auditorium. She was an entertaining speaker—combining intellectual rigor with considerable humor.

She was also an excellent teacher, and it was this talent that led to the two-year full-time appointment to the school system. At the end of the two years, she would be eligible for consideration as a full curator at the Museum. This position carried tenure, and it was only after consulting with Mr. Glatzner and being assured that her absence from the Museum would not affect her eligibility for tenure that she agreed to take on the assignment.[2]

❖ EQUAL OPPORTUNITY

Through the years Bernice Demovsky had been concerned and outspoken on the issue of women's rights. She campaigned actively for the Equal Rights Amendment while at the University of Wisconsin, then, later, throughout the State of Colorado when that state was considering ratification of the amendment. She also did a considerable amount of research and concluded, to her dismay, that the City of Denver had apparently done little or nothing since passage of the 1964 Civil Rights Act to implement its provisions—especially in regard to the employment of women.

The school system had been seriously negligent, in her opinion—not in total employment but in promotions and raises in pay for female teachers. When Demovsky was appointed full-time to the schools, there were approximately 3,200 teachers in the Denver Public School system. Of these over half (1,716) were women. The women, on average, had 8.2 years of service. Men, doing similar work, averaged slightly less than seven years of service. However, the average salary for women was $32,492; for men it was over $36,484.

---

[2]According to personnel practices at the museum, consideration for a full curator's position was given after five years' service as an associate curator. The museum Director had the sole authority to recommend such appointment to the Board of Trustees. The Director's recommendations were to be based on consultation with all "appropriate" persons. Assignment of a full curator title by the Board was not automatic at the end of the five-year period, but historically the title had been granted only after vigorous scrutiny.

Among the top administrative positions in the State System—from the State Commissioner of Education to superintendents, assistant superintendents, principals and assistant principals—81 percent were male. No females were employed at the assistant superintendent level or above.

Demovsky found a similar situation among Museum employees. There were 18 members of the curatorial staff of the Mt. Hope Museum of Fine Arts in 1990, including herself. Ten of these were women. The average years of service of the women was 5.6 years; for men it was 4.1 years. The average salary for women was $32,630; for men it was $37,740. One of the three full curators was a woman, and she reached that position after 12 years with the Museum. Her male counterparts in the same position had reached the position after five and six years, respectively.

Bernice Demovsky's research uncovered considerable additional data. Perhaps the most significant had to do with the comparisons of educational background and experience of men and women in the school system and the Museum. According to Demovsky, the women were slightly better educated; a larger percentage had masters and doctoral degrees—though their number of years' experience, on average, was somewhat less.

These facts and others caused Bernice Demovsky to expand her efforts, to seek changes in the system of hiring, promotion and salary reviews in the city. She accumulated facts regarding city and state employment outside the Denver school system and was appalled to discover that there were only three women in the police and fire departments. African Americans, Hispanics and other minorities were employed in meager numbers and were apparent victims of discrimination by those departments. The city had undergone considerable demographic changes in recent years characterized especially by increased numbers of Hispanics in the community.

Halfway through her first year of the full-time appointment, Demovsky began pointing up her concerns to other teachers in the school system. She organized some meetings of members of the teaching corps and used the Mt. Hope Museum auditorium for this purpose. The meetings were carried on under the guise of art-education seminars, but they concentrated exclusively on women's and minority rights. All teachers were invited, but women regularly comprised an overwhelming majority in the audiences. Various civil rights lawyers were invited to speak, and film documentaries on the work of Martin Luther King and Cesar Chavez, leader of the Farm Workers Union, were shown, with discussions afterwards. In March, when Director Glatzner was on vacation, an all-day symposium on women's rights was held, featuring a discussion round table involving Robin Morgan, editor of *Ms.* Magazine, Florence Howe, director of the Feminist Press and Bella Abzug, the New York political leader.

Demovsky's concerns carried over to the classrooms as well. She assigned readings by Gloria Steinem, Saul Alinsky, Bernice Sandler and Malcolm X, and she encouraged her students to express themselves verbally and through their art regarding existing social injustices, pointing especially to the near-poverty level in Denver's Hispanic areas. Some students complained to their principals—saying that Ms. Demovsky was no longer teaching art or art appreciation. According to one principal, Bernice had apparently "flipped her lid" over minority and women's rights.

Many of the students talked about Ms. Demovsky's classes at home, and parents began to inquire among themselves and to ask questions of the principals. At first the questions were in the form of friendly inquiries, but concern among parents mounted as Demovsky spoke to them individually and in groups during various "parent" days at the schools. The intensity of her concern and the fervor with which she pursued it was considerable.

Despite requests from parents and various principals that she confine her social rights preachings to places outside the classroom, Demovsky persisted, so that when the school year drew to a close in June, several principals requested that Ms. Demovsky be reassigned. They complained that she was not doing the job for which she was hired and was sowing seeds of disruption in their schools. These complaints came from male and female principals alike and caused Superintendent of Schools Alan Boyd to investigate further. In July, Boyd asked Ms. Demovsky to meet with him.

Demovsky was candid with Boyd. She said the situation was appalling and that she had no intention of stopping her campaign until the school system acknowledged their abuses of civil rights and took affirmative action to "right" the situation. She indicated further that she had contacted the officers of Local 57 of AFT who were then negotiating for a new collective bargaining agreement with the School Board and urged them to insist on vigorous new affirmative action provisions in the contract. She reminded Boyd that she was on a two-year assignment to the school system from the Mt. Hope Museum and said that she intended to carry out that assignment. There was one more year to go. Regarding her classroom work, Demovsky allegedly made the following statement to Mr. Boyd.

> I am the Master in the classroom, and any effort to tell me what to teach or how to teach it is an infringement on basic academic freedom. Furthermore, if you or anyone else tries to muzzle me I will consider it an infringement on my constitutional rights to free speech and will go straight to the School Board and the media with the information.

Mr. Boyd thereupon contacted Jerome Glatzner and told him about the conversation. He asked Glatzner to reassign Demovsky for the coming school year. Glatzner did not make any commitments but said he would talk with her.

A conversation between Glatzner and Demovsky took place a few days later. In fact, it continued over a span of several days as the two came back together in Glatzner's office, at his home, and even in a Denver restaurant. In essence, Glatzner said he sympathized with Demovsky's concerns, and he encouraged her to pursue them "on her own time." He said the assignment to the school system, backed financially by the Arts Council, was an important part of the Museum's educational function and required her to teach art and art appreciation—nothing more. Demovsky, in turn, said she had no intention of curtailing her activities, and she criticized Glatzner for not actively joining in her efforts to secure change. Finally, in desperation, Glatzner said that he had been asked by Boyd to remove Demovsky from the school system assignment, and he intended to do so unless she promised to confine her political activities to her own time, outside the classroom: that she had an obligation to teach—to teach art! Demovsky finally asked Glatzner to take her off the assignment and to return her on a full-time basis to the Museum. Glatzner refused, saying he had no replacement for her, and his budget would not permit him to hire an additional person for the curatorial staff. "Furthermore, I cannot justify an expert in Oriental art on full-time assignment to the Museum. It is necessary for you to teach in the school system as a condition of further employment."

In early August, Glatzner met with Boyd and convinced him that Demovsky should be reassigned to the schools for the coming year—that she had given her word that she would stick to teaching art, and that he, Glatzner, would put his name and reputation on the line in assurance that there would be no further trouble. Boyd thereupon agreed. Later in August, a contract was agreed upon by Local 57's bargaining committee and submitted to the membership for ratification. It was approved by a 72% affirmative vote on September 9, the Sunday following the start of the school year.

When the fall term began on September 4, Bernice Demovsky returned to the classrooms. She fulfilled her agreement with Glatzner and confined her working time to teaching art. However, she did not give up her campaign. Joined by 50 or so committed teachers and several members of the Museum staff, she arranged meetings with various groups: the City Council, the School Board, Local 57's officers, the District Trades Council for Colorado, the Lions Club, the Kiwanis Club, and the Colorado Arts Council. An articulate person, Ms. Demovsky appeared several times on local radio and television and voiced strong criticism against the School Board, the school administrators, the unions, and even the "complacent" parents in the community.

By mid-October, Demovsky and her followers had stirred up considerable controversy in the community but she still remained true to the agreement with Glatzner and concentrated on teaching art and art appreciation in the classroom.

Demovsky and her followers had undertaken a mass rally of concerned citizens on Sunday, October 21. This was to be followed the next day, the 22nd, by a city-wide boycott of classes. Perhaps reluctantly, but yielding to considerable pressures, the Executive Board of Local 57 backed the rally and agreed to participate. Regarding the boycott, they let it be known that they were not in favor—that this would be a violation of the contract—but that they would be powerless to stop members if they participated in it.

Both actions proved a fizzle. The 21st was a cold, rainy, windy day— "hardly fit for a penguin," said Demovsky, so the rally attracted only a small group of people. The boycott the next day was equally unsuccessful. It had been badly organized, so that few people knew whether it would take place. Attendance in the schools among teachers and students was only slightly below normal for a Monday.

In early November, Bernice Demovsky went back on her agreement with Mr. Glatzner. She essentially stopped teaching art and started, once again, to assign readings and reports on civil rights laws and minority movements. And again, the principals started to receive complaints, and these were conveyed to the Superintendent. On the third Monday in November, at a regular meeting of the School Board—open to the public—Bernice Demovsky appeared. She thereupon engaged Alan Boyd, the superintendent, in a heated public debate, demanding to know what, if anything, he intended to do about the hiring, promotion and salary practices of the school system. The debate was publicized widely, and Boyd was incensed.

❖ GLATZNER'S DECISION

Jerome Glatzner heard about the School Board meeting on the car radio as he drove to work the next morning. He had received a call a few days earlier from Mr. Boyd reporting on the resumption of complaints about Bernice Demovsky and had asked for time to investigate. Now he was certain that he would get a call from Boyd demanding her immediate removal.

The day before, Glatzner had talked about the situation with his personnel director, Roslyn Temple. Temple threw out several caution flags. She was worried that if any disciplinary actions were taken Demovsky might file a charge under Title VII of the Civil Rights Act claiming discrimination because of her sex. It was also possible that Demovsky would sue the Museum on constitutional grounds. Temple cautioned Glatzner to consider the effect publicity might have on potential donors. Glatzner wondered what role, if any, Local 57 might play if he took action against Demovsky. She was not a member of the union, but she was assigned to the school system and was working in a position that was "covered" by the certificate of representation. According to Temple, "Local 57 might be forced to defend her by virtue of their obligations as exclusive bargaining representative." "They could be sued themselves if they don't help her out."

The conversation with Temple had been anything but reassuring. And, sure enough, when he arrived at his office that morning, there was a message for him to call Alan Boyd, Superintendent of Schools.

He called promptly.

Glatzner: Alan, I put myself on the line in asking you to give Bernice another chance. I take full responsibility for the situation.

Boyd: I am not angry with you Jerry, I am concerned more that the situation has now been publicized so much that it has shown the school system and the Museum in a bad light. We've been examining our affirmative action program trying to make sure that when the Human Rights Commission and Equal Employment Opportunities people knock on our door we'll have something positive to report. Our racial balance was thrown off during the last two years because of layoffs, and salaries of women reflect a high rate of turnover among them, so that the longer term and higher salaried teachers are mostly men. Demovsky is right. But the way she's gone about it forces the various commissions to come in now, before we're ready for them.

Glatzner: I want to do whatever I can to work with you. However, I intend to remove Demovsky from assignment to the school system. She's gone back on her word to me, and she has not done the job she was assigned to do.

Boyd: Okay Jerry, but please keep me posted on what's happening.

Later that day, Glatzner telephoned Bernice Demovsky and invited her to meet him at his home that evening. He invited Roslyn Temple, his personnel director, to be there too.

At about 8:00 on Tuesday, Demovsky came to Mr. Glatzner's home. Glatzner, in the presence of Temple, angrily upbraided Demovsky for betraying his trust. He said she had not been doing the job to which she was assigned and that she was being discharged, effective January 15, from the employment of the Museum. It was November 20. Meanwhile, she was not to report back to the schools for work, but she could use the time until January 15 to look for other work.

Demovsky, in tears, said she had done only what her conscience had directed her to do. She said she knew it might lead to her discharge but she hoped Glatzner and Temple would be more sympathetic—that they would share her concerns about the situation she was fighting to correct.

Glatzner said he did share the concerns, but said he was more concerned that people who worked for him should confine their political and other extra-curricular activities to time outside the work hours. "You have gone back on your word to me; you have lied to me about use of the Museum facilities, and you have taken your salary under false pretenses. For these reasons, I am forced to dismiss you."

❖ DEMOVSKY TAKES ACTION

Nearly two weeks later, Jerome Glatzner received a call from Marvin Feldheim, President of the Colorado Federation of Teachers. Feldheim said he had been approached by several employees of the Museum about forming a union of Museum employees. He indicated further that he had signed authorization cards from over 60 percent of the employees and asked for a meeting with Mr. Glatzner for the purpose of bargaining with Local 57. Glatzner registered surprise, but he did not make any commitments, nor did he agree to a meeting. Rather, he took Feldheim's phone number and said he would call him back within three days.

Glatzner promptly called Roslyn Temple to his office, told her about the conversation and asked her to get the best possible legal advice. "This was not part of the job description for the Museum director's position," said Glatzner. "I haven't the slightest idea what to do."

Glatzner suspected Bernice Demovsky had been responsible for the phone call by Feldheim, and this suspicion was confirmed the next day when Demovsky, accompanied by three active Museum employees, appeared in front of the Museum's main entrance distributing leaflets. The leaflets, in the form of letters, announced that the Museum employees were in the process of organizing a union and pointed up some of the alleged abuses that had taken place—including the "unjustified dismissal of a distinguished associate curator for exercising her constitutional rights to self-expression."

Meanwhile, Alan Boyd received a call from one of his principals, Alice Kirsten of Hightower High School, stating that the union had filed a grievance with her regarding the discharge of Bernice Demovsky. Kirsten had been one of the principals who urged that Demovsky be reassigned because she had not done the job she had been asked to do. Kirsten said she was unaware that Demovsky had been discharged, but, more important, she wanted advice on how to respond to the request for a grievance meeting. She said the union representative, Mr. Feldheim, indicated he would call her back on Monday.

Alan Boyd thereupon called Stephen Shatkin, the Assistant Superintendent, to his office. He told Shatkin to personally oversee the Demovsky situation and keep him informed. Shatkin agreed—saying that he had heard Demovsky was going to take at least two additional actions. One—to bring charges against the Museum and the school system, jointly, before the Equal Employment Opportunity Commission for alleged discrimination against her because of her sex. In addition, Shatkin said he understood Demovsky planned to file a suit in Federal District Court naming the School Board, the Superintendent, the Museum, the Museum's Trustees and the Museum's Director as defendants in a charge alleging violation of Demovsky's constitutional rights.

❖ CASE PREPARATION QUESTIONS

1. Who is responsible for the evaluation of Bernice Demovsky's performance?
2. How can a principal balance a teacher's right of freedom of speech and the best interests of students?

◆ ◆ ◆

Ascot School District (A)

Richard Fossey and Katherine K. Merseth

On Thursday, August 31, James Roeske, Superintendent of the Ascot School District (ASD), sat alone in his office pondering a set of recommendations given to him earlier in the day by Gordon Schwalke, the District's Director of Personnel and Labor Relations. The recommendations dealt with Milton Botsford, a teacher of English and Journalism at the John F. Craig High School. According to Schwalke, Botsford had engaged in sex with at least three teen-age students at the high school during the past year.

Milton Botsford had been teaching at the school for 17 years. His alleged sexual encounters were brought to Roeske's attention in late July by Arthur Cooper, Principal of the Craig School. At that time, Cooper reported to Roeske that he had been visited by Jack Hurst, father of Denise Hurst, a recent graduate of the school. Hurst told Cooper that he suspected his daughter had been having an affair with Botsford. He said that while his daughter had apparently consented to the relationship he believed that Botsford's conduct was improper. While Hurst did not blame the school system for what had apparently taken place, he made it clear that he expected Cooper to initiate an inquiry into the situation and, if his suspicions were accurate, to take actions which would remove Botsford as a teacher.

After listening to Cooper's report, Superintendent Roeske asked Clara Hanson, Director of Secondary Education and Cooper's immediate superior, to conduct a thorough, but discreet, investigation. He advised Hanson to include Howard Koppa, the school system's attorney in the probe. Roeske wanted the attorney involved because of possible legal ramifications.

By mid-August Hanson and Koppa had obtained signed statements from three young women, including Denise Hurst, all stating that they had been sexually involved with Botsford during the past year. Each of the women had been interviewed separately, and each stated that the encounters had taken place with her consent. All three said they were over the age of 16 (Alaska's age of legal consent) at the time of the encounters. Denise Hurst was 17; the other two women were 18.

According to Hanson and Koppa, each woman expressed the desire that the information be treated confidentially, motivated in part by their concerns for Botsford's career.

After obtaining the statements, Hanson and Koppa conferred with Gordon Schwalke who, in turn, sought to contact Milton Botsford. Botsford was vacationing in Europe at the time, but on Tuesday, August 29 Schwalke received a telephone call from Howard Koppa reporting that he'd been contacted by attorney Joanne Rider, who said she represented Botsford. Rider told Koppa that Botsford wished to negotiate a resignation. This, then, led to a meeting of Schwalke, Koppa and Rider.

Two days later, on August 31, Schwalke presented a set of written recommendations to Superintendent Roeske. They called for Botsford's immediate resignation in return for payment by the school system of $43,000 in early retirement benefits plus a lump sum severance payment of $1,850. The entire matter would be kept confidential, but Botsford would agree never to apply for another teaching position in the State of Alaska.

Roeske's initial reaction bordered on outrage. However, he had great confidence in Gordon Schwalke's judgment, and when Schwalke told him that state laws required these payments, Roeske said he wanted to ponder the matter before giving the go-ahead. Teachers would report for the fall semester on Tuesday, September 5. It was clear to Roeske that any agreement would have to be finalized before that time or Botsford would, most likely, show up in his classroom on the 5th ready for his 18th year of teaching.

❖ THE ASCOT SCHOOL DISTRICT
AND SUPERINTENDENT ROESKE

The Ascot School District (ASD) was one of the larger school districts in Alaska, serving approximately 30 percent of the state's public school students. Enrollment for the upcoming school year would be around 30,000 students. The district operated six high schools: the John F. Craig High School, where Milton Botsford taught, was its second largest.

Two and one-half years earlier, the ASD school board hired James A. Roeske to be its new superintendent. Roeske was 48 years old at the time. He came from Iowa, where he had been superintendent in two school districts. He had also been a Professor of Education at Iowa State University, in Ames, and had authored more than 300 articles in journals, trade publications, and newspapers.

Roeske looked, dressed, and acted like a successful business executive. Exuding confidence, he immediately began to win friends among teachers and administrators in Ascot. Under his leadership, many changes took place. ASD implemented all-day kindergarten programs and created guidance positions in nine of the elementary schools. The district also initiated a take-home computer program for underachieving elementary students and opened parent assistance centers at five elementary school libraries. At these centers, parents could receive information about raising children and helping them with school work. Roeske promised to redistribute ASD's resources to schools and students in need; indeed, many of the innovative programs introduced under his administration were directed toward schools in lower-income neighborhoods.

During Roeske's administration, ASD's budget grew, in spite of tightening fiscal constraints on the city. The school district's budget for the next academic year was already set at $276 million. In contrast, the entire non-school municipal budget was $185 million. Roeske and the School Board had been able to increase their budget, because the community generally had confidence in the quality of education in Ascot and respect for the Board. In addition, Roeske demonstrated skills in building strong political ties in the Ascot business community.

❖ ASCOT, ALASKA

The city of Ascot is surrounded by spectacular natural beauty and is the medical, financial, and business center of the state. Ascot has a population of almost 150,000. A high percentage of its work force is employed by the federal, state, or municipal government.

During the 1980s, Ascot shared in the economic boom that came with high oil prices. Because 85 percent of state revenues came from taxes and royalties paid by the oil industry, Alaska used its oil wealth to expand governmental services. By 1990, the state had 402 state employees for every 10,000 citizens, three times the national average.

Alaska's teachers were the highest paid in the nation, and they enjoyed a state-financed pension plan which permitted them to retire with full benefits after 20 years of service. In addition, in 1989, the legislature approved a retirement incentive program allowing teachers who were over 40 years old to retire with full benefits after 17 years of service.

Ascot's private sector did not share the prosperity enjoyed by people working in the public sector. A principal reason for this disparity was a dramatic and unexpected plunge in international oil prices in the mid-80s. Prices plummeted from more than $38 to $13 per barrel. Users then turned to lower cost suppliers, mostly from the Middle East, causing Alaska's oil production and exploration to decline. Concurrently, private sector jobs and the real estate market collapsed. In essence, Ascot had become two communities, distinguished by their economic status. In the public sector, civil servants had high-paying, secure jobs with excellent benefits. In the private sector, bankruptcies were being filed at record rates, families were losing their properties, and businesses were closing.

While the Alaskan economic recession had some effect on the school district budget and on the job security of non-tenured teachers, the tenured teachers in the Ascot School District were affected very little and continued to enjoy high salaries. For the most part, citizens of Ascot did not resent these salaries, because Roeske, who consistently advocated and obtained more money for schools, was popular among teachers and other school employees.

❖ MILTON BOTSFORD

With 17 years of service and in his early 40s, Milton Botsford was eligible for retirement under the state's new retirement incentive program. He was described by one ASD administrator as an uninspired teacher, who relied mostly on lectures and quizzes to instruct his students.

In addition to being a teacher, Botsford was a newspaper columnist for the *Ascot Daily News,* Ascot's most liberal newspaper. He specialized in witty, acerbic news commentary from a liberal perspective. Ascot's political scene was a frequent target of ridicule for Botsford. The mayor of Ascot was just one of many elected officials who had been pricked by Botsford's editorial barbs. So too, had been the police chief, Paul Sullivan, and lower-ranking members of the police department.

The *Ascot Daily News* was one of two papers in Ascot, the other being the *Ascot Times.* Both papers were distributed statewide. Where the *Times* encouraged economic growth in Alaska and was positively disposed to area industry, the *Daily News* was more critical of industry and private money.

Roeske exercised care in his efforts to treat both papers on an equal footing. As a result, he enjoyed excellent relations and coverage from each. In general, newspaper coverage of ASD and the activities of its administrators and school board members was positive.

❖ FLASHBACK

Milton Botsford's alleged relationship with Denise Hurst had first been brought to the attention of Arthur Cooper in early May, nearly three months before Mr. Hurst visited the high school. At that time, a friend of Ms. Hurst told the Assistant Principal that she believed Botsford and Denise were having an affair. The Assistant Principal informed Principal Cooper who, in turn, questioned Denise and Botsford. Hurst and Botsford both adamantly denied the allegations. Botsford demanded to know who had started the rumor and said he would consult his attorney to find out if he could sue for slander. Cooper told Botsford at the time that if the rumor were true, it would cost Botsford his teaching career. He also advised Botsford not to invite students to his home or engage in any other activity that might give the appearance of impropriety.

At that point Cooper concluded that the allegations were untrue. After reporting his findings to Clara Hanson, his immediate superior, Cooper put the incident out of his mind.

❖ ARTHUR COOPER'S MEETING WITH MR. HURST

It was July 29 when Principal Arthur Cooper received a call from Jack Hurst, requesting a meeting to "discuss an issue regarding his daughter, Denise."

Cooper met with Hurst the next day. According to Cooper, Hurst seemed quite rational about a matter which, said Cooper, "obviously caused him a great deal of anguish." Hurst calmly told the principal he was certain his daughter had been involved sexually with Mr. Botsford. He also informed Principal Cooper that the teacher had "manipulated" other female students and identified two young women who had attended the high school. Hurst wanted the school district to take some action against Botsford, but he also wanted to protect his daughter from publicity. Hurst told Cooper that Botsford might be a good teacher, but he should be given a position where he wasn't around children. Hurst didn't ask that Botsford be punished; instead, he suggested that the District offer Botsford counseling.

❖ THE INTERVIEWS

Clara Hanson, the Director of Secondary Education, and District Attorney Howard Koppa had met a number of times to plan and prepare their investigation. Time was critical if they were going to confirm or repudiate Jack Hurst's allegations prior to the new school year. Having prepared their inquiry, they promptly contacted Gloria Damen and Sue Skinner, the two former ASD students whose names had been given to Arthur Cooper by Jack Hurst. Both agreed to be interviewed. On Saturday, August 12, Koppa and Hanson questioned Damen and Skinner. Both admitted to having sex with Botsford, but both stressed that they were 18 years old before their sexual involvement with Botsford began. Skinner said that she did not become sexually involved with Botsford until after she graduated from high school.

When Koppa asked the two young women to sign statements, both of them did so, but they insisted on confidentiality. Skinner said that she did not want to see Botsford go to jail. She just wanted him out of the school. She said that she did not consider herself to be Botsford's victim. "I knew exactly what I was doing," she said.

In response to the women's concerns, Koppa said that ASD would take all possible steps to ensure confidentiality, but that he could not guarantee it. Hanson told the women that ASD might be required to report the allegations to the Division of Family and Youth Services.

On Sunday, August 13, Hanson and Koppa traveled to Provo, Utah to interview Denise Hurst at Brigham Young University, where she was attending summer school. At first reluctant to talk, Denise Hurst ultimately admitted that she had been romantically involved with Botsford and had sex with him. She also admitted that she had lied when Principal Cooper asked her several months earlier whether she was involved with Botsford. She had lied, she said, to protect herself and Botsford.

During the interview, Hurst made it clear that she did not want any of this information to become public. In fact, her reluctance to talk about Botsford was so evident that Hanson and Koppa later shared hunches that Denise would refuse to testify if ASD attempted to dismiss Botsford, and the teacher demanded a hearing. Koppa prepared a complete statement of Hurst's testimony during the interview, and on the following day Denise Hurst signed it.

By late August, having interviewed the three women Mr. Hurst identified as having had sexual relations with Botsford, Howard Koppa sought to locate Botsford and discovered the teacher had gone to Europe for the summer. However, Botsford somehow learned that the school district was trying to contact him, and by phone hired attorney, Joanne Rider, to represent him. Rider immediately contacted Koppa on Botsford's behalf. From this point forward, all contacts between ASD and Botsford were made through attorneys.

❖ THE INVESTIGATION CONTINUES

As the investigation proceeded, Roeske was briefed from time to time. He was not directly involved in gathering information. In late August, in light of the findings of Hanson's and Koppa's interviews, Roeske met with Schwalke, Hanson, Cooper and other members of his staff to establish priorities. First, the group agreed that Botsford should not return to the classroom. Second, they agreed to attempt to protect the young women and their families from embarrassment, trauma and publicity. Lastly, they agreed to resolve the case as efficiently and inexpensively as possible. Earlier experiences with dismissal hearings for tenured teachers had taught many in the group that such efforts could be exceedingly expensive. They were also aware that a lengthy proceeding might undermine the positive attitude toward the school district which then existed in the community.

Roeske informed his team of his intent to inform the School Board and did so at the Board's next meeting. Roeske announced to Board members that Botsford was under investigation based on an "alleged relationship with a female high school student." Superintendent Roeske urged the members to keep the information to themselves, lest harm be done from disclosure.

❖ DIVISION OF FAMILY AND YOUTH SERVICES

Alaska law required educators to report suspected child abuse to the Division of Family and Youth Services (DFYS). Failure to report constituted a Class B misdemeanor punishable by a fine of up to $1,000 and imprisonment of up to 90 days. However, there was a question of interpretation in the cases of Hurst, Skinner and Damen. Although the statutory age of consent for sexual relations in Alaska was 16 years of age, Alaska's criminal laws defined the age of consent as 18 or older for persons "entrusted to the offender's care by authority of law." According to legislative history, this latter provision was intended to prohibit sexual relations between someone who had a legal relationship with a person under the age of 18, such as the relationship between a guardian and his ward. In such a case criminal penalties applied. Curiously, the provision had never been applied to persons in a student-teacher relationship. Indeed, in similar cases involving sexual relations between teachers and students over the age of 16, prosecutors had decided that there had been no criminal offense.

❖ DISCIPLINARY REGULATIONS

Teachers in the Ascot School District were represented by the Ascot Education Association (AEA), an affiliate of the National Education Association (NEA). The collective bargaining agreement between AEA and the Ascot School District contained no language concerning teacher conduct toward students. As with many contracts, it did contain language permitting discipline of a teacher for "just and reasonable cause," subject to a grievance procedure regarding matters dealing with terms and conditions of the collective bargaining agreement.

Apart from provisions of collective bargaining agreements, tenured teachers in Alaska's public schools could be dismissed for three reasons: 1) incompetence, 2) immorality, or 3) insubordination. The word "insubordination" did not appear in the statutes but was generally used by lawyers as a "catch all" for far more cumbersome wording contained in the statutes, as follows:

> . . . substantial noncompliance with school laws of the State, the regulations of the Department of Education, the bylaws of the district or the written rules of the superintendent.

Alaska's public school teachers were required by law to abide by professional teaching standards set forth by the Alaska Professional Teaching Practices Commission (PTPC). The PTPC had a code of ethics which was almost identical to that of the National Education Association (NEA), and one of its provisions contained language requiring teachers to safeguard the welfare of students. In 1980, the Alaska Supreme Court held that a violation of the PTPC code of ethics was evidence of "incompetence" under the laws governing teacher conduct. However, no case had been brought before Alaskan courts involving sexual misconduct by a teacher.

If Botsford was to be dismissed, the ASD School Board policy provided for a hearing by an officer appointed by the Board. Such a hearing was available irrespective of any labor contract which contained protections against improper discipline. The teacher could elect to have the hearing closed or open and would be entitled to representation by counsel, to subpoena witnesses, to have the proceedings recorded, and to cross-examine witnesses. Following the hearing, the officer was required to make non-binding recommendations to the Board.

If the Board upheld disciplinary action under this procedure, the teacher would have 30 days to appeal to the Superior Court. In the event of such an appeal, the Court would consider the matter in a trial *de novo* and would be free to conduct proceedings afresh. Sometimes in the past, trial judges had accepted the administrative record from the prior hearing and allowed the teacher to supplement that record before the Court.

During the past ten years only one non-retention case in the Ascot School District had been taken to a public hearing. In that case, NEA-Alaska became involved, and the hearing lasted two weeks. The process cost the District over $100,000 in attorneys' fees.

❖ A TENTATIVE AGREEMENT

At 3:30 p.m. on August 29, Howard Koppa, Gordon Schwalke and Clara Hanson, all representing the school district, met with Joanne Rider in Koppa's office. All agreed that Botsford was eligible for early retirement. If he did so, his participation in the early retirement plan would cost the School District $43,000 in additional contributions to the Teachers Retirement System on his behalf.

The School District had already participated in and approved early retirement for others, so no precedent would be involved in Botsford's case. Attorney Rider pointed out that, as an added incentive to early retirees, the School Board had passed a resolution giving a bonus to any teacher who retired early. The bonus amounted to 2.5 percent of a teacher's current annual salary plus $50 for each year of Alaska teaching service. The bonus was to be given in the form of a lump-sum payment. In Botsford's case this would be $1,850.

The two attorneys—Koppa and Rider—had researched the need to report the matter to the Division of Family and Youth Services (DFYS). They both believed there was no need to report. Rider understood from the conversation that the School District would not file a report. However, no one representing the District ever explicitly agreed not to do so.

Another important consideration entered the discussions when Clara Hanson raised the question of whether to seek revocation of Milton Botsford's teaching certificate. Hanson said she believed the District had a moral responsibility which extended past Ascot and that the matter ought to be brought before the Professional Teaching Practices Commission (PTPC). After some resistance by Rider, the parties reached an understanding that there would be no reporting to PTPC unless Botsford sought employment in another district.

Following the August 29 meeting Gordon Schwalke drafted a tentative agreement. Its provisions are summarized here:

1. Milton Botsford would voluntarily retire effective September 1;
2. Botsford would be eligible for early retirement and therefore would be the beneficiary of:
   a. added contributions to the Teachers Retirement System on his behalf amounting to $43,000;
   b. a lump-sum bonus of $1,850.

3. The matter would *not* be reported to the Professional Teaching and Practices Commission (PTPC) unless Botsford sought employment as a teacher in another school district.

Joanne Rider telephoned Milton Botsford, conveyed the proposed terms to him and he accepted. Schwalke said he would sign on the District's behalf pending approval of the superintendent.

❖ THE SUPERINTENDENT'S DILEMMA

James Roeske felt deeply ambivalent about Gordon Schwalke's recommendations for the resolution of the Milton Botsford case. On one hand he was relieved to know that the case might be settled discreetly and that the persons representing the District had substantially complied with the priorities agreed upon earlier in the month. Moreover, he was confident that the proposed settlement was lawful. On the other hand, he personally believed the cost of settlement was too high. Roeske knew full well that if the terms of Botsford's departure ever became public knowledge, the School District would be severely, and perhaps rightly, criticized. Roeske's decision was not an easy one.

❖ CASE PREPARATION QUESTIONS

1. What are Superintendant Roeske's problems? Are some of the problems more urgent than others?

2. What role does the teachers' association play in this case? How are the actions of the central administrators influenced by the contract and the teachers' association?

3. How would you respond to Jack Hurst's request that the information about his daughter be kept confidential?

◆ ◆ ◆

Ascot School District (B)

Richard Fossey and Katherine K. Merseth

On Friday, September 1, Superintendent James Roeske of the Ascot School District (ASD) told Gordon Schwalke, the district's Director of Personnel and Labor Relations, that he would support Schwalke's recommendations regarding the case of Milton Botsford. Schwalke then informed Joanne Rider, Botsford's attorney. Later that afternoon Botsford (who had returned from Europe), Rider and Schwalke met in Schwalke's office, and a formal written agreement was signed, witnessed, and notarized.

Under the terms of the agreement Botsford would resign immediately, before the commencement of the upcoming school year. Because he had 17 years of service, ASD agreed to allow Botsford to retire with full benefits under the State of Alaska's Retirement Incentive Program (R.I.P.). This program required participating school districts and teachers to pay additional retirement contributions equal to the amount the Alaska Teachers Retirement System (TRS) would have received if a participating teacher had been employed an additional three years. Thus, ASD would be required to pay $43,000. In addition, Botsford was given a lump-sum severance bonus of $1,850, amounting to 2.5% of his salary for the prior school year plus $50 for each of his 17 years of service.

As part of the agreement ASD agreed to keep the circumstances of Botsford's termination confidential, except for any reports required to be filed by law. Specifically, ASD agreed not to report Botsford to the Professional Teaching Practices Commission (PTPC), unless Botsford sought another teaching position. In return, Botsford agreed to allow his teaching certificate to lapse and not to seek another teaching job in the State of Alaska. The settlement terms additionally foreclosed any disciplinary or legal action against Botsford by the school system.

Superintendent Roeske played no role in the negotiations or signings. He did ask Schwalke some questions before giving approval—all dealing with his concerns about the apparent high costs. Schwalke explained that retirement bonuses were required both by Alaska statute and by resolution of the Ascot School Board. According to Schwalke, the school system's next best alternative would have been disciplinary action against Botsford for violation of the code of conduct of the Alaska Professional Teaching Practices Commission (PTPC) for insubordination or immorality. Schwalke reminded Roeske of their earlier discussions, saying:

I think we agreed that disciplinary action would almost certainly lead to unwanted publicity. Most likely the teachers' union would get involved. There could be public hearings. We would be required to pay Botsford's salary while the proceedings took place. Furthermore, we might lose the case—especially if the young women who were involved with Botsford refused to testify against him. Remember, Jim, this guy has a public voice through his newspaper column.

Roeske said nothing in response, signaling Schwalke with his hand that he would go along with the agreement.

On Tuesday, September 5, ASD teachers reported back to work to prepare for their students' arrival the next day. Botsford had gone into retirement, and so far, matters had been kept quiet.

Six days later, on Monday, September 11, Howard Koppa, the school system's lawyer, contacted Gordon Schwalke expressing concern that the Botsford affair could become public knowledge in spite of efforts by all parties to the agreed-upon resignation. Koppa pointed out that while he believed there was no requirement for reporting the matter to the Division of Family and Youth Services (DFYS), there was some slim chance that failure to report could have serious consequences for the school district. Koppa reminded Schwalke that the DFYS was charged with responsibility to investigate *all* cases of alleged child abuse.

Koppa:　These women involved in the Botsford situation are not "children" under the law's definition of the age of consent, but some people might make a case that schools are the same as "guardians" and that the appropriate age of consent is 18 when teachers and students are involved.

Schwalke:　Didn't you tell me some weeks ago that this "guardianship" concept had never been applied in a student–teacher relationship?

Koppa:　Yes, that's true. But there are a few attorneys in this city who might try to make a name for themselves by seeking its application at Botsford's expense. This could certainly arouse media attention, and our effort to keep the matter quiet could explode in all of our faces!

Schwalke:　I think we had an understanding with Joanne Rider that we would not report the matter to DFYS.

Koppa:　There is *nothing* in the agreement to reflect that understanding. In fact, we specifically avoided saying anything that would prohibit the district from filing a report.

After further conversation Schwalke and Koppa became convinced that "out of an abundance of caution" the allegations against Milton Botsford should be reported to DFYS. Koppa made a convincing argument when he reminded Schwalke, "The Alaska law requires doctors, nurses, counselors, school teachers and school employees to report suspected instances of child abuse. The law does not define the word child."

The next day, Tuesday, September 12, Schwalke met with Clara Hanson, Director of Secondary Education, and related his conversation with Howard

Koppa. Hanson, as a result, prepared a report to be submitted to DFYS. The report gave Botsford's name along with the names of Denise Hurst and her father, Jack. It did not give details of ASD's own investigations, nor did it mention names of the other two women who had been interviewed by Hanson and Koppa. Clara Hanson also advised Arthur Cooper, Principal of John F. Craig High School, to file a separate report to DFYS. This meant that Cooper, himself, would be immunized from liability. Hanson's and Cooper's reports were both filed with DFYS on Wednesday, September 13.

DFYS policy required investigation by the Division of suspected child abuse within families. However, charges against a person not related to the alleged victim were referred, as a matter of agency policy, to the police. Thus, DFYS passed on ASD's reports to the Ascot Police Department.

❖ OFFICER CHARLES BARNETT

The next afternoon, Thursday, September 14, Officer Charles Barnett, head of the Ascot Police Department's Exploited Children's Unit, went to Craig High School to interview Arthur Cooper and his Assistant Principal about the Botsford report. Barnett taped the interviews, but according to Cooper, he occasionally switched off the tape recorder.

Cooper later told Clara Hanson that Barnett seemed to be on a "fishing expedition." According to Cooper, Barnett went far beyond any inquiry related to Milton Botsford and sought to learn about possible drug rings within the school system. In what he called a "spirit of cooperation," Cooper provided Barnett with copies of all of his investigation files and notes dealing with the Botsford case.

❖ A POLICE SEARCH

Tuesday, October 3, was election day. Two school board members were running for reelection, and a $29 million bond issue for school construction was on the ballot. At 10:00 a.m., Ascot Police Chief Paul Sullivan arrived at the ASD central administration building, wearing a side arm and a bullet-proof vest. Sullivan was accompanied by 12 police officers. Pushing past a secretary, the officers burst into Superintendent Roeske's staff meeting. There, in front of startled administrators and office staff, Sullivan handed seven search warrants to the superintendent. The warrants authorized searches of the administration building and the personal offices of Clara Hanson and Gordon Schwalke.

Roeske sensed immediately that the police were looking for evidence about the Botsford case. Not wanting to impede a police investigation, Roeske called off his staff meeting and promptly offered to provide all the information ASD had on the Botsford investigation. According to Roeske, it took something less than 15 minutes to provide the officers with all available information on the Botsford case which was in possession of the school district.

But this did not satisfy Police Chief Sullivan, who insisted on conducting a search of ASD offices and files. Roeske had no recourse. While officers were emptying his drawers he read the search warrants thoroughly and realized that the police had come, not only to obtain information about Botsford, but to find evidence that school officials had broken laws, as well. One warrant, for example, authorized the police to search for evidence showing:

> ... that the following persons may have committed the crime of Failure to Immediately Report said Sexual Abuse of a Minor in violation of AS 47.17.020: 1) Clara Hanson, 2) Gordon Schwalke, 3) Arthur Cooper, 4) James Roeske.

Police officers made a room-by-room search of the central administration building. They scoured rooms and records that contained nothing to do with Milton Botsford. They scrutinized students' confidential records, examined personnel files, and even tried to read discarded typewriter ribbons.

James Roeske was stunned. "There must be some misunderstanding," he thought to himself. It was the first time in his life that he felt deeply threatened. He had never been accused of criminal conduct before. "Why wasn't the school district contacted in a more professional manner?" he asked. "I feel like I'm in a Rambo movie."

At the same time as Chief Sullivan and the officers were searching the administration building, three officers arrived at Craig High School to serve Principal Arthur Cooper with a search warrant. Two plainclothes officers began searching Cooper's office while a uniformed officer stood outside. Across the city, a similar scene was taking place in the law offices of Koppa, Spence and Mendelssohn, where ASD's attorney Howard Koppa was a senior partner. There, the police removed the law firm's files on the Botsford investigation, including the affidavits signed by the three former ASD students who alleged that they had engaged in sexual activities with Botsford.

At 10:00 that evening, the officers left the school district's central administration building, chaining the office doors shut behind them. As many as 17 police officers had participated in the search and, according to Roeske, they substantially disrupted ASD operations. When Roeske arrived at the administration building the next morning for a staff meeting at 7:30 a.m., police officers were already there, and they advised him he could not enter until 8:00. His office was no longer his own.

Police officers had resumed the search and continued examining records throughout the day. ASD administrators did not know how much material had been reviewed, but the police had the opportunity to inspect hundreds of employee files and student records.

That same day, attorney Howard Koppa sought to contact Police Chief Sullivan without success. However, Koppa did succeed in reaching District Attorney Gerald Brushert and learned from Brushert that he believed Milton Botsford's alleged conduct constituted a crime. Koppa asked Brushert why he had not communicated this opinion to the Ascot School Board or James Roeske. The District Attorney responded that he thought such action was unnecessary.

❖ THE MEDIA REACTS

Both the *Ascot Daily News* and the *Ascot Times* reported the events related to the police investigations in the Thursday, October 5 editions. In the reports, they disclosed the allegations against Milton Botsford without naming the young women who had been involved. Roeske was quoted as being "outraged" and "incredulous" at the investigations. The stories were not front page but public reaction was immediate.

Jack Hurst was furious that the incident had become public knowledge. He made his feelings known to Arthur Cooper in a phone call that afternoon, stating that it would be only a matter of time before his daughter's name was published. Cooper promptly passed Hurst's message on to Roeske.

By Saturday, October 7, the story reached the front page of the *Ascot Daily News*. However, the *News* focused solely on the police raids of the school buildings. Neither Botsford's name nor the names of the women were mentioned.

❖ A MEETING OF THE SCHOOL BOARD

On Thursday afternoon, October 5, members of the Ascot School Board met in a hastily called emergency session requested by Superintendent Roeske. Attorney Howard Koppa was in attendance. Koppa advised the Board to hire George Young, a well-known criminal lawyer, to provide advice regarding the actions by Police Chief Sullivan and members of the Ascot Police Department.

School board members stood solidly behind Superintendent Roeske and urged him to contact attorney Young. Roeske did so, asking Koppa and Young to work together to prepare whatever legal actions they deemed appropriate for the situation. On Friday afternoon, attorneys Young and Koppa held a press conference. They announced that Ascot School District was considering bringing a lawsuit against the police.

❖ ANOTHER SEARCH

On Saturday afternoon, October 7, police officers went to the John F. Craig High School with still another search warrant. According to newspaper accounts, Monday, October 9, the police were looking for evidence of "sexual activity." One article in the *Ascot Times* said the police, using "technical equipment," looked for "pubic hairs, blood, and semen." They cut samples from the carpet and sawed a piece out of a counter-top in Room 119 "formerly used by English teacher, Milton Botsford." The newspapers reported that the police had found "specimens" and that they had taken blood and hair samples for comparison from Mr. Botsford.

❖ ROESKE'S RECOMMENDATION

Over the weekend Roeske pondered the possibility of filing a lawsuit. Young and Koppa had informed him that it would be necessary to file a civil lawsuit to obtain information from the police that would explain their actions. The attorneys had already discovered that the initial search warrants had been based on the testimony of Officer Charles Barnett. They wanted to learn what Barnett had said that had persuaded an Ascot judge to allow the police investigations.

The lawyers urged Roeske to authorize a suit. According to Young, a lawsuit had a number of benefits. It would persuade a judge to order a stop to the police searches; protect the privacy interests of students, teachers, and administrators; and bar the police from prosecuting school officials. The attorneys reminded Roeske that ASD reported over 600 cases of suspected child abuse or neglect each year, and these could become subjects for continued media attention.

Roeske had reservations. He knew that legal actions could be expensive, both in dollars and in damage to the image of the school system and himself. He wondered how the public would view a legal battle between two municipal agencies. Would the public come to understand the importance of protecting the constitutional and privacy rights of students and employees, or would it rally behind the police? Roeske also feared too much of his own time would be dedicated to providing depositions, testifying in court and attending hearings. Jim Roeske was an educator. He wasn't trained for legal maneuvering. He needed to be focusing on the operations of the schools.

❖ CITIZEN REACTIONS

Although the actions of the police in the Ascot School District investigations were the initial focus of media attention, journalists began probing into the circumstances that triggered the investigations. They began to ask about Milton Botsford, his relationships with students, and Botsford's decision to retire. On Wednesday, October 11, the details of Botsford's retirement were revealed, and public dismay erupted. Citizens were outraged and they directed their anger at the superintendent and members of the school board.

❖ THE SCHOOL BOARD ACTION

On Thursday evening, October 12, the Ascot School Board assembled for a regularly scheduled meeting. Two items were on the agenda: the superintendent's recommendation regarding legal action against the police department and, a motion to increase the school budget.

Board members had been briefed previously by Attorneys Koppa and Young that the lawsuit would: seek prosecution of the officers for violating the constitutional rights of school administrators and the persons whose files were viewed; request a judge to rule that sex between a teacher and a 17-year-old student was not against the law; seek a court order directing the police not to prosecute school officials for the way they reported Botsford to DFYS; and seek to obtain the return of items seized by the police.

The budget motion being considered was an increase of $8 million over the previous year's budget, bringing the total school budget to $276 million.

Roeske's throat tightened as the meeting was called to order. After preliminary business, the Chairman turned to Roeske and said: "At this time the Board wishes to hear the recommendation of the superintendent regarding the proposed legal action suggested by attorneys Koppa and Young. Mr. Roeske?"

◆ ◆ ◆

The Case of Jack Buick

Katherine K. Merseth

Katrina Quinn didn't notice the robins outside her office window that spring day—somehow the beauty of the weather seemed insignificant as she sat at her desk. Instead, Katrina was deep in thought about herself, the Hudson mathematics program, and the professional future of one of Hudson's high school teachers, Jack Buick. "What should I do?" she thought, "What should I do with Jack's schedule?"

Katrina had just completed nine months as the mathematics curriculum coordinator in the Hudson Public Schools. With the exception of Buick, she felt good about her accomplishments in the position. She had successfully launched an ambitious in-service training program for elementary teachers, guided the reorganization of the junior high program and planned to increase the offerings at the senior high level for students who had tested below the advanced placement level.

The quiet in Katrina's office was shattered by the ring of the telephone. "Hello, Katrina?" the voice said, "this is Manny." "Oh, Hi," Katrina responded, "What's up?" Manny Olivero was the director of personnel for the school system. "Well, you're not going to believe this, but we've just received word from the union that Jack Buick is grieving his evaluation that you and Sam Gregory wrote." Gregory was principal of Hudson High. "Really?" Katrina responded, not really sure what a grievance meant. "Why?"

"Well," Manny continued, "he claims that the reference to his inability to communicate with supervisors had already been covered in the reprimand and that your evaluation of his teaching performance was biased and unfounded. There's nothing for us to do just yet, but I thought you'd better know." Katrina thanked Olivero for calling and hung up.

Katrina was angry and discouraged. What right did Buick have to question her evaluation? Her responsibility to evaluate him was clearly outlined in the contract and her job description. Was this a personal attack? Were her concerns about Buick's stability well-founded?

❖ THE REPRIMAND

At the request of the superintendent, Dr. Ralph Thompson, and Manny Olivero, Katrina had observed and evaluated all the mathematics teachers at Hudson High. Some teachers appreciated the personal comments and suggestions, but others were threatened by the increased supervision. Katrina's observation of Buick's basic math class had been most discouraging and disappointing. The students seemed hopelessly lost and bewildered by Buick's examples. He took no time to explain how he arrived at the answers, but continued to present problems, timing each by the clock. Katrina did not look forward to the conference to discuss the observation with Buick.

When she arrived at Buick's room for the scheduled appointment, he motioned her in and closed the door. Katrina sensed immediately that she did not want to be secluded with Buick. Without reading the observation that she handed to him, Buick demanded to know why Katrina was evaluating *him*. Buick pointed out that he was the most senior member of the department and that he was clearly the best teacher in the state (as evidenced by the Math League awards). Katrina sat quietly and listened. She had learned in previous conversations that Buick could be difficult if a disagreement arose.

Buick demanded to know what his teaching assignment would be for the coming year. She responded that she was planning to give one of the upper division calculus classes that Jack had always taught to a young woman in the department, Barbara Gomez. Hearing this, Buick leapt to his feet and shouted, "You can't do that, those are *my* classes! I began the calculus program here and it's *mine*. No one else is going to teach any of those classes. No one is going to tell me what to do!" Buick was pacing the room, shaking with rage. "Besides," he continued, "I'm the best teacher in the state, so it's my right to teach anything or any way I want!" With that, he stormed out of the room.

Katrina stopped by the principal's office on her way out of the building to report on Buick's behavior. Three other administrators happened to be present in the office. Just as she began to explain the incident, Buick burst into the outer office and threw open the door to the principal's inner office. His face was red, his voice loud and tense. He was shouting and making little sense. The principal tried to quiet him, which only caused Buick to challenge him. "If you think I'm being insubordinate, Gregory, why don't you fire me?" Buick marched around the office. Finally, as he started toward the door, he turned, pointing a finger at Katrina and said, "No broad will ever take any class away from me!" As he left the room, he flipped out the lights and slammed the door, leaving five administrators sitting in the dark in a windowless office.

Gregory called Olivero, director of personnel, to report the situation. Olivero asked Gregory, Buick's direct supervisor, if Buick had been suspended for conduct unbecoming a teacher according to Section 1-03 of the teachers' contract (see Exhibit 1 on page 287). "No," Gregory said. "What?" Olivero responded incredulously. Gregory continued, "Well, I guess I didn't think of it. Besides, tomorrow is the State Mathematics Contest which we have a good chance of winning. We need Buick there as coach. He'll settle down." Olivero groaned, "Well, for God's sake, Sam, make sure you reprimand him. It certainly sounds like unprofessional conduct to me. You know we didn't work long and hard to get those sections in the contract just so you could ignore them!" A letter of reprimand was presented the next day at a hearing in the superintendent's office (see Exhibit 2 on page 288).

❖ HUDSON

Hudson was a "bedroom" community within commuting distance of a large metropolitan area. Many of the families were second generation Greeks, Armenians and Italians who had moved into Hudson from the metropolitan area. The homes in Hudson were parts of large developments and were moderately priced. Although many of the parents had not gone to college, there was a very strong interest in the school system and the graduates' potential for post-secondary education. Consequently, tax rates were higher in this community than in surrounding areas, and schools and education were revered. The district's educational achievement was somewhat less lofty, however. Only about 40% of the students continued to four year colleges. The remaining graduates joined the armed forces, attended secretarial and other training schools, enrolled in junior colleges or went directly into the work force.

❖ JACK BUICK

Jack Buick was a veteran teacher. He was born, raised and educated in Milford, only 30 miles from Hudson. He had done his student teaching in a neighboring town and began to work in Hudson some 13 years ago. Jack still lived in Milford, was married, about 35 years old and had no children.

Jack's appearance was noteworthy. He wore the same jacket and tie to school every day. To many, he had the look of an "absent-minded" professor with unkempt hair. It was not uncommon to see him talking to himself. When Jack became excited (particularly in discussing pro football or math contests), the area above his right eye would twitch. Many students picked up on these traits and imitated him, although never to his face because of another important characteristic—his temper. Everyone in the school either knew first hand or by reputation about Jack's temper. Some students described him as "wicked mean" and parents often called the principal or coordinator to complain about his classroom demeanor. Gregory's typical response was a shrug of the shoulders and a promise to "look into it." Nothing, however, was ever done because "that's just the way Jack is."

Jack's teaching evaluations had received good ratings prior to Katrina's tenure as coordinator. In previous years, evaluations were not taken seriously either by administrators or teachers as it was generally assumed that comments would be positive unless a teacher's performance was very poor. This situation was changing, however. With declining enrollments and the increasing power of the union, there were frequent discussions about reductions in force. The administration maintained that layoffs would be based on evaluations, while the union argued for seniority. Katrina had been directed by Superintendent Thompson to evaluate all secondary teachers (see Exhibit 3 on page 289). Dr. Thompson told her it was very important that the administrators demonstrate that an evaluation system could be enforced.

❖ MATHEMATICS LEAGUE

The mathematics league was an interscholastic, extracurricular activity in which selected student teams would meet and compete over the solutions to mathematics problems. Jack Buick was the advisor to the team. The twelve members of the team had daily "practice" after school where Jack insisted he be called "coach" and the students be called "mathletes." The majority of the students on the team came from Buick's top calculus sections. Katrina had been told that math league practice often replaced the regular teaching in these sections, but because observations were announced, she had never directly observed this. To Jack, the success of the math team meant much more than the $200 he received as extra-curricular advisor; it meant everything. Any threat to the team, like the reassignment of a calculus section, could devastate him.

The teams were very successful in regional and state competitions and had filled the town newspaper and a trophy case outside the principal's office with symbols of their achievements. Gregory, hungry for a positive image for his school, was most supportive of the team, even to the point of overlooking some of Buick's outbursts and behavior with basic math students.

❖ THE MATHEMATICS PROGRAM

Katrina's assessment of the mathematics program at the high school level in Hudson focused on two issues: the allocation of resources to advanced and upper level students, and the relative ability of department members to teach both calculus and low remedial students.

The program at the high school offered a total of sixteen courses with six centering on various levels of calculus, and three on basic remedial mathematics. The sections in the calculus classes were small, with 8–10 students in each, while the sections in basic math were very large, ranging from 28 to 32 students. Katrina planned to reorganize the curriculum, giving greater emphasis and resources to the less able students. She had received verbal support for this change from Dr. Thompson and from the majority of the teachers. Although she knew that Jack Buick was philosophically opposed to the reorganization, he never came to department meetings when the changes were discussed.

The curriculum reorganization plan specifically called for a reduction in the number of calculus classes from six to two. This change brought the calculus program more in line with a model program for advanced placement students suggested by the College Entrance Examination Board. The teachers of the four extra calculus classes would be reassigned to additional sections for the less able students. This action would have the effect of reducing class size for basic math groups. Katrina felt strongly that students having difficulty in mathematics needed the smaller classes.

The mathematics teaching staff had twelve members—eight men and four women. Katrina's evaluations of the teachers had uncovered a number of teachers with training and ability to teach both the lower and upper students. In particular, there were two women and one man as well qualified as Buick to teach the advanced calculus students, and all three had requested these calculus assignments. In previous years, these requests had been ignored and the advanced calculus classes given automatically to Buick. Katrina had not yet made any commitments to these individuals because she hadn't decided what to do with Buick's schedule. One issue was clear, however: the reorganization of the curriculum meant that there would be fewer advanced calculus classes to assign and that skills to teach less proficient students now would be of greater importance to the department strategy.

❖ THE DECISION

Katrina looked back at the papers for the new high school schedule on her desk. The next name on the list was Jack Buick. As Katrina pondered the schedule, three possible strategies for dealing with Buick occurred to her:

1) Ignore Buick. Even though her evaluation of his teaching and the parental complaints had led her to believe that he was potentially harmful to some students, she could simply give him both top calculus classes and complete his schedule with random average groups. Hopefully no one who was politically powerful in the town would have a child in one of Buick's classes. Although this might alienate others who had requested the classes, it could be defended on the basis of past practice. Katrina tried not to think of the basic and average students or about the morale of the other teachers.

2) Work with Buick. Perhaps, through close supervision and counseling, Buick could become more accepting of average students. Would it be possible to interest Jack in anything else besides math league, calculus and football? As Katrina contemplated this situation, her shoulders sank. "He already grieved my evaluation, stating that I improperly evaluated him. How realistic is it to think he'd be willing to work with me or anyone, for that matter?"

3) Remove Buick. Because Buick had twelve years' seniority and tenure, he could only be removed for "just cause" (Section 1-03 of the teachers' contract). Just cause was difficult to prove, but she did see a way. If she reassigned all of Buick's calculus classes to other teachers, selected a new advisor for the math team and continued to evaluate him, chances were good he would lose control and jeopardize his position as he had done previously. Dr. Thompson was known to have little patience with "second chances," so a loss of control would probably mean termination for "conduct unbecoming a teacher." "After all," she thought, "he was warned in the letter of reprimand."

Katrina felt this action could be justified in the name of quality education for all students, but she also wondered about its effect on Buick's personal life and self-esteem. What was her responsibility to Buick as a human being?

The high school teaching schedules were due for the first computer run the next morning. The task of making out the department's schedule was not difficult as Katrina had done it frequently in her previous position. This time, however, she hesitated as she began to write the course numbers next to Jack Buick's name.

❖ CASE PREPARATION QUESTIONS

1. What should Katrina Quinn do?
2. What responsibility does a supervisor have to ensure a productive learning environment for students? What responsibility does a supervisor have to a career teacher who is no longer growing professionally?
3. From whom can Katrina Quinn expect to receive support?

EXHIBIT 1

Section 1-03 of the Teachers' Contract

No tenured teacher will be discharged, disciplined, reprimanded, or reduced in rank or compensation without just cause; just cause including, but not being limited to inefficiency, incapacity, conduct unbecoming a teacher, or insubordination. A non-tenured teacher, after ninety (90) calendar days of continuous employment, and during his contract year, shall not be discharged, disciplined, reprimanded, or reduced in rank or compensation without just cause; just cause including but not being limited to inefficiency, incapacity, conduct unbecoming a teacher, or insubordination. Upon action by the School Committee against an employee pursuant to Section 42 or 42(D) of Chapter 71, the employee may at his discretion within thirty (30) days following the final action by the School Committee appeal the matter to the Superior Court, or within such time period file for arbitration with the American Arbitration Association without complying with the other procedural provisions of the grievance procedure. If arbitration is elected, it will be conducted as set forth in the Contract. The election of the method of appeal by the employee shall be the exclusive method of resolving the dispute. In the event of any action against an employee by the School Committee pursuant to the terms of this paragraph, but not pursuant to Section 42 or 42(D) of Chapter

71, the employee shall be required to file a grievance in accordance with the procedures set forth in the Contract.

EXHIBIT 2

Letter of Reprimand

Hudson Public Schools
Administration Building

TO: Mr. Jack Buick
FROM: Mr. Sam Gregory, Principal and Mr. M. C. Olivero, Director of Personnel
SUBJECT: Mr. Jack Buick's behavior unbecoming a teacher

This letter is to summarize the events of April 6th leading to the meeting held at the Superintendent's Office on April 7, at which were present Mr. Jack Buick, Mr. Roger Quip, Mr. Sam Gregory, Mrs. Ruth Smith, Mrs. Katrina Quinn, Mr. John Concord, Jr., Mr. Manny Olivero.

On Wednesday, April 6th an incident occurred at the office of Mr. Sam Gregory, Principal of Hudson High School, during which time Mr. Buick displayed rude behavior and conduct unbecoming a teacher. The action that precipitated this behavior resulted from a conference held between Mrs. Katrina Quinn, Coordinator of Mathematics, and Mr. Buick at which time they discussed the probability of his teaching assignment for the 1987–88 school year and an upcoming supervisory observation. At this conference Mr. Buick was very rude toward Mrs. Quinn. Mrs. Quinn reported this to the principal who decided, along with Mr. Steve Batson, Assistant Principal, to call Mr. Buick to discuss this incident. However, prior to Mr. Gregory's contacting Mr. Buick, Mr. Buick, on his own, came to Mr. Gregory's office to discuss his teaching assignment for the next year. Present in Mr. Gregory's office at the time were Mr. Batson, Mr. Bill French, Mr. Gregory, Mr. John Concord, and Mrs. Quinn. When Mr. Buick asked about his teaching assignment for the next year, Mr. Gregory answered that he would probably be teaching fewer Calculus AP Courses. At this point, Mr. Buick became very loud, emotional and rude, as evidenced by statements such as: "Mrs. Quinn doesn't know what she is doing" and "I can run circles around this dame." After a few minutes of this behavior, he also stated, "Gregory, if you think I am being insubordinate, go ahead and fire me." After a few minutes of this, Mr. Buick left the office and as he did, turned off the lights and slammed the door shut behind him. Mr. Gregory immediately telephoned Mr. Olivero from his office. While Mr. Gregory was discussing the incident with Mr. Olivero, Mr. Buick burst into the office and repeated his previous behavior, shouting and being very rude again. The same people were present as before. After a few minutes of the same type of behavior, he again stormed out of the office slamming the door behind him.

As a result of the above incidents, Mr. Buick was requested to appear on the morning of April 7 at the Superintendent's Office to discuss his behavior unbecoming a teacher. At this meeting, Mr. Olivero indicated that it was important for Mr. Buick to understand that when disagreements occur, the solution is not achieved through rude, loud, irrational behavior. The Administration expects that its faculty will conduct themselves in a professional manner becoming a teacher. Since the role of a teacher carries with it a great responsibility and represents a model for students to follow, the type of behavior that Mr. Buick displayed *cannot be tolerated and will not be tolerated again.* Should there be a reoccurrence of this type of behavior, for whatever reason, it will require the Administration to take further disciplinary action.

(Signature)
John J. Buick

I have read the above.

Exhibit 3

Job Description of Coordinator

Responsible for the design, development, implementation, supervision and coordination of assigned departmental objectives to provide a continuous and articulate program for the department working within the framework of the school system's guidelines, to provide optimum growth of students, teachers and department heads.

Provide consultant services for assigned department heads and classroom teachers. Develop and revise long-range plans, utilizing current research in the assigned field, observe classroom lessons, analyze and evaluate the program utilizing formal evaluation criteria.

Chair, attend and/or participate on system-wide administrating Committees, and other meetings as required or directed. Direct and/or attend administrative and curriculum workshops. Participate in development of federally funded programs. Assist in the organizational planning at the classroom, unit, department, school and system levels. Provide in-service training for assigned staff. Assume responsibility for all receipts and expenditures of departmental activities, and for maintenance and control of departmental equipment and materials. Initiate, organize and oversee all pilot programs for the department. Teach demonstration lessons. Prepare educational specifications for materials, equipment and plant design of new schools.

Participate in the recruitment, selection, assignment and organization of new teachers. Supervise teachers' performance by employing analysis for professional growth procedures, techniques and materials. Evaluate teachers using formal procedures. Provide counsel and guidance in matters of personnel procedures.

Keep abreast of current trends in curriculum, through attendance at various local, state and national professional meetings and by reading professional materials. Disseminate ideas gained through these activities to all teachers.

Prepare reports and materials to inform administration and school committee of instructional programs and related activities.

Perform related duties as directed by the superintendent.

Supporting Teachers at Somerset High

John Ritchie

It was October 4, 11:30 p.m. Richard Dargon, the principal of Somerset High School had gone to bed early that night and was in a deep sleep when his phone rang. It was Ed Walsh, one of his veteran English teachers: "Richard, I thought I should let you know. The building reps met tonight and decided to go to work-to-rule. We're starting in the morning. All the School Committee will offer us next year is zero percent so they're about to find out just how much extra work they've been getting. We've decided only to do what's in the contract, nothing more. No papers graded at night, no extra meetings, no staying after school. This could get bad, Richard. You've got an angry bunch of high school teachers on your hands. I'll see you tomorrow, but don't expect me before the bell. Good night." Dargon stared at the phone after he hung up. "Great, just great," he said to himself. "But who's going to look out for the kids?"

❖ THE NEGOTIATIONS IN SOMERSET

Over the past year the Somerset Teachers Association and the School Committee had been unable to come to terms on a new contract for teachers. Worse, the negotiations had been bitter. Ultimately, the Committee was holding firm in its position that Somerset teachers had been treated well in the past, but that current fiscal circumstances called for belt-tightening. The Committee was offering a two-year contract, with a zero percent raise in the first year and a three percent increase in the second. For its part, the Association argued that average teacher salaries were near the bottom of a list of comparable communities and that a percentage increase equal to the cost of living was in order. The last contract had expired weeks earlier on September 1 and negotiations had not been held since June 30, when the School Committee had rejected an Association proposal of a nine percent raise spread over three years. On October 4, a meeting of the Association leadership to discuss possible options resulted in the decision to follow the letter of the now expired contract. This meant "work-to-rule."

❖ THE PRINCIPAL'S SLEEPLESS NIGHT

The call from Walsh kept Dargon up most of the night. He couldn't help think-ing about the work-to-rule situation he'd experienced as a young teacher. It had been a time full of doubt and conflict. Lying awake, he ruefully recalled the pain he experienced. As a young teacher, he wasn't sure he agreed with the action, but he also knew that he had no choice. If he wanted a job the next year, he had to abide by his union's action. He recalled that teachers per-formed only those duties specified in the contract, and no more. They arrived ten minutes before the bell in the morning and left ten minutes after the bell in the afternoon. Students who needed help after school found locked class-rooms; dances were canceled for lack of chaperons; evening meetings were postponed or attended only by administrators. Parents grew angry at teach-ers, teachers became divided, students stopped working. The damage to the morale of the school, Dargon recalled, had never been repaired. Ironically, he couldn't remember if the strategy had ultimately benefited the settlement of the teachers' contract. The principal worried that this work-to-rule action would be just as damaging at Somerset High.

❖ THE TOWN OF SOMERSET AND SOMERSET SCHOOLS

Somerset was primarily a residential suburb with a population of twenty five thousand situated about twenty miles from a major metropolitan area. It was generally regarded as being affluent and white, though over the past two decades the population had grown more diverse. The development of low cost housing units on the south side of town had attracted an influx of families from less affluent communities interested in taking advantage of Somerset's schools. Almost all of these newer residents were either African-American, Hispanic, or Asian. This demographic change, though not profound in numbers, had led to grumbling among some of the town's long-time residents about how Somerset "wasn't what it used to be." Many complained that "lots of these new kids have special education needs that are driving our school budget through the roof." There was a small but growing trend among the more affluent residents of the town to send their children to private schools, a trend that could potentially have dire implications for school enrollment and funding.

Somerset had always prided itself on its schools, which were generally rated among the top ten or fifteen school systems in the state, based on data including per pupil expenditures, which approached $6,000 a year; college board scores, which were 1,008 for the combined Scholastic Aptitude Test; drop-out rate, which was below 3% annually; and percentages of graduates enrolling in four year colleges, which was 84%. The Teachers Association reg-ularly pointed out, however, that while the system was ranked highly in these categories, it was twenty-fifth on the list in teachers' salaries in comparable communities. The average teacher salary was $35,927.

Historically, the relationship between the community and the school system had been a workable one, though not without deep and long-standing strains and tensions. Many residents felt that the steadily expanding school budget—which in the current year was roughly $15.5 million—could and should be reduced, and that programs in Home Economics, Industrial Arts, Business, and other elective areas should be eliminated to save money. Teachers' salaries were viewed with concern in many quarters, and it was often pointed out at local board meetings that "teachers, after all, only work for a part of the year."

For their part, many teachers in Somerset felt that the town expected too much from its schools and teachers. It was not difficult to find a number of teachers at any of the town's seven schools who would say, "They keep telling us that they expect excellence, and pushing us to do more. But they don't recognize what that requires and they're not willing to pay for it."

❖ SOMERSET HIGH SCHOOL AND RICHARD DARGON, PRINCIPAL

Somerset High School was the only high school in the Somerset School District and housed grades nine through twelve. Approximately 850 students were enrolled in the four grades; faculty included 65 teachers. Richard Dargon had come to the district five years earlier from a neighboring district where he had been a high school history teacher and had served as the school's assistant principal for four years.

Dargon's tenure at Somerset High had always been something of a struggle. He had worked hard creating new projects, appointing task forces, and arguing vociferously to maintain programs but the town's ever-tightening fiscal constraints seemed to encroach more and more on Dargon's hopes for the school. In fact, while Dargon was at the helm, four teaching positions had been eliminated and class size had steadily drifted upwards, from an average of twenty two students per class to twenty eight. Moreover, the budget for extracurricular activities had been reduced by twenty percent two years earlier, prompting many complaints from parents. Dargon had said repeatedly, it was all he could do to "keep the ship from moving backwards."

Despite these challenges, the principal felt he enjoyed a positive relationship with his staff, though he had been told more than once by teachers that "he just doesn't know what it's like to be a teacher." This criticism always stung and perplexed Dargon. He had loved teaching and, even though he'd been an administrator for nearly 10 years, he still felt close to the classroom. He wondered why his teachers didn't see this.

Moreover, Dargon believed deeply in the teaching profession and supported activities that developed teachers' professionalism. He was convinced that the best way for teachers to achieve more status and better pay was to do just what he'd been asking them repeatedly to do: pitch in, share more, act like true professionals. And yet, in Dargon's mind, the school's faculty had become increasingly disinclined to take on new or different challenges or responsibilities. When he exhorted his teachers to contribute more, many would argue, "Why? Then more will be expected. You really think they'll pay us more?"

To the principal, and to others in the community, an important symbolic change had occurred the previous year, when the annual Faculty Follies, a twenty five year tradition at Somerset High, had been canceled because of lack of faculty interest. The spring event, a fundraiser for the Somerset Scholarship Foundation, had always been a high point of the year, bringing together parents, students, and teachers for a cordial, and often hilarious, evening. Its cancellation had not gone unnoticed by the town's local newspaper, *The Somerset Ledger*, which featured an editorial lamenting the end of an important local tradition. The article had been headlined "More and More Teachers Unwilling to Go the Extra Mile."

❖ WORK-TO-RULE BEGINS

Ordinarily, by 7:30 in the morning, Somerset High was busy with teachers arranging their classrooms, running off copies of tests, meeting in committees, or simply talking with each other about the news, the weather, the assembly schedule. Students would also arrive early to meet with a teacher, or finish homework. However, on the morning of October 5, the high school was deserted, save for the fifty or so students gathered in the hall outside the locked library.

Dargon himself had arrived especially early at 6:30 in the morning. He wanted to be available for anyone who needed guidance and, if some teachers actually arrived early, he hoped to find out what people were feeling. However, when no teachers had arrived by 7:30, he went out for a stroll through the corridors. As he passed the students grouped outside the library, Jason Cayler, an eleventh grader, said, "Hey, Mr. Dargon, where's Miss McVean? She said she'd meet me at 7:10 to go over our test." Dargon could only reply, "Sorry, Jason. I don't know where she is. But if I see her I'll let her know you're waiting for her." Another student, Moira Hedley said, "Hey, Mr. D, is there gonna' be a strike? Are you going to call off school?" This question was met with hopeful cheers from the crowd of teenagers. "Of course we're not going to call off school," Dargon responded. "We want you here with us, exercising your brains!" The students groaned, and the principal walked away, telling them classes would begin at the regular time.

In fact, Dargon had a good idea where Janet McVean was, and where the rest of his staff was, and his suspicion was confirmed when he got back to his office. Looking through the window at the front sidewalk, he could see what seemed to be the entire faculty gathered on the sidewalk in front of the school. Some held signs with slogans such as "Pay now or pay later. How important are your children?"

It hurt the principal to see such a display outside the school. Hadn't they all entered the field of education for the growth and well being of the children? Dargon wanted to support his teachers. He knew their morale had been impacted by the perceived animosity of the School Board—but this demonstration was reducing his school to a political circus.

Ten minutes later, with the warning bell about to ring, the principal placed himself at the front door. He wanted to greet the teachers, to let them know he was there at his post. He'd decided he also wanted to somehow acknowledge their situation while encouraging them to keep doing their best work. However, few of his staff members met his glance as they passed by, instead carrying on whispered conversations amongst themselves.

❖ THE JOB-ACTION CONTINUES

Within two weeks, the sight of teachers gathered each morning outside of the high school had become a familiar one. Coffee and doughnuts were brought on a revolving schedule. Dargon observed an increasing sense of solidarity in the morning line, teachers, at first reluctant to participate, now seemed enthusiastic about joining their colleagues. And parents, dropping their kids off at school, seemed more and more grim.

But while the outlook among the faculty outside the school seemed strong and cohesive, attitudes in the building were growing more tense and negative with each passing day. Some teachers were rabid in their support of the labor action and vigilant in making sure everyone followed the agreed-upon procedures. If teachers remained in the building more than twenty minutes after the closing bell, they would inevitably receive requests in their mailboxes asking them not to stay longer than was absolutely required by contract. A banner also appeared in the faculty lounge one morning, an apparent reference to *The Somerset Ledger's* editorial from the previous spring. "Not Willing to Go the Extra Mile? Try Walking a Mile in Our Shoes!!" It had been signed by at least fifty of the school's sixty-five teachers.

❖ A BREAK IN THE RANKS

Nevertheless, Dargon soon discovered that the teachers' apparent solidarity, was belied by some strong sentiment against the job-action. Two highly respected, veteran members of the English Department had come to see him to express their deep discomfort with their colleagues' action. Because of the esteem in which they were held by their colleagues, and their support of many of the principal's initiatives, Dargon listened carefully.

"We consider ourselves professionals," said Jan Dolan. "Sure, we'd love to be paid more, but we didn't go into this for the money. We can't refuse kids what we're professionally committed to give them. Also, when you see some of the people who are so actively behind this, and think about what kind of teachers they are, it shakes you up. Steve Talbot? I don't think he's come up with a new lesson plan in ten years. There are a number of us who are really uncomfortable with what is going on." "I don't think it is fair to the six new teachers either," stated Albert Marcus. "Not being able to work after hours, kids in their classes are really going to miss out."

Two days later, Gladys Healey, the French teacher, appeared in Dargon's office in tears. She told the principal how she was being shunned by a number of veterans in the building because she was unwilling to join the assemblage in front of the school each morning. "I used to have so many friends here," she said. "Now it seems like we're turning on each other instead of working together. It hurts and it's really sad." Dargon said, "I know what you mean. We're circling the wagons and turning the guns inward."

❖ THE YEAR'S FIRST FACULTY MEETING

Tuesday, October 23, was the third Tuesday of the month—the day set aside for the monthly faculty meeting. Dargon looked forward to the opportunity to bring his teachers together, and offer them, if not support, at least implied understanding of their situation. He knew, from his conversations with the English and French teachers, that the faculty was somewhat divided, and he felt the meeting might be a chance to air concerns and do some team building. However, on Friday afternoon, October 19, Dargon was approached by Ed Walsh and Tom O'Connor, two of the most militant members of the Teachers Association.

"Richard, I hope you're not expecting much of a turnout on Tuesday," Walsh said. "We're out of here by 2:30, exactly twenty minutes after school ends. That's what the contract says." Dargon was stunned but pleased that he could so readily answer, "No, that's not what the contract says. The contract says teachers, given reasonable notice, are required to attend meetings scheduled by the administration. So, in fact, I do expect a big turnout on Tuesday. I expect everyone there." O'Connor said, "Well, I think the problem is going to be that we were given no notice, so we aren't required to come." Dargon felt his voice rising, his patience waning, "What do you mean no notice? We meet every third Tuesday. Have been for years." "Well," said Walsh, "things are a little different now. You never sent a memo about holding a meeting, never informed us in writing that you planned to go ahead, so don't count on us showing up. And by the way, 'circling the wagons and turning the guns inward?' How about a little understanding of our position?" Before Dargon could respond, Walsh and O'Connor abruptly left his office.

❖ THE PRINCIPAL ACTS

Richard Dargon was speechless, staring at the door that Walsh and O'Connor pulled shut behind them. He was both surprised and disappointed that his comment about circled wagons had gotten around, and wished he'd remembered the words of a mentor when he'd first become a principal: "There's no such thing as a casual comment from the leader of an organization."

Dargon contemplated the challenge made by Walsh and O'Connor to Tuesday's faculty meeting. The principal knew it was time for the faculty to come together but wasn't sure how to force the issue. After a few minutes, he reached for the phone on his desk and called the Superintendent, Morton Ashman, to ask for his advice. Ashman was blunt and angry, telling him by all means to hold the meeting, to direct teachers to come, and to place a note in the file of any teacher who refused to attend. "Dargon, I don't want you playing into the union's hands. Faculty meetings are a regular part of a teacher's responsibilities. Tell them to show up, and make sure they do. I want that meeting held, and I want to know who doesn't come. In fact, I hope you're keeping some sort of list of who's causing the biggest problems during this thing. I hope you're not siding with those teachers."

Ashman had been Superintendent for ten years, and was not regarded as a strong advocate by the Somerset teachers. He was viewed as someone who would do anything to please the School Committee, and Dargon himself had been troubled by his regular references to teachers not knowing how good they had it, and his comments that "firing a few people would do a world of good around here."

Dargon said little during his conversation with Ashman, realizing Ashman's stance was anything but constructive. At the same time, Ashman's remark that "faculty meetings are a regular part of a teacher's responsibilities" struck a note with the principal.

The principal sat thinking for a few minutes more and then decided to call John Montgomery, the district's attorney. Montgomery was calmer, and advised Dargon that it was well within his rights to hold the meeting. Even without a written announcement, such meetings were clearly past practice. As such, teachers could be expected to attend. As to whether he should hold the meeting, Montgomery said, that was a different matter. The attorney ended the conversation with, "It's your call, Richard."

As Dargon reflected on the reactions of the two men, it became more and more clear to him that his decisions and actions had consequence. If he held the meeting, he risked alienating his staff, and creating a situation that might result in teachers having to choose between attending the meeting or risking the possibility of being considered "insubordinate." If Dargon canceled the meeting, he risked looking as though he were caving in, failing to move the school ahead as best he could, and disobeying the orders of his Superintendent. Up until this point, the principal had imagined he could play a positive but neutral role in the conflict. Now he realized he was going to be faced with more and more decisions, and each decision would have important implications in the conflict. "Why can't they just separate their professional activity from their contract issues," Dargon thought to himself.

❖ THE FACULTY MEETING

At 10:00 on Monday morning, a memo (shown on p. 298) was placed in the mailboxes of all of the teachers at Somerset High School.

From Dargon's point of view, the meeting was a disaster. He was relieved to see that most of the teachers were present, though Walsh, O'Connor, and

> REMINDER: FACULTY MEETING TOMORROW AFTERNOON AT 2:30
> P.M. IN THE FACULTY ROOM. PLEASE LET ME KNOW IF YOU CANNOT
> ATTEND.
>
> R. DARGON

perhaps ten others on the sixty-five member staff were absent. The usual attendance procedure of passing around a pad of paper for sign-in was followed. The atmosphere was heavy, the silence palpable. Dargon began by talking about how difficult the situation was, and how he himself had experienced the trauma of work-to-rule when he was a teacher. He knew how committed the staff was, and how difficult it was to have to withhold services that they would ordinarily give freely. He went on to describe how hard it was for him, as principal, to have so many cooperative and exciting projects put on hold, but said that he understood also that working without a contract was very compromising.

As the principal spoke, he noticed that no one looked up at him, or seemed to greet his words with any sort of sympathy. It wasn't long before Don Slaven, a veteran science teacher, interrupted him. "Richard, we don't really care how hard this is for you. This isn't about you, although frankly a lot of us have been looking for a lot more support from you. Why did you hold this meeting in the first place? Just to show us you could? Or because you were told you had to?"

Before Dargon could respond, Jan Dolan, one of the English teachers who had spoken to him earlier about her discomfort with the job-action, leaped to her feet. "I can't believe you'd talk to Richard that way. And I can't believe the way you force your views on everyone else. Not everyone thinks this is a great idea, you know, and there's a lot of us who think the union's doing a lot more harm than good. Do you have any idea how much public support we've lost standing around with those stupid signs every morning?"

Following Dolan's comments, the meeting degenerated into what seemed like a free-for-all, involving the heated exchange of various points of view about the effect of the teachers' strategy, the role of the school committee, the need for parents to back the teachers, and the importance of not breaking ranks under pressure. Though Richard Dargon had feared this result, he did nothing to stop it, hoping that an opportunity to vent would be by itself, constructive. But tempers were hot; opinions strong. People weren't hearing each other. Dargon tried to mediate but was ignored. He felt pointless and out of the loop. At one point, Don Slaven interjected that from talking to the people he knew, a strike was the next logical step. "It's not very far off, either," he declared.

For Dargon, this was the breaking point. He said angrily, "Listen, you're not going to use a faculty meeting as a place to discuss a strike. I understand your frustration, but my job is to make sure the kids in this school get an education. That's what we're here for, the kids."

Someone in the back—it was not clear who—then shouted, "For once, forget the kids. What about us? You're the principal, what are you going to do for us?" Dargon began to stammer a response but most of the teachers got up to leave. The clock on the wall showed 2:51 p.m.

Though the meeting had been humbling, Dargon did gain some insights. It was clear to him now that, though a few found the job-action distasteful and unprofessional, the majority of the teachers on his staff were fully committed to work-to-rule. It was also clear to the principal that everyone expected something from him, and that he would have to choose his course of action carefully.

❖ THE CONFLICT ESCALATES

As the work-to-rule action continued over the next few weeks, Dargon spent increasingly more time fielding phone calls from parents. Mostly, they were concerned that their children's education was being impaired by the teachers working-to-rule. Dargon felt reasonably confident that he had managed to allay most of his parents' concerns, and had convinced them that the job-action would soon be resolved with no lasting damage. Several calls had particularly disturbed him, though, for they came from parents angry that some teachers were spending class time detailing the specifics of the dispute, and presenting their position. In these cases, Dargon spoke directly to the teachers involved, and told them that it was entirely inappropriate to politicize classrooms by presenting individual views about the work-action. In each case, the teacher claimed that he or she had merely been using the current situation as a case study for class discussion. "What are we supposed to do?" one teacher asked. "Pretend this isn't going on?" The next day, Dargon informed his teachers in a memo that any statement they made about the work-action could be misinterpreted and, in their own best interest, they should make every effort to not discuss it.

On a Tuesday night, early in November, members of the Somerset Teachers Association negotiating team met with representatives of the Somerset School Committee. The meeting lasted until 3:30 in the morning. No progress was made, and the Teachers Association issued a bulletin the next day, Wednesday, suggesting that "more serious measures may have to be taken to get what we deserve." Dargon saw the memo when it was brought to him by Ed Walsh. He immediately asked what "more serious measures" were being contemplated. Walsh said he didn't feel comfortable talking about it yet, but would try to keep Dargon informed. He went on to say that no teachers planned to attend the Open House for parents scheduled the following week, and that Dargon should avoid embarrassment by canceling it. "Unless," Walsh said, "you think you can handle a thousand parents on your own."

Dargon chided himself for not having anticipated the difficulties that the upcoming Open House would present. He had thought of it as a regular part of a teacher's duties and hadn't considered the possibility that people would boycott it. He had been concerned about what teachers might say to the parents in their classrooms, but hadn't imagined that the event would have to be canceled. This was, after all, the centerpiece of the school year, the evening when parents got a chance to see what their children's school was really like.

Dargon wondered what to do but, just then, Mrs. Flynn, his secretary, rang through to tell him that three students needed to see him immediately. John Hanley, a senior, Maureen Mason, a junior and Dennis Lopez, a senior, entered his office. The three kids clearly had an agenda and were eager to talk. John began by informing his principal that they were the editors of the student newspaper, *The Sagamore*, and that they were publishing a special edition of the paper that focused on the teachers' work-action. Maureen interjected that the edition presented student reactions to it. John handed the principal a copy. Dargon quickly perused the collection of stories and editorials and saw instantly that the paper would cause a firestorm. The common themes expressed were anger and resentment. Each piece stressed the fact that students felt they were being deprived of needed services, and that teachers were being selfish. One editorial, in particular, troubled him deeply. It mentioned five teachers by name—teachers that Dargon knew were among the weakest on his staff—and said, "How can these people, who everybody knows haven't taught anything new in years, be asking for more money?"

Dargon took a deep breath and asked, "How does your advisor feel about this?"

"He doesn't have anything to do with it. We're publishing this on our own," replied John. "Yeah," said Dennis, "and we checked with a lawyer who says we have the right to print our views, as long as we say clearly that it's just opinion. We wanted to tell you what we're doing just so you know."

"Well, I appreciate you informing me, but you know there's a meeting between the School Committee and the Association the day after tomorrow. This thing might be settled." The kids seemed reluctant to postpone publication for the meeting. Dargon tried another tact, telling them that he needed to check to see whether they could be charged with libel for mentioning specific teacher's names. The editors agreed to wait two days. Dargon honestly hoped that during that time he could come up with some strategy to prevent or delay the publication of the paper. He could only see its publication creating a deep and painful rift between teachers and students.

Unfortunately, the principal didn't have long to mull over this newest dilemma because, with the students' exit, Mrs. Flynn put through another call. Mrs. Flynn said, "Another parent for you, Richard." Dargon sighed and said, "Okay, let's see what this one has to say."

"Mr. Dargon, this is Mrs. Stuart, Laura's mother. I'm so upset. What's happened to education in this town? I am furious—and so are the other parents I've spoken to this morning. Trying to get better pay is one thing, but messing up our kids' chances to get into college is quite another."

The principal was dumbfounded, "What do you mean, Mrs. Stuart?" The mother informed Dargon that her daughter had asked her English teacher,

Mr. Walsh, to write a college recommendation and was told that because such responsibilities were not specified in the teachers' contract, teachers would not write recommendations until the contract dispute was settled.

Dargon assured the mother that he would immediately look into the situation. "I'll get back to you on this as soon as I can, Mrs. Stuart," he said. Before he was able to leave his office, however, another angry parent called. This was the father of Sean Lindover, president of the senior class, a young woman with great potential. "My daughter has applications at Cornell, and Brown and Stanford! She needs those recommendations!" By the end of the day, Dargon had received calls from at least twenty other parents, angrily demanding that he "do something."

The principal reluctantly called the Superintendent of Schools to describe the latest turn of events. Ashman was unequivocal, "That's absurd. Writing college recommendations is a regular part of every teacher's responsibility. I want you to direct them to do it and, if they refuse, tell them they will face serious consequences. It is well within your authority to direct teachers to write recommendations. Make no mistake about it. Good lord, don't these people understand they could be fired for insubordination? Where's the list I asked for with the names of the biggest troublemakers?"

The conversation was long and intense. Dargon hung up the phone without making any commitment to the list of "troublemakers."

❖ WHAT TO DO

Richard Dargon put a note in the mailboxes of Ed Walsh and three other union representatives for the high school, asking them to meet with him the next morning.

"Listen, Richard, we're not playing games here," said Walsh. "If the only way to get this community to take our position seriously is to hit them where it really hurts, that's what we're going to do."

"But Ed," Dargon responded, "recommendations have always been part of your job. You know how critical they are for kids. Why the hell doesn't anyone think about kids?" Having said this, the principal regretted it immediately. He knew within an hour it would have been repeated throughout the building.

"They're not required by contract. We've been doing that kind of extra work for years. If the School Committee wants to be tough, they'd better think about what they're up against," replied Walsh.

"But don't you know how much support you'll lose if you don't write recommendations? Talk about cutting off your nose," Dargon said, getting up and beginning to pace.

"Frankly, we haven't finally decided what we're going to do, but for now, recommendations are on hold. To tell you the truth, we're waiting to see what stance you're going to take. I think if you show us a little support for what we're going through, we could persuade teachers to write for kids. If you try to play hardball on this, and direct us to write them, then we'll either refuse or just submit a simple checklist for each student."

After the four teachers left his office, Dargon rose and took a walk around the school. Students had just passed to first hour classes and Dargon needed the quiet corridors to clear his head. With the complex issues he was facing, clear thinking was essential. Richard Dargon knew that the issues he faced—the job-action itself, the divisions on the staff, the recommendation conflict, the Open House, the student newspaper, Ashman's request for a list—were interconnected in very intricate ways. How could he support his teachers and do what was best for the kids? Lots of questions swirled around in the principal's head. However, one thing was for sure, Richard Dargon needed a consistent and thoughtful plan of action and he needed one now.

❖ CASE PREPARATION QUESTIONS

1. Richard Dargon is caught in the middle between his teachers and his superintendent. What advice do you have for him?

2. How can the principal show support for his teachers and do what is best for the students of Somerset High School?

3. Work-to-rule and other job actions can color a community's perception of a school district and its teachers. Outline a strategy for Richard Dargon that will minimize the negative impact of the Somerset teacher's job action in the community and enhance his role as the instructional leader of Somerset High.

Selected Readings and Bibliography

◆ ◆ ◆

Badaracco, J. and Ellsworth, R. (1989). *Leadership and the quest for integrity.* Boston: Harvard Business School Press.

Carter, K. and Unklesbay, R. (1989). Cases in teaching and law. *Journal of American Studies, 21,* 527–536.

Christensen, C. (1981). *Teaching by the case method.* Boston: Harvard Business School Case Services, Harvard Business School.

Christensen, C., Garvin , D., and Sweet, A. (Eds.). (1991). *Education for judgment: The artistry of discussion leadership.* Boston: Harvard Business School.

Christensen, C. and Hansen, A. (1987). *Teaching and the case method.* Boston: Harvard University School Publishing Division.

Christensen, C. and Hansen, A. (1994). *Teaching and the case method.* Boston: Harvard University School Publishing Division.

Christensen, C. and Zaleznick, A. (1954). The case method and its administrative environment. In M. McNair (Ed.), *The case method at Harvard Business School* (pp. 212–222). New York: McGraw-Hill Book Company, Inc.

Culbertson, J., Jacobson P., and Reller, T. (1960). *Administrative relationships.* Englewood Cliffs, NJ: Prentice Hall, Inc.

Doyle, W. (1990). Case methods in the education of teachers. *Teacher Education Quarterly, 17,* 7–16.

Frederick, P. (1981). The dreaded discussion: Ten ways to start. *Improving College and University Teaching, 29,* 109–114.

Gragg, C. (1940). Teachers must also learn. *Harvard Educational Review,* 10, 30–47

Gragg, C. (1954). Because wisdom can't be told. In M. McNair (Ed.), *The case method at the Harvard Business School* (pp. 6–14). New York: McGraw-Hill Book Company, Inc.

Greenwood, G. and Parkay, F. (1989). *Case studies for teaching decision making.* NY: Random House.

Hansen, A. (1987). Reflections of a case writer: Writing teaching cases. In C. Christensen and A. Hansen (Eds.), *Teaching and the case method* (pp. 264–270). Boston: Harvard Business School Press.

Hunt, P. (1951). The case method of instruction. *Harvard Educational Review, 21,* 175–192.

Kleinfeld, J. (1991). "Changes in problem solving abilities of students taught through case methods." Paper presented at the annual meeting of the American Educational Research Association of Chicago.

Kotter, J. (1995). Leading change: Why transformation efforts fail. *Harvard Business Review, 73,* 59–67.

Lampert, M. (1985). How do teachers manage to teach? Perspectives on problems in practice. *Harvard Educational Review, 55,* 178–194.

Lawrence, P. (1960). The preparation of case material. In K. Andrews (Ed.), *The case method of teaching human relations and administration* (pp. 215–224). Cambridge, MA: Harvard University Press.

McNair, M. (Ed.). (1954). *The case method at the Harvard Business School.* New York: McGraw-Hill Book Company, Inc.

Merseth, K. (1990). Case studies and teacher education. *Teacher Educational Quarterly, 17,* 53–62.

Merseth, K. (1991). *The case for cases in teacher education.* Washington, DC: American Association of Colleges for Teacher Education.

Merseth, K. (1996). Cases and case methods in teacher education. In J. Sikula (Ed.), *Handbook of research on teacher education: A project of the Association of Teacher Educators* (pp. 722-744). New York: Macmillan.

Richert, A. (1991). Case methods and teacher education: Using cases to teach teacher reflection. In B. Tabachnik and K. Zeichner (Eds.), *Issues and practices in inquiry-oriented teacher education* (pp. 130–150). London: Falmer Press.

Sargent, C., and Belisle, E. (1955). *Educational administration: Cases and concepts.* Boston: Houghton Mifflin Company.

Schön, D. (1983). *The reflective practitioner: How professionals think in action.* New York: Basic Books.

Schön, D. (1987). *Educating the reflective practitioner: Toward a new design for teaching and learning in the professions.* San Francisco: Jossey-Bass.

Schön, D. (Ed.). (1991). *The reflective turn: Case studies in and on educational practice.* New York: Teachers College Press.

Schwab, J. (1969). *College curriculum and student protest.* Chicago: University of Chicago Press.

Sykes, G. (1989). Learning to teach with cases. *NCRTE Colloquy, 2,* 7–13.

Sykes, G., and Bird, T. (1992). Teacher educators and the case idea. In G. Grant (Ed.), *Review of research in education, 18,* 457–521.

Wassermann, S. (1990). *Asking the right question: The essence of teaching* (Phi Delta Kappa Fastback 343). Bloomington, IN: Phi Delta Kappa.

Wassermann, S. (1993). *Getting down to cases: Learning to teach with case studies.* New York: Teachers College Press.

Wassermann, S. (1994). Using cases to study teaching. *Phi Delta Kappa, 75,* 602–611.

Welty, W. (1989). Discussion method teaching: How to make it work. *Change, 21,* 40–49.